VS COBOL II

Other Wiley Books You Might Find Helpful

VS COBOL II: Highlights and Techniques by Jim Janossy is a companion to Gary Brown's *Structured Programming in VS COBOL II* (John Wiley & Sons, Inc., 1992). Gary Brown's book is referential in nature; Jim Janossy's book is designed for you to use for rapid, focused learning of crucial VS COBOL II differences from VS COBOL.

Structured COBOL Programming (6th Edition), by Robert and Nancy Stern (John Wiley & Sons, Inc., 1991) is an excellent beginner's textbook for learning the COBOL language. Consider it if you don't already know COBOL.

Jim Janossy has written several other books dealing with the IBM mainframe and VAX environments, published by John Wiley & Sons:

Practical MVS JCL (1987, second edition in 1992)

Practical VSAM For Today's Programmer (1988)

Practical TSO/ISPF For Programmers and the Information Center (1988)

VAX COBOL On-Line (1992)

VS COBOL II

Highlights and Techniques

James G. Janossy
DePaul University, Chicago

John Wiley & Sons, Inc.
New York • Chichester • Brisbane • Toronto • Singapore

This book is dedicated to the memory of
Grace Murray Hopper (1906–1992)

ab uno disce omnes

In recognition of the importance of preserving what has been written, it is a policy of John Wiley & Sons, Inc., to have books of enduring value published in the United States printed on acid-free paper, and we exert our best efforts to that end.

Library of Congress Cataloging-in-Publication Data

Janossy, James G. (James Gustav), 1947–
    VS COBOL II : highlights and techniques / James G. Janossy.
      p. cm.
    Includes index.
    ISBN 0-471-57205-5 (book/disk set : alk. paper)   ISBN
0-471-55892-3 (pbk. : alk. paper)
     1. VS COBOL II (Computer program language) I. Title. II. Title:
VS COBOL 2. III. Title: VS COBOL two.
QA76.73.V77J36 1992   91-40990
005.2'22—dc20

Printed in the United States of America
10 9 8 7 6 5 4 3 2 1
Printed and bound by Courier Companies, Inc.

Preface

Why did I write this book? And why should you read it? VS COBOL II will affect thousands of mainframe sites and hundreds of thousands of programmers in the 1990s. VS COBOL II has been available since 1984 but few people have paid attention to it. IBM confused people with its different versions. With VS COBOL II Release 3, things have settled down. It's time for everyone to start making the switch because VS COBOL II gives you access to greatly expanded machine memory.

If you are a professional programmer who already knows COBOL, this concise book is aimed at you. The point of this book is to:

- Tell you the important things you need to know about VS COBOL II
- Show you how to use it in a hands-on way
- Demonstrate step-by-step how to use new interactive debugging techniques
- Identify problem areas and show you how to avoid them
- Provide trivia in the appendixes or tell you where to find it in manuals

IBM manuals and many fine books, such as *Structured VS COBOL II Programming* by Gary Brown (John Wiley & Sons, Inc., 1991) provide you with complete references to the new language version. I didn't set out to compete with those books. Instead, I designed and wrote this book as a *rapid learning tool* for you.

All of the example programs in this book are designed to produce demonstration output. You can actually run all of them. You can even obtain the programs on diskette with this book and upload them to your system. You can then modify the programs if you like to try out and confirm features. There is no better way for you to learn quickly.

If you are like most of the personnel I train, you need to learn VS COBOL II Release 3 as quickly as possible. You need important information first and you don't need trivia getting in the way. That's my approach!

With thanks . . .

I'd like to thank Dr. Helmut Epp, Chairman of the Department of Computer Science and Information Systems of DePaul University, and Dr. L. Edward Allemand, head of the Information Systems Division at DePaul, for their support in my book-writing projects. I would also like to thank Steve Samuels of DePaul's Computer Career Program for his suggestions and advice on COBOL techniques, pedagogy, and exercise ideas, and Norm Noerper of Caliber Data Training for his assistance in arranging corporate training sessions based on this and my other books.

JAMES G. JANOSSY

Lincolnwood, Illinois
March 1992

Contents

About the Author   **xvii**

1   Perspective: Why VS COBOL II?   **1**
1.1   The Evolution of COBOL   1
1.2   Evolution of the Mainframe Environment   2
1.3   Computer System Memory Growth   2
1.4   What "Addressing" Means   4
1.5   Accessing System Memory:
       AMODE and RMODE   5
1.6   *Try It!* Learn By Running My Programs!   6
1.7   Learning With PC-Based 1985
       COBOL Compilers   7

2   What You Lose in VS COBOL II   **8**
2.1   How IBM Changed Your COBOL World   8
2.2   IBM Took Away Some Conveniences   8
2.3   REMARKS and NOTE   9
2.4   You Lose CURRENT-DATE!   9
2.5   You Lose TIME-OF-DAY   11
2.6   You Lose TRANSFORM and EXAMINE   12
2.7   ISAM Is Dead!   12
2.8   No READY TRACE or EXHIBIT!   12
2.9   FLOW Option, Verb COUNT: Gone!   13
2.10   Report Writer: It's Now in a Precompiler   14
2.11   COMMUNICATION SECTION Is Gone   16
2.12   MIGR Option and Conversion Assistance   16
2.13   *Try It!* Using the MIGR Option   17
2.14   *Try It!* Seeing VS COBOL II
        Incompatibilities   17
2.15   *Try It!* Converting VS COBOL to
        VS COBOL II   17
2.16   VS COBOL II Procs and Libraries   26

**3 VS COBOL II Release 3 Compiler Listings
and Options**   **30**
3.1   Meet the VS COBOL II Compiler!   30
3.2   Program A1NEW:
       A Complete Example   30
3.3   VS COBOL II Compiler Listing for
       A1NEW   31
3.4   New Compiler Messages and Codes   33
3.5   The PROCESS Statement   33
3.6   Important VS COBOL II Compiler Options   57
3.7   Other VS COBOL II Compile Options You
       Should Know About   58
3.8   Execution and Runtime Options   59
3.9   The TITLE Statement   60

4 User Return Codes and the FDUMP Option   **61**
4.1   *Try It!* User Return Codes in VS COBOL   61
4.2   *Try It!* User Return Codes in VS COBOL II   76
4.3   User Return Code Messages and
       Documentation   76
4.4   Don't Use Return Codes 1000 to 1999!   76
4.5   When Does FDUMP Kick In?   76
4.6   How an FDUMP Looks   77
4.7   *Try It!* Seeing How Statement Level
       and FDUMP Work   77

5 Source Code Simplification   **84**
5.1   Use a Minimal IDENTIFICATION
       DIVISION   84
5.2   Simplification of the File Description (FD)   85
5.3   Simplification of WORKING-STORAGE   86
5.4   Eliminating the Word FILLER   86
5.5   Plainer Packed Decimal Coding and When
       to Use It   86
5.6   Plainer Binary Field Coding and When to
       Use It   87
5.7   *Try It!* Using Hexadecimal Literals   88
5.8   Simplification of the PROCEDURE
       DIVISION   89
5.9   NOT AT END and NOT INVALID KEY   91
5.10   The INITIALIZE Verb   91
5.11   *Try It!* Using the INITIALIZE Verb   92
5.12   INITIALIZE Verb with
       REPLACING Option   96

5.13   An Enhancement to EXIT?   96
5.14   You Can Code With Lowercase Letters   98

6 PERFORM Enhancements   **100**
6.1   Traditional "Out-of-Line" PERFORMs   100
6.2   How You Code an In-Line PERFORM   102
6.3   When Should You Use In-Line
        PERFORMs?   102
6.4   In-Line PERFORM with VARYING   102
6.5   END-IF Scope Delimiter in In-Line
        PERFORMs   104
6.6   *Try It!* Using the In-Line PERFORM   104
6.7   Nested In-Line PERFORM   105
6.8   PERFORM ... WITH TEST BEFORE   106
6.9   PERFORM ... WITH TEST AFTER   107
6.10   *Try It!* Deciphering In-Line PERFORMs   108

7 IF/ELSE, Scope Terminators, EVALUATE, and SET   115
7.1   New: < = and > = IF/ELSE Operations!   115
7.2   Negated Logical Complement Tests   117
7.3   Simplified Range Tests in VS COBOL II   117
7.4   END-IF: An Explicit Scope Terminator   118
7.5   Adding Clarity With END-IF   118
7.6   Explicit Scope Terminators   119
7.7   END-: Making a Conditional Statement
        Into Imperative   121
7.8   NEXT SENTENCE and CONTINUE   122
7.9   IF/ELSE Trivia   123
7.10   Comparing EVALUATE and IF/ELSE   124
7.11   Syntax Reference for EVALUATE Variations   127
7.12   EVALUATE With TRUE and
        Relation Coding   127
7.13   EVALUATE With TRUE and
        88-Level Condition Names   127
7.14   A Common EVALUATE Mistake   128
7.15   *Try It!* Replacing IF/ELSE with EVALUATE   131
7.16   *Try It!* EVALUATE With Compound
        Conditions   133
7.17   CONTINUE and OTHER in
        EVALUATE Statements   137
7.18   Syntax Reference for 88-Levels   138
7.19   *Try It!* Use SET to Control 88-Level Names   139

8 Tables and Syntax Improvements   **142**
8.1   Table Size Limits Expanded   142

8.2   You Can Now Use VALUE on a
       Table Definition   144
8.3   *Try It!* VALUE and Relative Subscripting/
       Indexing   145
8.4   Lookup Tables   147
8.5   VS COBOL II SEARCH and SEARCH ALL   150
8.6   Table Dimensions   153
8.7   *Try It!* Subscript/Index Validity
       Checking With SSRANGE   154
8.8   Why SSRANGE Doesn't Always Work   157
8.9   SSRANGE, NOSSRANGE, and Efficiency   167

9 Numeric Handling Differences   168
9.1   New Ways to Code COMP-3
       and COMP   168
9.2   Speeding Up Your Calculations   170
9.3   De-Editing During MOVE   171
9.4   *Try It!* De-Editing in VS COBOL II   172
9.5   Computational Precision and Accuracy:
       No Improvement!   173
9.6   *Try It!* COMPUTE Precision Problems and
       Solution   178
9.7   VS COBOL II Rounding Problems   178
9.8   Changes in ON SIZE ERROR   183
9.9   NUMPROC Compiler Option   184
       9.9.1 NUMPROC(PFD)   184
       9.9.2 NUMPROC(NOPFD)   186
       9.9.3 NUMPROC(MIG)   186

10 User-Defined Data Classes   187
10.1   Establishing a User-Defined Data Class   187
10.2   Accessing a User-Defined Data Class   188
10.3   *Try It!* See How a User-Defined
        Data Class Works   189
10.4   *Try It!* Creating User-Defined Data Classes   189
10.5   Hexadecimal Coding in User-Defined
        Data Classes   195
10.6   User-Defined Data Class Definitions
        in Copy Libraries   195

11 Character Handling Changes and Enhancements   196
11.1   INSPECT Replaces EXAMINE   196
11.2   *Try It!* Seeing How INSPECT
        With CONVERTING Works   197

11.3   *Try It!* Character Replacement For
        Encryption   198
11.4   The New REPLACE Feature   200
11.5   *Try It!* A REPLACE Demonstration   201
11.6   REPLACE Can Cure New Reserved Word
        Problems   201
11.7   *Try It!* Reference Modification   203
11.8   Guidelines for Reference Modification   207
11.9   *Try It!* You Can Overdo Reference
        Modification   209
11.10   You Can Nest COPY Directives   212
11.11   Double Byte Character Set and
        KANJI   212
11.12   Alphabetic Now Includes
        Lowercase Letters   214
11.13   WHEN-COMPILED Register   215

**12 VSAM Changes: Communication Codes
and File Status   216**
12.1   VSAM Background   216
12.2   The VSAM/Program Interface   217
12.3   VS COBOL II Extended VSAM Status
        Codes   217
12.4   File Status Replaces INVALID KEY   218
12.5   The Importance of File Status   220
12.6   File Status: Anticipate Before Acting!   221
12.7   Standard File Status Checking Pattern   222
12.8   VS COBOL II Expands the Set of
        File Status Values!   226
12.9   You Lose if You Emulate Release 2
        with CMPR2   226
12.10   *Try It!* Seeing VSAM Extended
        Communication Codes   227
12.11   *Try It!* Interpreting Expanded File
        Status Values   234
12.12   File Status for QSAM (Sequential) Files   235
12.13   Optional Files: New for VS COBOL II
        Release 3   236
12.14   Alternate Index SELECT/ASSIGN Coding
        and JCL   237
12.15   READ ... NEXT and DYNAMIC Access   237
12.16   Current Record Pointer and
        Key of Reference   238
12.17   Using the START Verb   240

12.18   Relational Conditions Available
        With START   241
12.19   Reading a VSAM KSDS Sequentially
        Via Alternate Key   242
12.20   *Try It!* Experimenting With START and
        Alternate Keys   243

13 Changes for CICS, IMS, and IMS/DC   **247**
13.1   CICS Code Restrictions for VS COBOL II   247
13.2   New STOP RUN, EXIT PROGRAM,
        GOBACK Usage   248
13.3   CICS Gets the CALL Verb!   249
13.4   Using CALL in CICS Programs   249
13.5   Use Locate Mode Without Coding
        BLL Cells!   250
13.6   LENGTH OF Register Simplifies
        CICS I/O   251
13.7   Pointer Fields and ADDRESS OF   252
13.8   CICS Program Translation, Compile and
        Linkage Edit   254
13.9   Tools for Debugging VS COBOL II
        CICS Programs   256
13.10   IMS/DC Restrictions   256
13.11   IMS Program Compiling   257
13.12   Linkage Editor Options for IMS   258
13.13   Runtime Options for IMS   258

14 Using SORT Without SECTIONs   **259**
14.1   What Is a SECTION?   259
14.2   Why Are SECTIONs Obsolete?   260
14.3   Restrictions and Features of SECTIONs   260
14.4   Why SECTIONs for SORT Input and
        Output Procedures?   261
14.5   Why You Should Abandon SECTIONs
        Now   261
14.6   *Try It!* ECAR3035: A No-SECTION
        Internal Sort Example   262
14.7   VS2DATE: A Handy CALLable Date Subroutine
        for VS COBOL II   272

15 COBTEST Batch Mode Debugging   **273**
15.1   What Is COBTEST?   273
15.2   Batch and Interactive Debugging   273
15.3   READY TRACE Not Supported!   276
15.4   *Try It!* Simulating READY TRACE
        Output With COBTEST   277

15.5   COBTEST Batch Mode Debugging JCL   277
15.6   Explanation of COBTEST and
        QUALIFY Coding   284
15.7   *Try It!* FREQ, LISTFREQ,
        and AT Debugging Commands   285
15.8   Batch Debugging Advantages and
        Disadvantages   286

16 Interactive COBTEST Debugging   287
16.1   COBTEST Modes   287
16.2   TSO/ISPF Foreground Operations   288
16.3   TSO/ISPF Foreground Compile and
        Link Naming Conventions   289
16.4   Interactive Foreground VS COBOL II
        Compile   290
16.5   Interactive Foreground Linkage Edit   294
16.6   Interactive Debugging   294
16.7   The COBTEST Full Screen   295
16.8   TSO ALLOCATE Commands for
        Program Files   295
16.9   TSO/ISPF PF Key Setup for Interactive
        Debugging   299
16.10   Source Code Window in Debugging   299
16.11   AUTOLIST to See Data-Name Contents   300
16.12   On-Line Debugger Command HELP   302
16.13   Leaving a Debugging Session   302
16.14   *Try It!* COBTEST Interactive Debugging   302
16.15   Going Beyond a COBTEST Demonstration   305

**Appendix A: VSAM Return, Function,
            and Feedback Codes   306**
A.1   VSAM Return Codes   307
A.2   VSAM Function Codes   307
A.3   VSAM Feedback Codes for OPEN/CLOSE
       (RC=0004)   308
A.4   VSAM Feedback Codes for Logical Errors
       (RC=0008)   309
A.5   VSAM Feedback Codes for Physical Errors
       (RC=0012)   310

Appendix B: Expanded VSAM File Status Values   311
B.1   Successful Conditions (00, 02, 04, 05, 07, 97)   311
B.2   AT END, Sequential Processing (10, 14)   312
B.3   INVALID KEY, Random Processing
       (21, 22, 23, 24)   312

B.4   I/O Errors (30 through 39)   313
B.5   Logic Errors (41 through 49)   314
B.6   Implementation Errors (90 through 96)   315

Appendix C: CALL by Content or Reference   316

C.1   CALL by Reference   316
C.2   CALL by Content   316
C.3   Mixing Data References in a Single CALL   317
C.4   LENGTH OF Feature   317
C.5   How You Code the CALLed Program   317
C.6   INITIAL and CANCEL   318

Appendix D: Nested Programs   319

D.1   What Are Nested Programs?   319
D.2   An Example of Nested Programs   319
D.3   Invoking Nested Programs   319
D.4   EXTERNAL   320
D.5   GLOBAL   321
D.6   COMMON   321
D.7   Should You Use Nested Programs?   321

Appendix E: Using Microcomputer-Based 1985 COBOL Compilers   322

E.1   Microcomputer-Based Compilers Versus
      IBM VS COBOL II   322
E.2   Building Your Source Code   322
E.3   Microcomputer-Based Program Testing   323
E.4   Compiler Options   324
E.5   Compile Listing   324
E.6   Error Messages   324
E.7   Product-Specific Information   324
E.8   Micro Focus COBOL   327
      E.8.1   SELECT/ASSIGN Statement and the
              DOS SET Command   327
      E.8.2   Clearing the Sequential File Buffer   328
      E.8.3   File Status   329
      E.8.4   Indexed File Creation   329
      E.8.5   Procedure for Compiling and
              Linkage Editing   330
      E.8.6   Debugging Environment   333
E.9   Ryan/McFarland COBOL-85   333
      E.9.1   SELECT/ASSIGN Statement   334
      E.9.2   Declaratives and File Status   334
      E.9.3   Indexed File Creation   334

E.9.4 Procedure for Compiling and
Linkage Editing   335

E.9.5 Debugging Environment   336

E.10 CA-Realia COBOL   337

E.10.1 SELECT/ASSIGN Statement   337

E.10.2 Declaratives, File Status,
and Index Files   338

E.10.3 Procedure for Compiling and
Linkage Editing   338

E.10.4 Debugging Environment   339

**Appendix F: Summary of COBTEST
Debugging Commands   340**

Appendix G: Suggested Shop Standards   341

G.1 Actions You Should Take Immediately   341

G.2 Actions for a Standards Committee
to Consider   342

G.3 Things You Should Have Your Systems
Programmers Do Now   345

Index   346

About the Author

James Janossy is a fulltime faculty member of the Department of Computer Science and Information Systems at DePaul University, Chicago. He teaches COBOL, MVS JCL, systems analysis and design, software testing, project management, relational database, and on-line programming on IBM and VAX systems. Prior to joining DePaul he worked in the industry for 17 years as manager of systems and programming and data processing project leader and programmer. Jim earned his B.A. at Northwestern University, his M.S. at California State University, Los Angeles, and is completing a Ph.D. in computer science.

Jim has written several books including *Practical MVS JCL, Practical VSAM* (with Richard Guzik), *Practical TSO/ISPF For Programmers and the Information Center, VS COBOL II: Highlights and Techniques,* and *VAX COBOL On-Line,* published by John Wiley & Sons. He also wrote *COBOL: A Software Engineering Introduction* for Dryden Press, Inc. He has authored columns and numerous articles for *Data Training* magazine, and given presentations on course development at the annual Data Training conference.

1

Perspective:
Why VS COBOL II?

VS COBOL, IBM's long-standard COBOL compiler, has provided you
with a stable environment for more than a decade. Why fix something
that isn't broken?

Simply put, while VS COBOL isn't actually broken, it is very hobbled.
It's not good enough anymore. Its limits in accessing available memory
have made it obsolescent. In a few years, VS COBOL will be entirely
obsolete.

Figure 1.1 shows you how IBM has changed many parts of its software
environment since 1964. In this introductory chapter, I'll show you why
IBM released VS COBOL II and why you'll be using it in the near future.
And in the rest of this book, I will show you how to put VS COBOL II
to work without a lot of fuss!

1.1 THE EVOLUTION OF COBOL

COBOL originated in 1959. It was developed by a committee of computer
manufacturers, academicians, and government personnel. It was always
intended that the language would be revised as hardware capabilities
improved.

COBOL was revised in 1968, but the 1968 COBOL standard did not
cover random access disk, which was still in its infancy then.

COBOL was revised a second time in 1974. The 1974 COBOL standard
has been the most popular version of the language. It set standards for
random access disk files. **VS COBOL is 1974 COBOL.**

COBOL was again revised in 1980–85. **VS COBOL II gives you 1985 COBOL**. The new COBOL standards provide some programming conveniences. I'll show you the "extras" of 1985 COBOL that you need to know to do effective work. I'll also show you how to overcome some of its defects.

But new programming features are not the real reason you will start using VS COBOL II. The real reason IBM has provided VS COBOL II lies in the need to deal with the expanding memory environment. So before we get into VS COBOL II itself, I will explain some terminology and concepts involving mainframe memory and operating system evolution.

1.2 EVOLUTION OF THE MAINFRAME ENVIRONMENT

IBM invented the System/360 computer architecture in 1963 and delivered the first computer of this family in April 1964. That computer offered two operating systems:

- OS (Operating System) for large mainframes
- DOS "Disk Operating System" for smaller mainframes

The VM (virtual machine) operating system was developed as a system programming tool and commercialized much later.

OS was and continues to be IBM's flagship mainframe operating system. OS became MVS (Multiple Virtual Storages) in 1972 and memory (storage) began to be called "virtual storage." MVS memory management techniques let programs see and use 16 megabytes of space regardless of the actual amount of machine memory installed on the system. IBM's VS COBOL (1974 COBOL) was developed to work well within the MVS environment.

MVS has been upgraded to MVS/XA and MVS/ESA to take advantage of memory growth. By today's standards, the limits of the original OS/MVS operating system are quite constrained. MVS/XA and MVS/ESA overcome these limits at the *operating system level*. VS COBOL II overcomes the memory limits at the *applications programming level*.

1.3 COMPUTER SYSTEM MEMORY GROWTH

The single most significant factor pushing operating system and software upgrade is progress in manufacturing electronic memory.

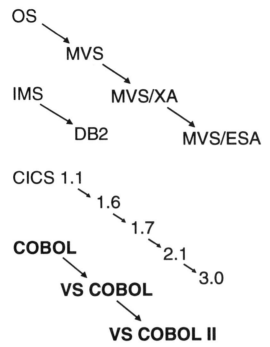

Figure 1.1 Progression of major IBM mainframe system software since the development of the System/360 in 1964.

In the 1960s computer memory consisted of separately manufactured magnetic cores each about a millimeter in diameter. Each core had several wires threaded through it. Core memory was expensive to make, it was physically large, and it consumed a lot of power. Its heat generation limited computers to a few megabytes of memory at most. In the 1960s many mainframes were equipped with 512K of memory or less! (Yes, *kilobytes*, not *megabytes!*)

In the 1970s semiconductor chip memory replaced magnetic cores in mainframes. With this technology a few hundred transistors (bits) were first placed on one circuit element. In the 1980s semiconductor memory density rapidly increased. 4K chips led to 16K chips, then 64K-bit chips. If you have a microcomputer you probably now have 256K-bit chips or one megabit chips in its memory. Chips containing 4 megabits of storage will soon become common.

IBM and other manufacturers have already produced 64-megabit chips. By the year 2000 the approximately 2″ square 256-megabit chips sketched in Figure 1.2 will be available in large machines. That's 32 megabytes of 8-bit memory in a chip that you can hold in your hand. But VS COBOL could only access much less than half of it!

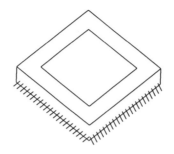

1 megabit chips (1990)

4 megabit chips (1992?)

16 megabit chips (1993?)

64 megabit chips (1995?)

256 megabit chips (1998?)

Figure 1.2   Progression of memory chip capacity.

This progression of machine memory has been underway for several years. All of the software changes in the operating system, IMS, DB2, CICS, and VS COBOL are aimed at making effective use of greatly expanded memory resources.

1.4   WHAT "ADDRESSING" MEANS

When the System/360 architecture was designed in 1964, memory addresses expressed with 24 binary digits (three 8-bit bytes) seemed very generous. After all, this supports $2^{24} = 16,777,216$ bytes; 16 megabytes. Back then, a machine with one-tenth this memory size was considered huge!

MVS/XA and MVS/ESA provide 31-bit addressing, which makes $2^{31} = 2,147,482,048$ bytes addressable. Now mainframe addresses (not just the annual national debt) can range into the billions. Figure 1.3 gives you some idea of the expansion in addressing range that 31-bit addresses provide.

Using the expanded memory range is important to your installation even if you don't write huge programs. Your organization's mainframes will become larger and larger repositories of information vital to your organization. Your installation will run more and more on-line systems

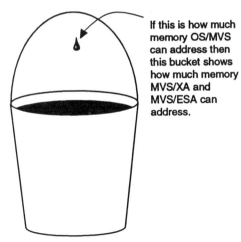

If this is how much memory OS/MVS can address then this bucket shows how much memory MVS/XA and MVS/ESA can address.

Figure 1.3 OS/MVS could access memory represented by a drop of water. MVS/XA and MVS/ESA can access a quantity of computer memory represented by the entire bucket.

and will store increasing quantities of data in databases. All of these uses will demand that your mainframes make the most effective use of the large memory resources that your mainframe computer system contains.

1.5 ACCESSING SYSTEM MEMORY: AMODE AND RMODE

You will become aware of the transition to greater memory sizes because you will see the terms AMODE and RMODE associated with your programs:

AMODE (addressing mode) The space that a program can access for data. AMODE(24) means 24-bit addresses for data; a program with AMODE(24) can access data only in memory below the 16 megabyte line. AMODE(31) means 31-bit data addresses; data can be accessed anywhere in memory.

RMODE (residence mode) The area of virtual storage in which the program can live. RMODE(24) means that a program must be put into memory below the 16 megabyte line, hogging memory that the operating system would prefer to use for other things. RMODE(ANY) means a program can execute anywhere in memory.

As you can see in Figure 1.4, the messages from the linkage editor (which processes your program after the COBOL compiler) tells you what AMODE and RMODE your program uses. You'll see AMODE(31) and

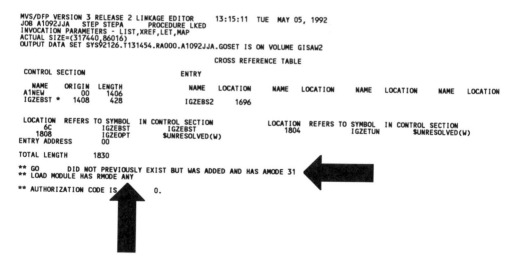

```
MVS/DFP VERSION 3 RELEASE 2 LINKAGE EDITOR     13:15:11  TUE  MAY 05, 1992
JOB A1092JJA    STEP STEPA      PROCEDURE LKED
INVOCATION PARAMETERS - LIST,XREF,LET,MAP
ACTUAL SIZE=(317440,86016)
OUTPUT DATA SET SYS92126.T131454.RA000.A1092JJA.GOSET IS ON VOLUME GISAW2
                                   CROSS REFERENCE TABLE

CONTROL SECTION                  ENTRY

  NAME     ORIGIN  LENGTH            NAME   LOCATION    NAME  LOCATION    NAME  LOCATION    NAME  LOCATION
A1NEW          00    1406
IGZEBST  *   1408     428          IGZEBS2    1696


LOCATION  REFERS TO SYMBOL  IN CONTROL SECTION           LOCATION  REFERS TO SYMBOL  IN CONTROL SECTION
    6C            IGZEBST      IGZEBST                        1804          IGZETUN      $UNRESOLVED(W)
  1808            IGZEOPT      $UNRESOLVED(W)
ENTRY ADDRESS          00

TOTAL LENGTH         1830

** GO        DID NOT PREVIOUSLY EXIST BUT WAS ADDED AND HAS AMODE 31
** LOAD MODULE HAS RMODE ANY

** AUTHORIZATION CODE IS        0.
```

Figure 1.4   AMODE and RMODE Linkage Editor Messages.

You see these types of messages from the linkage editor, which completes the handling of your program after you compile it. AMODE(24) means the data address mode of the program is limited to 24 bits while AMODE(31) means 31-bit data addressing. RMODE(24) means that the residence mode (where the program can be put into memory) is limited to a 24-bit address (below the 16 megabyte line) while RMODE(ANY) lets the program execute in any part of memory. VS COBOL can only provide AMODE(24) and RMODE(24). You need VS COBOL II to get AMODE(31) and RMODE(ANY)!

RMODE(ANY) only when you use the VS COBOL II compiler. VS COBOL II is IBM's first COBOL compiler that lets your programs use 31-bit address space.

Access to memory above the 16 megabyte line is the real reason IBM has provided VS COBOL II. And this is the real reason you will eventually have to use VS COBOL II!

1.6   *TRY IT!* LEARN BY RUNNING MY PROGRAMS!

I wrote this book to help professionals such as you quickly learn how to use VS COBOL II. All of the *Try It!* sections in the following chapters show you actual executable programs that demonstrate important features and techniques. Some of these programs also prove to you that you can get unexpected and potentially damaging results from some VS COBOL II facilities. You can actually run all of my *Try It!* programs to learn about VS COBOL II quickly.

To make your learning of VS COBOL II as rapid as possible, the publishers have arranged to make a version of this book available with source code in machine readable form. All of my programs are on diskette as plain ASCII files. You can run them directly with any PC-based 1985 COBOL compiler or you can upload them to your mainframe and run them with VS COBOL II. And speaking of PC-based 1985 COBOL compilers . . .

1.7 LEARNING WITH PC-BASED 1985 COBOL COMPILERS

Some installations now develop VS COBOL and VS COBOL II applications on PCs, test and debug them there, and then upload the source code to the mainframe for final compilation, testing, and production use. This is a good method for some types of work. It is also a very effective way to learn the 1985 COBOL coding aspects of VS COBOL II.

You'll be pleasantly surprised to learn that you can actually experiment with all 1985 COBOL coding features by using an educational version of the Ryan-McFarland COBOL-85 compiler, available for less than $20 with the sixth edition of *Structured COBOL Programming* by Nancy and Robert Stern (John Wiley & Sons, Inc., 1991). The RM/COBOL-85 compiler can run on any MS-DOS PC, even an 8088-based machine with only 384K memory. The educational version of this compiler is constrained by artificial limits to prevent its use commercially, but it provides an excellent way to see and try out many 1985 COBOL features and techniques.

I provided Appendix E in this book to help you use Ryan-McFarland COBOL-85, Microfocus COBOL 2, or Realia VS COBOL II. That appendix gives you specific information about SELECT/ASSIGN statement variations between these compilers. All of these compilers accept source code as plain ASCII text files. You can use any text editor or word processor (such as WordPerfect, Wordstar, Multimate, PC-Write, SPF-PC, or even MS-DOS EDLIN) to create programs as DOS files for these compilers.

2

What You Lose in VS COBOL II

Most VS COBOL programs will not work with the VS COBOL II compiler. Before you can make much progress in using the new compiler you have to know what is no longer available and how to do certain things a different way. In this chapter, I'll tell you what changes VS COBOL II presents in your life.

2.1 HOW IBM CHANGED YOUR COBOL WORLD

IBM seemed somewhat high-handed and arbitrary when it produced its first VS COBOL II compiler in 1984. In addition to dropping support for ISAM, it eliminated support for other features that programmers had found very useful. Customers complained loudly about IBM's handling of VS COBOL II Release 1. IBM restored a few of the features (but not all of them) when it offered VS COBOL Release 2 in 1986. But Release 2 also received lukewarm response in many installations.

VS COBOL II Release 3 now provides a stable product for your use. It permanently eliminates some VS COBOL features.

2.2 IBM TOOK AWAY SOME CONVENIENCES

IBM has permanently removed support for some common language features I have shown in Figure 2.1. Why did IBM make problems for you by doing this? That's a good question. Perhaps, since the compiler already had to be very large to support 1985 standards, IBM's software engineers

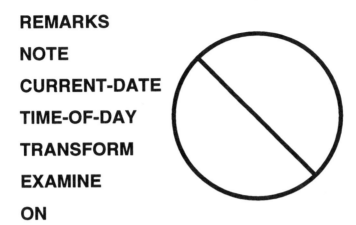

REMARKS

NOTE

CURRENT-DATE

TIME-OF-DAY

TRANSFORM

EXAMINE

ON

Figure 2.1   Summary of the most troublesome feature cuts made by IBM. You can no longer use any of these syntax features in your programs!

needed to trim somewhere. Still, as you will see, some of the feature cuts seem to make needless work for you in trivial areas. Here's what you have to do:

- Stop using the features that have been eliminated even in programs you now write in (old) VS COBOL. By not using these features, programs you write now will be easier to convert later.
- When you do program maintenance you may be required to upgrade a program from VS COBOL to VS COBOL II. You will need to change the parts of the program affected by feature deletions.

I show you here how to avoid problems with the most commonly used features that have been cut.

2.3 REMARKS AND NOTE

Both REMARKS and NOTE statements are documentation. You need to code these as comments now, by putting an asterisk in column 7. VS COBOL II won't recognize either of these as legal statement types.

2.4 YOU LOSE CURRENT-DATE!

The most unfortunate change made by IBM in VS COBOL II is dropping CURRENT-DATE. Up to now, you have been able to get today's date already formatted with slashes for page headings by moving CURRENT-DATE to a PIC X(8) field. For example, for August 23, 1992 MOVE CURRENT-DATE TO WS-MY-DATE would give you this in WS-MY-DATE:

```
08/23/92
```

But the only way to obtain the date with VS COBOL II is:

```
ACCEPT WS-DATE FROM DATE.
```

DATE is a PIC 9(6) or PIC X(6) special register that contains the Gregorian date in the form YYMMDD. For example, you will receive August 23, 1992 as:

```
920823
```

You'll have to ACCEPT this date into a field you code in WORKING-STORAGE, such as WS-DATE:

```
01 WS-DATE.
    05 WS-DATE-YR    PIC X(2).
    05 WS-DATE-MO    PIC X(2).
    05 WS-DATE-DA    PIC X(2).
```

Once you ACCEPT the date you can move the separate PIC X(2) parts of the date to build up the current date in a page heading in a traditional way:

```
MOVE WS-DATE-MO TO . . .
MOVE WS-DATE-DA TO . . .
MOVE WS-DATE-YR TO . . .
```

But I suggest that you achieve the format of date that you want by using STRING with literal slashes in between:

```
01 PAGE-HEADING-1.
    05 . . .
    05 . . .
    05 . . .
    05 PH1-DATE     PIC X(8).
------------------------------------------
```

```
ACCEPT WS-DATE FROM DATE.
STRING WS-DATE-MO '/'
       WS-DATE-DA '/'
       WS-DATE-YR    DELIMITED BY SIZE
   INTO PH1-DATE.
```

With this technique you have complete flexibility to select what mark you use between parts of the date (such as / or -) and how you format the date (MM/DD/YY or DD/MM/YY).

2.5 YOU LOSE TIME-OF-DAY

IBM has also removed the already-formatted TIME-OF-DAY. Instead, you now have to obtain the time like this:

```
ACCEPT WS-TIME FROM TIME.
```

TIME is a special register you can describe as PIC 9(8) or X(8). It contains hours, minutes, seconds, and hundredths since the previous midnight as HHMMSSHH. Once again, you must format it yourself if you want to print it with punctuation:

```
01  WS-TIME.
    05 WS-TIME-HRS    PIC X(2).
    05 WS-TIME-MIN    PIC X(2).
    05 WS-TIME-SEC    PIC X(2).
    05 WS-TIME-HUN    PIC X(2).
*
01  WS-TIME-FORMATTED PIC X(7).

------------------------------------------

  ACCEPT WS-TIME FROM TIME.
  STRING WS-TIME-HRS ':'
         WS-TIME-MIN '.'
         WS-TIME-SEC    DELIMITED BY SIZE
     INTO WS-TIME-FORMATTED.
```

As with VS COBOL you can't use ACCEPT in a CICS program for either DATE or TIME. You still need to use CICS commands to obtain date and time in on-line programs.

2.6 YOU LOSE TRANSFORM AND EXAMINE

TRANSFORM and EXAMINE are two of VS COBOL's specialized character handling verbs. You have not really lost the character substitution capabilities they provided. Instead, the 1985 COBOL standards required these capabilities to be provided by new options of the INSPECT verb. I'll show you in Chapter 11 how to use INSPECT to do the same things that you would have used TRANSFORM and INSPECT for in the past.

2.7 ISAM IS DEAD!

ISAM (Indexed Sequential Access Method) was IBM's software for indexed files from 1968 to 1973. IBM provided VSAM (Virtual Storage Access Method) in 1973 but continued supporting ISAM for many years. IBM finally dropped CICS support for ISAM in 1987. In a parallel move it dropped COBOL support for ISAM from the VS COBOL II compiler. Figure 2.2 just makes plain the unalterable fact that ISAM is dead, now completely replaced by VSAM.

There is a chance that you might still be caught in a source code conversion involving ISAM even if you work only on VSAM applications. Some installations changed from ISAM to VSAM and used a feature called the "ISAM Interface" of VS COBOL to minimize source code changes. This convenience was inefficient but provided a faster way to switch to VSAM files.

VS COBOL II drops support for the reserved words NOMINAL KEY, TRACK-AREA, FILE-LIMITS, PROCESSING MODE, and SEEK. Some of these were only treated as documentation by VS COBOL already.

2.8 NO READY TRACE OR EXHIBIT!

You can no longer use READY TRACE for debugging because VS COBOL II has eliminated it. READY TRACE activated a listing that showed each paragraph name as it received control. You might have used it to examine logic flow when test results were incorrect.

VS COBOL II also drops support for the EXHIBIT verb. EXHIBIT NAMED provided a display of data field contents prefaced by the WORKING-STORAGE name of the field. It was also handy for debugging. To achieve the same effect now, use DISPLAY. But to make a field label print, you can explicitly code the name:

```
DISPLAY 'WS-COUNTER = ', WS-COUNTER.
```

Figure 2.2 VSAM was released in 1973 as a replacement for ISAM. IBM has dropped all COBOL language support for ISAM in VS COBOL II. You can't use VS COBOL II to access an ISAM file.

In VS COBOL, EXHIBIT CHANGED WS-COUNTER would cause print only when executed and when the contents of the field cited had been modified since it was last exhibited. DISPLAY doesn't have this special capability. If you want to duplicate EXHIBIT you can develop your own logic to print selected items. But this is very burdensome and not really practical. So what are you going to do for debugging?

You will have to learn the new debugging techniques that VS COBOL II provides you! I show you in Chapter 15 how to use the COBTEST debugger in batch mode to duplicate what READY TRACE used to do. For many purposes this will be as painless as your old READY TRACE and EXHIBIT debugging.

In Chapter 16 I take you through an interactive debugging session. In interactive debugging you run COBTEST under TSO/ISPF and can immediately start running, stop, peek into, poke values into, and otherwise probe your program in a modern hands-on way.

2.9 FLOW OPTION, VERB COUNT: GONE!

IBM has drastically altered and/or renamed the parm (parameter) options you can use to control the compiler's operation. We'll cover VS COBOL II parm options in detail in the next chapter. But one of the most significant changes in VS COBOL II has been the elimination of the FLOW/COUNT option.

The VS COBOL compiler option FLOW was helpful in identifying the flow of control in a program prior to abend (abnormal ending). If a program abended, you could see the line numbers of the 100 instructions leading up to the failure. Now, you'll get this from COBTEST batch debugging.

At runtime, the COUNT option produced a list of verbs in the program, in source code sequence, and provided a count of the number of times each was executed during the run. With this tabulation you could readily locate "dead" or insufficiently executed code in the program. Now, the compiler automatically identifies and ignores dead (logically unreachable) code. Once again, the COBTEST debugging environment provides a solution for verb execution counting, and I will show you how to use it in Chapter 15.

2.10   REPORT WRITER: IT'S NOW IN A PRECOMPILER

Report Writer is a feature that makes it easy to produce control break reports. It's part of the ANSI standard for COBOL and has been present in VS COBOL all along. You may or may not have used it. If you did use it you might have been told that it has been dropped from VS COBOL II. Not so! In fact, Report Writer has been given even better support in the VS COBOL II environment.

It's true that Report Writer is not supported by the VS COBOL II compiler. Instead, IBM has put it into a separate piece of software named the Report Writer Precompiler (Product 5798-DYR). It reads a VS COBOL or VS COBOL II program that contains Report Writer coding and generates an equivalent VS COBOL II program without Report Writer syntax.

You don't have to change old programs that use Report Writer to "roll your own" page control and subtotaling logic. Just run your program through the precompiler and feed the newly-generated program source code into the VS COBOL II compiler as illustrated in Figure 2.3. If you use this precompiler your life doesn't change, just your JCL.

The Report Writer precompiler provides more features than VS COBOL Report Writer did. It supports 1974 and 1985 COBOL standards for Report Writer while VS COBOL implemented only the 1968 features. The precompiler also provides better error messages that carry the original line numbers of the program. A feature of the precompiler is called the "collator." It merges the source code listing of the precompiler and the compiler to produce a single consolidated source code listing for your use in debugging.

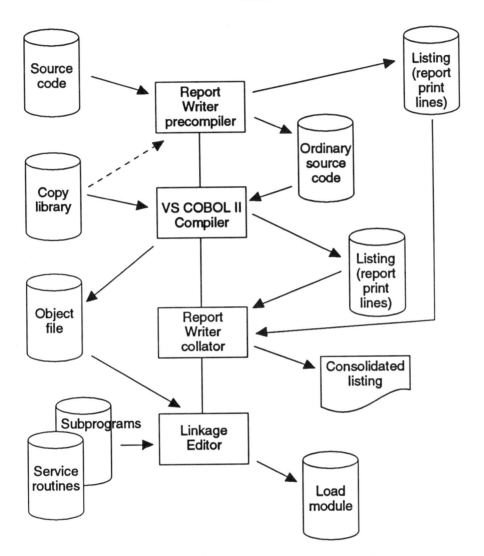

Figure 2.3   Report Writer Support by the VS COBOL II Environment.

Report Writer is not eliminated by the VS COBOL II environment but instead is supported by a precompiler. You write your program using standard Report Writer features. The precompiler reads your program and from it creates a new set of ordinary COBOL source code that will compile correctly. The collator produces a consolidated source code listing by merging report printing from the precompiler and the compiler. All you need to continue using Report Writer is the precompiler, collator and the JCL to run it. You can set the precompiler to handle your copy statements.

If your installation management does not want to pay the extra money to license the Report Writer precompiler, you will have to eliminate the REPORT SECTION, the INITIATE, GENERATE, and TERMINATE verbs, and all other Report Writer syntax elements from your programs. To convert such a program you'll have to install data-names and use your own logic to handle page control and subtotaling. That's usually a big job. If you are a Report Writer user, make sure your installation management is aware of the precompiler and budgets money to pay its separate license fee.

2.11   COMMUNICATION SECTION IS GONE

The COMMUNICATION SECTION of the DATA DIVISION was originally intended by COBOL's designers as a feature for computer terminal communication. But the purpose of this section was ultimately handled by CICS on IBM mainframes. ACCEPT MESSAGE COUNT, DISABLE, ENABLE, RECEIVE, and SEND are not supported by VS COBOL II.

2.12   MIGR OPTION AND CONVERSION ASSISTANCE

The (old) VS COBOL compiler will help you prepare for working with VS COBOL II. An option named MIGR was added to it several years ago. If you turn on this option, it gives you informational messages about any feature that you are using that will not work with the VS COBOL II compiler. In the next section I provide a *Try It!* program for you to see how MIGR works.

Your installation may license an IBM product named the CICS and COBOL Conversion Aid (CCCA) to help you convert VS COBOL programs to VS COBOL II. Other vendors have also aimed at the vast market of COBOL conversions with conversion products. These include Advance II from Language Technology Corporation and CA-Optimizer/ COBOL Migration Option from Computer Associates.

Conversion products may not provide complete conversion. You might still have to convert some CICS, IMS, IDMS, or DB2 code manually. And of course you have to check the operation of any converted code thoroughly to make sure you still get the same results from your compiled code. In the chapters that follow, I highlight for you the kinds of unexpected results that even a properly converted VS COBOL II might give you.

2.13 *TRY IT!* USING THE MIGR OPTION

In moving to VS COBOL II, IBM has eliminated some features that you may be using now. In this exercise you'll practice identifying these changes even before you start using VS COBOL II.

With little documentation, IBM added a new PARM option named MIGR to Release 2.4 of the existing VS COBOL compiler. If you use this option you will get informational messages warning you about the things that the program has in it that will be rejected by VS COBOL II. If you are still working mostly in VS COBOL, the MIGR option can start telling you how compatible (or incompatible) your programs are to VS COBOL II.

Program A1OLD, listed in Figure 2.4, is a program that creates a simple listing of some data that it reads from a file. The data read by this program is listed in Figure 2.5 on page 26. I have illustrated the output produced by it in Figure 2.6 on page 27.

Use JCL such as shown in Figure 2.7 (page 28) to compile, linkage edit, and run A1OLD with your existing VS COBOL compiler. See if you can find the informational messages about problems this program would have if processed by the VS COBOL II compiler. (As a hint, I have listed the informational messages in Figure 2.8 on page 28.)

2.14 *TRY IT!* SEEING VS COBOL II INCOMPATIBILITIES

VS COBOL II will complain if you use features that it does not support. The old VS COBOL compiler can tell you about these unsupported features using the MIGR option. Let's see what happens if you didn't use that advance warning but instead left unsupported features in a program and compiled it with VS COBOL II.

Use JCL similar to that listed in Figure 2.9 on page 29 to compile, linkage edit, and run A1OLD with the VS COBOL II compiler. When your job runs, you'll note that only the compile step functioned; the link edit and run didn't occur.

Take a look at how the new compiler reports errors right under their occurrence, rather than at the end of the compile listing. This is just one of the improvements IBM made in the output of the new compiler. We'll examine many more of the compiler output enhancements in the next chapter.

2.15 *TRY IT!* CONVERTING VS COBOL TO VS COBOL II

A1OLD is a straightforward reporting program that works well under VS COBOL. Let's pretend that you recently received an assignment to do a little maintenance on it to enhance its functionality.

(*text continues on page 26*)

VS COBOL Compile of Program A1OLD
(Compare to Figure 3.3)

```
00001 000100 IDENTIFICATION DIVISION.
00002 000200 PROGRAM-ID.    A1OLD.
00003 000300 AUTHOR.        J JANOSSY.
00004 000400 INSTALLATION.  DEPAUL UNIVERSITY.
00005 000500 DATE-WRITTEN.  DEC 1989.
00006 000600 DATE-COMPILED. MAY 5,1992.
00007 000700 REMARKS.       THIS PROGRAM READS A FILE OF TICKET RECORDS
00008                       FOR A PLEASURE CRUISE AND PRINTS A REPORT LISTING
00009                       EACH PASSENGER WITH VALIDATION OF QUANTITY FIELD
00010 001000*
00011 001100 ENVIRONMENT DIVISION.
00012 001200 CONFIGURATION SECTION.
00013 001300 SOURCE-COMPUTER. IBM-3090.
00014 001400 OBJECT-COMPUTER. IBM-3090.
00015 001500 INPUT-OUTPUT SECTION.
00016 001600 FILE-CONTROL.
00017 001700     SELECT MASTER-FILE       ASSIGN TO TICKDATA.
00018 001800     SELECT PASSENGER-REPORT  ASSIGN TO TICKLIST.
00019 001900*
00020 002000 DATA DIVISION.
00021 002100 FILE SECTION.
00022 002200*
00023 002300 FD MASTER-FILE
00024 002400    LABEL RECORDS ARE STANDARD
00025 002500    BLOCK CONTAINS 0 RECORDS
00026 002600    RECORD CONTAINS 80 CHARACTERS.
00027 002700 01 MASTER-RECORD                PIC X(80).
00028 002800*
00029 002900 FD PASSENGER-REPORT
00030 003000    LABEL RECORDS ARE OMITTED
00031 003100    BLOCK CONTAINS 0 RECORDS
00032 003200    RECORD CONTAINS 133 CHARACTERS.
00033 003300 01 PASSENGER-REPORT-PRINTLINE   PIC X(133).
```

```
00034 003400/
00035 003500 WORKING-STORAGE SECTION.
00036 003600 01 FILLER  PIC X(21)  VALUE 'WORKING STORAGE START'.
00037 003700*
00038 003800 01 WS-EOF-FLAG           PIC X(1)    VALUE 'M'.
00039 003900 88 WS-EOF-MORE-DATA                  VALUE 'M'.
00040 004000 88 WS-EOF                            VALUE 'E'.
00041 004100*
00042 004200 01 WS-COUNTERS.
00043 004300 05 WS-MF-REC-COUNT       PIC S9(5) COMP-3  VALUE +0.
00044 004400 05 WS-REC-LISTED-COUNT   PIC S9(5) COMP-3  VALUE +0.
00045 004500*
00046 004600 01 PASSENGER-REPORT-COUNTERS.
```

```
00047  004700    05  PR-LINES-REMAINING                  PIC S9(3)  COMP-3  VALUE +0.
00048  004800    05  PR-PAGE-COUNT                       PIC S9(3)  COMP-3  VALUE +0.
00049  004900*
00050  005000 01  MASTER-RECORD-INPUT-AREA.
00051  005100    05  MR-KEY.
00052  005200    05  MR-LAST-NAME                        PIC X(5).
00053  005300    05  MR-FIRST-NAME                       PIC X(14).
00054  005400    05  MR-CRUISE-DATE.                     PIC X(15).
00055  005500        10  MR-CRUISE-DATE-YR               PIC X(2).
00056  005600        10  MR-CRUISE-DATE-MO               PIC X(2).
00057  005700        10  MR-CRUISE-DATE-DA               PIC X(2).
00058  005800    05  MR-TICKET-QTY-X                     PIC X(3).
00059  005900    05  MR-TICKET-QTY-9  REDEFINES  MR-TICKET-QTY-X  PIC 9(3).
00060  006000    05  MR-DECK-CODE                        PIC X(2).
00061  006100    05  MR-SALES-AGENT                      PIC X(23).
00062  006200    05  MR-DATE-BOUGHT.
00063  006300        10  MR-DATE-BOUGHT-YR               PIC X(2).
00064  006400        10  MR-DATE-BOUGHT-MO               PIC X(2).
00065  006500        10  MR-DATE-BOUGHT-DA               PIC X(2).
00066  006600    05  FILLER                              PIC X(6).
00067  006700*
00068  006800 01  DECK-TABLE-SETUP.
00069  006900    05  FILLER  PIC X(17)  VALUE 'B  BRIDGE DECK    '.
00070  007000    05  FILLER  PIC X(17)  VALUE 'B1 BOAT DECK      '.
00071  007100    05  FILLER  PIC X(17)  VALUE 'B2 PROMENADE DECK '.
00072  007200    05  FILLER  PIC X(17)  VALUE 'S  SHELTER DECK   '.
00073  007300    05  FILLER  PIC X(17)  VALUE 'S1 FREEBOARD DECK '.
00074  007400    05  FILLER  PIC X(17)  VALUE 'C  MAIN DECK      '.
00075  007500    05  FILLER  PIC X(17)  VALUE 'C1 LOWER DECK     '.
00076  007600    05  FILLER  PIC X(17)  VALUE 'C2 ORLOP DECK     '.
00077  007700*
00078  007800 01  DECK-TABLE REDEFINES DECK-TABLE-SETUP.
00079  007900    05  DECK-TABLE-ROW     OCCURS 8 TIMES
00080  008000                           INDEXED BY DT-IX.
00081  008100        10  DT-DECK-CODE   PIC X(2).
00082  008200        10  FILLER         PIC X(1).
00083  008300        10  DT-DECK-NAME   PIC X(14).
00084  008400*
00085  008500 01  PR-PAGE-HEADING.
00086  008600    05  PR-HEADING-BORDER.
00087  008700        10  FILLER                          PIC X(1).
00088  008800        10  FILLER                          PIC X(132) VALUE ALL '*'.
00089  008900    05  PR-HEADING-INFO.
00090  009000        10  FILLER                          PIC X(1).


3         A1OLD              17.26.50       MAY  5,1992

00091  009100        10  FILLER  PIC X(22)  VALUE '*    MIRACLE PLEASURE C'.
00092  009200        10  FILLER  PIC X(22)  VALUE 'RUISES, INC.      *   PAS'.
00093  009300        10  FILLER  PIC X(22)  VALUE 'SENGER TICKET LIST'.
00094  009400        10  FILLER  PIC X(22)  VALUE '*    PROGRAM A1OLD'.
00095  009500        10  FILLER  PIC X(17)  VALUE 'REPORT R-1  '.
00096  009600    05  PR-HEADING-DATE                     PIC X(8).
```

Figure 2.4 A1OLD is a simple file-to-print program that you can use to experiment with the VS COBOL MIGR option and VS COBOL II error reporting. This program will successfully run with VS COBOL but will give you MIGR messages. It will not compile with VS COBOL II until you convert it.

19

```
00097  009700          10  FILLER               PIC X(12)  VALUE ' * PAGE '.
00098  009800          10  PR-HEADING-PAGE-NO   PIC ZZ9.
00099  009900          10  FILLER               PIC X(4)   VALUE ' *'.
00100  010000*
00101  010100   01  PR-COLUMN-HEADING.
00102  010200       05  PR-COL-HDR-1.
00103  010300          10  FILLER               PIC X(1).
00104  010400          10  FILLER               PIC X(22)  VALUE
00105  010500          10  FILLER               PIC X(22)  VALUE
00106  010600          10  FILLER               PIC X(22)  VALUE '         CRUISE'.
00107  010700          10  FILLER               PIC X(22)  VALUE
00108  010800          10  FILLER               PIC X(22)  VALUE '           DATE'.
00109  010900          10  FILLER               PIC X(22)  VALUE
00110  011000*
00111  011100       05  PR-COL-HDR-2.
00112  011200          10  FILLER               PIC X(22)  VALUE
00113  011300          10  FILLER               PIC X(22)  VALUE
00114  011400          10  FILLER               PIC X(22)  VALUE
00115  011500          10  FILLER               PIC X(22)  VALUE
00116  011600          10  FILLER               PIC X(22)  VALUE
00117  011700          10  FILLER               PIC X(22)  VALUE
00118  011800          10  FILLER               PIC X(1).  PASSENGER BO
00119  011900*                                  ID#        DATE
00120  012000       05  PR-COL-HDR-3.           OKING NAME     DEC
00121  012100          10  FILLER               PIC X(22)  VALUE
00122  012200          10  FILLER               PIC X(22)  VALUE
00123  012300          10  FILLER               PIC X(22)  VALUE
00124  012400          10  FILLER               PIC X(22)  VALUE
00125  012500          10  FILLER               PIC X(22)  VALUE
00126  012600          10  FILLER               PIC X(22)  VALUE
00127  012700          10  FILLER               PIC X(22)  VALUE
00128  012800*
00129  012900   01  PASSENGER-REPORT-DETAIL-LINE.
00130  013000       05  FILLER                  PIC X(1).
00131  013100       05  PR-KEY                  PIC X(5).
00132  013200       05  PR-PASSENGER-BOOKING-NAME   PIC X(28).  VALUE SPACES.
00133  013300       05  FILLER                  PIC X(2)   VALUE SPACES.
00134  013400       05  PR-CRUISE-DATE-MO       PIC X(2)   VALUE '-'.
00135  013500       05  FILLER                  PIC X(1)   VALUE '-'.
00136  013600       05  PR-CRUISE-DATE-DA       PIC X(2).
00137  013700       05  FILLER                  PIC X(1)   VALUE '-'.
00138  013800       05  PR-CRUISE-DATE-YR       PIC X(2).
00139  013900       05  FILLER                  PIC X(2)   VALUE SPACES.
00140  014000       05  PR-TICKET-QTY-X         PIC X(4).
00141  014100       05  PR-TICKET-QTY-9 REDEFINES  PR-TICKET-QTY-X  PIC ZZ9.
00142  014200          PR-TICKET-QTY-X          PIC X(4)   VALUE SPACES.
00143  014300       05  FILLER                  PIC X(2)   VALUE SPACES.
00144  014400       05  PR-DECK-CODE            PIC X(1)   VALUE SPACE.
00145  014500       05  FILLER                  PIC X(1)   VALUE SPACE.
00146  014600       05  PR-DECK-NAME            PIC X(14).
00147  014700       05  FILLER                  PIC X(2)   VALUE SPACES.
```

4   A1OLD   17.26.50   MAY 5,1992

20

```
00148  014800    05 PR-SALES-AGENT          PIC X(23).
00149  014900    05 FILLER                  PIC X(2)   VALUE SPACES.
00150  015000    05 PR-DATE-BOUGHT-MO       PIC X(2).
00151  015100    05 FILLER                  PIC X(1)   VALUE '-'.
00152  015200    05 PR-DATE-BOUGHT-DA       PIC X(2).
00153  015300    05 FILLER                  PIC X(1)   VALUE '-'.
00154  015400    05 PR-DATE-BOUGHT-YR       PIC X(2).
00155  015500    05 FILLER                  PIC X(3)   VALUE SPACES.
00156  015600    05 PR-ERROR-MSG            PIC X(21).
00157  015700*
00158  015800 01 PR-ENDLINE.
00159  015900    05 FILLER                  PIC X(1)   VALUE SPACE.
00160  016000    05 PR-EL-MESSAGE           PIC X(20).
00161  016100    05 FILLER                  PIC X(3)   VALUE SPACES.
00162  016200    05 PR-EL-COUNT             PIC Z,ZZZ,ZZ9.
00163  016300    05 FILLER                  PIC X(100) VALUE SPACES.
```

```
5      A1OLD        17.26.50      MAY 5,1992

00164  016400/ PROCEDURE DIVISION.
00165  016500 0000-MAINLINE.
00166  016600    READY TRACE.
00167  016700    PERFORM 1000-BOJ.
00168  016800    PERFORM 2000-PROCESS-A-RECORD
00169  016900       UNTIL WS-EOF-FLAG = 'E'.
00170  017000    PERFORM 3000-EOJ.
00171  017100    STOP RUN.
00172  017200*
00173  017300*
00174  017400 1000-BOJ.
00175  017500    OPEN   INPUT  MASTER-FILE   OUTPUT  PASSENGER-REPORT.
00176  017600    MOVE CURRENT-DATE TO PR-HEADING-DATE.
00177  017700    EXAMINE PR-HEADING-DATE REPLACING ALL '/' BY '-'.
00178  017800    PERFORM 2900-PR-NEWPAGE.
00179  017900    PERFORM 2700-READ-MASTER-FILE.
00180  018000*
00181  018100 2000-PROCESS-A-RECORD.
00182  018200    PERFORM 2100-FORM-A-PRINTLINE.
00183  018300    IF PR-LINES-REMAINING IS LESS THAN +1
00184  018400       PERFORM 2900-PR-NEWPAGE.
00185  018500    WRITE PASSENGER-REPORT-PRINTLINE
00186  018600       FROM PASSENGER-REPORT-DETAIL-LINE
00187  018700       AFTER ADVANCING 1 LINES.
00188  018800    SUBTRACT +1 FROM PR-LINES-REMAINING.
00189  018900    ADD +1 TO WS-REC-LISTED-COUNT.
00190  019000    PERFORM 2700-READ-MASTER-FILE.
00191  019100*
00192  019200 2100-FORM-A-PRINTLINE.
00193  019300    MOVE MR-KEY                TO PR-KEY.
00194  019400    MOVE SPACES                TO PR-PASSENGER-BOOKING-NAME.
00195  019500    STRING MR-FIRST-NAME   DELIMITED BY SPACE
00196  019600                           DELIMITED BY SIZE
```

Figure 2.4 *Continued*

```
00197                          MR-LAST-NAME     DELIMITED BY SPACE
00198                                           INTO PR-PASSENGER-BOOKING-NAME.
00199           MOVE MR-CRUISE-DATE-MO     TO PR-CRUISE-DATE-MO.
00200           MOVE MR-CRUISE-DATE-DA     TO PR-CRUISE-DATE-DA.
00201           MOVE MR-CRUISE-DATE-YR     TO PR-CRUISE-DATE-YR.
00202*
00203           IF MR-TICKET-QTY-9 IS NUMERIC
00204               MOVE MR-TICKET-QTY-9 TO PR-TICKET-QTY-9
00205               MOVE SPACES TO PR-ERROR-MSG
00206           ELSE
00207               MOVE MR-TICKET-QTY-X TO PR-TICKET-QTY-X
00208               MOVE '** QTY NOT NUMERIC **' TO PR-ERROR-MSG.
00209*
00210           MOVE MR-DECK-CODE              TO PR-DECK-CODE.
00211           SET DT-IX TO 1.
00212           SEARCH DECK-TABLE-ROW
00213               AT END
00214                   MOVE ALL '*DECK CODE ERR' TO PR-DECK-NAME
00215               WHEN MR-DECK-CODE = DT-DECK-CODE(DT-IX)
00216                   MOVE DT-DECK-NAME(DT-IX) TO PR-DECK-NAME.
00217*
00218           MOVE MR-SALES-AGENT       TO PR-SALES-AGENT.
00219           MOVE MR-DATE-BOUGHT-MO    TO PR-DATE-BOUGHT-MO.
00220           MOVE MR-DATE-BOUGHT-DA    TO PR-DATE-BOUGHT-DA.

6       A10LD        17.26.50        MAY  5,1992

00221           MOVE MR-DATE-BOUGHT-YR    TO PR-DATE-BOUGHT-YR.
00222*
00223       2700-READ-MASTER-FILE.
00224           READ MASTER-FILE INTO MASTER-RECORD-INPUT-AREA
00225               AT END
00226                   MOVE 'E' TO WS-EOF-FLAG.
00227           IF WS-EOF-FLAG NOT = 'E'
00228               ADD +1 TO WS-MF-REC-COUNT.
00229*
00230       2900-PR-NEWPAGE.
00231           ADD +1 TO PR-PAGE-COUNT.
00232           MOVE PR-PAGE-COUNT TO PR-HEADING-PAGE-NO.
00233           WRITE PASSENGER-REPORT-PRINTLINE FROM PR-HEADING-BORDER
00234               AFTER ADVANCING PAGE
00235           WRITE PASSENGER-REPORT-PRINTLINE FROM PR-HEADING-INFO
00236               AFTER ADVANCING 1 LINES.
00237           WRITE PASSENGER-REPORT-PRINTLINE FROM PR-HEADING-BORDER
00238               AFTER ADVANCING 1 LINES.
00239           WRITE PASSENGER-REPORT-PRINTLINE FROM PR-COL-HDR-1
00240               AFTER ADVANCING 3 LINES.
00241           WRITE PASSENGER-REPORT-PRINTLINE FROM PR-COL-HDR-2
00242               AFTER ADVANCING 1 LINES.
00243           WRITE PASSENGER-REPORT-PRINTLINE FROM PR-COL-HDR-3
00244               AFTER ADVANCING 1 LINES.
00245           MOVE SPACES TO PASSENGER-REPORT-PRINTLINE.
00246           WRITE PASSENGER-REPORT-PRINTLINE
```

```
00247              AFTER ADVANCING 2 LINES.
00248         MOVE +50 TO PR-LINES-REMAINING.
00249*
00250   3000-EOJ.
00251         MOVE SPACES TO PR-ENDLINE.
00252         MOVE '**** END OF JOB.        ' TO PR-EL-MESSAGE
00253         IF PR-LINES-REMAINING IS LESS THAN +2
00254             PERFORM 2900-PR-NEWPAGE.
00255         WRITE PASSENGER-REPORT-PRINTLINE FROM PR-ENDLINE
00256             AFTER ADVANCING 2 LINES.
00257         SUBTRACT +2 FROM PR-LINES-REMAINING.
00258*
00259         MOVE 'RECORDS READ         '      TO PR-EL-MESSAGE.
00260         MOVE WS-MF-REC-COUNT              TO PR-EL-COUNT.
00261         IF PR-LINES-REMAINING IS LESS THAN +1
00262             PERFORM 2900-PR-NEWPAGE.
00263         WRITE PASSENGER-REPORT-PRINTLINE FROM PR-ENDLINE
00264             AFTER ADVANCING 1 LINES.
00265         SUBTRACT +1 FROM PR-LINES-REMAINING.
00266*
00267         MOVE 'RECORDS PRINTED      '      TO PR-EL-MESSAGE.
00268         MOVE WS-REC-LISTED-COUNT         TO PR-EL-COUNT.
00269         IF PR-LINES-REMAINING IS LESS THAN +1
00270             PERFORM 2900-PR-NEWPAGE.
00271         WRITE PASSENGER-REPORT-PRINTLINE FROM PR-ENDLINE
00272             AFTER ADVANCING 1 LINES.
00273         SUBTRACT +1 FROM PR-LINES-REMAINING.
00274*
00275         CLOSE MASTER-FILE  PASSENGER-REPORT.
```

```
7      A10LD              17.26.50      MAY  5,1992

INTRNL NAME   LVL  SOURCE NAME                BASE    DISPL  INTRNL NAME  DEFINITION  USAGE   R O Q M
DNM=1-188     FD   MASTER-FILE                DCB=01         DNM=1-188    DS 80C      QSAM          F
DNM=1-213     01   MASTER-RECORD              BL=1           DNM=1-213    DS 135C     DISP
DNM=1-236     FD   PASSENGER-REPORT           DCB=02         DNM=1-236    DS 133C     QSAM          F
DNM=1-266     01   PASSENGER-REPORT-PRINTLINE BL=2    000    DNM=1-266    DS 21C      DISP
DNM=1-302     01   FILLER                     BL=3    000    DNM=1-302    DS 1C       DISP
DNM=1-313     88   WS-EOF-FLAG                BL=3    018    DNM=1-313    DS 1C       DISP
DNM=1-337     88   WS-EOF-MORE-DATA                          DNM=1-337
DNM=1-364     88   WS-EOF                                    DNM=1-364
DNM=1-381     01   WS-COUNTERS                BL=3    020    DNM=1-381    DS 0CL6     GROUP
DNM=1-405     02   WS-MF-REC-COUNT            BL=3    020    DNM=1-405    DS 3P       COMP-3
DNM=1-430     02   WS-REC-LISTED-COUNT        BL=3    023    DNM=1-430    DS 3P       COMP-3
DNM=1-459     01   PASSENGER-REPORT-COUNTERS  BL=3    028    DNM=1-459    DS 0CL4     GROUP
DNM=2-000     02   PR-LINES-REMAINING         BL=3    028    DNM=2-000    DS 2P       COMP-3
DNM=2-028     02   PR-PAGE-COUNT              BL=3    02A    DNM=2-028    DS 2P       COMP-3
DNM=2-051     01   MASTER-RECORD-INPUT-AREA   BL=3    030    DNM=2-051    DS 0CL80    GROUP
DNM=2-088     02   MR-KEY                     BL=3    030    DNM=2-088    DS 5C       DISP
DNM=2-104     02   MR-LAST-NAME               BL=3    035    DNM=2-104    DS 14C      DISP
DNM=2-126     02   MR-FIRST-NAME              BL=3    043    DNM=2-126    DS 15C      DISP
DNM=2-149     02   MR-CRUISE-DATE             BL=3    052    DNM=2-149    DS 0CL6     GROUP
DNM=2-176     03   MR-CRUISE-DATE-YR          BL=3    052    DNM=2-176    DS 2C       DISP
```

DMAP option (changes to the MAP option)

Figure 2.4 *Continued*

23

```
REG 7   BL =1
REG 8   BL =2

WORKING-STORAGE STARTS AT LOCATION 000A0 FOR A LENGTH OF 004B8.

12      A1OLD           17.26.50        MAY  5,1992

*STATISTICS*     SOURCE RECORDS = 275   DATA DIVISION STATEMENTS = 119   PROCEDURE DIVISION STATEMENTS =   72
*OPTIONS IN EFFECT*     SIZE = 1048576  BUF = 241664  LINECNT = 57   SPACE1, FLAGW, SEQ,  SOURCE
*OPTIONS IN EFFECT*     DMAP, NOPMAP, NOCLIST, NOSUPMAP, NOXREF   SXREF, LOAD, NODECK, APOST, NOTRUNC, FLOW= 30
*OPTIONS IN EFFECT*     NOTERM, NONUM, NOBATCH, NONAME, COMPILE=01   STATE, RESIDENT, DYNAM,  LIB, NOSYNTAX
*OPTIONS IN EFFECT*     NOOPTIMIZE, NOSYMDMP, NOTEST, VERB,  ZWB,  SYST, NOENDJOB, NOLVL
*OPTIONS IN EFFECT*     NOLST, NOFDECK, NOCDECK, LCOL2, L120,  DUMP, NOADV, NOPRINT,
*OPTIONS IN EFFECT*     NOCOUNT, NOVBSUM, NOVBREF, LANGLVL(2)
```

Compiler PARM option settings

```
13      A1OLD           17.26.50        MAY  5,1992

                        CROSS-REFERENCE DICTIONARY

DATA NAMES                      DEFN      REFERENCE

DECK-TABLE                      000078
DECK-TABLE-ROW                  000079
DECK-TABLE-SETUP                000068
DT-DECK-CODE                    000081    000214
DT-DECK-NAME                    000083    000216
DT-IX                           000079    000211    000214    000216
MASTER-FILE                     000017    000175
MASTER-RECORD                   000027    000224    000224    000275
MASTER-RECORD-INPUT-AREA        000050    000224
MR-CRUISE-DATE                  000054
MR-CRUISE-DATE-DA               000057    000200
MR-CRUISE-DATE-MO               000056    000199
MR-CRUISE-DATE-YR               000055    000201
MR-DATE-BOUGHT                  000062
MR-DATE-BOUGHT-DA               000065    000220
MR-DATE-BOUGHT-MO               000064    000219
MR-DATE-BOUGHT-YR               000063    000221
MR-DECK-CODE                    000060    000210    000214
MR-FIRST-NAME                   000053
MR-KEY                          000051    000193
MR-LAST-NAME                    000052
MR-SALES-AGENT                  000061    000218
MR-TICKET-QTY-X                 000058    000207
MR-TICKET-QTY-9                 000059    000203    000204
PASSENGER-REPORT                000018    000175    000185    000233  000235  000237  000239  000241  000243  000246  000255
```

SXREF option changes to XREF but is still sorted by data name

```
15      A1OLD        17.26.50      MAY  5,1992

PROCEDURE NAMES         DEFN        REFERENCE

0000-MAINLINE           000166      000168
1000-BOJ                000174      000169
2000-PROCESS-A-RECORD   000181      000182
2100-FORM-A-PRINTLINE   000192      000179   000190
2700-READ-MASTER-FILE   000223      000178   000184   000254   000262   000270
2900-PR-NEWPAGE         000230      000171
3000-EOJ                000250
```

(MIGR option messages are printed here if you activate them ... see Figure 2.8)

```
H96-LEVEL LINKAGE EDITOR OPTIONS SPECIFIED SIZE=1024K
    DEFAULT OPTION(S) USED -  SIZE=(1048576,65536)

****NEWPROG   DOES NOT EXIST BUT HAS BEEN ADDED TO DATA SET      AMODE 24
RMODE IS 24
AUTHORIZATION CODE IS    0.
```

(Program output follows ... see Figure 2.6)

```
1000-BOJ ,2900-PR-NEWPAGE ,2700-READ-MASTER-FILE ,2000-PROCESS-A-RECORD ,2100-FORM-A-PRINTLINE ,
2700-READ-MASTER-FILE ,2000-PROCESS-A-RECORD ,2100-FORM-A-PRINTLINE ,2700-READ-MASTER-FILE ,
2000-PROCESS-A-RECORD ,2100-FORM-A-PRINTLINE ,2700-READ-MASTER-FILE ,2000-PROCESS-A-RECORD ,
2700-READ-MASTER-FILE ,2000-PROCESS-A-RECORD ,2100-FORM-A-PRINTLINE ,2700-READ-MASTER-FILE ,
2000-PROCESS-A-RECORD ,2100-FORM-A-PRINTLINE ,2700-READ-MASTER-FILE ,2000-PROCESS-A-RECORD ,
2700-READ-MASTER-FILE ,2000-PROCESS-A-RECORD ,2100-FORM-A-PRINTLINE ,2700-READ-MASTER-FILE ,
2000-PROCESS-A-RECORD ,2100-FORM-A-PRINTLINE ,2700-READ-MASTER-FILE ,3000-EOJ ,
2100-FORM-A-PRINTLINE ,2700-READ-MASTER-FILE ,3000-EOJ ,
```

READY TRACE is not supported by VS COBOL II but you can use the COBTEST debugger to replicate it (see Chapter 15)

Figure 2.4 *Continued*

```
      1           2         3         4           5            6           7          8
----+----0----+----0----+----0----+----0---+----0---+----0----+----0----+----0----+----0
43102|IFORNIA    |CAL       |920317|007|B2|ULTIMATE TRAVEL AGENCY|910807|
43261|CANNON     |LUCE      |920317|001|C |FOX VALLEY TRAVEL     |911004|
43345|TOTALLER   |T.        |920317|002|C1|ULTIMATE TRAVEL AGENCY|911017|
43377|WHIZ       |G.        |920317|001|S |WORLD TRAVEL, INC.    |911123|
43480|TOUR       |D.        |920415|Xa |C1|HOLIDAY TOURS, INC.   |920117|
43483|INA        |CAROL     |920415|002|S |FOX VALLEY TRAVEL     |920118|
43484|ZONA       |HARRY     |920415|010|C2|UNRAVEL TRAVEL, INC.  |920222|
43507|RITA       |MARGA     |920415|002|&X|WORLD TRAVEL, INC.    |920401|
49257|FOOEY      |O.        |920507|004|B1|JACK SPRAT TRAVEL     |910803|
49321|ABAMA      |AL        |920507|-PQ|B |UWANNAGO TRAVEL AGENCY|911105|
49322|TUCKY      |KEN       |920507|002|C |ULTIMATE TRAVEL AGENCY|911105|
49467|LURKI      |TURKI     |920507|015|B1|HOLIDAY TOURS, INC.   |911224|
```

Figure 2.5 These data records will be read by program A1OLD. Each record documents the purchase of one or more tickets for a pleasure cruise.

Our end user likes the report produced by A1OLD, shown in Figure 2.6, especially the fact that it identifies records that have invalid data in the ticket quantity field. The content of this field should be numeric. If it's not, A1OLD clearly indicates the problem with a message on the report. Unfortunately, the program doesn't provide a count of the records that are flawed in this way. You'll need to install such a count and arrange to have it print with the label RECORDS WITH BAD TICKET QUAN-TITY at the end of the report.

Enhance A1OLD as required and make it work under VS COBOL II. Use JCL to compile, link, and run your converted program with the new compiler. This is very typical of the kind of "convert when you modify it" chore you will soon face in program maintenance!

2.16 VS COBOL II PROCS AND LIBRARIES

New cataloged procedures have been installed to access the VS COBOL II compiler. These procedures are named:

COB2UC   Compile only
COB2UCL   Compile and linkage edit
COB2UCLG   Compile, linkage edit, and go
COB2UCG   Compile, load, and go
COB2ULG   Linkage edit and go

The new compiler always needs a DD statement named //SYSUT5, whereas the old compiler needed this only if you used the SYMDMP

```
*************************************************************************************
*  MIRACLE PLEASURE CRUISES, INC.  *  PASSENGER TICKET LIST  *  PROGRAM A1OLD   REPORT R-1  *  05-05-92  *  PAGE   1  *
*************************************************************************************

                                   CRUISE    QTY                                              DATE
ID#    PASSENGER BOOKING NAME       DATE     PEOPLE   DECK              SALES AGENT            BOUGHT     QTY ERROR?
<--->  <------------------------>   <----->  <--->    <------------->   <------------------->  <----->    <----------------->

43102  CAL IFORNIA                  03-17-92    7     B2 PROMENADE DECK  ULTIMATE TRAVEL AGENCY  08-07-91
43261  LUCE CANNON                  03-17-92    1     C  MAIN DECK       FOX VALLEY TRAVEL       10-04-91
43345  T. TOTALLER                  03-17-92    2     C1 LOWER DECK      ULTIMATE TRAVEL AGENCY  10-17-91
43377  G. WHIZ                      03-17-92    1     S  SHELTER DECK    WORLD TRAVEL, INC.      11-23-91
43480  D. TOUR                      04-15-92   X@     C1 LOWER DECK      HOLIDAY TOURS, INC.     01-17-92   ** QTY NOT NUMERIC **
43483  CAROL INA                    04-15-92    2     S  SHELTER DECK    FOX VALLEY TRAVEL       01-18-92
43484  HARRY ZONA                   04-15-92   10     C2 ORLOP DECK      UNRAVEL TRAVEL, INC.    02-22-92
43507  MARGA RITA                   05-07-92    2     &X *DECK CODE ERR  WORLD TRAVEL, INC.      04-01-92
49257  O. FOOEY                     05-07-92    4     B1 BOAT DECK       JACK SPRAT TRAVEL       08-03-91
49321  AL ABAMA                     05-07-92  -PQ     B  BRIDGE DECK     UWANNAGO TRAVEL AGENCY  11-05-91   ** QTY NOT NUMERIC **
49322  KEN TUCKY                    05-07-92    2     C  MAIN DECK       ULTIMATE TRAVEL AGENCY  11-05-91
49467  TURKI LURKI                  05-07-92   15     B1 BOAT DECK       HOLIDAY TOURS, INC.     12-24-91

*** END OF JOB
RECORDS READ        12
RECORDS PRINTED     12
```

Figure 2.6 This output is produced by a successful run of program A1OLD.

```
EDIT --- CSCJGJ.CSC.CNTL(A1OLD) - 01.01 -------------------- COLUMNS 001 072
COMMAND ===>                                               SCROLL ===> PAGE
****** ***************************** TOP OF DATA ********************************
000001 //CSCJGJA  JOB 1,'BIN 7 JANOSSY',MSGCLASS=X,MSGLEVEL=(1,1),
000002 //   NOTIFY=CSCJGJ
000003 //*
000004 //*   THIS JCL = CSCJGJ.CSC.CNTL(A1OLD)
000005 //*
000006 //STEPA   EXEC  PROC=COBUCLG,
000007 // PARM.COB=('SIZE=1024K',
000008 //             'STATE',
000009 //             'FLOW=30',
000010 //             'SXR',
000011 //             'LIB',
000012 //             'DYN',
000013 //             'DMAP',
000014 //             'APOST',
000015 //             'MIGR'),
000016 //             PDS='CSCJGJ.CSC.COBOL',
000017 //   MEMBER='A1OLD'
000018 //GO.TICKDATA DD  DSN=CSCJGJ.CSC.CNTL(TICKDATA),DISP=SHR
000019 //GO.TICKLIST DD  SYSOUT=*
000020 //GO.SYSOUT   DD  SYSOUT=*
000021 //
```

> You may need to code your execution
> JCL with PARM.COB to override the
> VS COBOL compiler parameter setting
> for **MIGR**, the migration flagging
> parameter. (Your VS COBOL compile,
> link, and go proc is named COBUCLG
> or something similar.) When you code
> PARM.COB you have to supply the whole
> parameter string, not just changes!

Figure 2.7 MVS JCL is used to execute the standard compile/link/go IBM cataloged procedure for the VS COBOL compiler. PARM.COB on the EXEC statement overrides the proc to turn on the MIGR option.

```
1000-BOJ                    000174  000168
2000-PROCESS-A-RECORD       000181  000169
2100-FORM-A-PRINTLINE       000192  000182
2700-READ-MASTER-FILE       000223  000179  000190
2900-PR-NEWPAGE             000230  000178  000184  000254  000262  00027
3000-EOJ                    000250  000171
```

```
   16       A1OLD           17.55.36      MAY  5,1992

*** MIGRATION FLAGGING IN EFFECT ***

CARD    ERROR MESSAGE

7       IKF1225I-I     *** MIGR-OTHR *** REMARKS  IS NOT SUPPORTED IN VS COBOL II.
167     IKF1228I-I     *** MIGR-OTHR *** READY IS NOT SUPPORTED IN VS COBOL II.
176     IKF1225I-I     *** MIGR-OTHR *** CURRENT-DATE  IS NOT SUPPORTED IN VS COBOL II.
177     IKF1225I-I     *** MIGR-OTHR *** EXAMINE  IS NOT SUPPORTED IN VS COBOL II.
```

```
H96-LEVEL LINKAGE EDITOR OPTIONS SPECIFIED SIZE=1024K
        DEFAULT OPTION(S) USED -  SIZE=(1048576,65536)

****NEWPROG   DOES NOT EXIST BUT HAS BEEN ADDED TO DATA SET    AMODE 24
RMODE IS 24
AUTHORIZATION CODE IS      0.
```

Figure 2.8 The informational messages produced for A1OLD by the VS COBOL compiler when you specify the MIGR "migration" option.

```
EDIT ---- A1092JJ.LIB.JCL(VS2CLG) - 01.01 ------------------- COLUMNS 001 072
COMMAND ===>                                              SCROLL ===> PAGE
****** **************************** TOP OF DATA ********************************
000001 //A1092JJA  JOB (1092,COB2),'JANOSSY',CLASS=A,MSGCLASS=X,
000002 // NOTIFY=A1092JJ
000003 //*
000004 //* THIS JCL = A1092JJ.LIB.JCL(VS2CLG)
000005 //*
000006 //STEPA    EXEC  COB2UCLG,
000007 // PARM.COB2=('NOADV',
000008 //             'NOCMPR2',
000009 //             'DATA(31)',
000010 //             'DYN',
000011 //             'FASTSRT',
000012 //             'LANGUAGE(UE)',
000013 //             'NUMPROC(PFD)',
000014 //             'NOMAP')
000015 //COB2.SYSIN  DD   DSN=A1092JJ.LIB.COBOL(A1OLD),DISP=SHR
000016 //GO.TICKDATA DD   DSN=A1092JJ.LIB.JCL(TICKDATA),DISP=SHR
000017 //GO.TICKLIST DD   SYSOUT=*
000018 //GO.SYSOUT   DD   SYSOUT=*
000019 //
```

Figure 2.9 Use JCL similar to this to try to compile Program A1OLD with your VS COBOL II compiler. The program works fine with VS COBOL but you will receive error messages from VS COBOL II. Program conversions like this will be a fact of life for you over the next few years!

option. Unlike VS COBOL, the VS COBOL II compiler also requires DD statements for work files at //SYSUT6 and //SYSUT7.

New libraries have been set up to house the compiler and service routines. SYS1.COB2COMP is the library where the compiler and its many modules are usually stored. SYS1.COB2LIB is where service routines needed at runtime are housed.

3

VS COBOL II Release 3 Compiler Listings and Options

In this chapter I will show you how to interpret the VS COBOL II compiler's listing and how it communicates problems to you. You'll get a lot more out of this chapter if you have already run the *Try It!* exercises at the end of Chapter 2, and have your listings handy. If you haven't done the exercises at the end of Chapter 2, just look at my complete example in Figure 3.3.

3.1 MEET THE VS COBOL II COMPILER!

The VS COBOL II compiler is named IGYCRCTL. IBM's naming convention for its system software gives the first three letters of any software name a special role. These letters become the prefix for all messages produced by the software. Any screen or print messages starting with IGY are from the VS COBOL II compiler. I have listed some of the most common software error code prefixes in Table 3.1. I'm just telling you this so that you can easily recognize what software is "talking" to you.

3.2 PROGRAM A1NEW: A COMPLETE EXAMPLE

The best way to become comfortable with the VS COBOL II compiler is actually to go through a complete compiler-produced listing of source

Message Prefix	Software Producing the Message
IGY	VS COBOL II compiler
IGZ	VS COBOL II runtime modules (not the compiler)
IKF	(Old) VS COBOL compiler
HEW	Linkage editor and program loader
DFH	CICS environment
DFS	IMS environment
DSN	DB2 environment
IDC	VSAM Access Method Services (IDCAMS)
IEA	MVS operating system supervisor
IEC	MVS data management subsystem
IEF	MVS job scheduler subsystem
IAT	Job Entry Subsystem 3 (JES3)
ICE	DFSORT utility
WER	Syncsort utility (not IBM)

Table 3.1 Software name and error code prefixes assigned by IBM and non-IBM third-party vendors. You'll see these letters on messages generated by software such as the VS COBOL II compiler.

code you have already seen. I'm going to use the job stream in Figure 3.1 for an extended example involving program A1NEW. This is my solution for the *Try It!* exercise in section 2.15 of this book. This program reads data from a file of pleasure cruise ticket sales and lists it to paper, creating a simple report. This job stream is represented by the MVS JCL in Figure 3.2.

3.3 VS COBOL II COMPILER LISTING FOR A1NEW

Figure 3.3 is the entire compiler listing produced by VS COBOL II for the A1NEW program. This figure is very important to this book and I want to explain something about it to you.

Publishing a book designed for rapid learning is a little tricky. Given the normal typesetting and page layout processes the author usually has minimal control over the placement of text and related figures. To get around this problem I have arranged Figure 3.3 differently than you would see in many books. I have formatted this long figure into parts and put explanations of its major points into the figure legends.

Figure 3.3 is completely explained in its legends on pages 34 through 55. There is no point in my repeating many of those same words here in text. At this point please examine Figure 3.3 carefully. Then return to this chapter at section 3.4 (page 33).

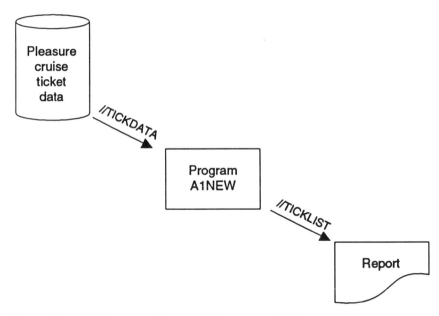

Figure 3.1 Job Stream Diagram of Program A1NEW.

A1NEW reads data from a file and lists it on a report. This is the program you could convert from VS COBOL to VS COBOL II in section 2.15 of this book. When I converted the program and compiled it, the VS COBOL II compiler produced the listing in Figure 3.3.

```
EDIT ---- A1092JJ.LIB.JCL(A1NEW) - 01.02 ------------------- COLUMNS 001 072
COMMAND ===>                                                 SCROLL ===> PAGE
****** ************************** TOP OF DATA ****************************
000001 //A1092JJA  JOB (1092,COB2),'JANOSSY',CLASS=A,MSGCLASS=X,
000002 //  NOTIFY=A1092JJ
000003 //*
000004 //* THIS JCL = A1092JJ.LIB.JCL(A1NEW)
000005 //*                                    ┌─────────────────────────────┐
000006 //STEPA   EXEC  COB2UCLG,              │ Use this type of JCL to execute│
000007 // PARM.COB2=('NOADV',  ───────────────│ your VS COBOL II compiler. Make │
000008 //          'NOCMPR2',                 │ sure that you code ".COB2" as the│
000009 //          'DATA(31)',                │ correct stepname of your compile │
000010 //          'DYN',                     │ proc. This lets you set the PARM │
000011 //          'FASTSRT',                 │ (parameter) options for compiling.│
000012 //          'LANGUAGE(UE)',            │ You can also use a PROCESS state-│
000013 //          'NUMPROC(PFD)',            │ ment in your program to set PARMs.│
000014 //          'NOMAP')                   └─────────────────────────────┘
000015 //COB2.SYSIN   DD  DSN=A1092JJ.LIB.COBOL(A1NEW),DISP=SHR
000016 //GO.TICKDATA  DD  DSN=A1092JJ.LIB.JCL(TICKDATA),DISP=SHR
000017 //GO.TICKLIST  DD  SYSOUT=*
000018 //GO.SYSOUT    DD  SYSOUT=*
000019 //
```

Figure 3.2 Use this type of job control language to compile, linkage edit, and execute your VS COBOL II programs. In Chapter 2 you saw the source code for program A1OLD, a VS COBOL program. I've converted A1OLD to VS COBOL II and named it A1NEW.

3.4   NEW COMPILER MESSAGES AND CODES

VS COBOL II supplies you with better and clearer information about your program than did the old VS COBOL compiler. For instance, error messages now always refer to field names by the real names, not names such as "DNM=1-234" as VS COBOL did. And the new compiler gives you informational and error messages embedded directly in the source code listing after the line referred to, as illustrated on page 38.

The suffix on an embedded or ending IGY message tells you if the message is informational, a warning, or an error. You can control how much of this information is embedded in your source code listing. Figure 3.4 (page 57) shows you the meaning of the message suffixes and how to use the FLAG(x,y) option to control embedding.

You get the maximum embedded messages from the compiler with FLAG(I,I). You get no embedded informational messages with FLAG(I,W). All messages always print at the end of the listing.

3.5   THE PROCESS STATEMENT

You can use the optional PROCESS statement to set compiler options, such as FLAG(I,W), within the source code instead of setting them by using JCL. This is a major convenience! You code PROCESS before the PROCEDURE DIVISION heading:

```
000100 PROCESS  FLAG(I,W)   MAP  OFFSET
000200 IDENTIFICATION DIVISION.
000200 PROGRAM-ID.  TABLE1.
000300 AUTHOR.        J. JANOSSY.
         -
         -
         -
```

You saw how I used this in my A1NEW program in Figure 3.3 (page 36) to set the XREF, MAP, LIST, and OFFSET options on. Some simple rules govern your use of the PROCESS statement:

- You can put more than one compiler option on a PROCESS statement.
- You can't continue options from one PROCESS statement to another but you can use multiple PROCESS statements if you group them all before the IDENTIFICATION DIVISION.

(text continues on page 57)

```
                    J E S 2   J O B   L O G  --  S Y S T E M   G I S A  --  N O D E   G I S A N J E

13.14.54 JOB 7244  IEF097I A1092JJA - USER A1092JJ ASSIGNED
13.14.55 JOB 7244  IEF677I WARNING MESSAGE(S) FOR JOB A1092JJA ISSUED
13.14.55 JOB 7244  $HASP373 A1092JJA STARTED - INIT 5 - CLASS A - SYS GISA - DATE 92126
13.14.55 JOB 7244  IEF403I A1092JJA STARTED - TIME 13.14.55
13.15.17 JOB 7244  $HASP395 A1092JJA ENDED - DATE 92126

----- JES2 JOB STATISTICS -----
06 MAY 92 JOB EXECUTION DATE
        20 CARDS READ
     1,000 SYSOUT PRINT RECORDS
         0 SYSOUT PUNCH RECORDS
        79 SYSOUT SPOOL KBYTES
      0.38 MINUTES EXECUTION TIME

 1 //A1092JJA JOB (1092,COB2),'JANOSSY',CLASS=A,MSGCLASS=X,                   JOB 7244
   //         NOTIFY=A1092JJ
 ***        THIS JCL = A1092JJ.LIB.JCL(A1NEW)
 ***
 2 //STEPA  EXEC COB2UCLG,                                                    00010000
   //  PARM.COB2=('NOADV',                                                    00020000
   //            'NOCMPR2',                                                   00030002
   //            'DATA(31)',                                                  00040000
   //            'DYN',                                                       00050000
   //            'FASTSRT',                                                   00060000
   //            'LANGUAGE(UE)',                                              00070000
   //            'NUMPROC(PFD)',                                              00080000
   //            'NOMAP',                                                     00090000
   //            'NOVBREF')                                                   00100000
 3 XXCOB2UCLG PROC                                                           00110000
   ***       PROC FOR COBOL II - COMPILE, LINK, AND GO                       00121001
 4 XXCOB2    EXEC PGM=IGYCRCTL,PARM='OBJECT',REGION=3500K                    00122004
 5 XXSTEPLIB DD  DSNAME=SYS1.COB2COMP,DISP=SHR                               00130001
 6 XXSYSPRINT DD SYSOUT=*                                                    00140000
 7 XXSYSLIN  DD  DSNAME=&&LOADSET,UNIT=SYSDA,DISP=(MOD,PASS)                  00150000
   XX            SPACE=(TRK,(3,3)),DCB=(BLKSIZE=80,LRECL=80,RECFM=FB)        00160000
 8 XXSYSUT1  DD  UNIT=SYSDA,SPACE=(CYL,(1,1))                                00170000
 9 XXSYSUT2  DD  UNIT=SYSDA,SPACE=(CYL,(1,1))                                00180000
10 XXSYSUT3  DD  UNIT=SYSDA,SPACE=(CYL,(1,1))                                00190000
11 XXSYSUT4  DD  UNIT=SYSDA,SPACE=(CYL,(1,1))                                00200000
12 XXSYSUT5  DD  UNIT=SYSDA,SPACE=(CYL,(1,1))                                00210000
13 XXSYSUT6  DD  UNIT=SYSDA,SPACE=(CYL,(1,1))                                00220000
14 XXSYSUT7  DD  UNIT=SYSDA,SPACE=(CYL,(1,1))                                00230000
15 //COB2.SYSIN DD DSN=A1092JJ.LIB.COBOL(A1NEW),DISP=SHR                     00240000
16 XXLKED    EXEC PGM=IEWL,PARM='LIST,XREF,LET,MAP',COND=(5,LT,COB2)         00250000
17 XXSYSLIN  DD  DSNAME=&&LOADSET,DISP=(OLD,DELETE)
   XX            DDNAME=SYSIN
18 XXSYSLMOD DD  DSNAME=&&GOSET(GO),DISP=(,PASS),UNIT=SYSDA,
   XX            SPACE=(CYL,(1,1,1))
19 XXSYSLIB  DD  DSNAME=SYS1.COB2LIB,DISP=SHR
20 XXSYSUT1  DD  UNIT=SYSDA,SPACE=(CYL,(1,1))
21 XXSYSPRINT DD SYSOUT=*
22 XXGO      EXEC PGM=*.LKED.SYSLMOD,COND=((5,LT,LKED),(5,LT,COB2))
23 XXSTEPLIB DD  DSNAME=SYS1.COB2LIB,DISP=SHR
24 XXSYSDBOUT DD SYSOUT=*
25 XXSYSABOUT DD SYSOUT=*
26 XXSYSDUMP DD  SYSOUT=*
27 XXSYSDUMP DD  SYSOUT=*
28 //GO.TICKDATA DD DSN=A1092JJ.LIB.JCL(TICKDATA),DISP=SHR
29 //GO.TICKLIST DD SYSOUT=*
30 //GO.SYSOUT  DD SYSOUT=*

STMT NO. MESSAGE

 23 IEF686I DDNAME REFERRED TO ON DDNAME KEYWORD IN PRIOR STEP WAS NOT RESOLVED

IEF236I ALLOC. FOR A1092JJA COB2 STEPA
IEF237I 301  ALLOCATED TO STEPLIB
IEF237I JES2 ALLOCATED TO SYSPRINT
IEF237I 834  ALLOCATED TO SYSLIN
IEF237I 70A  ALLOCATED TO SYSUT1
IEF237I 821  ALLOCATED TO SYSUT2
IEF237I 821  ALLOCATED TO SYSUT3
```

34

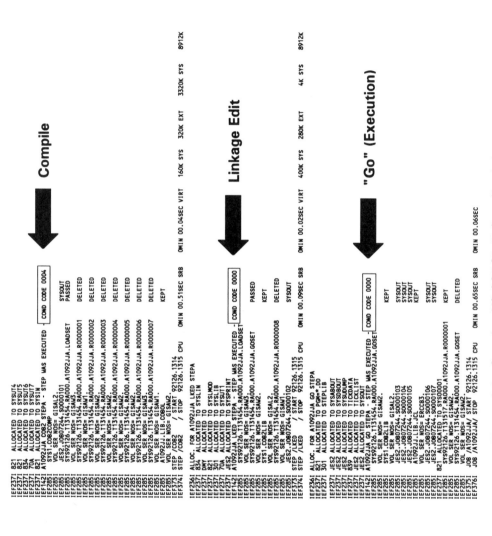

Figure 3.3 Complete VS COBOL II Compile Listing of A1NEW.

INVOCATION PARAMETERS:

NOADV,NOCMPR2,DATA(31),DYN,FASTSRT,LANGUAGE(UE),NUMPROC(PFD),NOMAP,NOVBREF

    IGYOS4001-W THE "FASTSRT" OPTION WAS NOT ALLOWED BY LOCAL INSTALLATION CONTROL. THIS OPTION WAS DISCARDED.

PROCESS(CBL) STATEMENTS:

000100 PROCESS XREF MAP LIST OFFSET

    IGYOS4022-W THE "LIST" OPTION WAS DISCARDED DUE TO OPTION CONFLICT RESOLUTION. THE "OFFSET" OPTION FROM "PROCESS/CBL"
                 STATEMENT TOOK PRECEDENCE.

OPTIONS IN EFFECT:
    NOADV
    APOST
    NOAMO
    BUFSIZE(4096)
    NOCMPR2
    COMPILE
    DATA(31)
    NODBCS
    NODECK
    NODUMP
    DYNAM
    NOEXIT
    NOFASTSRT
    NOFDUMP
    FLAG(I,I)
    NOFLAGMIG
    NOFLAGSAA
    NOFLAGSTD
    LANGUAGE(UE)
    LIB
    LINECOUNT(60)
    NOLIST
    MAP
    NONAME
    NONUMBER
    NUMPROC(PFD)
    OBJECT
    OFFSET
    OPTIMIZE
    OUTDD(SYSOUT)
    RENT
    RESIDENT
    NOSEQUENCE
    SIZE(3584000)
    SOURCE
    SPACE(1)
    NOSSRANGE
    NOTERM
    NOTEST
    TRUNC(OPT)
    NOVBREF
    NOWORD
    XREF(FULL)
    ZWB

(a)

Figure 3.3 Complete VS COBOL II Compile Listing of A1NEW

You'll get a listing like this if you compile A1NEW with VS COBOL II. In the several pages that follow I explain this listing to you via the circled letters. Follow these figure legends and you'll get the best "tour" of the VS COBOL II compiler listing that I can provide!

a. You can turn on compiler options with the PROCESS statement, which you put before the first line of your program. The PROCESS statement I used starts with the line number 000100. I have used it to turn on the XREF cross reference listing, data MAP, assembler LISTing, and condensed list OFFSET. Notice that the compiler warns me that the LIST option (the old "PMAP" assembler listing option) conflicts with the OFFSET listing (the old "CLIST" option) and OFFSET prevails here. VS COBOL II lists your options in a column before the source code. This is much nicer than VS COBOL! I cover many of the options important to you as a programmer in this chapter.

```
000001    000200 IDENTIFICATION DIVISION.
000002    000300 PROGRAM-ID.    A1NEW.
000003    000400*************************************************
000004    000500*                                               *
000005    000600*          BY JIM JANOSSY  DEPAUL UNIVERSITY  3/15/92  *
000006    000700*                                               *
000007    000800*    THIS PROGRAM READS A FILE OF TICKET RECORDS   *
000008    000900*    FOR A PLEASURE CRUISE AND PRINTS A REPORT THAT *
000009    001000*    LISTS EACH WITH VALIDATION OF QUANTITY FIELD   *
000010    001100*                                               *
000011    001200*    CHANGES:   5/05/92   CONVERTED TO VS COBOL II  *
000012    001300*                                               *
000013    001400*************************************************
000014    001500 ENVIRONMENT DIVISION.
000015    001600 INPUT-OUTPUT SECTION.
000016    001700 FILE-CONTROL.
000017    001800*
000018    001900* FOR MICRO FOCUS COBOL:
000019    002000*    SELECT MASTER-FILE        ASSIGN EXTERNAL TICKDATA
000020    002100*      ORGANIZATION IS LINE SEQUENTIAL.
000021    002200*    SELECT PASSENGER-REPORT   ASSIGN EXTERNAL TICKLIST
000022    002300*      ORGANIZATION IS LINE SEQUENTIAL.
000023    002400*
000024    002500* FOR VS COBOL II:
000025    002600    SELECT MASTER-FILE        ASSIGN TO TICKDATA.
000026    002700    SELECT PASSENGER-REPORT   ASSIGN TO TICKLIST.
000027    002800*
000028    002900*
```

Dual sets of SELECT/ASSIGN statements are handy if you work on a microcomputer and upload code to a mainframe

```
                                                                                33
                                                                                38
```

```
000030    003100 DATA DIVISION.
000031    003200 FILE SECTION.
000032    003300*
000033    003400 FD MASTER-FILE

==000033==> IGYGR1216-I A "RECORDING MODE" OF "F" WAS ASSUMED FOR FILE "MASTER-FILE".

000034    003500    BLOCK CONTAINS 0 RECORDS
000035    003600    RECORD CONTAINS 80 CHARACTERS.                           BLF=0000+000         80C
000036    003700 01 MASTER-RECORD                      PIC X(80).
000037    003800*
000038    003900 FD PASSENGER-REPORT

==000038==> IGYGR1216-I A "RECORDING MODE" OF "F" WAS ASSUMED FOR FILE "PASSENGER-REPORT".

000039    004000    BLOCK CONTAINS 0 RECORDS
000040    004100    RECORD CONTAINS 133 CHARACTERS.                          BLF=0001+000        133C
000041    004200 01 PASSENGER-REPORT-PRINTLINE  PIC X(133).
000042    004300*
```

Figure 3.3 *Continued*

b. VS COBOL II gives you a column ruler on all pages of your listing. This is very handy because it lets you see if you have coded statements beyond column 72, which is the last column in which the compiler "sees" actual source code. Eliminate REMARKS; make these lines comments.

c. You now get automatic cross-referencing in your listing! The 33 and 38 here on SELECT/ASSIGN lines point to the LINEIDs where I coded the corresponding FDs.

d. The ∗∗∗ DATA DIVISION ∗∗∗ title on this page comes from a TITLE statement I put at line 003000, which the compiler does not show as normal source code. You code TITLE statements as:

```
003000 TITLE '*** DATA DIVISION ***'.
```

You can put TITLE statements anywhere you like. They replace the compiler's labeling on the source code listing and cause a page eject of your listing. You can put any label up to 65 characters long on each TITLE statement.

Notice the embedded messages labeled IGYGR1216-I. The suffix "I" indicates that these are informational messages. You can control whether I, W, E, S, and U messages are embedded in source code or listed only at the end of the code (see chart on page 57).

e. The MAP option gives you a data map like the old VS COBOL "DMAP" option. But it lists within the source code, not afterward, so it is much handier! The BLF values are "base locator" cells that are useful only in dump analysis, but the 80C and 133C shown here are the assembler equivalents of field definitions.

39

```
                                                       A1NEW    DATE 05/05/92   TIME 13:14:57   PAGE    4
*** WORKING-STORAGE SECTION ***                                                                MAP AND CROSS REFERENCE
LINEID PL SL ----*A-1-B--+----2----+----3----+----4----+----5----+----6----+----7-|-+----8

000044      *** WORKING-STORAGE SECTION ***
000045 004500 WORKING-STORAGE SECTION.
000046 004600 01  FILLER  PIC X(21)   VALUE 'WORKING STORAGE START'.      BLW=0000+000          21C
000047 004700 01  WS-DATE.                                                BLW=0000+018          0CL6
000048 004800 05  WS-DATE-YR  PIC X(2).                                   BLW=0000+018,0000002  2C
000049 004900 05  WS-DATE-MO  PIC X(2).                                   BLW=0000+01A,0000002  2C
000050 005000 05  WS-DATE-DA  PIC X(2).                                   BLW=0000+01C,0000004  2C
000051 005100*01  WS-EOF-FLAG           PIC X(1)          VALUE 'M'.      BLW=0000+020,0000000  1C
000052 005200 88  WS-EOF-MORE-DATA                        VALUE 'M'.
000053 005300 88  WS-EOF                                  VALUE 'E'.
000054 005400*01  WS-COUNTERS.                                            BLW=0000+028          0CL6
000055 005600 05  WS-MF-REC-COUNT       PIC S9(5)  COMP-3 VALUE +0.       BLW=0000+028,0000003  3P
000056 005700 05  WS-REC-LISTED-COUNT   PIC S9(5)  COMP-3 VALUE +0.       BLW=0000+028,0000003  3P
000058 005900*01  PASSENGER-REPORT-COUNTERS.                              BLW=0000+030          0CL4
000059 006000 05  PR-LINES-REMAINING    PIC S9(3)  COMP-3 VALUE +0.       BLW=0000+030,0000002  2P
000060 006200 05  PR-PAGE-COUNT         PIC S9(3)  COMP-3 VALUE +0.       BLW=0000+032,0000002  2P

000063 006400 01  MASTER-RECORD-INPUT-AREA.                               BLW=0000+038          0CL80
000064 006600 05  MR-KEY.                                                 BLW=0000+038,0000005  5C
000065 006600 05  MR-LAST-NAME          PIC X(5).                         BLW=0000+038,0000005  14C
000066 006700 05  MR-FIRST-NAME         PIC X(14).                        BLW=0000+03D,0000005  15C
000067 006800 05  MR-CRUISE-DATE.                                         BLW=0000+048,0000013  21C
000068 006900 10  MR-CRUISE-DATE-YR     PIC X(2).
000069 007000 10  MR-CRUISE-DATE-MO     PIC X(2).
000070 007100 10  MR-CRUISE-DATE-DA     PIC X(2).
000071 007200 05  MR-TICKET-QTY-X       PIC X(3).                         BLW=0000+05A,0000022  2C
000072 007300 05  MR-TICKET-QTY-9 REDEFINES MR-TICKET-QTY-X  PIC 9(3).
000073 007400 05  MR-DECK-CODE          PIC X(2).                         BLW=0000+05C,0000024  2C
000074 007500 05  MR-SALES-AGENT        PIC X(25).                        BLW=0000+05E,0000026  2C
000075 007600 05  MR-DATE-BOUGHT.
000076 007700 10  MR-DATE-BOUGHT-YR     PIC X(2).
000077 007800 10  MR-DATE-BOUGHT-MO     PIC X(2).
000078 007900 10  MR-DATE-BOUGHT-DA     PIC X(2).
000079 008000 05  FILLER                PIC X(6).                         71

000081 008100 01  DECK-TABLE-SETUP.                                       —81
000082 008200 05  FILLER PIC X(17) VALUE 'B   BRIDGE DECK   '.
000083 008300 05  FILLER PIC X(17) VALUE 'B1  BOAT DECK     '.
000084 008400 05  FILLER PIC X(17) VALUE 'B2  PROMENADE DECK'.
000085 008500 05  FILLER PIC X(17) VALUE 'S   SHELTER DECK  '.
000086 008600 05  FILLER PIC X(17) VALUE 'S1  FREEBOARD DECK'.
000087 008700 05  FILLER PIC X(17) VALUE 'C   MAIN DECK     '.
000088 008800 05  FILLER PIC X(17) VALUE 'C1  LOWER DECK    '.
000089 008900 05  FILLER PIC X(17) VALUE 'C2  ORLOP DECK    '.
000091 009100*01  DECK-TABLE REDEFINES DECK-TABLE-SETUP.
000092 009200 05  DECK-TABLE-ROW                OCCURS 8 TIMES
000093 009300                                   INDEXED BY DT-IX.
000094 009400 10  DT-DECK-CODE    PIC X(2).
000095 009500 10  FILLER          PIC X(1).
000096 009600 10  DT-DECK-NAME    PIC X(14).
000098 009800*01  PR-PAGE-HEADING.
000099 009900 05  PR-HEADING-BORDER.
000100 010100 10  FILLER          PIC X(1).
000101 010200 10  FILLER          PIC X(132) VALUE ALL '*'.
```

(f) (g)

```
000102
000103 010300        05  PR-HEADING-INFO.
000104 010400           10  FILLER              PIC X(1).
000105 010500           10  FILLER              PIC X(22)  VALUE '* MIRACLE PLEASURE C'.
000106 010600           10  FILLER              PIC X(22)  VALUE 'RUISES, INC.      *  PAS'.
000107 010700           10  FILLER              PIC X(22)  VALUE 'SENGER TICKET LIST'.
000108 010800           10  FILLER              PIC X(17)  VALUE '*   PROGRAM A1NEW',
000109 010900                                              'REPORT R-1 *',
000110 011000           10  PR-HEADING-DATE     PIC X(8).
000111 011100           10  FILLER              PIC X(12)  VALUE '  * PAGE ',
000112 011200           10  PR-HEADING-PAGE-NO  PIC ZZ9.
000113 011300           10  FILLER              PIC X(4)   VALUE ' *'.
000114 011400
000115 011500 01  PR-COLUMN-HEADING.
000116 011600        05  PR-COL-HDR-1.
000117 011700           10  FILLER              PIC X(1).
000118 011800           10  FILLER              PIC X(22)  VALUE
000119 011900           10  FILLER              PIC X(22)  VALUE         'CRUISE'
000120 012000           10  FILLER              PIC X(22)  VALUE
000121 012100           10  FILLER              PIC X(22)  VALUE    'QTY'
000122 012200           10  FILLER              PIC X(22)  VALUE
000123 012300           10  FILLER              PIC X(22)  VALUE        'DATE'
000124 012400
000125 012500        05  PR-COL-HDR-2.
000126 012600           10  FILLER              PIC X(1).
000127 012700           10  FILLER              PIC X(22)  VALUE ' ID#  PASSENGER BO'
000128 012800           10  FILLER              PIC X(22)  VALUE 'OKING NAME      DATE'
000129 012900           10  FILLER              PIC X(22)  VALUE '      PEOPLE     DEC'
000130 013000           10  FILLER              PIC X(22)  VALUE 'K           SALES A'
000131 013100           10  FILLER              PIC X(22)  VALUE 'GENT      BOUGHT'
000132 013200           10  FILLER              PIC X(22)  VALUE ' QTY ERROR?'
       013300
```

(h)

Figure 3.3 *Continued*

f. The *** WORKING-STORAGE SECTION *** title on this page comes from a TITLE statement:

```
004400 TITLE '*** WORKING-STORAGE SECTION ***'.
```

You can put TITLE statements anywhere you like.

g. You get line number cross references whether or not you use the MAP option. Here the 81 tells you that DECK-TABLE, which redefines DECK-TABLE SETUP, refers back to line 81 where DECK-TABLE SETUP is defined. BLW ("base locator" cells for working storage) values clutter your listing. Don't use MAP and you'll get a listing that is easier to read.

h. Code literal lines like column and page headings using six lines of 22 bytes. This can save you a lot of time otherwise required to count the letters in words and to separately code each word and spaces in headings. (This is not required by VS COBOL II but is just a productive modern practice.)

```
000133  013400          05  PR-COL-HDR-3.
000134  013500              10  FILLER     PIC X(22)  VALUE
000135  013600              10  FILLER     PIC X(22)  VALUE
000136  013700              10  FILLER     PIC X(22)  VALUE
000137  013800              10  FILLER     PIC X(22)  VALUE
000138  013900              10  FILLER     PIC X(22)  VALUE
000139  014000              10  FILLER     PIC X(22)  VALUE
000140  014100              10  FILLER     PIC X(22)  VALUE
000141  014200*
000142  014300  01  PASSENGER-REPORT-DETAIL-LINE.
000143  014400      05  PR-KEY                     PIC X(1).
000144  014500      05  FILLER                     PIC X(5).       VALUE SPACES.     IMP
000145  014600      05  PR-PASSENGER-BOOKING-NAME  PIC X(28).      VALUE SPACES.     IMP
000146  014700      05  FILLER                     PIC X(2).       VALUE SPACES.
000147  014800      05  PR-CRUISE-DATE-MO          PIC X(2).
000148  014900      05  FILLER                     PIC X(1).       VALUE '-'.
000149  015000      05  PR-CRUISE-DATE-DA          PIC X(2).
000150  015100      05  FILLER                     PIC X(1).       VALUE '-'.
000151  015200      05  PR-CRUISE-DATE-YR          PIC X(2).
000152  015300      05  FILLER                     PIC X(4).       VALUE SPACES.     IMP
000153  015400      05  PR-TICKET-QTY-X            PIC X(3).                         154
000154  015500      05  PR-TICKET-QTY-9  REDEFINES PR-TICKET-QTY-X  PIC ZZ9.         IMP
000155  015600      05  FILLER                     PIC X(4).       VALUE SPACES.
000156  015700      05  PR-DECK-CODE               PIC X(2).
000157  015800      05  FILLER                     PIC X(1).       VALUE SPACE.      IMP
000158  015900
```

*** WORKING-STORAGE SECTION ***

```
000159  016000      05  PR-DECK-NAME         PIC X(14).
000160  016100      05  FILLER               PIC X(2).       VALUE SPACES.     IMP
000161  016200      05  PR-SALES-AGENT       PIC X(25).
000162  016300      05  FILLER               PIC X(2).       VALUE SPACES.     IMP
000163  016400      05  PR-DATE-BOUGHT-MO    PIC X(2).
000164  016500      05  FILLER               PIC X(1).       VALUE '-'.
000165  016600      05  PR-DATE-BOUGHT-DA    PIC X(2).
000166  016700      05  FILLER               PIC X(1).       VALUE '-'.
000167  016800      05  PR-DATE-BOUGHT-YR    PIC X(3).       VALUE SPACES.     IMP
000168  016900      05  FILLER               PIC X(21).
000169  017000      05  PR-ERROR-MSG
000170  017100  01  PR-ENDLINE.
000171  017200      05  FILLER               PIC X(1).       VALUE SPACE.
000172  017300      05  PR-EL-MESSAGE        PIC X(20).      VALUE SPACES.     IMP
000173  017400      05  FILLER               PIC X(3).       VALUE SPACES.     IMP
000174  017500      05  PR-EL-COUNT          PIC Z,ZZZ,ZZ9.
000175  017600      05  FILLER               PIC X(100)      VALUE SPACES.     IMP
000176  017700
000177  017800*
```

(circled callout letters: i, j, k)

```
LINEID PL SL ----*A-1-B--+----2----+----3----+----4----+----5----+----6----+----7-|--+----8
000179
000180 018000 PROCEDURE DIVISION.
000181 018100 0000-MAINLINE.
000182 018200     PERFORM 1000-BOJ.                                               187
000183 018300     PERFORM 2000-PROCESS-A-RECORD                                   197
000184 018400         UNTIL WS-EOF-FLAG = 'E'.                                    51
000185 018500     PERFORM 3000-EOJ.                                              267
000186 018600     STOP RUN.
000187 018700*
000188 018800 1000-BOJ.
000189 018900     OPEN  INPUT  MASTER-FILE   OUTPUT  PASSENGER-REPORT.          33 38
000190 019000     ACCEPT WS-DATE FROM DATE.                                      46
000191 019100     STRING WS-DATE-MO '-'                                          48
000192 019200        WS-DATE-DA '-'                                              49
000193 019300        WS-DATE-YR        DELIMITED BY SIZE                         47
000194 019400        INTO PR-HEADING-DATE.                                      109
000195 019500     PERFORM 2900-PR-NEWPAGE.                                      247
000196 019600     PERFORM 2700-READ-MASTER-FILE.                               239
000197 019700*
000198 019800 2000-PROCESS-A-RECORD.
000199 019900     PERFORM 2100-FORM-A-PRINTLINE.                               208
000200 020000   1 IF PR-LINES-REMAINING IS LESS THAN +1                         60
000201 020100       PERFORM 2900-PR-NEWPAGE.                                    247
000202 020200     WRITE PASSENGER-REPORT-PRINTLINE                              41
000203 020300       FROM PASSENGER-REPORT-DETAIL-LINE                          142
000204 020400       AFTER ADVANCING 1 LINES.
000205 020500     SUBTRACT +1 FROM PR-LINES-REMAINING.                          60
000206 020600     ADD +1 TO WS-REC-LISTED-COUNT.                                57
000207 020700     PERFORM 2700-READ-MASTER-FILE.                               239
000208 020800*
000209 020900 2100-FORM-A-PRINTLINE.
000210 021000     MOVE MR-KEY                  TO PR-KEY.                      64 144
000211 021100     MOVE SPACES                  TO PR-PASSENGER-BOOKING-NAME.   IMP 146
000212 021200     STRING MR-FIRST-NAME   DELIMITED BY SPACE                    66 IMP
000213 021300        MR-LAST-NAME        DELIMITED BY SIZE                     65 IMP
000214 021400        MR-LAST-NAME        DELIMITED BY SPACE                   146
000215 021500        INTO PR-PASSENGER-BOOKING-NAME.                          69 148
000216 021600     MOVE MR-CRUISE-DATE-MO    TO PR-CRUISE-DATE-MO.             70 150
000217 021700     MOVE MR-CRUISE-DATE-DA    TO PR-CRUISE-DATE-DA.             68 152
000218 021800     MOVE MR-CRUISE-DATE-YR    TO PR-CRUISE-DATE-YR.
000219 021900*
000220 022000   1 IF MR-TICKET-QTY-9 IS NUMERIC                               72 155
000221 022100   1   MOVE MR-TICKET-QTY-9 TO PR-TICKET-QTY-9                    IMP 169
000222 022200     ELSE
000223 022300   1   MOVE SPACES TO PR-ERROR-MSG                               71 154
000224 022400   1   MOVE MR-TICKET-QTY-X TO PR-TICKET-QTY-X                   169
000225 022500     MOVE '*** QTY NOT NUMERIC ***' TO PR-ERROR-MSG.
000226 022600*
000227 022700     MOVE MR-DECK-CODE          TO PR-DECK-CODE.                 73 157
000228 022800     SET DT-IX TO 1.                                             93
000229 022900     SEARCH DECK-TABLE-ROW                                       92
000230 023000       AT END
000231 023100   1     MOVE ALL '*DECK CODE ERR' TO PR-DECK-NAME              159
000232 023200   1     WHEN MR-DECK-CODE = DT-DECK-CODE(DT-IX)                73 94 93
000233 023300        MOVE DT-DECK-NAME(DT-IX) TO PR-DECK-NAME.               96 93 159
000234 023400*
000235 023500     MOVE MR-SALES-AGENT       TO PR-SALES-AGENT.               74 161
000236 023600     MOVE MR-DATE-BOUGHT-MO    TO PR-DATE-BOUGHT-MO.            77 163
       023700     MOVE MR-DATE-BOUGHT-DA    TO PR-DATE-BOUGHT-DA.            78 165
```

Figure 3.3 *Continued*

43

```
000237 023800        MOVE MR-DATE-BOUGHT-YR    TO PR-DATE-BOUGHT-YR.              76 167
000238 023900*
000239 024000 2700-READ-MASTER-FILE.
000240 024100        MOVE SPACES TO MASTER-RECORD.
000241 024200        READ MASTER-FILE INTO MASTER-RECORD-INPUT-AREA               IMP 36
000242 024300           AT END                                                    33 63
000243 024400              MOVE 'E' TO WS-EOF-FLAG                                 51
000244 024500           NOT AT END
000245 024600              ADD +1 TO WS-MF-REC-COUNT.                             56
000246 024700*
000247 024800 2900-PR-NEWPAGE.
000248 024900        ADD +1 TO PR-PAGE-COUNT.                                     61
000249 025000        MOVE PR-PAGE-COUNT TO PR-HEADING-PAGE-NO.                    61 111
000250 025100        WRITE PASSENGER-REPORT-PRINTLINE FROM PR-HEADING-BORDER      41 99
000251 025200           AFTER ADVANCING PAGE.
000252 025300        WRITE PASSENGER-REPORT-PRINTLINE FROM PR-HEADING-INFO        41 102
000253 025400           AFTER ADVANCING 1 LINES.
000254 025500        WRITE PASSENGER-REPORT-PRINTLINE FROM PR-HEADING-BORDER      41 99
000255 025600           AFTER ADVANCING 1 LINES.
000256 025700        WRITE PASSENGER-REPORT-PRINTLINE FROM PR-COL-HDR-1           41 115
000257 025800           AFTER ADVANCING 3 LINES.
000258 025900        WRITE PASSENGER-REPORT-PRINTLINE FROM PR-COL-HDR-2           41 124
000259 026000           AFTER ADVANCING 1 LINES.
000260 026100        WRITE PASSENGER-REPORT-PRINTLINE FROM PR-COL-HDR-3           41 133
000261 026200           AFTER ADVANCING 1 LINES.
000262 026300        MOVE SPACES TO PASSENGER-REPORT-PRINTLINE.
000263 026400        WRITE PASSENGER-REPORT-PRINTLINE
000264 026500           AFTER ADVANCING 2 LINES.
000265 026600        MOVE +50 TO PR-LINES-REMAINING.                             60
000266 026700*
000267 026800 3000-EOJ.
000268 026900        MOVE SPACES TO PR-ENDLINE.                                   IMP 171
000269 027000        MOVE '*** END OF JOB '          TO PR-EL-MESSAGE            173
000270 027100        IF PR-LINES-REMAINING IS LESS THAN +2                        60
000271 027200           PERFORM 2900-PR-NEWPAGE.                                  247
000272 027300        WRITE PASSENGER-REPORT-PRINTLINE FROM PR-ENDLINE             41 171
000273 027400           AFTER ADVANCING 2 LINES.
000274 027500        SUBTRACT +2 FROM PR-LINES-REMAINING.                        60
000275 027600*
000276 027700        MOVE 'RECORDS READ       '      TO PR-EL-MESSAGE.           173
000277 027800        MOVE WS-MF-REC-COUNT            TO PR-EL-COUNT.             56 175
000278 027900        IF PR-LINES-REMAINING IS LESS THAN +1                        60
000279 028000           PERFORM 2900-PR-NEWPAGE.                                  247
000280 028100        WRITE PASSENGER-REPORT-PRINTLINE FROM PR-ENDLINE             41 171
000281 028200           AFTER ADVANCING 1 LINES.
000282 028300        SUBTRACT +1 FROM PR-LINES-REMAINING.                        60
000283 028400*
000284 028500        MOVE 'RECORDS PRINTED    '      TO PR-EL-MESSAGE.           173
000285 028600        MOVE WS-REC-LISTED-COUNT        TO PR-EL-COUNT.             57 175
000286 028700        IF PR-LINES-REMAINING IS LESS THAN +1                        60
000287 028800           PERFORM 2900-PR-NEWPAGE.                                  247
000288 028900        WRITE PASSENGER-REPORT-PRINTLINE FROM PR-ENDLINE             41 171
000289 029000           AFTER ADVANCING 1 LINES.
000290 029100        SUBTRACT +1 FROM PR-LINES-REMAINING.                        60
000291 029200*
000292 029300        CLOSE  MASTER-FILE  PASSENGER-REPORT.                        33 38
```

Figure 3.3 *Continued*

i. (Page 43) The ***PROCEDURE DIVISION*** title on this page comes from a TITLE statement I put at line 017900:

```
017900 TITLE '*** PROCEDURE DIVISION ***'.
```

You can put TITLE statements anywhere you like.

j. (Page 43) These automatic cross-reference numbers tell you the line where the PERFORMed paragraph is coded, or the line in the DATA DIVISION where the data names have been defined. For example, paragraph 1000-BOJ starts at line 187. Notice that the compiler uses LINEID line numbers it has applied in the far left column, not the six-digit COBOL line numbers in the code itself!

Line number 197 refers to where the paragraph 2000-PROCESS-A-RECORD starts. Line 51 refers to where 88-level name WS-EOF-FLAG is defined. Lines 33 and 38 refer to where the FDs for the files being OPENed are coded.

You get this automatic cross-reference whether or not you use the MAP option. It's an extremely convenient feature of VS COBOL II!

k. (Page 43) The "1's" in the SL column refer to "statement level." You'll see them on any IF/ELSE's and other types of statements where decision-making is involved. These numbers appear on any lines within (after) a decision-making statement. The numbers tell you after how many decisions the line of code is placed. These numbers may help you decipher complex logic.

l. (Page 44) IMP in the cross-reference means "implicit definition." Notice that this line involves moving SPACES to a data name. IMP refers to SPACES. The line number refers to the destination of the move, which is PASSENGER-REPORT-PRINTLINE defined at line 41.

45

(m)

AN "M" PRECEDING A DATA-NAME REFERENCE INDICATES THAT THE DATA-NAME IS MODIFIED BY THIS REFERENCE.

DEFINED	CROSS-REFERENCE OF DATA NAMES	REFERENCES
91	DECK-TABLE	228
92	DECK-TABLE-ROW	91
81	DECK-TABLE-SETUP	231
94	DT-DECK-CODE	232
96	DT-DECK-NAME	M227 231 232
93	DT-IX	25 188 241 292
33	MASTER-FILE	M240
36	MASTER-RECORD	M241
63	MASTER-RECORD-INPUT-AREA . . .	
67	MR-CRUISE-DATE	216
70	MR-CRUISE-DATE-DA	215
69	MR-CRUISE-DATE-MO	217
68	MR-CRUISE-DATE-YR.	
78	MR-DATE-BOUGHT-DA.	236
77	MR-DATE-BOUGHT-MO.	235
76	MR-DATE-BOUGHT-YR.	237
73	MR-DECK-CODE	226 231
66	MR-FIRST-NAME.	211
64	MR-KEY	209
65	MR-LAST-NAME	213
74	MR-SALES-AGENT	234
71	MR-TICKET-QTY-X.	72 223
72	MR-TICKET-QTY-9.	219 220
38	PASSENGER-REPORT	26 188 292
59	PASSENGER-REPORT-COUNTERS. . .	202
142	PASSENGER-REPORT-DETAIL-LINE .	M201 M250 M252 M254 M256 M258 M260 M262 M263 M272 M280 M288
41	PASSENGER-REPORT-PRINTLINE . .	256
115	PR-COL-HDR-1	258
124	PR-COL-HDR-2	260
133	PR-COL-HDR-3	
114	PR-COLUMN-HEADING.	M216
150	PR-CRUISE-DATE-DA.	M215
148	PR-CRUISE-DATE-MO.	M217
152	PR-CRUISE-DATE-YR.	M236
165	PR-DATE-BOUGHT-DA.	M235
163	PR-DATE-BOUGHT-MO.	M237
167	PR-DATE-BOUGHT-YR.	M226
157	PR-DECK-CODE	M230 M232
159	PR-DECK-NAME	M277 M285
175	PR-EL-COUNT.	M269 M276 M284
173	PR-EL-MESSAGE.	M268 272 280 288
171	PR-ENDLINE	M221 M224
169	PR-ERROR-MSG	250 254
99	PR-HEADING-BORDER.	M193
109	PR-HEADING-DATE.	252
102	PR-HEADING-INFO.	M249
111	PR-HEADING-PAGE-NO	M209
144	PR-KEY	199 M204 M265 270 274 278 M282 286 M290
60	PR-LINES-REMAINING	M248 249
61	PR-PAGE-COUNT.	M210 M214
98	PR-PAGE-HEADING.	M234
146	PR-PASSENGER-BOOKING-NAME. . .	
161	PR-SALES-AGENT	

(n)

Figure 3.3 *Continued*

m. The ***PROCEDURE DIVISION*** title on this page comes from the TITLE statement I used at line 017900 at the beginning of the PROCEDURE DIVISION. The title will continue to carry over throughout the listing. If you use TITLE statements you can put a blank TITLE statement like this at the end of your program:

999999 TITLE ' '.

so that the XREF and other pages that follow don't carry your last real title.

n. The VS COBOL II XREF is like the old VS COBOL SXREF. The XREF lists data names sorted alphabetically by name, not in the order you defined them. (The VS COBOL XREF gave you an unsorted cross-reference, which is not available in VS COBOL II.)

The DEFINED column shows you where a data name is defined. REFERENCES shows you every line where the data name is used. "M" next to the line number where a data name is used means that the value of the data name might be changed at that point (it is the target of a MOVE or COMPUTE).

No line numbers under REFERENCES for a data name means that the program doesn't ever refer to the data name. This might tip you off to an error. On the other hand, group names over a series of flag fields or counters would not ordinarily be referenced elsewhere.

DEFINED	CROSS-REFERENCE OF DATA NAMES	REFERENCES
154	PR-TICKET-QTY-X.	155 M223
155	PR-TICKET-QTY-9.	M220
55	WS-COUNTERS	
46	WS-DATE.	
49	WS-DATE-DA	M189
48	WS-DATE-MO	191
47	WS-DATE-YR	190
53	WS-EOF	192
51	WS-EOF-FLAG.	183 M243
52	WS-EOF-MORE-DATA	
56	WS-WF-REC-COUNT.	M245 277
57	WS-REC-LISTED-COUNT.	M205 285

CONTEXT USAGE IS INDICATED BY THE LETTER PRECEDING A PROCEDURE-NAME REFERENCE.
THESE LETTERS AND THEIR MEANINGS ARE:
A = ALTER (PROCEDURE-NAME)
D = GO TO (PROCEDURE-NAME) DEPENDING ON
E = END OF RANGE OF (PERFORM) THROUGH (PROCEDURE-NAME)
G = GO TO (PROCEDURE-NAME)
P = PERFORM (PROCEDURE-NAME)
T = (ALTER) TO PROCEED TO (PROCEDURE-NAME)
U = USE FOR DEBUGGING (PROCEDURE-NAME)

DEFINED	CROSS-REFERENCE OF PROCEDURES	REFERENCES
180	0000-MAINLINE	
187	1000-BOJ	P181
197	2000-PROCESS-A-RECORD.	P182
208	2100-FORM-A-PRINTLINE.	P198
239	2700-READ-MASTER-FILE.	P195 P206
247	2900-PR-NEWPAGE.	P194 P200 P271 P279 P287
267	3000-EOJ	P184

DEFINED	CROSS-REFERENCE OF PROGRAMS	REFERENCES
2	A1NEW	

Figure 3.3 *Continued*

o. This material is produced only when you activate the XREF option. It is like the old VS COBOL "SXREF" option with some minor differences.

The * * * PROCEDURE DIVISION * * * title on this page comes from the TITLE statement I used at line 017900 at the beginning of the PROCEDURE DIVISION. The last title will continue to carry over throughout the remainder of the listing. See items (i) and (m).

p. DEFINED tells you where each paragraph starts in your source code, using the line number applied by the compiler.

REFERENCES tells you primarily the line numbers where PERFORMs of the paragraph are coded, indicated by a "P" in front of the line. The only other letter you'll commonly see in front of the referencing line number is "E," which means the paragraph is the end of a PERFORM . . . THRU, such as an exit coded like

1000-EXIT. EXIT.

The meaning of other letters is printed in the legend at the top of the procedure name cross-reference.

q. VS COBOL II supports nested programs (see Appendix D). Nested programs are unusual in COBOL and your shop standards may prohibit you from using them. If you do use them you will see more than just the main program name listed here.

DATA DIVISION MAP

DATA DEFINITION ATTRIBUTE CODES (RIGHTMOST COLUMN) HAVE THE FOLLOWING MEANINGS:
```
D = OBJECT OF OCCURS DEPENDING   G = GLOBAL                            S = SPANNED FILE
E = EXTERNAL                     O = HAS OCCURS CLAUSE                 U = UNDEFINED FORMAT FILE
F = FIXED LENGTH FILE            OG= GROUP HAS OWN LENGTH DEFINITION   V = VARIABLE LENGTH FILE
FB= FIXED LENGTH BLOCKED FILE    R = REDEFINES                        VB= VARIABLE LENGTH BLOCKED FILE
```

SOURCE LINEID	HIERARCHY AND DATA NAME	BASE LOCATOR	HEX-DISPLACEMENT BLK	STRUCTURE	ASMBLR DATA DEFINITION	DATA TYPE	DATA DEF ATTRIBUTES
33	FD MASTER-FILE	BLF=0000	001		DS 80C	QSAM	FB
36	01 MASTER-RECORD		000			DISPLAY	
38	FD PASSENGER-REPORT	BLF=0001	001		DS 133C	QSAM	FB
41	01 PASSENGER-REPORT-PRINTLINE	BLW=0000	001		DS 21C	DISPLAY	
45	01 FILLER	BLW=0000	018		DS 0CL6	GROUP	
46	01 WS-DATE	BLW=0000	018		DS 2C	DISPLAY	
47	02 WS-DATE-YR	BLW=0000	01A		DS 2C	DISPLAY	
48	02 WS-DATE-MO	BLW=0000	01C		DS 2C	DISPLAY	
49	02 WS-DATE-DA	BLW=0000	020		DS 1C	DISPLAY	
51	01 WS-EOF-FLAG	BLW=0000	020	000 000			
52	88 WS-EOF-MORE-DATA	BLW=0000	020				
53	88 WS-EOF	BLW=0000	020	000 000			
55	01 WS-COUNTERS	BLW=0000	028		DS 0CL6	GROUP	
56	02 WS-MF-REC-COUNT	BLW=0000	028	000 000	DS 3P	PACKED-DEC	
57	02 WS-REC-LISTED-COUNT	BLW=0000	028	000 003	DS 3P	PACKED-DEC	
59	01 PASSENGER-REPORT-COUNTERS	BLW=0000	030		DS 0CL4	GROUP	
60	02 PR-LINES-REMAINING	BLW=0000	030	000 000	DS 2P	PACKED-DEC	
61	02 PR-PAGE-COUNT	BLW=0000	032	000 002	DS 2P	PACKED-DEC	
63	01 MASTER-RECORD-INPUT-AREA	BLW=0000	038		DS 0CL80	GROUP	
64	02 MR-KEY	BLW=0000	038		DS 5C	DISPLAY	
65	02 MR-LAST-NAME	BLW=0000	030	000 005	DS 14C	DISPLAY	
66	02 MR-FIRST-NAME	BLW=0000	048	000 013	DS 15C	DISPLAY	
67	02 MR-CRUISE-DATE	BLW=0000	05A	000 022	DS 0CL6	GROUP	
68	03 MR-CRUISE-DATE-YR	BLW=0000	05A	000 022	DS 2C	DISPLAY	
69	03 MR-CRUISE-DATE-MO	BLW=0000	05C	000 024	DS 2C	DISPLAY	
70	03 MR-CRUISE-DATE-DA	BLW=0000	05E	000 026	DS 2C	DISPLAY	
71	02 MR-TICKET-QTY-X	BLW=0000	060	000 028	DS 3C	DISPLAY	
72	02 MR-TICKET-QTY-9	BLW=0000	060	000 028	DS 3C	DISP-NUM	
73	02 MR-DECK-CODE	BLW=0000	063	000 02B	DS 2C	DISPLAY	
74	02 MR-SALES-AGENT	BLW=0000	065	000 02D	DS 23C	DISPLAY	
75	02 MR-DATE-BOUGHT	BLW=0000	07C	000 044	DS 0CL6	GROUP	
76	03 MR-DATE-BOUGHT-YR	BLW=0000	07C	000 044	DS 2C	DISPLAY	
77	03 MR-DATE-BOUGHT-MO	BLW=0000	07E	000 046	DS 2C	DISPLAY	
78	03 MR-DATE-BOUGHT-DA	BLW=0000	080	000 048	DS 2C	DISPLAY	
79	02 FILLER	BLW=0000	082	000 04A	DS 6C	DISPLAY	
81	01 DECK-TABLE-SETUP	BLW=0000	088		DS 0CL136	GROUP	
82	02 FILLER	BLW=0000	088	000 000	DS 17C	DISPLAY	
83	02 FILLER	BLW=0000	099	000 011	DS 17C	DISPLAY	
84	02 FILLER	BLW=0000	0AA	000 022	DS 17C	DISPLAY	
85	02 FILLER	BLW=0000	0BB	000 033	DS 17C	DISPLAY	
86	02 FILLER	BLW=0000	0CC	000 044	DS 17C	DISPLAY	
87	02 FILLER	BLW=0000	0DD	000 055	DS 17C	DISPLAY	
88	02 FILLER	BLW=0000	0EE	000 066	DS 17C	DISPLAY	
89	02 FILLER	BLW=0000	0FF	000 077	DS 17C	DISPLAY	
91	01 DECK-TABLE	BLW=0000	088		DS 0CL136	GROUP	R
92	02 DECK-TABLE-ROW	BLW=0001	000	000 000	DS 0CL17	GROUP	R O
93	DT-IX	IDX=0001	000		DS	INDEX-NAME	R

Figure 3.3 *Continued*

r. This material is produced only when you activate the MAP option. It is like the old VS COBOL "DMAP" option with some minor differences.

The ★★PROCEDURE DIVISION ★★★ title on this page comes from the TITLE statement I used at line 017900 at the beginning of the PROCEDURE DIVISION. The last title will continue to carry over throughout the remainder of the listing. See items (i), (m) and (o).

s. MAP lists your FDs and WORKING-STORAGE data names in the order you coded them. But it "normalizes" the level numbers to show you how the compiler has actually interpreted them. This has the advantage of showing you exactly how your data structures are being treated, but it results in loss of the 05, 10, and 15 level numbers you might have used.

t. The right side of the MAP confirms for you the data type of each data name. These include "QSAM" for sequential files, "DISPLAY" for character data, "GROUP" for group data name (no PIC on it) "PACKED-DECIMAL" for COMP-3, and "NUM-EDIT" for numeric edited, such as $ZZ,ZZ9.

The letters in the last column are described at the top of the page in a legend. One of the handiest is the letter "R" which means that the item on this line redefines some other data item defined earlier.

u. The ASMBLR DATA DEFINITION column shows you the "define storage" definitions the compiler has decided to use for each of your data items. You don't have to understand assembler to find this useful. One of the handiest uses of this column on the MAP is to check that your printlines are coded at the correct length. "0CL" means a group name. All of your printlines should normally receive 0CL133 here. If they don't, you probably have made a mistake in coding the printline.

For non-group data names, "C" means "characters" (bytes) of storage. For PIC X and PIC 9 fields, the number in front of the C, such as "17C," means 17 bytes of storage.

For COMP-3 (packed decimal) data, the assembler definition such as "3P" (see WS-MF-REC-count above) shows how many *bytes of storage* are being used for the data, **not** how many digits of numeric precision or size are involved. For example, a field defined as PIC S9(5) COMP-3 receives "3P" for its assembler definition since it takes three bytes of storage (five half-byte digits and one half-byte for the sign).

51

PROGRAM GLOBAL TABLE BEGINS AT LOCATION 000080 FOR 000008 BYTES
THE PGT CONTAINS 000001 CELL(S) FOR ADDRESSABILITY TO THE CGT
PBL1   AT LOCATION 000790 FOR LINE 2

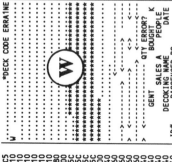

CONSTANT GLOBAL TABLE BEGINS AT LOCATION 000088 FOR 00059A BYTES
LITERAL POOL MAP FOR LITERALS IN THE CGT:

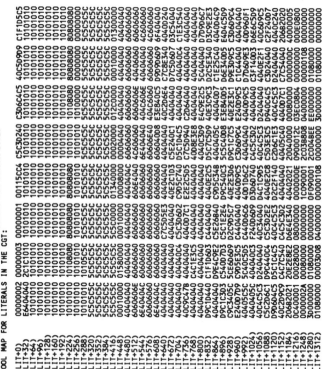

0000A4 (LIT+0)   00000002 00000003 00000001 00115CC4 C5C3D240 C3D6C4C5 40C5D9D9 C1F1D5C5
0000C4 (LIT+32)   E6404040 2C1C1010 10101010 10101010 10101010 10101010 10101010 10101010
0000E4 (LIT+64)   10101010 10101010 10101010 10101010 10101010 10101010 10101010 10101010
000104 (LIT+96)   10101010 10101010 10101010 10101010 10101010 10101010 10101010 10101010
000124 (LIT+128)   10101010 10101010 10101010 10101010 10101010 10101010 10101010 10101010
000144 (LIT+160)   10101010 10101010 10101010 80808080 10101010 10101010 10101010 10101010
000164 (LIT+192)   10101010 10101010 10101010 80808080 80808080 10101010 10101010 80808080
000184 (LIT+224)   10101010 10108080 80808080 10101010 10100000 10108080 80808080 80808080
0001A4 (LIT+256)   10101010 10105C5C 5C5C5C5C 5C5C5C5C 5C5C5C5C 00000000 00000000 00000000
0001C4 (LIT+288)   5C5C5C5C 5C5C5C5C 5C5C5C5C 5C5C5C5C 5C5C5C5C 5C5C5C5C 5C5C5C5C 5C5C5C5C
0001E4 (LIT+320)   5C5C5C5C 5C5C5C5C 5C5C5C5C 5C5C5C5C 5C5C5C5C 5C5C5C5C 5C5C5C5C 5C5C5C5C
000204 (LIT+352)   5C5C5C5C 5C5C5C5C 5C5C5C5C 5C5C5C5C 5C5C5C5C 5C5C5C5C 5C5C5C5C 5C5C5C5C
000224 (LIT+384)   5C5C5C5C 5C5C5C5C 5C5C5C5C 0134040 01200000 00010000 01300000 5C5C5C5C
000244 (LIT+416)   5C5C5C5C 5C5C5C5C 01580000 00100000 0002040 00020000 00000000 01300000
000264 (LIT+448)   00010000 40404040 40404040 4060040C 60606060 40404040 40404040 40404040
000284 (LIT+480)   40404040 40404040 60606060 606E4040 60606060 60606060 60606060 4040040
0002A4 (LIT+512)   6060606E 60606060 60606060 60606060 40404040 40606060 60606060 60606060
0002C4 (LIT+544)   6E40404C 6E404040 6E404040 6E40404C 6E404040 4040040 40C60060 60606060
0002E4 (LIT+576)   6060606E 60606060 6060606E 6060606E 606E6F40 60606E40 40C60060 4C60060
000304 (LIT+608)   6E40404C 60606060 60606060 60604008 D9D9D609 D9D9D609 6F40040 6F40040
000324 (LIT+640)   40404040 40404040 C7C5D5E3 C7C5D5E3 40202064 40202D64 6F40D240 4040D240
000344 (LIT+672)   40404040 40404040 40E2C1D3 5E2640C1 5E2640C1 D7C5D607 D3C5D607 D3C5D607
000364 (LIT+704)   40404004 40404004 C5C3D602 D5C1D4C5 D5C1D4C5 C1E3C540 C1E3C540 C1E3C540
000384 (LIT+736)   4C9C678 40404040 40404040 C7C5D940 C2D64404 C2D64040 40404040 40404040
0003A4 (LIT+768)   40404040 40404040 40404040 40804040 40804008 D7D906C7 D7D906C7 D7D906C7
0003C4 (LIT+800)   40404040 40404040 C4C1E3C5 4040C3D9 4040C3D9 5C4C4040 5C404040 D7D906C7
0003E4 (LIT+832)   D9C1D440 C4C1E3C5 5E2640C5 40E3C9C3 40E3C9C3 D2C5E340 D2C5E340 D3C5E2E3
000404 (LIT+864)   40404040 D9E4C9E2 C5E26840 C905C34B C905C34B 40404007 40404007 4040D4C9
000424 (LIT+896)   D9C1C303 C540D7D3 C5C1E2E4 D2C5E306 D9C1D4C5 D9C1D4C5 D7E309C5 C3D609C4
000444 (LIT+928)   C9C3405C 5CE60609 D2C9D5C7 40E2E306 40106C2 E240D9C5 E240D9C5 40404040
000464 (LIT+960)   E240D7D9 C905E3C5 C440D5D9 C4C5C3D2 C4C5C3D2 E240D9C5 C1C44040 404040F6
000484 (LIT+992)   40405C5C 5C40C505 5C40C505 4D0106C2 40404040 40404040 D7D609E3 40960F1
0004A4 (LIT+1024) 40405C5C 40404040 40404040 D3060740 D4C1C9D5 D4C1C9D5 C3F14003 D6E6C5D9
0004C4 (LIT+1056) 40C4C5C3 D2404040 40C34040 D4C1C9D5 40C4C5C3 D2404040 40E2F1 40C0965
0004E4 (LIT+1088) C5C2D6C1 D9C44040 C5C3C8 D9C1C9D5 D940C4C5 C3C9 C3024040 C2F24007
000504 (LIT+1120) D9D6D4C5 D5C1C4C5 40C4C5C3 D2C2F140 C2D64040 40C45C3 D2404040 4040C240
000524 (LIT+1152) 40C2D9C9 C4C7C540 40C4C5C3 D2404040 40404040 40C4C5C3 D2C240 20682020
000544 (LIT+1184) 20682021 20E2E8E2 D6E4E340 00000000 00000000 00000000 40000005 40000000
000564 (LIT+1216) 0C400001 0C028400 08000000 00000000 09000012 03EC0804 00000000 000E0800
000584 (LIT+1248) 0000002A 00080000 01080000 1C090001 2C03B808 04000000 00000108 00000000
0005A4 (LIT+1280) 30000000 01080000 00000000 0F090001 2C004BEE EE000000 01080000 00000000
0005C4 (LIT+1312) 01080000 00003D08 04000000 00000108 00000000 3D000000 01080000 00000000

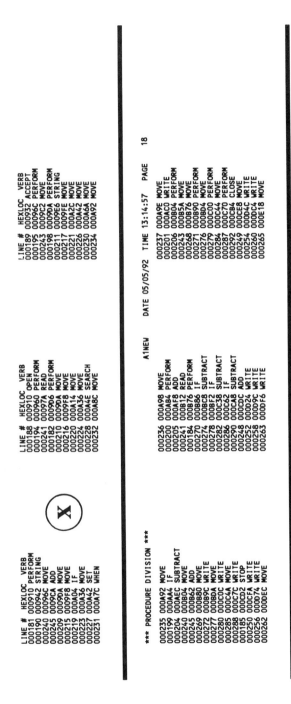

```
LINE #  HEXLOC  VERB          LINE #  HEXLOC  VERB          LINE #  HEXLOC  VERB
000181  000910  PERFORM       000188  000910  OPEN          000189  000932  ACCEPT
000190  000942  STRING        000194  000960  PERFORM       000195  00096C  PERFORM
000240  00096C  MOVE          000241  00097A  READ          000243  0009C2  MOVE
000245  0009CA  ADD           000182  0009D6  PERFORM       000198  0009DA  PERFORM
000209  0009DA  MOVE          000210  0009DA  MOVE          000211  0009E6  STRING
000215  0009F8  MOVE          000220  0009F8  MOVE          000217  0009FF  MOVE
000219  000A04  IF            000224  000A14  MOVE          000221  000A2C  MOVE
000223  000A36  MOVE          000228  000A36  MOVE          000226  000A42  MOVE
000227  000A42  SET           000230  000A4E  SEARCH        000230  000A6A  MOVE
000231  000A7C  WHEN          000232  000A8C  MOVE          000234  000A92  MOVE
```

```
*** PROCEDURE DIVISION ***          A1NEW        DATE 05/05/92   TIME 13:14:57   PAGE  18

000235  000A92  MOVE          000236  000A98  MOVE          000237  000A9E  MOVE
000199  000AA4  IF            000200  000AB4  PERFORM       000201  000AC0  WRITE
000204  000AEC  SUBTRACT      000205  000AF8  ADD           000206  000B04  PERFORM
000240  000B04  MOVE          000241  000B12  READ          000243  000B5A  MOVE
000245  000B62  ADD           000184  000B76  PERFORM       000268  000B76  MOVE
000269  000B80  MOVE          000269  000B86  IF            000271  000B90  PERFORM
000272  000B9C  WRITE         000274  000BC8  SUBTRACT      000276  000BD4  MOVE
000277  000BDA  MOVE          000278  000BE8  IF            000279  000C00  PERFORM
000280  000C0C  WRITE         000282  000C38  SUBTRACT      000284  000C44  MOVE
000285  000C4A  MOVE          000286  000C62  IF            000287  000C70  PERFORM
000288  000C7C  WRITE         000290  000CA8  SUBTRACT      000292  000CB4  CLOSE
000185  000CD2  STOP          000248  000CDC  ADD           000249  000CE8  MOVE
000250  000CFA  WRITE         000252  000D24  WRITE         000254  000D4C  WRITE
000256  000D74  WRITE         000258  000D9C  WRITE         000260  000DC4  WRITE
000262  000DEC  MOVE          000263  000DF6  WRITE         000265  000E18  MOVE
```

Figure 3.3   *Continued*

v. This material is produced only when you activate the OFFSET option. It is like the old VS COBOL "CLIST" (condensed listing) option with some minor differences.

The *** * PROCEDURE DIVISION ***** title on this page comes from the TITLE statement I used at line 017900 at the beginning of the PROCEDURE DIVISION. See items (i), (m), (r) and (o).

w. OFFSET gives you a character and hex dump of the "Constant Global Table" created by the compiler for your literal values in working storage. This is not very useful but is produced unavoidably by the OFFSET option.

x. This is the useful part of the listing generated by the OFFSET option. It is printed in three columns, but you have to read across a whole line before you read down in a column. This listing gives you the source code line number (LINE #), hexadecimal displacement into the load module (HEXLOC), and verb name (VERB) for each COBOL instruction.

*** PROCEDURE DIVISION ***

LINEID MESSAGE CODE MESSAGE TEXT

     IGYDS0139-W   DIAGNOSTIC MESSAGES WERE ISSUED DURING PROCESSING OF COMPILER OPTIONS. THESE MESSAGES ARE LOCATED AT THE
                   BEGINNING OF THE LISTING.

  33 IGYGR1216-I   A "RECORDING MODE" OF "F" WAS ASSUMED FOR FILE "MASTER-FILE".
  38 IGYGR1216-I   A "RECORDING MODE" OF "F" WAS ASSUMED FOR FILE "PASSENGER-REPORT".

MESSAGES   TOTAL   INFORMATIONAL   WARNING   ERROR   SEVERE   TERMINATING
PRINTED: 5   2   3

* STATISTICS FOR COBOL PROGRAM A1NEW:
*   SOURCE RECORDS = 292
*   DATA DIVISION STATEMENTS = 63
*   PROCEDURE DIVISION STATEMENTS = 70

END OF COMPILATION 1, PROGRAM A1NEW, HIGHEST SEVERITY 4.

RETURN CODE 4

MVS/DFP VERSION 3 RELEASE 2 LINKAGE EDITOR   13:15:11 TUE MAY 05, 1992
JOB A1092JA   STEP STEPA   PROCEDURE LKED
INVOCATION PARAMETERS - LIST,XREF,LET,MAP
ACTUAL SIZE=(317440,86016)
OUTPUT DATA SET SYS92126.T131454.RA000.A1092JA.GOSET IS ON VOLUME GISAW2

                                          CROSS REFERENCE TABLE

CONTROL SECTION   ENTRY
  NAME   ORIGIN LENGTH   NAME   LOCATION   NAME   LOCATION   NAME   LOCATION   NAME   LOCATION
A1NEW   00   1406
IGZEBST *   1408   428   IGZEBS2   1696

LOCATION REFERS TO SYMBOL IN CONTROL SECTION   LOCATION REFERS TO SYMBOL IN CONTROL SECTION
    6C   IGZEBST $UNRESOLVED(W)   1804   IGZETUN $UNRESOLVED(W)
  1808   IGZEOPT $UNRESOLVED(W)
ENTRY ADDRESS   00

TOTAL LENGTH   1830
** GO   DID NOT PREVIOUSLY EXIST BUT WAS ADDED AND HAS AMODE 31
** LOAD MODULE HAS RMODE ANY

** AUTHORIZATION CODE IS   0.

Figure 3.3 *Continued*

y. The IGYDS0139-W diagnostic messages warning refers to the fact that I specified conflicting compiler options OFFSET and LIST.

The IGYGR1216-I informational messages were embedded in the source code listing, but all messages always print at the end of the listing, too. You can use the FLAG option (page 57) to eliminate embedded informational messages.

z. The VS COBOL II compiler gives you these statistics about the compile. RETURN CODE 4 means that a COND CODE of 0004 is being communicated to the operating system. You'll get a return code of 0 (0000) for a completely clean compile and 4 (0004) for a compile with warning messages like IGYDS0139-W. Figure 3.4 on page 57 shows you how return code values are associated with message suffixes such as -I and -W.

```
                                   CRUISE   QTY                                          DATE
ID#   PASSENGER BOOKING NAME        DATE     PEOPLE         DECK           SALES AGENT          BOUGHT     QTY ERROR?
<--->  <------------------------>  <------>  <-->   <------------------>  <------------------>  <------>   <------------------>

43102  CALIFORNIA                  03-17-92    7     B2 PROMENADE DECK     ULTIMATE TRAVEL AGENCY  08-07-91
43261  LUCE CANNON                 03-17-92    1     C  MAIN DECK          FOX VALLEY TRAVEL       10-04-91
43345  T. TOTALLER                 03-17-92    2     C1 LOWER DECK         ULTIMATE TRAVEL AGENCY  10-17-91
43377  G. WHIZ                     03-17-92    1     S  SHELTER DECK       WORLD TRAVEL, INC.      11-23-91
43480  D. TOUR                     04-15-92   xa     C1 LOWER DECK         HOLIDAY TOURS, INC.     01-17-92   ** QTY NOT NUMERIC **
43483  CAROL INA                   04-15-92    2     S  SHELTER DECK       FOX VALLEY TRAVEL       01-18-92
43484  HARRY ZONA                  04-15-92   10     C2 ORLOP DECK         UNRAVEL TRAVEL, INC.    02-22-92
43507  MARGA RITA                  04-15-92    4     &X *DECK CODE  ERR    WORLD TRAVEL, INC.      04-01-92
49257  O. FOOEY                    05-07-92   -PQ    B1 BOAT DECK          JACK SPRAT TRAVEL       08-03-91
49321  AL ABAMA                    05-07-92    2     B  BRIDGE DECK        UNANNAGO TRAVEL AGENCY  11-05-91
49322  KEN TUCKY                   05-07-92    2     C  MAIN DECK          ULTIMATE TRAVEL AGENCY  11-05-91   ** QTY NOT NUMERIC **
49467  TURKI LURKI                 05-07-92   15     B1 BOAT DECK          HOLIDAY TOURS, INC.     12-24-91


*** END OF JOB
RECORDS READ      12
RECORDS PRINTED   12
```

Figure 3.3 Continued

- You can use spaces or commas between options on the PROCESS statement.
- You can't code options with embedded spaces. For example, you could not code FLAG(I,W) as FLAG(I W).

But PROCESS may not work in your programs. When an installation puts in the VS COBOL II compiler, its management can decide to disallow PROCESS statements. As a standard, some shops prefer to have all compile options visible in JCL rather than hiding them in source code.

3.6 IMPORTANT VS COBOL II COMPILER OPTIONS

Figure 3.3 (page 36) lists the 44 options for the VS COBOL II compiler and tells you how they were set for this particular run. "NO" in front of

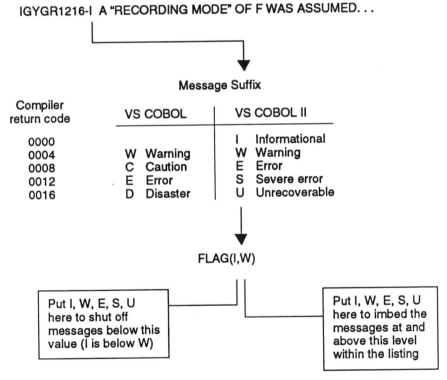

Figure 3.4 VS COBOL II Return Codes and Related Message Suffixes.

VS COBOL II message suffixes are different from those of VS COBOL. You can control the level of error messages you get and whether or not they are embedded in the listing using the FLAG compiler option.

VS COBOL	VS COBOL-II	What the Option Does
PMAP	LIST	Produces an assembler language listing of the program
CLIST	OFFSET	Produces a condensed listing of verbs and hex offsets
SXREF	XREF	Sorted cross-reference
XREF	(gone!)	Non-sorted cross-reference
DMAP	MAP	Produces a data map showing hex displacement in the DATA DIVISION, field size and usage in the order fields are defined.
FLAGW	FLAG(W)	Note syntax warnings => 0004
FLAGE	FLAG(E)	Note syntax errors > 0004 only
SYNTAX	NOCOMPILE	Check syntax but don't produce any object code (efficient for first time compile)
LOAD	OBJECT	Produce object file at //SYSLIN

Figure 3.5   Important compile options renamed or changed from VS COBOL to VS COBOL II Release 3 and what they do.

an option means that it was turned off. As with VS COBOL, the new compiler gives you dozens of parameter options that tailor the way it works for you. IBM has changed, eliminated, or arbitrarily renamed many of the compiler options from VS COBOL to VS COBOL II.

All of the VS COBOL/VS COBOL II compiler options and name changes are described in IBM's manual *VS COBOL II Application Programming Guide Release 3*, SC26–4045. The name changes shown in Figure 3.5 are the ones that will most likely affect you.

3.7   OTHER VS COBOL II COMPILE OPTIONS YOU SHOULD KNOW ABOUT

Some other useful VS COBOL II compiler options can eliminate excess warning messages in your listings or improve the efficiency of your programs:

NUMBER—If you specify NUMBER, the compiler will use your COBOL line numbers for error messages; NONUMBER lets the compiler assign its own sequential line numbers and uses them for messages.

NOSEQ—Turns off warnings about out of sequence source code line numbers. You should use NOSEQ or you will get needless warning messages when you use copy library members since you can't control the line numbers on them.

TEST—If you are going to debug a program either in batch or interactive mode, you must specify the TEST option when you compile the program as I explain in Chapters 15 and 16.

FASTSRT—Lets the sort utility handle I/O instead of COBOL when you do an internal sort. This improvement only works if you use both USING and GIVING options in the SORT verb. Always specify FASTSRT since it disables itself if it can't operate.

LANGUAGE(UE)—Uses only uppercase (capital) letters for source code headings and error messages. LANGUAGE(EN) lets the compiler use lowercase letters in source code listing headings and error messages. This option has nothing to do with your use of lowercase letters in programs! All it controls is how the compiler prints your source code listing.

FLAGSAA—Identifies any incompatibilities between your program and System Application Architecture standards, in the same way that MIGR in VS COBOL identifies incompatibilities between the old and new compiler versions. SAA is IBM's set of standards for program language portability between different levels of hardware.

CMPR2—IBM introduced many changes in VS COBOL II between its Releases 2 and 3. If you already have converted some VS COBOL programs to VS COBOL II Release 2, you can use the compiler option CMPR2 to force the Release 3 compiler to operate exactly as it did with Release 2. It's not a good idea to use CMPR2 as more than a temporary crutch since it prevents you from accessing the many new features of Release 3!

3.8 EXECUTION AND RUNTIME OPTIONS

You can specify several other compiler options at program compile time, such as DATA(24/31), SSRANGE, NUMPROC, TRUNC, DYNAM, RESIDENT, RENT, and OPTIMIZE, but they affect the program only when it is linkage edited or executed. Most of these options are preset by your installation systems group and you do not need to worry about them.

You can shut off certain options with NODEBUG, NOSSRANGE, NOSTAE, NOAIXBLD, NOSPOUT, and NOLIBKEEP when you execute a program even if the options had been turned on during the compile.

This requires coding a special PARM on the JCL EXEC statement that executes the program. I will show you how to do this for SSRANGE in Chapter 8.

3.9 THE TITLE STATEMENT

VS COBOL II gives you a very handy way to label all or part of your source code listing. You can put a statement such as:

```
001500 TITLE 'WORKING-STORAGE FOR XYZ RECORD UPDATE'.
```

in the program to cause a labeling printline to appear at the upper left corner of the source code listing. The title you code will automatically be left-justified at the upper left corner of the listing and will replace the COBOL II compiler identification after the first page of the program. If you code TITLE lines, start them in column 8 or beyond. You can't continue a TITLE line and you can't put any other statement on the same line.

TITLE works as shown in Figure 3.3. The TITLE line will not appear as a part of your source code in the compiler's listing. It will force the listing to begin on a new page at the point, just like EJECT or a slash (/) in column 7. TITLE statements have no effect on logic.

You can use any number of TITLE statements in a program. They give you a handy way to label parts of a large program. They are a good (and cost-free) way to gain readability and documentation in source code listings.

4

User Return Codes and the FDUMP Option

You probably know that in a COBOL program you can move a value from 0 to 4095 to a special register called RETURN-CODE. RETURN-CODE is automatically passed to the operating system and becomes visible as the COND CODE for the step at which the program is executed. This makes it possible for a program to communicate to subsequent job steps via JCL (and COND on EXEC statements) to shut off subsequent job steps.

You may not have known that the old VS COBOL compiler, unseen by you, inserted logic into your program to activate a return code such as 0519 if the program loses control and falls out its bottom. You get such a return code during a run, not during compiling. In VS COBOL, about ten such return codes were possible. They were confusing because their meaning was difficult to find in VS COBOL documentation.

VS COBOL II expands its runtime error usage of user return codes. Now the user return codes all give you a code in the format U1nnn; in other words, return codes in the range 1000 to 1999. In this chapter, I will explain what you need to know about VS COBOL II user return codes to make sense of them.

4.1 *TRY IT!* USER RETURN CODES IN VS COBOL

The program I have listed in Figure 4.1 is named B1OLDRC. It will abend if you run it. Its logic jumps out of a PERFORMed paragraph to an EXIT but no PERFORM . . . THRU was active! This means that the

(text continues on page 76)

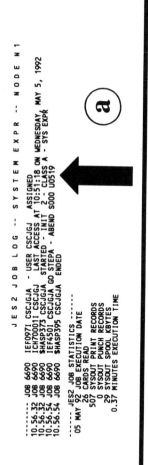

```
J E S 2   J O B   L O G  --  S Y S T E M   E X P R  --  N O D E  N 1

------ JOB 6690  IEF097I CSCJGJA - USER CSCJGJ  ASSIGNED
10.56.32 JOB 6690  ICH70001I CSCJGJ  LAST ACCESS AT 10:51:18 ON WEDNESDAY MAY 5, 1992
10.56.32 JOB 6690  $HASP373 CSCJGJA  STARTED - INIT  2 - CLASS A - SYS EXPR
10.56.54 JOB 6690  IEF450I CSCJGJA GO STEPA - ABEND S000 U0519
10.56.54 JOB 6690  $HASP395 CSCJGJA ENDED

------ JES2 JOB STATISTICS ------
05 MAY 92 JOB EXECUTION DATE
      26 CARDS READ
     507 SYSOUT PRINT RECORDS
       0 SYSOUT PUNCH RECORDS
      29 SYSOUT SPOOL KBYTES
    0.37 MINUTES EXECUTION TIME
```

```
1   //CSCJGJA  JOB 1,'BIN 7 JANOSSY',MSGCLASS=X,MSGLEVEL=(1,1),     JOB 6690
    //         NOTIFY=CSCJGJ
    ***     THIS JCL = CSCJGJ.CSC.CNTL(B1OLDRC)
    ***
2   //STEPA   EXEC PROC=CLINKGO,
    // PARM.COB=('SIZE=1024K',
    //          'STATE',
    //          'FLOW=30',
    //          'SYM',           <=== VS COBOL SYMBOLIC DUMP "SYMDMP" OPTION
    //          'SXR',                (REQUIRES USE OF SYSUT5 AND "SYM" PDS)
    //          'LIB',
    //          'DYN',
    //          'DMAP',
    //          'APOST',
    //          'MIGR')
    //          PDS=CSCJGJ.CSC.COBOL',
    //          MEMBER=B1OLDRC'
3   XXCLINKGO  PROC SYSOUT='*',
    XX          PDS=
    XX          MEMBER=
    XX          COPYLIB='SYS1.VSCOLIB'
    . . .
```

```
IEF236I ALLOC. FOR CSCJGJA GO STEPA
IEF237I 128 ALLOCATED TO PGM=*.DD
IEF237I 120 ALLOCATED TO STEPLIB
IEF237I JES2 ALLOCATED TO SYSOUT
IEF237I JES2 ALLOCATED TO SYSDBOUT
IEF237I 122 ALLOCATED TO SORTWK01
IEF237I 128 ALLOCATED TO SORTWK02
IEF237I 123 ALLOCATED TO SYSUT5
IEF237I 121 ALLOCATED TO SYS13583
IEF237I JES2 ALLOCATED TO SYSOUT
IEF237I JES2 ALLOCATED TO SYSDTERM
```

00010000
00020000
00030000
00040000

62

Figure 4.1 A Program Losing Control Gives You U0519 in VS COBOL.

This figure shows you how program B1OLDRC loses control and how VS COBOL tells you about it. The same program in Figure 4.2 produces different results in VS COBOL II!

a. User completion code 0519 is embedded in the job log at the start of the system print you get when you run the program. 0519 is a return code automatically moved to RETURN-CODE by the VS COBOL compiler in this type of situation. Documentation for the VS COBOL user return codes was hard to find in the IBM programmers's manual.

b. I used the SYMDMP option (SYM) of VS COBOL for this run to produce a "symbolic dump." If you turn on SYM like this, your compile step and the "go" step need access to a special partitioned data set at DDname //SYSUT5. See chapter 17 of *Practical MVS JCL* (Janossy, John Wiley & Sons, Inc., 1987, 1992) for more information on using the old VS COBOL symbolic dump option.

```
IEF237I JES2 ALLOCATED TO SYSDBOUT
IEF237I JES2 ALLOCATED TO SYSDBG
IEF472I CSCJGJA GO STEPA - COMPLETION CODE - SYSTEM=000 USER=0519
IEF285I SYS92126.T105632.RA000.CSCJGJA.TEMPPDS         KEPT
IEF285I VOL SER NOS= ACSCAF.
IEF285I SYS1.VSCLLIB                                    KEPT
IEF285I VOL SER NOS= ACSRES,
IEF285I JES2.JOB06690.SO0104                            SYSOUT
IEF285I JES2.JOB06690.SO0105                            SYSOUT
IEF285I SYS92126.T105632.RA000.CSCJGJA.R0000006        DELETED
IEF285I VOL SER NOS= ACSDLB.
IEF285I SYS92126.T105632.RA000.CSCJGJA.R0000007        DELETED
IEF285I VOL SER NOS= ACSCAI.
IEF285I CSCJGJ.CSC.SYM                                  KEPT
IEF285I VOL SER NOS= ACSCAA.
IEF285I CATALOG.USER                                    KEPT
IEF285I VOL SER NOS= ACSCAT.
IEF285I JES2.JOB06690.SO0106                            SYSOUT
IEF285I JES2.JOB06690.SO0107                            SYSOUT
IEF285I JES2.JOB06690.SO0108                            SYSOUT
IEF285I JES2.JOB06690.SI0101                            SYSIN
IEF373I STEP /GO       / START 92126.1056
IEF374I STEP /GO       / STOP  92126.1056 CPU    0MIN 00.16SEC SRB    0MIN 00.01SEC VIRT    36K SYS    308K
IEF237I 128  ALLOCATED TO SYS00001
IEF285I SYS92126.T105654.RA000.CSCJGJA.R0000001        KEPT
IEF285I VOL SER NOS= ACSCAF.
IEF285I SYS92126.T105632.RA000.CSCJGJA.TEMPPDS         DELETED
IEF285I VOL SER NOS= ACSCAF.
IEF373I JOB /CSCJGJA / START 92126.1056
IEF376I JOB /CSCJGJA / STOP  92126.1056 CPU    0MIN 00.88SEC SRB    0MIN 00.09SEC
```

```
PP 5740-CB1 RELEASE 2.4                           IBM OS/VS COBOL  JULY  1, 1982

1                  10.56.36         MAY  5,1992                                10.56.36  DATE MAY  5,1992

00001 000100 IDENTIFICATION DIVISION.
00002 000200 PROGRAM-ID.   B10LDRC.
00003 000300 AUTHOR.       J JANOSSY.
00004 000400 INSTALLATION. DEPAUL UNIVERSITY.
00005 000500 DATE-WRITTEN. SEP 1986.
00006 000600 DATE-COMPILED. MAY  5,1992.
00007 000700*REMARKS.      THIS PROGRAM JUMPS OUT OF A PERFORMED ROUTINE
00008 000800*              TO DEMONSTRATE A VS COBOL USER 0519 ERROR
00009 000900*              FOR COMPUTER CAREER PROGRAM TRAINING PURPOSES.
00010 001000*
00011 001100 ENVIRONMENT DIVISION.
00012 001200*
00013 001300 DATA DIVISION.
00014 001400 WORKING-STORAGE SECTION.
00015 001500 01  WS-START-MSG            PIC X(11)  VALUE 'HERE IS WS!'.
00016 001600 01  WS-HERE-IS-DISPLAY-NUM  PIC 9(3)   VALUE 0.
00017 001700 01  WS-HERE-IS-PACKED-NUM   PIC S9(5)  COMP-3  VALUE +0.
00018 001800*
00019 001900 PROCEDURE DIVISION.
00020 002000 0000-MAINLINE.
00021 002100     MOVE 123      TO WS-HERE-IS-DISPLAY-NUM.
00022 002200     MOVE +98765   TO WS-HERE-IS-PACKED-NUM.
00023 002300     DISPLAY '***1** B10LDRC PROGRAM STARTING ****'.
```

```
00024    002400    PERFORM 1000-ROUTINE.
00025    002500    DISPLAY '**3** PROGRAM ENDED NORMALLY ***'.
00026    002600    STOP RUN.
00027    002700*
00028    002800 1000-ROUTINE.
00029    002900    DISPLAY '**2** WE GOT TO THE 1000-ROUTINE ***'.
00030    003000    GO TO 1000-EXIT.
00031    003100    DISPLAY '**4** THIS DISPLAY IS AFTER GO TO OUT OF ROUTINE'.
00032    003200*
00033    003300*   I DID NOT PERFORM "THRU" 1000-EXIT SO BRANCHING HERE IS WRONG.
00034    003400*   THE PROGRAM WILL LOSE CONTROL AS A RESULT:
00035    003500*
00036    003600 1000-EXIT.    EXIT.

         . . .
```

```
H96-LEVEL LINKAGE EDITOR OPTIONS SPECIFIED SIZE=1024K
      DEFAULT OPTION(S) USED - SIZE=(1048576,65536)                 AMODE 24
****NEWPROG  DOES NOT EXIST BUT HAS BEEN ADDED TO DATA SET
RMODE IS 24
AUTHORIZATION CODE IS        0.


***1** B1OLDRC PROGRAM STARTING ***
**2** WE GOT TO THE 1000-ROUTINE ***
```

```
                          COBOL ABEND DIAGNOSTIC AIDS

PROGRAM     B1OLDRC

LAST PSW BEFORE ABEND = FF85000D50115EB8        USER COMPLETION CODE = 0519

LAST CARD NUMBER/VERB NUMBER EXECUTED -- CARD NUMBER 000036/VERB NUMBER 01.

                                    FLOW TRACE

B1OLDRC  000020 000028 000036
```

Figure 4.1 *Continued*
```
```

TYPE CODES USED IN SYMDMP OUTPUT

CODE	MEANING
A	= ALPHABETIC
AN	= ALPHANUMERIC
ANE	= ALPHANUMERIC EDITED
D	= DISPLAY (STERLING NONREPORT)
DE	= DISPLAY EDITED (STERLING REPORT)
F	= FLOATING POINT (COMP-1/COMP-2)
FD	= FLOATING POINT DISPLAY (EXTERNAL FLOATING POINT)
NB	= NUMERIC BINARY UNSIGNED (COMP)
NB-S	= NUMERIC BINARY SIGNED
ND	= NUMERIC DISPLAY UNSIGNED (EXTERNAL DECIMAL)
ND-OL	= NUMERIC DISPLAY OVERPUNCH SIGN LEADING
ND-OT	= NUMERIC DISPLAY OVERPUNCH SIGN TRAILING
ND-SL	= NUMERIC DISPLAY SEPARATE SIGN LEADING
ND-ST	= NUMERIC DISPLAY SEPARATE SIGN TRAILING
NE	= NUMERIC EDITED
NP	= NUMERIC PACKED DECIMAL UNSIGNED (COMP-3)
NP-S	= NUMERIC PACKED DECIMAL SIGNED
*	= SUBSCRIPTED

DATA DIVISION DUMP OF B1OLDRC

TASK GLOBAL TABLE

	LOC	VALUE							
SAVE AREA	115AA0	0030C4C2	00114FB0	00114A08	00115EA8	00117SD6	00115E26	70115EA4	00115868
	115AC0	00115CF8	00115E9E	5015FC0	00115A80	00115CA7	00115CA8	00115F72	00115SE0
	115AE0	00115DE0	00115CC8						
SWITCH	115AE8	3D02004B							
TALLY	115AEC	00000000							

DATA DIVISION DUMP OF B1OLDRC

LOC	CARD	LV NAME	TYPE	VALUE
115A80	000015	01 WS-START-MSG	AN	HERE IS WS!
115A90	000016	01 WS-HERE-IS-DISPLAY-NUM	ND	123
115A98	000017	01 WS-HERE-IS-PACKED-NUM	NP-S	+98765

END OF COBOL DIAGNOSTIC AIDS

SYMDMP CONTROL CARDS

B1OLDRC SYSUT5

NO ERRORS FOUND IN CONTROL CARDS

Figure 4.1 *Continued*

c. (Page 64) You can also find the user return code within the body of the system print, but this is much harder to locate.

d. (Page 64) I put WORKING-STORAGE into program B1OLDRC just so that you could see the result of a symbolic dump in VS COBOL and compare it to the FDUMP (formatted dump) of VS COBOL II; see (h).

e. (Page 65) The logic of B1OLDRC jumps out of a PERFORMed loop at line 003000, to 1000-EXIT, an empty paragraph. The program would have worked fine if I had coded the PERFORM as "PERFORM 1000-ROUTINE THRU 1000-EXIT". As it stands, my GO TO 1000-EXIT makes it impossible for control to return to the PERFORM. I "drop out of the bottom" of the program, losing control.

f. (Page 65) The output produced by the program does not include the DISPLAYed information at line 003100, which is never executed due to the GO TO above it.

g. (Page 65) The STATE and FLOW options provide these abend diagnostic messages if your program abends. When you use VS COBOL you don't need to specify SYM with STATE and FLOW since they work independently of SYM. Notice that VS COBOL still talks about "cards" as if your code was punched on cards!

h. (Page 66) VS COBOL's SYMDMP option produces this data division dump. It is called a "formatted" dump because the contents of numeric and packed decimal fields are converted to printable form for you to interpret, as opposed to a raw memory dump where you would see these values in hexadecimal. VS COBOL II changes the name of the compiler option SYMDMP to FDUMP and changes the format of the dump.

```
EDIT ---- A1092JJ.LIB.JCL(B1NEWRC) - 01.01 -------------------- COLUMNS 001 072
COMMAND ===>                                                   SCROLL ===> PAGE
****** ************************************ TOP OF DATA ************************************
000001 //A1092JJA JOB (1092,COB2),'JANOSSY',CLASS=A,MSGCLASS=X,
000002 // NOTIFY=A1092JJ
000003 //*
000004 //*     THIS JCL = A1092JJ.LIB.JCL(B1NEWRC)
000005 //*
000006 //STEPA   EXEC COB2UCLG,
000007 // PARM.COB2=('NOADV',
000008 //          'NOCMPR2',
000009 //          'DATA(31)',
000010 //          'DYN',
000011 //          'FASTSRT',
000012 //          'LANGUAGE(UE)',
000013 //          'NUMPROC(PFD)',
000014 //          'NOMAP',
000015 //          'FDUMP',         <=== COMMENT OUT IF DON'T WANT FDUMP
000016 //          'NOVBREF',)
000017 //COB2.SYSIN DD DSN=A1092JJ.LIB.COBOL(B1NEWRC),DISP=SHR
000018 //GO.SYSOUT DD SYSOUT=*
000019 //
```

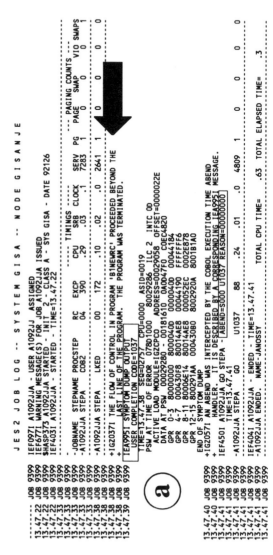

```
                J E S 2   J O B   L O G  --  S Y S T E M   G I S A  --  N O D E   G I S A N J E

13.47.22 JOB 9399  IEF097I A1092JJA - USER A1092JJ ASSIGNED
13.47.22 JOB 9399  IEF677I WARNING MESSAGE(S) FOR JOB A1092JJA ISSUED
13.47.22 JOB 9399  $HASP373 A1092JJA STARTED - INIT 2 - CLASS A - SYS GISA - DATE 92126
13.47.22 JOB 9399  IEF403I A1092JJA - STARTED - TIME=13.47.22
```

					--- TIMINGS ---				PG	--- PAGING COUNTS ---			SWAPS
-JOBNAME	STEPNAME	PROCSTEP	RC	EXCP	CPU	SRB	CLOCK	SERV		PAGE	SWAP	VIO	
-A1092JJA	STEPA	COB2	04	390	.29	.03	.1	7283	0	0	0	0	1
-A1092JJA	STEPA	LKED	00	172	.10	.02	.0	2661	1	0	0	0	0

```
13.47.38 JOB 9399  +IGZ037I THE FLOW OF CONTROL IN PROGRAM 'B1NEWRC' PROCEEDED BEYOND THE
13.47.38 JOB 9399  +       LAST LINE OF THE PROGRAM.  THE PROGRAM WAS TERMINATED.
13.47.38 JOB 9399  IEA995I SYMPTOM DUMP OUTPUT
                   USER COMPLETION CODE=1037
13.47.38 JOB 9399   TIME=13.47.38 SEQ=02757 CPU=0000 ASID=0019
13.47.38 JOB 9399   PSW AT TIME OF ERROR 078D1000 8002928B  ILC 2  INTC 0D
13.47.39 JOB 9399    ACTIVE LOAD MODULE=IGZCPCO ADDRESS=00029058 OFFSET=0000022E
                     DATA AT PSW 0002928D - 00181610 0A0047F0 C0EC4820
                     GPR 0-3  80000000 8000040D 0000040D 00044184
                     GPR 4-7  000430F8 8001AAE8 00044190 FFFFFFF6
                     GPR 8-11 80006E14 8001AAE8 000052EC 0002E878
                     GPR 12-15 800291AA 00043080 8002992A 8001B1A0
                    END OF SYMPTOM DUMP
13.47.40 JOB 9399  +IGZ057I AN ABEND WAS INTERCEPTED BY THE COBOL EXECUTION TIME ABEND
13.47.40 JOB 9399  +       HANDLER.  IT IS DESCRIBED BY A CORRESPONDING IEA995I MESSAGE.
13.47.41 JOB 9399  IEF450I A1092JJA GO STEPA - ABEND=S000 U1037 REASON=00000000
                   TIME=13.47.41
```

| -A1092JJA | STEPA | GO | U1037 | 88 | .24 | .01 | .0 | 4809 | 1 | 0 | 0 | 0 | 0 |

```
13.47.41 JOB 9399  IEF404I A1092JJA - ENDED - TIME=13.47.41
13.47.41 JOB 9399  -A1092JJA ENDED. NAME-JANOSSY TOTAL CPU TIME=   .63 TOTAL ELAPSED TIME=   .3
```

Figure 4.2 U1037: Loss of Control Reported By VS COBOL II.

VS COBOL II uses more user return code values than VS COBOL, and it uses entirely different values. It reports loss of control with user completion code U1037, automatically generated by the compiler. The meaning of the code is clearly stated in the system output. The code value U1037 is related to the IGZ message by its last three digits. That is, IGZ037I is the corresponding message number.

a. You could look up message IGZ037I in IBM's debugging manual for VS COBOL II but there is no reason to. All you would find is the same message that is already printed for you here in the job log! IBM software engineers did a good job in this area. The message is very explicit about the problem that caused the posting of the user return code.

b. (Page 70) You will also see the IGZ messages for a user abend completion code in the body of the system output for your job. This just repeats the information in the job log, but is less convenient to find.

c. (Page 71) I turned on the FDUMP option with the JCL I used to invoke the VS COBOL II compiler. Compiler PARMs set by the JCL are called "invocation parameters."

```
13.47.41 JOB 9399 $HASP395 A1092JJA ENDED - DATE 92126

----- JES2 JOB STATISTICS -----

05 MAY 92 JOB EXECUTION DATE
     19 CARDS READ
    609 SYSOUT PRINT RECORDS
      0 SYSOUT PUNCH RECORDS
     37 SYSOUT SPOOL KBYTES
   0.32 MINUTES EXECUTION TIME


  1 //A1092JJA  JOB (1092,COB2),'JANOSSY',CLASS=A,MSGCLASS=X,          JOB 9399
    //          NOTIFY=A1092JJ
    ***         $ACFJ219 ACF2 ACTIVE GISANJE                            ACF2
    ***
    ***         THIS JCL = A1092JJ.LIB.JCL(B1NEWRC)
    ***
  2 //STEPA     EXEC  COB2UCLG,
    //          PARM.COB2=('NOADV',
    ///                    'NOCMPR2',
    ///                    'DATA(31)',
    ///                    'DYN',
    ///                    'FASTSRT',
    ///                    'LANGUAGE(UE)',
    ///                    'NUMPROC(PFD)',
    ///                    'NOMAP',
    ///                    'FDUMP',           <=== COMMENT OUT IF DON'T WANT FDUMP
    ///                    'NOVBREF')
  3 XXCOB2UCLG PROC
    ***        PROC FOR COBOL II - COMPILE, LINK, AND GO
  4 XXCOB2     EXEC  PGM=IGYCRCTL,PARM='OBJECT',REGION=3500K
  5 XXSTEPLIB  DD    DSNAME=SYS1.COB2COMP,DISP=SHR


IEF236I ALLOC. FOR A1092JJA GO STEPA
IEF237I 834 ALLOCATED TO PGM=*.DD
IEF237I 301 ALLOCATED TO STEPLIB
IEF237I JES2 ALLOCATED TO SYSABOUT
IEF237I JES2 ALLOCATED TO SYSDBOUT
IEF237I JES2 ALLOCATED TO SYSUDUMP
IEF237I JES2 ALLOCATED TO SYSOUT
```
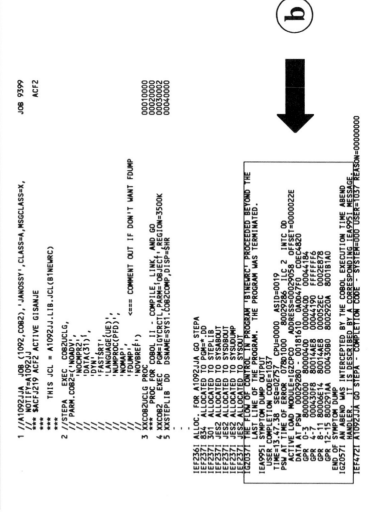
```
IGZ057I THE FLOW OF CONTROL IN PROGRAM 'B1NEWRC' PROCEEDED BEYOND THE
        LAST LINE OF THE PROGRAM.  THE PROGRAM WAS TERMINATED.

IEA995I SYMPTOM DUMP OUTPUT
  USER COMPLETION CODE=1037
  TIME=13.47.38  SEQ=02757       CPU=0000  ASID=0019
  PSW AT TIME OF ERROR  07B01000  80029286 ILC 2  INTC 0D
    ACTIVE LOAD MODULE=IGZCPCO     ADDRESS=00029058  OFFSET=0000022E
    DATA AT PSW  00029280 - 0018161D 0A0D47F0 C0EC4820
    GPR 0-3   80000000 80000400 0000040D 00044184
    GPR 4-7   000430F8 80014AE8 00044190 FFFFFFF6
    GPR 8-11  80006E14 80014AE8 0005052EC 0002E878
    GPR 12-15 80029100 800430B0 0002920A 8001B1A0
END OF SYMPTOM DUMP
IGZ057I AN ABEND WAS INTERCEPTED BY THE COBOL EXECUTION TIME ABEND
        HANDLER.  IT IS DESCRIBED BY A CORRESPONDING IEA995I MESSAGE.
IEF472I A1092JJA GO STEPA - COMPLETION CODE - SYSTEM=000 USER=1037 REASON=00000000
```

```
IEF285I   SYS92126.T134722.RA000.A1092JJA.GOSET          KEPT
IEF285I   VOL SER NOS= GISAW3.
IEF285I   SYS1.COB2LIB                                    KEPT
IEF285I   VOL SER NOS= GISAL2.
IEF285I   JES2.JOB09399.S0000103                          SYSOUT
IEF285I   JES2.JOB09399.S0000104                          SYSOUT
IEF285I   JES2.JOB09399.S0000105                          SYSOUT
IEF285I   JES2.JOB09399.S0000106                          SYSOUT
IEF237I   834  ALLOCATED TO SYS00001
IEF285I   SYS92126.T134741.RA000.A1092JJA.R0000001        KEPT
IEF285I   VOL SER NOS= GISAW3.
IEF285I   SYS92126.T134722.RA000.A1092JJA.GOSET           DELETED
IEF285I   VOL SER NOS= GISAW3.
IEF375I   JOB /A1092JJA/ START 92126.1347
IEF376I   JOB /A1092JJA/ STOP  92126.1347 CPU  0MIN 00.63SEC SRB   0MIN 00.06SEC


PP 5668-958 IBM VS COBOL II RELEASE 3.2 09/05/90          DATE 05/05/92  TIME 13:47:24  PAGE    1

INVOCATION PARAMETERS:

NOADV,NOCMPR2,DATA(31),DYN,FASTSRT,LANGUAGE(UE),NUMPROC(PFD),NOMAP,FDUMP,NOVBREF

     IGYOS4001-W  THE "FASTSRT" OPTION WAS NOT ALLOWED BY LOCAL INSTALLATION CONTROL.  THIS OPTION WAS DISCARDED.

OPTIONS IN EFFECT:

     NOADV
      APOST
     NOAWO
     NOCMPR2
      BUFSIZE(4096)
      COMPILE
      DATA(31)
     NODBCS
     NODECK
     NODUMP
      DYNAM
     NOEXIT
     NOFASTSRT
      FDUMP
      FLAG(I,I)
     NOFLAGMIG
      . .
      . .
```

Figure 4.2 *Continued*

```
PP 5668-958 IBM VS COBOL II RELEASE 3.2 09/05/90                    B1NEWRC   DATE 05/05/92   TIME 13:47:24   PAGE    2
LINEID  PL SL  ----+-*A-1-B--+----2----+----3----+----4----+----5----+----6----+----7-|--+----8 MAP AND CROSS REFERENCE

000001         000100 IDENTIFICATION DIVISION.
000002         000200 PROGRAM-ID.    B1NEWRC.
000003         000300 AUTHOR.        J JANOSSY.
000004         000400 INSTALLATION.  DEPAUL UNIVERSITY.
000005         000500 DATE-WRITTEN.  SEP 1986.
000006         000600*
000007         000700*REMARKS.        THIS PROGRAM JUMPS OUT OF A PERFORMED ROUTINE
000008         000800*                TO DEMONSTRATE A VS COBOL USER 0519 ERROR
000009         000900*                FOR COMPUTER CAREER PROGRAM TRAINING PURPOSES.
000010         001000*
000011         001100 ENVIRONMENT DIVISION.
000012         001200*
000013         001300 DATA DIVISION.
000014         001400 WORKING-STORAGE SECTION.
000015         001500 01  WS-START-MSG                 PIC X(11)  VALUE 'HERE IS WS!'.
000016         001600 01  WS-HERE-IS-DISPLAY-NUM        PIC 9(3)   VALUE 0.
000017         001700 01  WS-HERE-IS-PACKED-NUM         PIC S9(5)  COMP-3  VALUE +0.
000018         001800*
000019         001900 PROCEDURE DIVISION.
000020         002000 0000-MAINLINE.
000021         002100     MOVE 123      TO WS-HERE-IS-DISPLAY-NUM.
000022         002200     MOVE +98765   TO WS-HERE-IS-PACKED-NUM.
000023         002300     DISPLAY '**1** B1NEWRC PROGRAM STARTING ***'.
000024         002400     PERFORM 1000-ROUTINE.
==000024==> IGYOP3093-W THE "PERFORM" STATEMENT AT ""PERFORM" (LINE 24.01)" CANNOT REACH ITS
            EXIT.
000025         002500     DISPLAY '**3** PROGRAM ENDED NORMALLY ***'.
000026         002600     STOP RUN.
000027         002700*
000028         002800 1000-ROUTINE.
000029         002900     DISPLAY '**2** WE GOT TO THE 1000-ROUTINE ***'.
000030         003000     GO TO 1000-EXIT.
000031         003100     DISPLAY '**4** THIS DISPLAY IS AFTER GO TO OUT OF ROUTINE'.
==000031==> IGYOP3091-W CODE FROM ""DISPLAY" (LINE 31.01)" TO ""DISPLAY" (LINE 31.01)" CAN NEVER
            BE EXECUTED, AND WAS THEREFORE DISCARDED.
000032         003200*
000033         003300* I DID NOT PERFORM "THRU" 1000-EXIT SO BRANCHING HERE IS WRONG.
000034         003400* THE PROGRAM WILL LOSE CONTROL AS A RESULT:
000035         003500*
000036         003600 1000-EXIT.    EXIT.
```

d ▼

e ▼

16
17

28

36

```
MVS/DFP VERSION 3 RELEASE 2 LINKAGE EDITOR      13:47:34  TUE  MAY 05, 1992
JOB A1092JJA  STEP STEPA  PROCEDURE LKED
INVOCATION PARAMETERS - LIST,XREF,LET,MAP
ACTUAL SIZE=(317440,86016)
OUTPUT DATA SET SYS92126.T134722.RA000.A1092JJA.GOSET IS ON VOLUME GISAN3

                              CROSS REFERENCE TABLE

CONTROL SECTION                    ENTRY
 NAME     ORIGIN  LENGTH    NAME    LOCATION   NAME   LOCATION   NAME   LOCATION   NAME   LOCATION
B1NEWRC    00     1B28
IGZEBST *  1B28    428     IGZEBS2   1DB6

LOCATION REFERS TO SYMBOL   IN CONTROL SECTION        LOCATION  REFERS TO SYMBOL  IN CONTROL SECTION
   6C      IGZEBST           IGZEBST                     1F24      IGZETUN          $UNRESOLVED(W)
   1F28    IGZEOPT           $UNRESOLVED(W)
ENTRY ADDRESS      00

TOTAL LENGTH      1F50
** GO       DID NOT PREVIOUSLY EXIST BUT WAS ADDED AND HAS AMODE 31
** LOAD MODULE HAS RMODE ANY
** AUTHORIZATION CODE IS      0.
```

```
--- VS COBOL II ABEND INFORMATION ---

PROGRAM = 'B1NEWRC' COMPILED ON '05/05/92' AT '13:47:24'

   TGT = '03102028'

NO FILES WERE USED IN THIS PROGRAM.

CONTENTS OF BASE LOCATORS FOR WORKING STORAGE ARE:
   0-00043E88

CONTENTS OF BASE LOCATORS FOR THE LINKAGE SECTION ARE:
   0-00000000

NO VARIABLY LOCATED AREAS WERE USED IN THIS PROGRAM.

NO EXTERNAL DATA WAS USED IN THIS PROGRAM.

NO INDEXES WERE USED IN THIS PROGRAM.

--- END OF VS COBOL II ABEND INFORMATION ---
```

Figure 4.2 *Continued*

```
--- VS COBOL II FORMATTED DUMP AT ABEND ---

PROGRAM = 'B1NEWRC'

COMPLETION CODE = 'U1037'

PSW AT ABEND = '078D100080029286'

THE ABEND ADDRESS WAS OUTSIDE OF MAINLINE COBOL CODE.

OPTIMIZATION WAS IN EFFECT FOR THIS PROGRAM.

THE RELATIVE ADDRESS OF THE NEXT INSTRUCTION TO BE EXECUTED:

'FCF291D6'

THE GP REGISTERS AT ENTRY TO ABEND WERE

   Regs  0 -  3  - '80000000  80000400  00000400  00044184'

   Regs  4 -  7  - '000430F8  80014AE8  00044190  FFFFFFF6'

   Regs  8 - 11  - '80006E14  80014AE8  000052EC  0002E878'

   Regs 12 - 15  - '800291AA  000430B0  8002920A  8001B1A0'

DATA DIVISION DUMP OF 'B1NEWRC'
000015 01 B1NEWRC.WS-START-MSG X(11)
       DISP    ===>HERE IS WS!
000016 01 B1NEWRC.WS-HERE-IS-DISPLAY-NUM 999
       DISP    ==>123
000017 01 B1NEWRC.WS-HERE-IS-PACKED-NUM S9(5)
       CMP3    ===>+98765

--- END OF VS COBOL II FORMATTED DUMP AT ABEND ---
```

(g)

```
***1** B1NEWRC PROGRAM STARTING ***
***2** WE GOT TO THE 1000-ROUTINE ***
```

Figure 4.2 VS COBOL II Compiler Enhancements and U1037.

d. (Page 72) IGYOP messages like IGYOP3093-W come from VS COBOL II's own internal optimizer component. The optimizer has figured out that in this program I have jumped out of a PERFORMed loop and the loop can never reach its end. This is a pretty smart observation by the optimizer.

e. (Page 72) This optimizer message tells you that some code in the program can never be reached ("dead" code) and has been dropped from the compile. The dead code does not result in any machine language in the load module.

f. (Page 73) VS COBOL II gives you summary information like this when your program fails with a user return code or with a system completion code. You'll get this even if you don't use the FDUMP option.

g. (Page 74) When your program abends, or ends with a user return code generated by a problem, FDUMP prints a formatted dump for every item in WORKING-STORAGE. You see the line number of each WORKING-STORAGE item, the code that defines it, what its format is, and at the arrow = = = > its interpreted contents. While the format of the FDUMP is a little more cluttered than the SYMDMP listing of VS COBOL, FDUMP is much easier to use. With SYMDMP you had to turn on a compiler option, and also preallocate and refer to a special partitioned data set at //SYSUT5 in both your compile and execution steps. All you have to do to get a formatted abend dump with VS COBOL II is to turn on the FDUMP option either in JCL or in a PROCESS statement.

program loses control. The GO TO sends control out of a loop and control eventually goes crashing through the bottom of the program.

If you compile, link, and run this program with your VS COBOL proc, you will get a user return code of 0519. Try it. You'll get error reporting similar to Figure 4.1 at notes (a) and (b) on page 62.

4.2   *TRY IT!* USER RETURN CODES IN VS COBOL II

Figure 4.2 lists B1NEWRC as processed by VS COBOL II. This is exactly the same program as in Figure 4.1, except that I added a PROCESS statement with FDUMP to activate a formatted dump. Figure 4.2 note (a) on page 68 shows you U1037, the new user return code analogous to the old U0519.

I have included extensive notes about Figure 4.2 in its legends. Look over this figure and its legends now since I haven't repeated that same material in text form.

4.3   USER RETURN CODE MESSAGES AND DOCUMENTATION

Each U1nnn code is associated with a message labeled IGZnnnI using the last three digits. For example, U1037 refers to message IGZ037I. All of the IGZ messages are documented in Appendix C of *VS COBOL II Application Programming: Debugging,* SC26–4049.

But don't reach for your manuals when you receive a user return code! VS COBOL II prints the complete text of the relevant message in your output, as you can see in Figure 4.2 (a). This makes it unnecessary for you to refer to the debugging manual. Just look into the job log closely!

4.4   DON'T USE RETURN CODES 1000 TO 1999!

Since the VS COBOL II compiler has now staked its claim to user return codes 1000 through 1999, you are well advised not to use values in this range for your own purposes. If you code new programs or modify existing ones to be used with VS COBOL II you have to avoid this return code number range. This may make it necessary for you to revise documentation about return codes posted by production programs.

4.5   WHEN DOES FDUMP KICK IN?

The VS COBOL II FDUMP option produces a formatted dump of your program's memory if the program fails. "Fails" includes two situations:

- Your program abends and you receive a system completion code such as 0CB (attempt to divide by zero).
- Your program receives a compiler-inserted user return code.

You will not get an FDUMP just because you move a value to RETURN-CODE yourself. You can still continue to use RETURN-CODE for communication to JCL and to the outside world as long as you use values less than 1000 or greater than 1999.

4.6 HOW AN FDUMP LOOKS

I turned on the FDUMP option in B1NEWRC using a PROCESS statement. I could have just as well activated FDUMP with JCL overriding the PARM to the compiler. Since the program receives a compiler-inserted user return code at runtime, the FDUMP option gives me a dump. Take a look at Figure 4.2, (page 74) where I illustrate an FDUMP.

In an FDUMP you see the WORKING-STORAGE of your program printed in a formatted manner. The FDUMP will show you line numbers if you have not used the OPT (optimize) option, or hexadecimal displacements in memory if you have used OPT.

4.7 *TRY IT!* SEEING HOW STATEMENT LEVEL AND FDUMP WORK

Here is a pleasant way to explore many new compiler and listing features. I designed program B2COINS to produce some interesting results. It's based on the following scenario.

When Uncle Droesselmeyer visits his relatives he walks in with pockets bulging with coins. He made his fortune in gold mining and he always carries a lot of his wealth around with him. And he likes to spoil his nieces and nephews.

The rich uncle plays a simple game to give each niece and nephew a monetary gift. He takes the kids one at a time and plays "penny-dime-dollar" with each one. To do this he puts three cups upside down on a table. He puts a penny under one cup, a dime under the second cup, and a silver dollar under the third cup. He then moves the cups around and lets the child pick one cup and keep the money under it. He does this four times for each child. Each child can receive as much as four dollars or as little as four cents. Most of the time each child receives some value in between these extremes.

Little nephew Jimmy has gotten curious about all the possible combinations of coins he might receive from his rich uncle. He's written a small COBOL program to analyze the possibilities, see how many different money gift totals there might be, and find out which values are more likely to occur than others. The program is called B2COINS.

When B2COINS is run, the program produces a listing with 81 lines of output, showing every combination of coins possible with four rounds of play. Figure 4.3 shows you this output. Figure 4.4 shows the source code as it appears when compiled with VS COBOL II. Examine Figure 4.4 closely to see the information I have put in notes (a), (b), and (c).

You can do the following things with B2COINS to reinforce your understanding of the VS COBOL II compiler features and FDUMP options described in Chapters 3 and 4. (You can key in the program from Figure 4.4 or obtain the source code in machine-readable form from the diskette-based version of this book.)

1. Run B2COINS with no PROCESS statement. This will show you how your installation has set the default VS COBOL II compiler options.
2. Run B2COINS with the XREF, MAP, and FDUMP options. Do you prefer XREF but not MAP due to MAP clutter in your WORK-ING-STORAGE?
3. Look at the source code listing produced by VS COBOL II and see the embedded cross-reference and statement nesting level numbers (See Figure 4.4).
4. Modify your copy of the B2COINS so that it uses the convention of PERFORM ... THRU exits. To do this, install empty "exit" paragraphs immediately after each paragraph. Then change each PERFORM to a PERFORM ... THRU the exit. See what effect this change makes on the procedure-name cross reference.
5. Make WS-VAL1, WS-VAL2, WS-VAL3, and WS-VAL4 into packed decimal fields by putting COMP-3 after the PIC on each one. But don't put a VALUE clause on any of these definitions. Then force the program to abend immediately when it starts by including the statement:

```
004010   ADD WS-VAL1 TO WS-VAL2.
```

after line 004000. Explore these questions by looking at the result of this run:
1. Do you get a 0C7 system completion code as with VS COBOL?
2. What value do uninitialized numeric fields assume?
3. How does your FDUMP show you the contents of your WORK-ING-STORAGE fields?

```
PENNY   PENNY   PENNY   PENNY   VALUE =  $  .04
PENNY   PENNY   PENNY   DIME    VALUE =  $  .13
PENNY   PENNY   PENNY   DOLLAR  VALUE =  $ 1.03
------------------------------------------------
PENNY   PENNY   DIME    PENNY   VALUE =  $  .13
PENNY   PENNY   DIME    DIME    VALUE =  $  .22
PENNY   PENNY   DIME    DOLLAR  VALUE =  $ 1.12
------------------------------------------------
PENNY   PENNY   DOLLAR  PENNY   VALUE =  $ 1.03
PENNY   PENNY   DOLLAR  DIME    VALUE =  $ 1.12
PENNY   PENNY   DOLLAR  DOLLAR  VALUE =  $ 2.02
------------------------------------------------
PENNY   DIME    PENNY   PENNY   VALUE =  $  .13
PENNY   DIME    PENNY   DIME    VALUE =  $  .22
PENNY   DIME    PENNY   DOLLAR  VALUE =  $ 1.12
------------------------------------------------
PENNY   DIME    DIME    PENNY   VALUE =  $  .22
PENNY   DIME    DIME    DIME    VALUE =  $  .31
PENNY   DIME    DIME    DOLLAR  VALUE =  $ 1.21
------------------------------------------------
PENNY   DIME    DOLLAR  PENNY   VALUE =  $ 1.12
PENNY   DIME    DOLLAR  DIME    VALUE =  $ 1.21
PENNY   DIME    DOLLAR  DOLLAR  VALUE =  $ 2.11
------------------------------------------------
PENNY   DOLLAR  PENNY   PENNY   VALUE =  $ 1.03
PENNY   DOLLAR  PENNY   DIME    VALUE =  $ 1.12
PENNY   DOLLAR  PENNY   DOLLAR  VALUE =  $ 2.02
------------------------------------------------
PENNY   DOLLAR  DIME    PENNY   VALUE =  $ 1.12
PENNY   DOLLAR  DIME    DIME    VALUE =  $ 1.21
PENNY   DOLLAR  DIME    DOLLAR  VALUE =  $ 2.11
------------------------------------------------
PENNY   DOLLAR  DOLLAR  PENNY   VALUE =  $ 2.02
PENNY   DOLLAR  DOLLAR  DIME    VALUE =  $ 2.11
PENNY   DOLLAR  DOLLAR  DOLLAR  VALUE =  $ 3.01
------------------------------------------------
DIME    PENNY   PENNY   PENNY   VALUE =  $  .13
DIME    PENNY   PENNY   DIME    VALUE =  $  .22
DIME    PENNY   PENNY   DOLLAR  VALUE =  $ 1.12
------------------------------------------------
DIME    PENNY   DIME    PENNY   VALUE =  $  .22
DIME    PENNY   DIME    DIME    VALUE =  $  .31
DIME    PENNY   DIME    DOLLAR  VALUE =  $ 1.21
------------------------------------------------
DIME    PENNY   DOLLAR  PENNY   VALUE =  $ 1.12
DIME    PENNY   DOLLAR  DIME    VALUE =  $ 1.21
DIME    PENNY   DOLLAR  DOLLAR  VALUE =  $ 2.11
------------------------------------------------
DIME    DIME    PENNY   PENNY   VALUE =  $  .22
DIME    DIME    PENNY   DIME    VALUE =  $  .31
DIME    DIME    PENNY   DOLLAR  VALUE =  $ 1.21
------------------------------------------------
DIME    DIME    DIME    PENNY   VALUE =  $  .31
DIME    DIME    DIME    DIME    VALUE =  $  .40
DIME    DIME    DIME    DOLLAR  VALUE =  $ 1.30
------------------------------------------------
DIME    DIME    DOLLAR  PENNY   VALUE =  $ 1.21
DIME    DIME    DOLLAR  DIME    VALUE =  $ 1.30
DIME    DIME    DOLLAR  DOLLAR  VALUE =  $ 2.20


------------------------------------------------
DIME    DOLLAR  PENNY   PENNY   VALUE =  $ 1.12
DIME    DOLLAR  PENNY   DIME    VALUE =  $ 1.21
DIME    DOLLAR  PENNY   DOLLAR  VALUE =  $ 2.11
------------------------------------------------
DIME    DOLLAR  DIME    PENNY   VALUE =  $ 1.21
DIME    DOLLAR  DIME    DIME    VALUE =  $ 1.30
DIME    DOLLAR  DIME    DOLLAR  VALUE =  $ 2.20
------------------------------------------------
DIME    DOLLAR  DOLLAR  PENNY   VALUE =  $ 2.11
DIME    DOLLAR  DOLLAR  DIME    VALUE =  $ 2.20
DIME    DOLLAR  DOLLAR  DOLLAR  VALUE =  $ 3.10
------------------------------------------------
DOLLAR  PENNY   PENNY   PENNY   VALUE =  $ 1.03
DOLLAR  PENNY   PENNY   DIME    VALUE =  $ 1.12
DOLLAR  PENNY   PENNY   DOLLAR  VALUE =  $ 2.02
------------------------------------------------
DOLLAR  PENNY   DIME    PENNY   VALUE =  $ 1.12
DOLLAR  PENNY   DIME    DIME    VALUE =  $ 1.21
DOLLAR  PENNY   DIME    DOLLAR  VALUE =  $ 2.11
------------------------------------------------
DOLLAR  PENNY   DOLLAR  PENNY   VALUE =  $ 2.02
DOLLAR  PENNY   DOLLAR  DIME    VALUE =  $ 2.11
DOLLAR  PENNY   DOLLAR  DOLLAR  VALUE =  $ 3.01
------------------------------------------------
DOLLAR  DIME    PENNY   PENNY   VALUE =  $ 1.12
DOLLAR  DIME    PENNY   DIME    VALUE =  $ 1.21
DOLLAR  DIME    PENNY   DOLLAR  VALUE =  $ 2.11
------------------------------------------------
DOLLAR  DIME    DIME    PENNY   VALUE =  $ 1.21
DOLLAR  DIME    DIME    DIME    VALUE =  $ 1.30
DOLLAR  DIME    DIME    DOLLAR  VALUE =  $ 2.20
------------------------------------------------
DOLLAR  DIME    DOLLAR  PENNY   VALUE =  $ 2.11
DOLLAR  DIME    DOLLAR  DIME    VALUE =  $ 2.20
DOLLAR  DIME    DOLLAR  DOLLAR  VALUE =  $ 3.10
------------------------------------------------
DOLLAR  DOLLAR  PENNY   PENNY   VALUE =  $ 2.02
DOLLAR  DOLLAR  PENNY   DIME    VALUE =  $ 2.11
DOLLAR  DOLLAR  PENNY   DOLLAR  VALUE =  $ 3.01
------------------------------------------------
DOLLAR  DOLLAR  DIME    PENNY   VALUE =  $ 2.11
DOLLAR  DOLLAR  DIME    DIME    VALUE =  $ 2.20
DOLLAR  DOLLAR  DIME    DOLLAR  VALUE =  $ 3.10
------------------------------------------------
DOLLAR  DOLLAR  DOLLAR  PENNY   VALUE =  $ 3.01
DOLLAR  DOLLAR  DOLLAR  DIME    VALUE =  $ 3.10
DOLLAR  DOLLAR  DOLLAR  DOLLAR  VALUE =  $ 4.00
```

Figure 4.3 Output of B2COINS: the Penny-Dime-Dollar Game.

This output shows all of the combinations of coins and winnings possible with four rounds of the game of penny-dime-dollar. A rich uncle puts a penny under one cup, a dime under another cup, and a dollar under a third cup and moves around the cups. A niece or nephew chooses one cup and gets to keep the coin under it. The rich uncle puts another similar coin under the chosen cup, moves the cups, and the child chooses again. Four rounds of play make up one game. The child can win as little as four cents or as much as four dollars.

```
PP 5668-958 IBM VS COBOL II RELEASE 3.2 09/05/90          B2COINS   DATE 05/05/92   TIME 17:52:01   PAGE   2
 LINEID PL SL ---+--*A-1-B--+----2----+----3----+----4----+----5----+----6----+----7-|-+----8  MAP AND CROSS REFERENCE

000001  000100 IDENTIFICATION DIVISION.
000002  000200 PROGRAM-ID.  B2COINS.
000003  000300************************************************************
000004  000400*                                                          *
000005  000500*           BY JIM JANOSSY   DEPAUL UNIVERSITY    5/5/92    *
000006  000600*                                                          *
000007  000700*          DROESSELMEYER'S GENEROUS COIN GAME FOR          *
000008  000800*          NIECES AND NEPHEWS                              *
000009  000900*                                                          *
000010  001000************************************************************
000011  001100 ENVIRONMENT DIVISION.
000012  001200*
000013  001300 DATA DIVISION.
000014  001400 WORKING-STORAGE SECTION.
000015  001500 01  PR-LINE.
000016  001600     12  PR-NAME1        PIC X(6).
000017  001700     12  FILLER          PIC X(2).
000018  001800     12  PR-NAME2        PIC X(6).          VALUE SPACES.          IMP
000019  001900     12  FILLER          PIC X(2).
000020  002000     12  PR-NAME3        PIC X(6).          VALUE SPACES.          IMP
000021  002100     12  FILLER          PIC X(2).
000022  002200     12  PR-NAME4        PIC X(6).          VALUE SPACES.          IMP
000023  002300     12  FILLER          PIC X(2).
000024  002400     12  PR-TOTAL        PIC $22.99.        VALUE ' VALUE = '.
000025  002500*
000026  002600 01  WS-COINS.
000027  002700     12  WS-COIN1        PIC 9(1).
000028  002800     12  WS-COIN2        PIC 9(1).
000029  002900     12  WS-COIN3        PIC 9(1).
000030  003000     12  WS-COIN4        PIC 9(1).
000031  003100*
000032  003200 01  WS-VALUES.
000033  003300     12  WS-VAL1         PIC S9(3)V99.
000034  003400     12  WS-VAL2         PIC S9(3)V99.
000035  003500     12  WS-VAL3         PIC S9(3)V99.
000036  003600     12  WS-VAL4         PIC S9(3)V99.
000037  003700     12  WS-TOTAL        PIC S9(3)V99.
000038  003800/
000039  003900 PROCEDURE DIVISION.
000040  004000 0000-MAINLINE.
000041  004100     DISPLAY '*** PROGRAM B2COINS STARTING'.
000042  004200     PERFORM 1000-COIN1
000043  004300         VARYING WS-COIN1
000044  004400             FROM 1 BY 1
000045  004500         UNTIL WS-COIN1 > 3.
000046  004600     DISPLAY '*** PROGRAM ENDING'.
000047  004700     STOP RUN.
000048  004800*
000049  004900 1000-COIN1.
000050  005000     IF WS-COIN1 = +1
000051  005100         MOVE 'PENNY'  TO PR-NAME1
000052  005200         MOVE +.01 TO WS-VAL1
000053  005300     ELSE
000054  005400     IF WS-COIN1 = +2
000055  005500         MOVE 'DIME' TO PR-NAME1
000056  005600         MOVE +.10 TO WS-VAL1
000057  005700     ELSE
000058  005800     IF WS-COIN1 = +3
000059  005900         MOVE 'DOLLAR' TO PR-NAME1
000060  006000         MOVE +1.00 TO WS-VAL1.
000061  006100     PERFORM 2000-COIN2
```

(a)

(b)

```
49
27

27

27
16
33

27
16
33
66
```

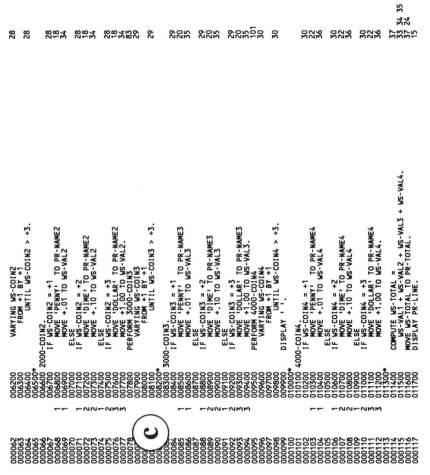

Figure 4.4 Source code for program B2COINS.

```
*** PROGRAM B2COINS STARTING

PENNY  PENNY  PENNY  PENNY   VALUE = $  .04
PENNY  PENNY  PENNY  DIME    VALUE = $  .13
PENNY  PENNY  PENNY  DOLLAR  VALUE = $ 1.03

PENNY  PENNY  DIME   PENNY   VALUE = $  .13
PENNY  PENNY  DIME   DIME    VALUE = $  .22
PENNY  PENNY  DIME   DOLLAR  VALUE = $ 1.12

PENNY  PENNY  DOLLAR PENNY   VALUE = $ 1.03
PENNY  PENNY  DOLLAR DIME    VALUE = $ 1.12
PENNY  PENNY  DOLLAR DOLLAR  VALUE = $ 2.02

PENNY  DIME   PENNY  PENNY   VALUE = $  .13
PENNY  DIME   PENNY  DIME    VALUE = $  .22
PENNY  DIME   PENNY  DOLLAR  VALUE = $ 1.12

PENNY  DIME   DIME   PENNY   VALUE = $  .22
PENNY  DIME   DIME   DIME    VALUE = $  .31
PENNY  DIME   DIME   DOLLAR  VALUE = $ 1.21

PENNY  DIME   DOLLAR PENNY   VALUE = $ 1.12
PENNY  DIME   DOLLAR DIME    VALUE = $ 1.21
PENNY  DIME   DOLLAR DOLLAR  VALUE = $ 2.11

PENNY  DOLLAR PENNY  PENNY   VALUE = $ 1.03
PENNY  DOLLAR PENNY  DIME    VALUE = $ 1.12
PENNY  DOLLAR PENNY  DOLLAR  VALUE = $ 2.02

PENNY  DOLLAR DIME   PENNY   VALUE = $ 1.12
PENNY  DOLLAR DIME   DIME    VALUE = $ 1.21
PENNY  DOLLAR DIME   DOLLAR  VALUE = $ 2.11

PENNY  DOLLAR DOLLAR PENNY   VALUE = $ 2.02
PENNY  DOLLAR DOLLAR DIME    VALUE = $ 2.11
PENNY  DOLLAR DOLLAR DOLLAR  VALUE = $ 3.01

DIME   PENNY  PENNY  PENNY   VALUE = $  .13
DIME   PENNY  PENNY  DIME    VALUE = $  .22
DIME   PENNY  PENNY  DOLLAR  VALUE = $ 1.12

DIME   PENNY  DIME   PENNY   VALUE = $  .22
DIME   PENNY  DIME   DIME    VALUE = $  .31
DIME   PENNY  DIME   DOLLAR  VALUE = $ 1.21

. . .
```

Figure 4.4 *Continued*

a. (Page 80) The "IMP" in the automatic cross-reference column indicates a noteworthy characteristic of the data name being defined. You always get this automatic cross-reference, not just when you activate the MAP option. (In this run, I used NOMAP, not MAP.) The possible codes you may see here are:

IMP—Implicit definition: you used a figurative constant such as SPACES, ZEROS, HIGH-VALUES, LOW-VALUES, QUOTES, NULLS, or a special register such as RETURN CODE, LENGTH OF, ADDRESS OF, or SORT-MESSAGE.

UND—The data item or procedure (performed code) is undefined.

DUP "Duplicate"—The data item or procedure is defined more than once.

EXT—External program name is referenced in a CALL.

*—Same as EXT when you used the NOCOMPILE option.

b. (Page 80) The embedded cross reference shows you when every PERFORMed routine starts.

c. (Page 81) The "SL" statement level numbers printed by the compiler at the left side attempt to show you how far into a decision structure each IF is. For example, the MOVE at line 007600 has three IF's logically before it. But this is a serial IF/ELSE, not a nested IF/ELSE! You will find statement level numbers are more meaningful for true nested IF/ELSEs.

83

5

Source Code Simplification

One of the benefits of VS COBOL II is that it streamlines some of the elements of COBOL coding. This makes sense; COBOL has been around for 30 years and many code elements needed in the 1960s are no longer relevant. In this chapter I tell you how to eliminate excess verbiage from your code.

5.1 USE A MINIMAL IDENTIFICATION DIVISION

VS COBOL II strips the IDENTIFICATION DIVISION down to the bare minimum. It can now be as small as:

```
IDENTIFICATION DIVISION.
PROGRAM-ID.    B2COINS.
```

This is really all that is required. Most shops, however, have traditionally required coding some or all of these other paragraphs in the IDENTI-FICATION DIVISION for documentation purposes:

```
REMARKS.
AUTHOR.
INSTALLATION.
DATE-WRITTEN.
DATE-COMPILED.
SECURITY.
```

```
002000 DATA DIVISION.
002100 FILE SECTION.                          ┌─────────────┐
002200*                                       │  VS COBOL   │
002300 FD  MASTER-FILE                        └─────────────┘
002400     LABEL RECORDS ARE STANDARD
002500     RECORDING MODE IS F
002600     BLOCK CONTAINS 0 RECORDS
002700     RECORD CONTAINS 80 CHARACTERS
002800     DATA RECORD IS MASTER-RECORD.
002900 01  MASTER-RECORD                            PIC X(80).
```

```
002000 DATA DIVISION.
002100 FILE SECTION.                          ┌──────────────┐
002200*                                       │ VS COBOL II  │
002300 FD  MASTER-FILE                        └──────────────┘
002600     BLOCK CONTAINS 0 RECORDS
002700     RECORD CONTAINS 80 CHARACTERS.
002900 01  MASTER-RECORD                            PIC X(80).
```

Figure 5.1   You can simplify your File Descriptions (FD) with VS COBOL II.

VS COBOL II drops support for the REMARKS paragraph and will probably drop support for the others in future releases. Make all of these items into comments now by putting an asterisk * in column 7. Omit DATE-COMPILED. You already get the date (and time) printed on every page of the compiler's listing! I suggest a new top-of-program comments standard for your consideration in Appendix G.

5.2 SIMPLIFICATION OF THE FILE DESCRIPTION (FD)

VS COBOL II makes your life easier in FD coding because you don't have to code LABEL RECORDS ARE STANDARD or LABEL REC-ORDS ARE OMITTED anymore. In the past you might have coded an FD as in the upper part of Figure 5.1. Now you can code the FD as in the lower part of Figure 5.1.

You still need BLOCK CONTAINS 0 RECORDS in the FD for QSAM (sequential) files to tell MVS that the program is passing up its oppor-tunity to specify the block size. If you leave out this clause, the block size is taken to be the record length, that is, the default is reading an unblocked file! Leaving out this clause gives you an abend with system completion code 001–4 if you are actually reading a blocked file.

RECORD CONTAINS establishes the actual record length, but the length of record definitions no longer needs to match what the RECORD CONTAINS clause says. For example, the following code defines records in TIME-SHEET-FILE as fixed length 80 bytes, but you will only be able to access the first 65 bytes of each record, and the compiler will not complain:

```
002300 FD TIME-SHEET-FILE
002400    BLOCK CONTAINS 0 RECORDS
002500    RECORD CONTAINS 80 CHARACTERS.
002600 01 TIME-SHEET-RECORD          PIC X(65).
```

I suggest you continue to code RECORD CONTAINS for documentation, but realize that it no longer buys you any FD record layout length validation.

5.3 SIMPLIFICATION OF WORKING-STORAGE

VS COBOL II makes some of your WORKING-STORAGE coding more clear. You now can:

- Omit coding the word FILLER.
- Code COMP-3 as PACKED-DECIMAL.
- Code COMP as BINARY.
- Code hexadecimal literals like PIC X(3) VALUE X'F140F2'.

In the sections below, I'll consider each of these simplifications separately.

5.4 ELIMINATING THE WORD FILLER

In the past, you had to use the word FILLER in record descriptions to account for fields you did not need to access. You might have coded a line to print final counts in a program as in the upper part of Figure 5.2. Now you can code this line as in the lower part of Figure 5.2.

Is the ability to omit the word FILLER a significant benefit? It's easier, but you can accidentally omit a data-name that you intended to code. If you omit the word FILLER, it's harder to glance at your code and see if it is complete. I suggest that you do not eliminate FILLER name coding.

5.5 PLAINER PACKED DECIMAL CODING AND WHEN TO USE IT

VS COBOL II still supports the traditional ways of coding numbers. You have four ways to store numbers:

```
                                       ┌──────────┐
                                       │ VS COBOL │
                                       └──────────┘
012000 01  R1-ENDLINE.
012100        05 FILLER                PIC X(1) VALUE SPACE.
012200        05 R1-EL-MESSAGE         PIC X(20).
012300        05 FILLER                PIC X(3) VALUE SPACES.
012400        05 R1-EL-COUNT           PIC Z,ZZZ,ZZ9.
012500        05 FILLER                PIC X(100) VALUE SPACES.
```

```
                                       ┌─────────────┐
                                       │ VS COBOL II │
                                       └─────────────┘
012000 01  R1-ENDLINE.
012100        05                       PIC X(1) VALUE SPACE.
012200        05 R1-EL-MESSAGE         PIC X(20).
012300        05                       PIC X(3) VALUE SPACES.
012400        05 R1-EL-COUNT           PIC Z,ZZZ,ZZ9.
012500        05                       PIC X(100) VALUE SPACES.
```

Figure 5.2 You can eliminate coding the word FILLER on field definitions you won't access in the program.

```
01  WS-COUNT   PIC 9(5)             VALUE  0.     Display
01  WS-COUNT   PIC S9(5)            VALUE +0.     Zoned decimal
01  WS-COUNT   PIC S9(5) COMP-3 VALUE +0.         Packed decimal
01  WS-COUNT   PIC S9(4) COMP   VALUE +0.         Pure binary
```

The least efficient of these is "display" format (number storage in print format). It's the farthest away from the format in which the IBM mainframe actually does arithmetic.

The most efficient for general purposes is COMP-3, packed decimal. Packed decimal digits store in only four bits (not eight); numbers fit in just about half the space on disk, tape, or in memory. Packed decimal is the format that the System/390 (like the System/360 and System/370 before it) uses for ordinary arithmetic. If your number is not in this format already, the compiler has to convert it to packed decimal when you do arithmetic with it.

VS COBOL II gives you a plainer way to code packed decimal numbers besides the word "COMP-3":

```
01  WS-COUNT   PIC S9(5)  PACKED-DECIMAL  VALUE +0.
```

5.6 PLAINER BINARY FIELD CODING AND WHEN TO USE IT

Pure binary fields are different from other numeric formats because they come in definite increments of memory, as shown in Figure 5.3. The number you code within the parentheses for a binary field establishes

PICture	Decimal Capacity	Memory	Common IBM Term
S9(4) COMP	9,999	2 bytes	Half-word binary
S9(9) COMP	999,999,999	4 bytes	Full-word binary
S9(18) COMP	999,999,999,999,999,999	8 bytes	Double-word binary

Figure 5.3   Coding, Capacity, and Storage for Binary Fields.

Binary fields coded with COMP take either 2, 4, or 8 bytes of storage and have the decimal capacity shown. In VS COBOL II you can also code BINARY now instead of the word COMP to define these fields.

how large a decimal value you can store, but all binary-stored values take either 2, 4, or 8 bytes of storage. For example, a PIC S9(5) COMP and a PIC S9(9) COMP value both take 4 bytes of storage.

If you have to store a subscript or count that will be no larger than 9,999, you can code S9(4) COMP and achieve efficient processing. If the value will be up to 999,999,999 you can code S9(9) COMP and achieve almost as efficient processing. But if you specify a number size larger than nine digits, you will receive a double-word binary item. Aside from the extra memory it requires it will process much slower since a lot of extra work needs to be done to handle it.

Pure binary numbers are efficient for integers such as subscripts and counters. The System/390 does arithmetic for integer numbers less than ten digits long in binary. But don't code an implied decimal point and digits to the right of the decimal in the PIC for a binary field! Binary numbers can't adequately represent decimal precision.

Under VS COBOL II you can code binary numbers in a plainer way than using the word "COMP":

```
01  WS-COUNT   PIC S9(4)   BINARY  VALUE +0.
```

5.7   *TRY IT!* USING HEXADECIMAL LITERALS

VS COBOL II allows you to code literal values in WORKING-STORAGE in hexadecimal. Hexadecimal notation is something new to COBOL. It may help you if you need to work with special character printing on laser printers, escape sequences for printers or modems, or screen attribute values in CICS programs.

I have listed C1HEX in Figure 5.4. The two sets of FILLER items in this small program contain a message encoded in hexadecimal. The first item is encoded in ASCII, the information encoding scheme of PCs and minicomputers. The second item is encoded in EBCDIC, the encoding scheme of IBM mainframes.

Compile, linkage edit, and run C1HEX with VS COBOL II. The DISPLAYs in it will let you see the contents of both data tables in character form. You'll be able to read the EBCDIC version of the message. If you process this program with a PC-based COBOL-85 compiler, such as RM/COBOL-85, Micro Focus, or Realia, you'll be able to read the ASCII version of this message.

You can use hexadecimal literals in WORKING-STORAGE VALUE clauses as I've shown in Figure 5.4. You can also use them in MOVE statements such as:

```
MOVE X'C1C3D9' TO WS-NAME-FIELD.
```

and in IF/ELSE statements. When you use hex literals, you need to code each byte as two legitimate hex symbols or you will get a compiler error message.

5.8 SIMPLIFICATION OF THE PROCEDURE DIVISION

VS COBOL II provides many changes in the PROCEDURE DIVISION. Three important enhancements are:

- NOT AT END is now available to complement AT END.
- NOT INVALID KEY is now available to complement INVALID KEY.
- The INITIALIZE verb exists to reinitialize fields.

Two trivial changes are:

- EXIT has become a "noise" word.
- You can code using lowercase letters.

I'll cover each of these separately in the next several sections.

```
000100 IDENTIFICATION DIVISION.
000200 PROGRAM-ID.    C1HEX.
000300 AUTHOR.        J. JANOSSY.
000400*REMARKS.       DEMONSTRATE USE OF HEXADECIMAL LITERALS.
000500 ENVIRONMENT DIVISION.
000600*
000700 DATA DIVISION.
000800 WORKING-STORAGE SECTION.
000900 01  DATA-TABLE-1.
001000     05 FILLER           PIC X(1)  VALUE X'41'.
001100     05 FILLER           PIC X(1)  VALUE X'49'.
001200     05 FILLER           PIC X(1)  VALUE X'4E'.
001300     05 FILLER           PIC X(1)  VALUE X'27'.
001400     05 FILLER           PIC X(2)  VALUE X'5420'.
001500     05 FILLER           PIC X(1)  VALUE X'48'.
001600     05 FILLER           PIC X(1)  VALUE X'45'.
001700     05 FILLER           PIC X(4)  VALUE X'5820574F'.
001800     05 FILLER           PIC X(1)  VALUE X'4E'.
001900     05 FILLER           PIC X(1)  VALUE X'44'.
002000     05 FILLER           PIC X(1)  VALUE X'45'.
002100     05 FILLER           PIC X(2)  VALUE X'5246'.
002200     05 FILLER           PIC X(3)  VALUE X'554C21'.
002300*
002400 01  DATA-TABLE-2.
002500     05 FILLER           PIC X(4)  VALUE X'C1C9D57D'.
002600     05 FILLER           PIC X(4)  VALUE X'E340C8C5'.
002700     05 FILLER           PIC X(4)  VALUE X'E740E6D6'.
002800     05 FILLER           PIC X(4)  VALUE X'D5C4C5D9'.
002900     05 FILLER           PIC X(4)  VALUE X'C6E4D35A'.
003000/
003100 PROCEDURE DIVISION.
003200 0000-MAINLINE.
003300     DISPLAY 'C1HEX STARTING'.
003400     DISPLAY '---------------------------'.
003500     DISPLAY 'IN ASCII:'.
003600     DISPLAY DATA-TABLE-1.
003700     DISPLAY '---------------------------'.
003800     DISPLAY 'IN EBCDIC:'
003900     DISPLAY DATA-TABLE-2.
004000     STOP RUN.
```

Output (on a microcomputer with RM/COBOL-85):

```
C1HEX STARTING
---------------------------
IN ASCII:
AIN'T HEX WONDERFUL!
---------------------------
IN EBCDIC:
-++)¶ə++_ə̲µ++-++¦_+Z
```

Output (on the mainframe with VS COBOL II):

```
C1HEX STARTING
---------------------------
IN ASCII:
.....................
---------------------------
IN EBCDIC:
AIN'T HEX WONDERFUL!
```

Figure 5.4   Hexadecimal Literals are Supported by VS COBOL II.

You can run C1HEX to see how hexadecimal literals work in WORKING-STORAGE coding. This program has the same message coded in EBCDIC and ASCII. You can read the ASCII-encoded message if you run the program on a PC with a 1985 COBOL compiler such as RM/COBOL-85, MicroFocus, or Realia. You will see the EBCDIC-encoded message on an IBM mainframe with VS COBOL II.

5.9 NOT AT END AND NOT INVALID KEY

The syntax of the input/output verbs, such as READ and RETURN, has been enhanced so that you can avoid some awkward coding. The traditional structured method for coding a READ paragraph has been as shown in the upper part of Figure 5.5. You needed to test your end-of-file flag immediately so that you could add to the record counter only if you had not yet reached end of file. You can simplify this coding to be more straightforward, as shown in the lower part of Figure 5.5.

NOT INVALID KEY has also been provided to complement the INVALID KEY clause. This affects the direct access READ, WRITE, REWRITE, DELETE, and START verbs. But as you'll see in Chapter 12, INVALID KEY is now obsolete and you should use File Status checking for all VSAM I/O communication.

5.10 THE INITIALIZE VERB

The INITIALIZE verb is one of the most significant enhancements of VS COBOL II. It lets you reset the values of many WORKING-STORAGE fields coded under a group name to a standard value with just one statement. The standard value for each field is spaces or zero, depending on the type of PICture the field has. INITIALIZE sets these types of fields to spaces:

Alphabetic	PIC A(..)
Alphanumeric	PIC X(..)
Alphanumeric-edited	PIC XX/XX/XX

INITIALIZE sets these types of fields to zero:

Numeric	
DISPLAY	PIC 9(..)
Signed	PIC S9(..)
Packed decimal	PIC S9(..) COMP-3
Binary	PIC S9(4) COMP
Floating point	COMP-1 or COMP-2
Numeric-edited	PIC ZZ,ZZ9.99

But INITIALIZE does not affect FILLER fields or index items. It works on original field definitions, not data-names that are redefinitions.

VS COBOL

```
017200 2700-READ-MASTER-RECORD.
017300     READ MASTER-FILE INTO MASTER-RECORD-INPUT-AREA
017400         AT END
017500             MOVE 'E' TO WS-EOF-FLAG.
017600     IF WS-EOF-FLAG NOT = 'E'
017700         ADD +1 TO WS-MF-REC-COUNT.
```

VS COBOL II

```
017200 2700-READ-MASTER-RECORD.
017300     READ MASTER-FILE INTO MASTER-RECORD-INPUT-AREA
017400         AT END
017500             MOVE 'E' TO WS-EOF-FLAG
017600         NOT AT END
017700             ADD +1 TO WS-MF-REC-COUNT.
```

Figure 5.5   You can use NOT AT END in VS COBOL II to avoid an IF test in record counting.

Here is a common way to code INITIALIZE:

```
01  WS-GROUP.
    05 WSG-NAME     PIC X(15).
    05 WSG-AGE      PIC S9(3) COMP-3.
    05 WSG-INCOME   PIC 9(7)V99.
    05 WSG-DATE     PIC XX/XX/XX.
    05 WSG-CODE     PIC A(1).
```

```
INITIALIZE WS-GROUP.
```

5.11   *TRY IT!* USING THE INITIALIZE VERB

Many questions remain unanswered by a trivial example. Does INITIALIZE work on fields with subscripts? How about fields defined under an OCCURS clause? Can you initialize one row in a table? Does INITIALIZE affect FILLER fields?

The best way to see what INITIALIZE does is to run a test with all of these variations. That's exactly what program C2INIT does, illustrated in Figure 5.6. Take a close look at the annotations for that illustration and under the output it produces. C2INIT shows examples of INITIALIZE operation that answer questions most people have about how it works.

```
000100 IDENTIFICATION DIVISION.
000200 PROGRAM-ID.      C2INIT.
000300 AUTHOR.          J. JANOSSY.
000400*REMARKS.         DEMONSTRATE INITIALIZE VERB WITH OCCURS CLAUSE.
000500 ENVIRONMENT DIVISION.
000600*
000700 DATA DIVISION.
000800 WORKING-STORAGE SECTION.
000900*
001000 01  WS-SUB                        PIC 9(1)  VALUE 0.
001100*
001200 01  TEST-TABLE.
001300     05 TEST-ROW   OCCURS 5 TIMES.
001400        10 TR-ALPHABETIC           PIC A(3)  VALUE 'AAA'.
001500        10 FILLER                  PIC X(1)  VALUE '*'.
001600        10 TR-ALPHANUMERIC         PIC X(3)  VALUE 'XXX'.
001700        10                         PIC X(1)  VALUE '*'.
001800        10 TR-ALPHANUMERIC-EDITED  PIC X/X.
001900        10                         PIC X(1)  VALUE '*'.
002000        10 TR-NUMERIC-ZD           PIC 9(3)  VALUE 123.
002100        10                         PIC X(1)  VALUE '*'.
002200        10 TR-NUMERIC-SIGNED       PIC S9(3) VALUE +456.
002300        10 TR-ALL-X   REDEFINES  TR-NUMERIC-SIGNED  PIC X(3).
002400        10                         PIC X(1)  VALUE '*'.
002500        10 TR-NUMERIC-PACKED       PIC S9(3) COMP-3.
002600        10                         PIC X(1)  VALUE '*'.
002700        10 TR-NUMERIC-EDITED       PIC ZZ9.
002800        10                         PIC X(1)  VALUE '*'.
002900        10 TR-MULTIPLE  OCCURS 4 TIMES  PIC 9(3) VALUE 789.
003000        10                         PIC X(1)  VALUE '*'.
003100        10 TR-MULTIPLE-GROUP  OCCURS 2 TIMES.
003200           15 TR-MG-DATA           PIC 9(3)  VALUE 357.
003300/
003400 PROCEDURE DIVISION.
003500 0000-MAINLINE.
           DISPLAY '** C2INIT PROGRAM STARTING **'.
           DISPLAY 'TABLE CONTENTS BEFORE ANY INITIALIZE'.
           PERFORM
               VARYING WS-SUB FROM 1 BY 1
               UNTIL WS-SUB > 5
                   DISPLAY TEST-ROW(WS-SUB)
           END-PERFORM.
           DISPLAY '-------------------------------------------'.
       *
           INITIALIZE TEST-TABLE.
           DISPLAY 'TABLE CONTENTS AFTER INITIALIZE OF 01 LEVEL'.
           PERFORM
               VARYING WS-SUB FROM 1 BY 1
               UNTIL WS-SUB > 5
                   DISPLAY TEST-ROW(WS-SUB)
           END-PERFORM.
           DISPLAY '-------------------------------------------'.
       *
           MOVE ALL '*' TO TEST-TABLE.
           DISPLAY 'TABLE CONTENTS AFTER MOVING ALL "*" TO 01 LEVEL'.
           PERFORM
               VARYING WS-SUB FROM 1 BY 1
               UNTIL WS-SUB > 5
                   DISPLAY TEST-ROW(WS-SUB)
           END-PERFORM.
           DISPLAY '-------------------------------------------'.
       *
           INITIALIZE TEST-ROW(3).
           DISPLAY 'TABLE CONTENTS AFTER INITIALIZE OF ROW 3'.
           PERFORM
               VARYING WS-SUB FROM 1 BY 1
               UNTIL WS-SUB > 5
                   DISPLAY TEST-ROW(WS-SUB)
           END-PERFORM.
           DISPLAY '-------------------------------------------'.
       *
           MOVE ALL '*' TO TEST-TABLE.
           DISPLAY 'TABLE CONTENTS AFTER MOVING ALL "*" TO 01 LEVEL'.
           PERFORM
               VARYING WS-SUB FROM 1 BY 1
               UNTIL WS-SUB > 5
                   DISPLAY TEST-ROW(WS-SUB)
           END-PERFORM.
           DISPLAY '-------------------------------------------'.
       *
           INITIALIZE TEST-TABLE
               REPLACING NUMERIC BY 1.
           DISPLAY 'TABLE CONTENTS AFTER INITIALIZE NUMERIC BY 1'.
           PERFORM
               VARYING WS-SUB FROM 1 BY 1
               UNTIL WS-SUB > 5
                   DISPLAY TEST-ROW(WS-SUB)
           END-PERFORM.
           DISPLAY '-------------------------------------------'.
           STOP RUN.
```

(a) (b) (c) (d) (e) (f)

Figure 5.6   C2INIT program (see legend on page 95).

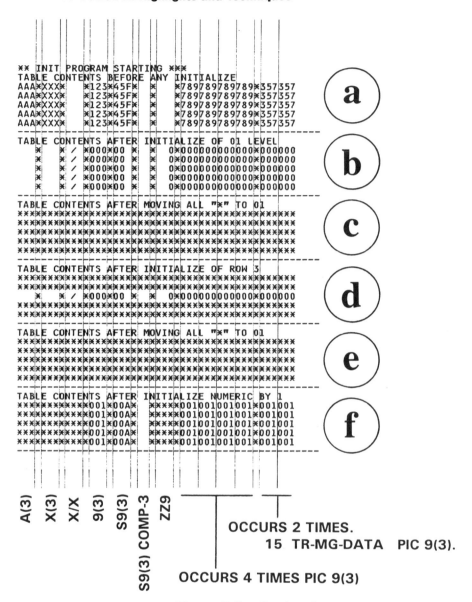

```
** INIT PROGRAM STARTING ***
TABLE CONTENTS BEFORE ANY INITIALIZE
AAA*XXX*   *123*45F*  *   *789789789789*357357
AAA*XXX*   *123*45F*  *   *789789789789*357357       ⓐ
AAA*XXX*   *123*45F*  *   *789789789789*357357
AAA*XXX*   *123*45F*  *   *789789789789*357357
AAA*XXX*   *123*45F*  *   *789789789789*357357
------------------------------------------------
TABLE CONTENTS AFTER INITIALIZE OF 01 LEVEL
  *   * / *000*00 *  *   0*000000000000*000000
  *   * / *000*00 *  *   0*000000000000*000000       ⓑ
  *   * / *000*00 *  *   0*000000000000*000000
  *   * / *000*00 *  *   0*000000000000*000000
  *   * / *000*00 *  *   0*000000000000*000000
------------------------------------------------
TABLE CONTENTS AFTER MOVING ALL "*" TO 01
************************************************
************************************************
************************************************       ⓒ
************************************************
************************************************
------------------------------------------------
TABLE CONTENTS AFTER INITIALIZE OF ROW 3
************************************************
************************************************
  *   * / *000*00 *  *   0*000000000000*000000       ⓓ
************************************************
************************************************
------------------------------------------------
TABLE CONTENTS AFTER MOVING ALL "*" TO 01
************************************************
************************************************
************************************************       ⓔ
************************************************
************************************************
------------------------------------------------
TABLE CONTENTS AFTER INITIALIZE NUMERIC BY 1
**********001*00A*  *****001001001001*001001
**********001*00A*  *****001001001001*001001
**********001*00A*  *****001001001001*001001       ⓕ
**********001*00A*  *****001001001001*001001
**********001*00A*  *****001001001001*001001
------------------------------------------------
```

A(3) X(3) X/X 9(3) S9(3) S9(3) COMP-3 ZZ9

OCCURS 2 TIMES.
   15 TR-MG-DATA   PIC 9(3).

OCCURS 4 TIMES PIC 9(3)

Figure 5.6 *Continued*

Figure 5.6   (See figure starting on page 93) Program C2INIT Shows How IN-ITIALIZE Works.

Program C2INIT contains a table named TEST-TABLE with five TEST-ROWs. It DISPLAYs the rows of the table six times by looping through it. The notes tell you about the actions leading up to each DISPLAY. Match up the noted letters to see what each INITIALIZE actually does.

a. This shows you the contents of TEST-TABLE before any INITIALIZE. The field contents result from VALUE clauses. Fields without VALUE clauses are cleared to hexadecimal zero (X'00') automatically by VS COBOL II (use HEX ON while viewing your output to confirm this).

b. INITIALIZE TEST-TABLE is acceptable. It makes alphanumeric fields contain spaces and numeric fields contain the value zero. FILLER fields are not changed. You can't see the contents of packed decimal (COMP-3) fields because the bits represent unprintable characters.

c. MOVE ALL '*' TO TEST-TABLE puts asterisks in every position of every row in the table.

d. Can you use INITIALIZE on just one row of a table? Yes, you can! Here you see the result of INITIALIZE TEST-ROW(3). Notice that INITIALIZE properly handles the fields defined under nested OCCURS at the end of each row.

e. This MOVE ALL '*' TO TEST-TABLE just makes the table full of asterisks again for another test.

f. INITIALIZE with the REPLACING option limits initialization actions to just the data types specified. You *don't* get default initialization values for the data types you do not cite! Only the pure numeric data types (any format) are set to 1 when you use REPLACING NUMERIC BY 1. Not even the NUMERIC-EDITED PIC ZZ9 is affected by this REPLACING. Notice that the fields defined under the nested OCCURS at the end of each row are processed normally by INITIALIZE.

Why not try to run C2INIT? You can copy the source code from this book or upload it from diskette. If you actually run C2INIT, you can explore some additional specifications for INITIALIZE, such as the RE-PLACING option I tell you about next. Look at your C2INIT output using hex on TSO/ISPF and you can see what hexadecimal values are contained in fields you don't affect with VALUE and INITIALIZE!

5.12 INITIALIZE VERB WITH REPLACING OPTION

You can code additional phrases with an INITIALIZE verb to limit its action to certain fields. You can also code clauses to specify what the initializing value will be:

```
INITIALIZE item-1 item-2 item-3
    REPLACING ALPHABETIC                    BY object-1
             ALPHANUMERIC                   BY object-2
             ALPHANUMERIC-EDITED            BY object-3
             NUMERIC                        BY object-4
             NUMERIC-EDITED                 BY object-5
             DCBS                           BY object-6
             EGCS                           BY object-7.
```

Where

"item-" is a data-item group name.

"object-" can be a literal or a data-item.

The seven different data types recognized by INITIALIZE are listed above. You can list only those types you need; you don't have to code all of them. You'll most likely require:

ALPHANUMERIC	such as PIC X(..)
ALPHANUMERIC-EDITED	such as PIC XX/XX/XX
NUMERIC	any numeric PIC
NUMERIC-EDITED	such as $ZZ,ZZZ.99

Important! When used with REPLACING, INITIALIZE limits its work to the field types you specify. INITIALIZE doesn't affect any field types in the group that you do not mention! In Figure 5.7, I have coded several variations of INITIALIZE to show you what the effect of each is.

5.13 AN ENHANCEMENT TO EXIT?

You can use EXIT to form an empty paragraph. If you put an empty paragraph at the end of a normal paragraph, it can serve as an end label.

```
01    WS-GROUP.
      05 WSG-NAME              PIC X(15).
      05 WSG-AGE               PIC S9(3) COMP-3.
      05 WSG-INCOME            PIC 9(7)V99.
      05 FILLER                PIC X(3).
      05 WSG-DATE              PIC XX/XX/XX.
      05 WSG-CODE              PIC A(1).



      ---------------------------------------------------------------------



      INITIALIZE WS-GROUP.


                     WSG-NAME          contains spaces
          Effect:    WSG-AGE           contains zero
                     WSG-INCOME        contains zero
                     FILLER            unchanged
                     WSG-DATE          contains ᵬᵬ/ᵬᵬ/ᵬᵬ
                     WSG-CODE          contains a space


      INITIALIZE WS-GROUP REPLACING NUMERIC BY 2.


                     WSG-NAME          unchanged
          Effect:    WSG-AGE           contains 2
                     WSG-INCOME        contains 2
                     FILLER            unchanged
                     WSG-DATE          unchanged
                     WSG-CODE          unchanged



      INITIALIZE WS-GROUP
         REPLACING ALPHANUMERIC BY '*'
                   NUMERIC BY 19.

                     WSG-NAME          contains ***************
          EFFECT:    WSG-AGE           contains 19
                     WSG-INCOME        contains 19
                     FILLER            unchanged
                     WSG-DATE          unchanged
                     WSG-CODE          unchanged
```

Figure 5.7   When you use INITIALIZE with the REPLACING option you can make the initializing values something other than space for alphanumeric fields and zero for numeric fields. But when you code REPLACING, the initializing action is limited to just the field types you specify. To get all fields processed with REPLACING you have to specify every data type!

```
0000-MAINLINE.
    PERFORM 1000-BOJ THRU 1000-BOJ-EXIT.
    PERFORM 2000-PROCESS THRU 2000-EXIT
        UNTIL WS-EOF-FLAG = 'E'.
    PERFORM 3000-EOJ THRU 3000-EOJ-EXIT.
    STOP RUN.
*
1000-BOJ.
    OPEN INPUT PHONE-FILE OUTPUT REPORT1.
    PERFORM 2700-READ THRU 2700-READ-EXIT.
    IF IN-TYPE = 'A'
        GO TO 1000-EXIT.
    MOVE SPACES TO INPUT-AREA.
    PERFORM 1200-NON-A-SETUP.
1000-EXIT.  EXIT.
    DISPLAY 'OOPS! I CODED SOMETHING AFTER THE EXIT!'.
```

```
┌──────────────────────────────────────────────────────┐
│ VS COBOL: Code after EXIT is an error.               │
│                                                      │
│ VS COBOL II: Code after EXIT is processed normally;  │
│              EXIT is treated as a "no operation."    │
└──────────────────────────────────────────────────────┘
```

Figure 5.8 VS COBOL rejected anything else in a paragraph if you coded the word EXIT in it. VS COBOL II won't complain if you put code in such a paragraph. Rather than being a benefit, this makes a greater potential for error in program maintenance!

Using PERFORM ... THRU this empty paragraph gives you a way to branch out of the paragraph's logic from anywhere within it. This style of code is handy for maintenance work and I've illustrated an example in Figure 5.8.

VS COBOL required that if you coded EXIT it could be the only thing in the paragraph. VS COBOL II has relaxed its enforcement of the rule. Now if code exists after EXIT in a paragraph, it will be executed. This can cause some problems in maintenance if you inadvertently put code after an EXIT, since the compiler will no longer complain about it.

5.14 YOU CAN CODE WITH LOWERCASE LETTERS

IBM System/390 software has its roots in the System/360 of 1964. The System/360 relied on printing devices that had originated in the days when bytes had only six data bits! A six-bit byte could represent only 2^6 = 64 different bit patterns. In those days printers couldn't support lowercase letters and they didn't have a real quotation mark ("). This is why IBM compilers and JCL have traditionally used only uppercase (capital) letters and the apostrophe instead of the quotation mark.

VS COBOL II has finally made it into the world of lowercase letters. It lets you write some or all of your source code using them. VS COBOL

```
018000 Procedure Division.
018100 0000-mainline.
018200         Perform 1000-boj.
018300         Perform 2000-process-a-record
018400             until ws-eof-flag = 'e'.
018500         Perform 3000-eoj.
018600         Stop run.
018700*
018800 1000-BOJ.
018900         Open  input master-file   output  passenger-report.
019000         Accept ws-date from date.
019100         String ws-date-mo '-'
019200                ws-date-da '-'
019300                ws-date-yr   delimited by size
019400         into pr-heading-date.
019500         Perform 2900-pr-newpage.
019600         Perform 2700-read-master-file.
019700*
019800 2000-process-a-record.
019900         Perform 2100-form-a-printline.
020000         If pr-lines-remaining is less than +1
020100             perform 2900-pr-newpage.
020200         Write passenger-report-printline
020300             from passenger-report-detail-line
020400             after advancing 1 lines.
020500         Subtract +1 from pr-lines-remaining.
020600         Add +1 to ws-rec-listed-count.
020700         Perform 2700-read-master-file.
```

Figure 5.9 You can now use lowercase ("small") letters in your actual source code statements. VS COBOL II is not case sensitive so you can mix uppercase (capitals) and lowercase letters freely. But the TSO/ISPF "CAPS ON" option will automatically make lowercase letters into uppercase letters. Unless you have a raving passion for lowercase letters, there is no benefit to coding VS COBOL II with them.

II is not case sensitive, so a field named TF-DEPARTURE-DATE is the same as Tf-Departure-Date.

I have listed some source code in Figure 5.9, showing how you can now code COBOL on the mainframe. There's no particular advantage to writing source code in lowercase letters unless you find it more readable. But there's a bit of awkwardness in doing so. TSO/ISPF is set to change your source code to uppercase with its CAPS ON option. This lets you see how much you have entered on the screen since you last pressed the <*Enter*> key. If you turn CAPS OFF in your editing profile to create programs using lowercase letters, you pass up the opportunity to see an indication on the screen as to how long you have been inactive from the system's point of view. Without this help, it's easier for you get timed out and logged off by TSO.

6

PERFORM
Enhancements

VS COBOL II gives you two new features for the PERFORM verb:

- "in-line" PERFORMs
- The WITH TEST AFTER option.

Neither of these is critical to your work. All of the existing ways you have used PERFORM in VS COBOL continue to be supported. In this chapter, I'll show you how each of these new features works. I'll also give you some examples of things you can but probably should not do with these new features.

6.1 TRADITIONAL "OUT-OF-LINE" PERFORMS

You have traditionally coded PERFORM as an "out-of-line" PER-FORM, illustrated in the upper part of Figure 6.1. Control passes from the place where your PERFORM is executed to another paragraph or a series of paragraphs. When the paragraph or SECTION you are performing completes execution, control returns to the statement following the PERFORM. Program D1PEROLD produces the output shown in Figure 6.1.

```
000100 IDENTIFICATION DIVISION.
000200 PROGRAM-ID.    D1PEROLD.
000300 AUTHOR.        J. JANOSSY.
000400*
000500*REMARKS.       DEMONSTRATE AN OUT-OF-LINE PERFORM
000600*
000700 ENVIRONMENT DIVISION.
000800 DATA DIVISION.
000900 WORKING-STORAGE SECTION.
001000 01  WS-COUNT                  PIC 9(2)   VALUE 0.
001100/
001200 PROCEDURE DIVISION.
001300 0000-MAINLINE.
001400     DISPLAY 'PROGRAM D1PEROLD STARTING'.
001500     PERFORM 2100-DISPLAY
001600        UNTIL WS-COUNT > 4.          ┌─────────────────────┐
001700     DISPLAY 'PROGRAM ENDING'.       │ Out-of-Line PERFORM │
001800     STOP RUN.                       └─────────────────────┘
001900*
002000 2100-DISPLAY.
002100     ADD 1 TO WS-COUNT.
002200     DISPLAY 'THE COUNT NOW = ', WS-COUNT.
```

```
000100 IDENTIFICATION DIVISION.
000200 PROGRAM-ID.    D1PERNEW.
000300 AUTHOR.        J. JANOSSY.
000400*
000500*REMARKS.       DEMONSTRATE AN OUT-OF-LINE PERFORM
000600*
000700 ENVIRONMENT DIVISION.
000800 DATA DIVISION.
000900 WORKING-STORAGE SECTION.
001000 01  WS-COUNT                  PIC 9(2)   VALUE 0.
001100/
001200 PROCEDURE DIVISION.
001300 0000-MAINLINE.
001400     DISPLAY 'PROGRAM D1PERNEW STARTING'.
001500     PERFORM
001600        UNTIL WS-COUNT > 4        ┌──────────────────┐
001700            ADD 1 TO WS-COUNT     │ In-Line PERFORM  │
001800            DISPLAY 'THE COUNT NOW = ', WS-COUNT
001900     END-PERFORM. ───────────┐   └──────────────────┘
002000     DISPLAY 'PROGRAM ENDING'.│
002100     STOP RUN.                │
                                    │
                       ┌────────────────────────────┐
                       │ You need this END-PERFORM   │
                       └────────────────────────────┘
```

```
Output:

    PROGRAM D1PERNEW STARTING
    THE COUNT NOW = 01
    THE COUNT NOW = 02
    THE COUNT NOW = 03
    THE COUNT NOW = 04
    THE COUNT NOW = 05
    PROGRAM ENDING
```

Figure 6.1 Out-of-Line PERFORMS and In-Line PERFORMS in VS COBOL II.

(*Top*) You can continue to code "traditional" out-of-line PERFORMS with VS COBOL II but (*bottom*) you can also use in-line PERFORMs ended by END-PERFORM.

6.2   HOW YOU CODE AN IN-LINE PERFORM

An in-line PERFORM makes it unnecessary to branch to a separate paragraph to invoke a PERFORM. Instead, you code the action to be taken after the word PERFORM and end it with the new "scope delimiter" END-PERFORM. You can see an in-line PERFORM in the lower part of Figure 6.1. Program D1PERNEW produces the same output as D1PEROLD.

VS COBOL II gives you 18 "explicit scope delimiters" such as END-PERFORM. Your use of all scope delimiters is optional, but you always need to end an in-line PERFORM with END-PERFORM. You'll see all of the explicit scope delimiters in the next chapter.

6.3   WHEN SHOULD YOU USE IN-LINE PERFORMS?

An in-line PERFORM is:

- More efficient than an out-of-line PERFORM since it allows VS COBOL II to optimize code to reduce virtual storage paging.
- Easier to read since all code is in one place.
- Better if the code being performed is only executed at one point and not from several points.

An out-of-line PERFORM is better when:

- You have to PERFORM the same logic from several places within a program.
- For clarity, you want to make each statement in the performed logic a freestanding sentence, perhaps making subsequent program maintenance or enhancement easier.

The VS COBOL compiler and optimizer often processes out-of-line PERFORMs into in-line PERFORMs in machine language to boost efficiency. The compiler does this when a routine is PERFORMed only once.

6.4   IN-LINE PERFORM WITH VARYING

The VARYING clause lets you manipulate the value of a field as a PERFORM executes. You use it to eliminate separate ADD instructions to vary a value, as shown in the upper part of Figure 6.2. The starting value,

```
000100 IDENTIFICATION DIVISION.
000200 PROGRAM-ID.     D2PEROLD.
000300 AUTHOR.         J. JANOSSY.
000400*
000500*REMARKS.        DEMONSTRATE AN OUT-OF-LINE PERFORM WITH VARYING
000600*
000700 ENVIRONMENT DIVISION.
000800 DATA DIVISION.
000900 WORKING-STORAGE SECTION.
001000 01  WS-COUNT                    PIC 9(2)    VALUE 0.
001100/
001200 PROCEDURE DIVISION.
001300 0000-MAINLINE.
001400     DISPLAY 'PROGRAM D2PEROLD STARTING'.
001500     PERFORM 2100-DISPLAY                    ┌──────────────┐
001600        VARYING WS-COUNT FROM 1 BY 1         │ Out-of-line  │
001700        UNTIL WS-COUNT > 5.                  │   PERFORM    │
001800     DISPLAY 'PROGRAM ENDING'.               │ with VARYING │
001900     STOP RUN.                               └──────────────┘
002000*
002100 2100-DISPLAY.
002200     DISPLAY 'THE COUNT NOW = ', WS-COUNT.
```

```
000100 IDENTIFICATION DIVISION.
000200 PROGRAM-ID.     D2PERNEW.
000300 AUTHOR.         J. JANOSSY.
000400*
000500*REMARKS.        DEMONSTRATE AN IN-LINE PERFORM WITH VARYING
000600*
000700 ENVIRONMENT DIVISION.
000800 DATA DIVISION.
000900 WORKING-STORAGE SECTION.
001000 01  WS-COUNT                    PIC 9(2)    VALUE 0.
001100/
001200 PROCEDURE DIVISION.
001300 0000-MAINLINE.                           ┌──────────────┐
001400     DISPLAY 'PROGRAM D2PERNEW STARTING'. │   In-Line    │
001500     PERFORM                              │   PERFORM    │
001600        VARYING WS-COUNT FROM 1 BY 1      │ with VARYING │
001700        UNTIL WS-COUNT > 5                └──────────────┘
001800           DISPLAY 'THE COUNT NOW = ', WS-COUNT
001900     END-PERFORM.
002000     DISPLAY 'PROGRAM ENDING'.
002100     STOP RUN.
```

```
Output:

    PROGRAM D2PERNEW STARTING
    THE COUNT NOW = 01
    THE COUNT NOW = 02
    THE COUNT NOW = 03
    THE COUNT NOW = 04
    THE COUNT NOW = 05
    PROGRAM ENDING
```

Figure 6.2   In-Line PERFORM With VARYING ... UNTIL Option.
The out-of-line PERFORM supports the VARYING and UNTIL options to sweep
a counter, subscript, or index value over a range. You can also use VARYING
and UNTIL with the VS COBOL II in-line PERFORM.

increment for each time through the processing loop, and ending value don't have to be literal values. You can use data-names in these places.

You can use the VARYING clause with an in-line PERFORM, as shown in the bottom part of Figure 6.2. As in all uses of the in-line PERFORM, you have to end this PERFORM with the explicit scope delimiter END-PERFORM.

6.5   END-IF SCOPE DELIMITER IN IN-LINE PERFORMS

A total of 18 new explicit scope delimiters like END-PERFORM exist. Technically, only END-PERFORM is absolutely required. But if you put an IF/ELSE into an in-line PERFORM, you need to end it with END-IF as I did in Figure 6.3.

6.6   *TRY IT! USING THE IN-LINE PERFORM*

You probably feel that in-line PERFORMs are a snap. They can be. But when I use the following demonstration in a VS COBOL II "differences" training class I conduct for various clients, about half of the programmers make a mistake in using in-line PERFORMs! Try your hand at it.

I wrote a small program named D3OLD to compress the non-space characters in a line of text to the left, eliminating embedded spaces. Here is the input and output of this compression routine:

```
STRING BEFORE =   AB C D  E FG H  I JKL  M N    O P Q
STRING AFTER = ABCDEFGHIJKLMNOPQ
```

Program D3OLD does this by using two work areas accessed byte-by-byte, and two independent subscripts. It scans the first work area with a PERFORM . . . VARYING that affects the first subscript, looking for non-blank positions. When it encounters a non-blank position, it increments the second subscript and copies the non-blank position into that position in the second work area, as Figure 6.4 shows.

I have listed D3OLD in Figure 6.5. It uses a traditional out-of-line PERFORM to look at each byte of the character string one-by-one and decide what to do with it. You can compile, linkage edit, and run this program.

After you run D3OLD as it exists, revise it so that it uses an in-line PERFORM and then compile, linkage edit, and run it again. You'll know you have done it correctly when you get a clean compile and the same output I've shown for "STRING AFTER."

```
000100 IDENTIFICATION DIVISION.
000200 PROGRAM-ID.    D2PERIF.
000300 AUTHOR.        J. JANOSSY.
000400*
000500*REMARKS.       DEMONSTRATE AN IN-LINE PERFORM WITH VARYING
000600*               HOUSING AN EMBEDDED IF STATEMENT
000700*
000800 ENVIRONMENT DIVISION.
000900 DATA DIVISION.
001000 WORKING-STORAGE SECTION.
001100 01  WS-COUNT                    PIC 9(2)    VALUE 0.
001200/
001300 PROCEDURE DIVISION.
001400 0000-MAINLINE.
001500     DISPLAY 'PROGRAM D2PERIF STARTING'.
001600     PERFORM
001700        VARYING WS-COUNT FROM 1 BY 1
001800        UNTIL WS-COUNT > 5
001900            DISPLAY 'THE COUNT NOW = ', WS-COUNT
002000            IF WS-COUNT = 3
002100                DISPLAY '*** THE COUNT IS NOW 3!'
002200            END-IF
002300     END-PERFORM.
002400     DISPLAY 'PROGRAM ENDING'.
002500     STOP RUN.
```

If you imbed an IF/ELSE in an in-line PERFORM you need to end the IF with the END-IF scope delimiter

Output:

```
PROGRAM D2PERIF STARTING
THE COUNT NOW = 01
THE COUNT NOW = 02
THE COUNT NOW = 03
*** THE COUNT IS NOW 3!
THE COUNT NOW = 04
THE COUNT NOW = 05
PROGRAM ENDING
```

Figure 6.3 You Need END-IF in a VS COBOL II In-Line PERFORM.

END-IF is another explicit scope terminator like END-PERFORM. If you use an IF/ELSE in an in-line PERFORM, you need to demarcate the end of the scope of the decision with END-IF before ending the in-line PERFORM with END-PERFORM.

6.7 NESTED IN-LINE PERFORM

The AFTER option has always existed in VS COBOL to allow you to "nest" the VARYING and UNTIL action of a PERFORM. (Don't confuse this use of the word AFTER with "WITH TEST AFTER" that is new in VS COBOL II, as I describe in the following two sections!)

The top part of Figure 6.6 (page 108) shows you how the AFTER option lets me vary three values, WS-A, WS-B, and WS-C, making WS-C vary most rapidly and WS-A least rapidly. The bottom part of Figure 6.6 shows you the output from this program.

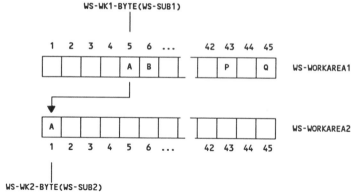

Figure 6.4   How Program D3OLD Left-Justifies a Character String.

D3OLD "squishes left" the text in WS-WORKAREA1, left-justifying it in WS-WORKAREA2, using a PERFORM . . . VARYING to sweep the WS-SUB1 subscript value over the range of 1 to 45. Can you modify the program to use an in-line PERFORM instead of a traditional out-of-line PERFORM? The source code for D3OLD is listed in Figure 6.5.

You can't use the AFTER clause with the in-line PERFORM to vary more than one data-name at a time. But you can get the same effect by nesting in-line PERFORMs within one another, as shown in the second part of Figure 6.6. When you nest in-line PERFORMs in this way, you end each PERFORM with a matching scope terminator END-PER-FORM.

Thus a new style of nested in-line coding becomes possible with VS COBOL II. Your installation probably doesn't have any standards guiding (or prohibiting) local use of this technique. But common sense would indicate that heavily nested PERFORMs can complicate program maintenance in the same way that heavily nested IF/ELSE can complicate it! See Appendix G for shop standards I suggest you consider for this and other VS COBOL II features.

6.8   PERFORM . . . WITH TEST BEFORE

VS COBOL's PERFORM always makes its test of the UNTIL condition before executing the code specified by the PERFORM. This is known as a "do until" loop, as shown in the upper part of Figure 6.7 (page 110). With VS COBOL II you get the same processing whether or not you code the new phrase WITH TEST BEFORE.

You don't have to pay any attention to the WITH TEST BEFORE phrase. It remains the default in VS COBOL II, and your PERFORMs will work the same way they have in VS COBOL.

```
000100 IDENTIFICATION DIVISION.
000200 PROGRAM-ID.       D3OLD.
000300 AUTHOR.           J. JANOSSY.
000400*REMARKS.          SQUISH A STRING TO THE LEFT.
000500 ENVIRONMENT DIVISION.
000600*
000700 DATA DIVISION.
000800 WORKING-STORAGE SECTION.
000900 01  WS-STRING                    PIC X(45)  VALUE
001000     '    AB  C D   E FG  H   I JKL   M N    O P Q'.
001100 01  WS-WORKAREA1.
001200     05 WS-WK1-BYTE    OCCURS 45 TIMES   PIC X(1).
001300 01  WS-WORKAREA2.
001400     05 WS-WK2-BYTE    OCCURS 45 TIMES   PIC X(1).
001500 01  WS-SUB1                       PIC 9(2)  VALUE 0.
001600 01  WS-SUB2                       PIC 9(2)  VALUE 0.
001700/
001800 PROCEDURE DIVISION.
001900 0000-MAINLINE.
002000     DISPLAY 'PROGRAM D3OLD STARTING'.
002100     DISPLAY 'STRING BEFORE = ', WS-STRING.
002200*
002300     MOVE WS-STRING TO WS-WORKAREA1.
002400     MOVE SPACES TO WS-WORKAREA2.
002500     PERFORM 1000-MOVE-BY-BYTE
002600        VARYING WS-SUB1 FROM 1 BY 1
002700           UNTIL WS-SUB1 > 45.
002800     DISPLAY 'STRING AFTER  = ', WS-WORKAREA2.
002900     STOP RUN.
003000*
003100 1000-MOVE-BY-BYTE.
003200     IF WS-WK1-BYTE(WS-SUB1) NOT = SPACE
003300        ADD 1 TO WS-SUB2
003400        MOVE WS-WK1-BYTE(WS-SUB1)
003500           TO WS-WK2-BYTE(WS-SUB2).
```

Output:

```
PROGRAM D3OLD STARTING
STRING BEFORE =    AB  C D   E FG  H   I JKL   M N    O P Q
STRING AFTER  = ABCDEFGHIJKLMNOPQ
```

Figure 6.5 Source Code for Program D3OLD Using Out-of-Line PERFORM.

The D3OLD program left-justifies text. Modify this program so that it uses an in-line PERFORM rather than an out-of-line PERFORM.

6.9 PERFORM . . . WITH TEST AFTER

VS COBOL II enhances the operation of PERFORM by letting you test the condition that ends a PERFORM . . . UNTIL after each execution of the loop code. When the ending condition test is made after the loop is executed, the loop always executes at least once. In formal software engineering terminology this is called a "repeat until" loop.

The lower part of Figure 6.7 (page 110) shows you how a repeat until loop works in VS COBOL II. Notice that the output of the program is different: you now see four outputs from the loop rather than three. Why? Because the comparison of the varied value to the ending value is made *after* the loop code is executed!

The WITH TEST AFTER feature has been included in VS COBOL II only to round out your tool kit of software engineering structures. You may not find much use for it. But be aware of the drastic change it makes in PERFORM operation. Do not use WITH TEST AFTER casually without understanding its impact!

```
000100 IDENTIFICATION DIVISION.
000200 PROGRAM-ID.     D4NESTOT.
000300 AUTHOR.         J. JANOSSY.
000400*
000500*REMARKS.        DEMONSTRATE COMPLEX PERFORM WITH "AFTER" CLAUSE
000600*                USING OUT-OF-LINE CODING
000700*
000800 ENVIRONMENT DIVISION.
000900 DATA DIVISION.
001000 WORKING-STORAGE SECTION.
001100 01  WS-COUNT            PIC 9(2)   VALUE 0.
001200 01  WS-A               PIC 9(2)   VALUE 0.
001300 01  WS-B               PIC 9(2)   VALUE 0.
001400 01  WS-C               PIC 9(2)   VALUE 0.
001500/
001600 PROCEDURE DIVISION.
001700 0000-MAINLINE.
001800     DISPLAY 'PROGRAM D4NESTOT STARTING'.
001900     PERFORM 2100-DISPLAY                        ┌─────────────────┐
002000         VARYING WS-A FROM 1 BY 1 UNTIL WS-A > 3 │ Out-of-line     │
002100         AFTER WS-B FROM 1 BY 1 UNTIL WS-B > 3   │ PERFORM with    │
002200             AFTER WS-C FROM 1 BY 1 UNTIL WS-C > 3. │ AFTER to "nest" │
002300     DISPLAY 'PROGRAM ENDING'.                    │ VARYING action  │
002400     STOP RUN.                                    └─────────────────┘
002500*
002600 2100-DISPLAY.
002700     ADD 1 TO WS-COUNT.
002800     DISPLAY 'LOOP COUNT=', WS-COUNT,
002900            ' A=',  WS-A,
003000            ' B=',  WS-B,
003100            ' C=',  WS-C.
```

Figure 6.6 Nested PERFORMS Simulate the VARYING . . . AFTER Option.

(*Above*) You can use the AFTER option in a traditional PERFORM to nest VARY-ing actions and sweep multiple values through all of their possible combinations. This is one way to reinitialize a multiple-level table. (*Next page*) You can't use the AFTER option to nest in-line PERFORMs, but you can nest in-line PER-FORMs within other in-line PERFORMs. Each nested in-line PERFORM ends with its matching END-PERFORM.

6.10 *TRY IT!* DECIPHERING IN-LINE PERFORMS

In-line PERFORMs can be more efficient than out-of-line PERFORMs. To some programmers, they seem more logical. You can write code using in-line PERFORMs similar to pseudocode and languages such as C, Pas-cal, and PL/I.

You may encounter in-line PERFORMs in programs that you have to maintain even if you don't choose to use them in programs you write. How can you analyze complex nested in-line PERFORMs?

Figure 6.8 (page 111) shows you the source code for program D5NESTED, a new version of the analysis for Uncle Droesselmeyer's coin game. You saw an early version of this program, named B2COINS, in Chapter 4, section 4.7. The program develops a listing of all possible combinations of winnings that a person might receive when choosing cups covering a penny, a dime, or a dollar, with four rounds of play. This

(text continues on page 114)

```
000100 IDENTIFICATION DIVISION.
000200 PROGRAM-ID.    D4NESTIN.
000300 AUTHOR.        J. JANOSSY.
000400*
000500*REMARKS.      DEMONSTRATE COMPLEX PERFORM WITH "AFTER" CLAUSE
000600*               USING IN-LINE CODING
000700*
000800 ENVIRONMENT DIVISION.
000900 DATA DIVISION.
001000 WORKING-STORAGE SECTION.
001100 01  WS-COUNT              PIC 9(2)   VALUE 0.
001200 01  WS-A                 PIC 9(2)   VALUE 0.
001300 01  WS-B                 PIC 9(2)   VALUE 0.
001400 01  WS-C                 PIC 9(2)   VALUE 0.
001500/
001600 PROCEDURE DIVISION.
001700 0000-MAINLINE.
001800     DISPLAY 'PROGRAM D4NESTIN STARTING'.
001900     PERFORM
002000       VARYING WS-A FROM 1 BY 1
002100       UNTIL WS-A > 3
002200         PERFORM
002300           VARYING WS-B FROM 1 BY 1
002400           UNTIL WS-B > 3
002500             PERFORM
002600               VARYING WS-C FROM 1 BY 1
002700               UNTIL WS-C > 3
002800                 ADD 1 TO WS-COUNT
002900                 DISPLAY 'LOOP COUNT='  WS-COUNT
003000                              '  A='   WS-A
003100                              '  B='   WS-B
003200                              '  C='   WS-C
003300             END-PERFORM
003400             DISPLAY '-------------------------------'
003500         END-PERFORM
003600     END-PERFORM.
003700     DISPLAY 'PROGRAM ENDING'.
003800     STOP RUN.
```

> How you can nest
> in-line PERFORMs
> to get the same
> action as with
> AFTER above

Output:

```
PROGRAM D4NESTIN STARTING
LOOP COUNT=01 A=01 B=01 C=01
LOOP COUNT=02 A=01 B=01 C=02
LOOP COUNT=03 A=01 B=01 C=03
-----------------------------
LOOP COUNT=04 A=01 B=02 C=01
LOOP COUNT=05 A=01 B=02 C=02
LOOP COUNT=06 A=01 B=02 C=03
-----------------------------
    -
    -
    -
-----------------------------
LOOP COUNT=25 A=03 B=03 C=01
LOOP COUNT=26 A=03 B=03 C=02
LOOP COUNT=27 A=03 B=03 C=03
PROGRAM ENDING
```

Figure 6.6   *Continued*

```
000100 IDENTIFICATION DIVISION.
000200 PROGRAM-ID.    D4BEFORE.
000300 AUTHOR.        J. JANOSSY.
000400*
000500*REMARKS.      ORDINARY PERFORM WITH TEST BEFORE.
000600*
000700 ENVIRONMENT DIVISION.
000800 DATA DIVISION.
000900 WORKING-STORAGE SECTION.
001000 01  WS-COUNT                 PIC 9(2)   VALUE 0.
001100/
001200 PROCEDURE DIVISION.
001300 0000-MAINLINE.
001400     DISPLAY 'PROGRAM D4BEFORE STARTING'.
001500     PERFORM 2100-DISPLAY
001600        WITH TEST BEFORE
001700           VARYING WS-COUNT FROM 1 BY 1
001800              UNTIL WS-COUNT > 3.
001900     STOP RUN.
002000*
002100 2100-DISPLAY.
002200     DISPLAY 'THE COUNT NOW = ', WS-COUNT.
```

> With test BEFORE
> the loop executes
> (this continues
> to be the default)

```
Output:

        PROGRAM D4BEFORE STARTING
        THE COUNT NOW = 01
        THE COUNT NOW = 02
        THE COUNT NOW = 03
```

```
000100 IDENTIFICATION DIVISION.
000200 PROGRAM-ID.    D4AFTER.
000300 AUTHOR.        J. JANOSSY.
000400*
000500*REMARKS.      ORDINARY PERFORM WITH TEST AFTER.
000600*
000700 ENVIRONMENT DIVISION.
000800 DATA DIVISION.
000900 WORKING-STORAGE SECTION.
001000 01  WS-COUNT                 PIC 9(2)   VALUE 0.
001100/
001200 PROCEDURE DIVISION.
001300 0000-MAINLINE.
001400     DISPLAY 'PROGRAM D4AFTER STARTING'.
001500     PERFORM 2100-DISPLAY
001600        WITH TEST AFTER
001700           VARYING WS-COUNT FROM 1 BY 1
001800              UNTIL WS-COUNT > 3.
001900     STOP RUN.
002000*
002100 2100-DISPLAY.
002200     DISPLAY 'THE COUNT NOW = ', WS-COUNT.
```

> With test
> AFTER
> loop logic

```
Output:

        PROGRAM D4AFTER STARTING
        THE COUNT NOW = 01
        THE COUNT NOW = 02
        THE COUNT NOW = 03
        THE COUNT NOW = 04
```

> Make sure you understand why
> AFTER makes this loop execute
> four times instead of three!

Figure 6.7   WITH TEST AFTER Alters PERFORM Operation.

(*Top*) The VS COBOL II PERFORM . . . UNTIL defaults to testing the condition ending the loop before executing the logic of the loop. If the condition is already satisfied on the first attempt to loop, the loop never executes. This is a "do-while" loop. (*Bottom*) VS COBOL II gives you the option of coding WITH TEST AFTER on any PERFORM. . . UNTIL. If you code this, the test of the condition satisfying the UNTIL is made *after* the loop logic executes. This is a "repeat-until" loop and its loop logic always executes at least once.

```
000001  000100  IDENTIFICATION DIVISION.
000002  000200  PROGRAM-ID.  D5NESTED.
000003  000300*********************************************************
000004  000400*                                                       *
000005  000500*          BY JIM JANOSSY   DEPAUL UNIVERSITY   5/5/92   *
000006  000600*                                                       *
000007  000700*       DROSSELMEYER'S GENEROUS COIN GAME USING          *
000008  000800*       NESTED IN-LINE PERFORMS (SEE ALSO B2COINS)       *
000009  000900*                                                       *
000010  001000*********************************************************
000011  001100  ENVIRONMENT DIVISION.
000012  001200*
000013  001300  DATA DIVISION.
000014  001400  WORKING-STORAGE SECTION.
000015  001500  01  MONEY-TABLE-SETUP.
000016  001600      12  FILLER          PIC X(10)   VALUE '001 PENNY '.
000017  001700      12  FILLER          PIC X(10)   VALUE '010 DIME  '.
000018  001800      12  FILLER          PIC X(10)   VALUE '100 DOLLAR'.
000019  001900  01  MONEY-TABLE REDEFINES MONEY-TABLE-SETUP.
000020  002000      12  MONEY-ELEMENT OCCURS 3 TIMES.              15
000021  002100          15  MONEY-VALUE   PIC 9V99.
000022  002200          15  FILLER        PIC X(1).
000023  002300          15  MONEY-NAME    PIC X(6).
000024  002400*
000025  002500  01  PR-LINE.
000026  002600      12  PR-NAME1        PIC X(6).
000027  002700      12  FILLER          PIC X(2).
000028  002800      12  PR-NAME2        PIC X(6).
000029  002900      12  FILLER          PIC X(2).
000030  003000      12  PR-NAME3        PIC X(6).
000031  003100      12  FILLER          PIC X(2).
000032  003200      12  PR-NAME4        PIC X(6).
000033  003300      12  FILLER          PIC X(11).
000034  003400      12  PR-TOTAL        PIC $ZZ.99.
000035  003500*
000036  003600  01  HYPHEN-LINE        PIC X(47)   VALUE ALL '-'.
000037  003700*
000038  003800  01  WS-COINS.                                     IMP
000039  003900      12  WS-COIN1        PIC 9(1).                 IMP
000040  004000      12  WS-COIN2        PIC 9(1).                 IMP
000041  004100      12  WS-COIN3        PIC 9(1).
000042  004200      12  WS-COIN4        PIC 9(1).
000043  004300*
000044  004400  01  WS-VALUES.
000045  004500      12  WS-VAL1         PIC 9(3)V99.
000046  004600      12  WS-VAL2         PIC 9(3)V99.
000047  004700      12  WS-VAL3         PIC 9(3)V99.
000048  004800      12  WS-VAL4         PIC 9(3)V99.
000049  004900      12  WS-TOTAL        PIC 9(3)V99.
```

(a) (b)

Figure 6.8 (see legend on page 113)

111

```
LINEID PL SL   ----+-*A-1-B-+----2----+----3----+----4----+----5----+----6----+----7-|--+----8  MAP AND CROSS REFERENCE
000050   005000/
000051   005100  PROCEDURE DIVISION.
000052   005200  0000-MAINLINE.
000053   005300      PERFORM
000054   005400          VARYING WS-COIN1                                39
000055   005500          FROM 1 BY 1
000056   005600          UNTIL WS-COIN1 > 3
000057 1 005700          MOVE MONEY-NAME(WS-COIN1) TO PR-NAME1           39 39 26
000058 1 005800          MOVE MONEY-VALUE(WS-COIN1) TO WS-VAL1           21 39 45
000059 1 005900      PERFORM
000060 1 006000          VARYING WS-COIN2                                40
000061 1 006100          FROM 1 BY 1
000062 2 006200          UNTIL WS-COIN2 > 3
000063 2 006300          MOVE MONEY-NAME(WS-COIN2) TO PR-NAME2           40 40 28
000064 2 006400          MOVE MONEY-VALUE(WS-COIN2) TO WS-VAL2           23 40 46
000065 2 006500      PERFORM
000066 2 006600          VARYING WS-COIN3                                41
000067 3 006700          FROM 1 BY 1
000068 3 006800          UNTIL WS-COIN3 > 3
000069 3 006900          MOVE MONEY-NAME(WS-COIN3) TO PR-NAME3           41 41 30
000070 3 007000          MOVE MONEY-VALUE(WS-COIN3) TO WS-VAL3           21 41 47
000071 3 007100      PERFORM
000072 3 007200          VARYING WS-COIN4                                42
000073 4 007300          FROM 1 BY 1
000074 4 007400          UNTIL WS-COIN4 > 3
000075 4 007500          MOVE MONEY-NAME(WS-COIN4) TO PR-NAME4           42 42 32
000076 4 007600          MOVE MONEY-VALUE(WS-COIN4) TO WS-VAL4           23 42 48
000077 4 007700          COMPUTE WS-TOTAL =                              49
000078 4 007800             WS-VAL1 + WS-VAL2 + WS-VAL3 + WS-VAL4        45 46 47 48
000079 4 007900          MOVE WS-TOTAL TO PR-TOTAL                       49 34
000080 3 008000          DISPLAY PR-LINE                                25
000081 3 008100      END-PERFORM
000082 2 008200      DISPLAY HYPHEN-LINE                                36
000083 2 008300      END-PERFORM
000084 1 008400      END-PERFORM
000085   008500      END-PERFORM
000086   008600      STOP RUN.
```

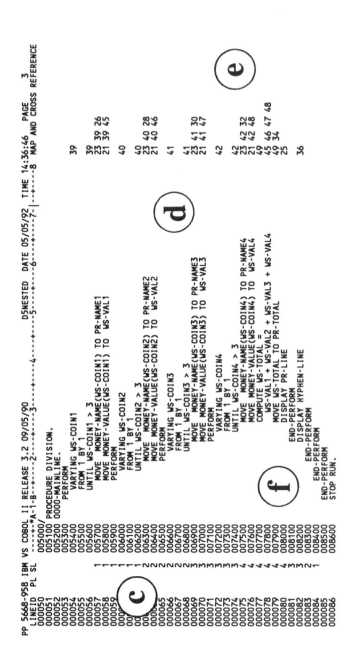

c d e f

112

Figure 6.8 Nested In-Line PERFORMs: Compiled Source Code for D5NESTED.

Program D5NESTED produces the same output as B2COINS in Chapter 4 (see Figure 4.3, page 79). The nested PERFORMs exhaust all possible combinations of three coins drawn four times ($3^4 = 81$ combinations).

a. This table with three rows is accessed with WS-COIN1, WS-COIN2, WS-COIN3, and WS-COIN4 as subscripts to directly look up the coin name and value represented by the digits 1, 2, and 3. The 15 in the MAP AND CROSS-REFERENCE column shows that MONEY-TABLE redefines the data name defined on line 15.

b. PR-LINE is repeatedly DISPLAYed much as a printline is written out, and produces the bulk of D5NESTED output. IMP refers to use of the figurative constant SPACES to initialize certain fields in PR-LINE.

c. The statement level number shows how deep each line of logic is within nested PERFORMs. Nesting values decrease at the end of the single large sentence as END-PERFORMs are encountered.

d. All four nested PERFORMs are housed in one single sentence in this program. Is this good or bad coding? Does it ease program maintenance or make it more difficult to accomplish reliably?

e. The MAP AND CROSS-REFERENCE values here show lines on which data items are defined. When multiple data names exist on a line, multiple definition line numbers appear, such as "23 42 32."

f. It's a good idea to indent each END-PERFORM at exactly the same position as the PERFORM it matches. This way the code can be analyzed by drawing vertical lines between matching PERFORMs and END-PERFORMs. But the VS COBOL II compiler does not use or recognize indentation; it pairs PERFORMs to END-PERFORMs from the innermost pair outward.

version of the program has a small table in it, accessed by subscripts WS-COIN1, WS-COIN2, WS-COIN3, and WS-COIN4. This replaces the use of IF/ELSE logic to interpret the numbers produced by the PERFORM ... VARYING logic.

In program D5NESTED, I have replaced all out-of-line PERFORMs with one in-line PERFORM. Examples in some language textbooks seem to recommend this style of coding, especially when logic is mapped out in pseudocode. Do you agree or disagree with the thought that the style of logic in D5NESTED is desirable? Does D5NESTED work? Do these things to find out and explore this area:

- Analyze the logic of program D5NESTED. Draw vertical lines connecting each PERFORM with its END-PERFORM.
- Compile, linkage edit, and run D5NESTED. Is your output reasonable?
- Look at the statement level numbers applied by the compiler to the nested in-line PERFORMs. Do these make any sense to you?

7

IF/ELSE, Scope Terminators, EVALUATE, and SET

VS COBOL II gives you capabilities to express decision-making logic far beyond those of VS COBOL. The improvements include direct "equal to or greater than" and "equal to or less than" coding, explicit scope delimiters, the new EVALUATE verb, and the expansion of SET to affect 88-level condition names. I have lumped my explanations of these related features into this chapter so you can rapidly see what they can do for you.

7.1 NEW: $<=$ AND $>=$ IF/ELSE OPERATIONS!

VS COBOL was constrained in its syntax. It allowed you to define relation conditions only for less than, equal to, and greater than. The negations of these were also supported:

```
IF A < B         or, in words:       IF A IS LESS THAN B
IF A = B         or, in words:       IF A IS EQUAL TO B
IF A > B         or, in words:       IF A IS GREATER THAN B


IF A NOT < B     or, in words:       IF A IS NOT LESS THAN B
IF A NOT = B     or, in words:       IF A IS NOT EQUAL TO B
IF A NOT > B     or, in words:       IF A IS NOT GREATER THAN B
```

But VS COBOL did not support "less than or equal to" or "equal to or greater than." Suppose you had to find out if A was less than or equal to B? In VS COBOL you could not state:

```
IF A < = B
IF A IS LESS THAN OR EQUAL TO B
```

You had to state such a test as the *negated complement* of the intended test:

Intended test	Negated complement
A < = B	A NOT > B
A > = B	A NOT < B

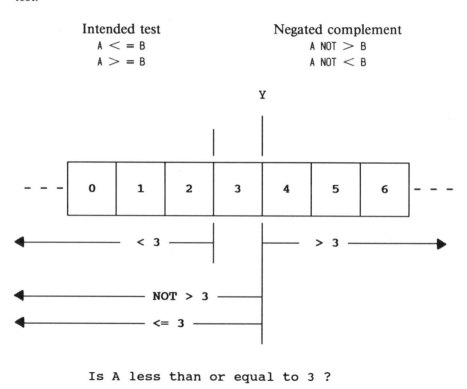

```
Is A less than or equal to 3 ?

    IF   A NOT > 3        in VS COBOL

    IF   A <= 3           in VS COBOL II
```

Figure 7.1   How NOT > and < = WORK.

A number line lets you see how NOT > means the same thing as < = . VS COBOL requires you to code NOT > for a test that said "equal to or less than" but VS COBOL II gives you the < = operator to say it directly. You can now also use > = for "equal to or greater than."

7.2 NEGATED LOGICAL COMPLEMENT TESTS

It helps to picture a number line to see why VS COBOL's negated complementary relation conditions work. Suppose we want to test a value named A to see if it is less than or equal to three. Look at Figure 7.1. Here is how to understand it:

(a) Everything right of line y is greater than 3.
(b) Everything left of line y is *not* greater than 3.
(c) Everything left of line y is less than or equal to three.

VS COBOL did not allow you to express (c) directly. To make an "equal to or less than" test in VS COBOL, you have to code (b) as IF A NOT > 3 . . . . Since > is the opposite of <, you can think of it as the "logical complement." NOT > is the negated logical complement of <. But VS COBOL II lets you code (c) directly:

```
IF A <= 3 . . .
```

Using <= and >= can simplify your logic! When one value is relevant to a decision, as in this example, it is called a limit test. Two values exist in the decision, forming a range. VS COBOL II simplifies range tests even more.

7.3 SIMPLIFIED RANGE TESTS IN VS COBOL II

Is WS-NUMBER a value in the range 2 through 4? To code this in VS COBOL you have to state:

```
IF ( (WS-NUMBER IS NOT < 2)
      AND
     (WS-NUMBER IS NOT > 4) )
        PERFORM . . .
```

or

```
IF ( (WS-NUMBER IS NOT LESS THAN 2)
      AND
     (WS-NUMBER IS NOT GREATER THAN 4) )
          PERFORM . . .
```

But in VS COBOL II your code becomes much more direct:

```
IF WS-NUMBER >= 2 AND WS-NUMBER <= 4
   PERFORM . . .
```

In coding "greater than or equal to" or "less than or equal to" always code the $>$ or $<$ sign first, before the $=$ sign, with no space between.

7.4   END-IF: AN EXPLICIT SCOPE TERMINATOR

You can code END-IF to mark the end of an IF/ELSE construct instead of using a period. For example, this is satisfactory coding under VS COBOL II:

```
IF WS-AGE-OF-UNCLE <= WS-AGE-OF-NIECE
   PERFORM 1200-PUNK-UNCLE
 ELSE
   PERFORM 1300-NORMAL.
```

But this coding is fine too:

```
IF WS-AGE-OF-UNCLE <= WS-AGE-OF-NIECE
   PERFORM 1200-PUNK-UNCLE
 ELSE
   PERFORM 1300-NORMAL
END-IF
```

In this case END-IF slightly improves clarity but that is not its main purpose. The main purpose of END-IF, and of the other "explicit scope delimiters" shown in Figure 7.2, is to *mark the end of the statement without using a period*. By ending an IF/ELSE with END-IF, you can embed the IF/ELSE within any other logic as a self-contained unit.

7.5   ADDING CLARITY WITH END-IF

You can use END-IF to add clarity to nested IF/ELSE logic. This can help in cases where you cannot avoid the use of large IF/ELSE structures. The upper part of Figure 7.3 represents the health risk factor predicted by three variables associated with an individual. The decision table at the bottom of this figure shows, in tabular form, the risk factor associated

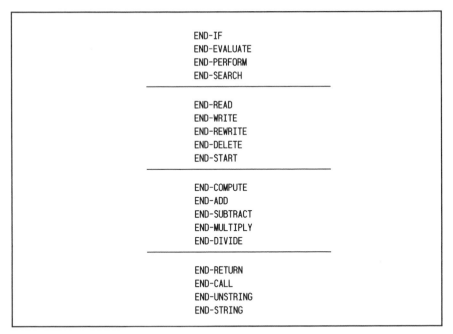

```
                         END-IF
                         END-EVALUATE
                         END-PERFORM
                         END-SEARCH

                         END-READ
                         END-WRITE
                         END-REWRITE
                         END-DELETE
                         END-START

                         END-COMPUTE
                         END-ADD
                         END-SUBTRACT
                         END-MULTIPLY
                         END-DIVIDE

                         END-RETURN
                         END-CALL
                         END-UNSTRING
                         END-STRING
```

Figure 7.2 Explicit Scope Delimiters.

You can use these 18 new reserved words in VS COBOL II to end the action of the matching verbs logically without using a period. Your main use of these delimiters will be to make IF and EVALUATE decisions into self-contained units that can be coded within other decisions or actions.

with each of the eight possible combinations of the variables. You could use an IF/ELSE as in Figure 7.4 to implement the decision testing. Each END-IF is paired with the nearest unpaired IF preceding it.

7.6 EXPLICIT SCOPE TERMINATORS

A conditional statement is like an IF/ELSE. What follows the IF and ELSE all become part of it until the statement is terminated. In VS COBOL you could only terminate a conditional statement with a period. The execution of all of that is conditioned on the outcome of a logic test is not definite.

An imperative statement is the opposite of a conditional statement. When you state MOVE A TO B there is no question about what will happen every time the statement is executed.

A major purpose of explicit scope delimiters, such as END-IF, is to let you terminate conditional statements without using a period. By ending the following types of statements with explicit scope terminators, you turn them into imperative statement groups that can be coded within other conditional statements:

```
IF/ELSE . . . END/IF
EVALUATE . . . END-EVALUATE
COMPUTE . . . ON SIZE ERROR . . . END-COMPUTE
STRING . . . ON OVERFLOW . . . END-STRING
READ . . . AT END . . . END-READ
READ . . . INVALID KEY . . . END-READ
SEARCH . . . AT END . . . WHEN . . . END-SEARCH
```

	Male	**Female**
No family history of heart disease	Smoker = .18 Nonsmoker = .01	Smoker = .14 Nonsmoker = .005
Family history of heart disease	Smoker = .32 Nonsmoker = .03	Smoker = .24 Nonsmoker = .02

Family history of heart disease?	**Sex**	**Smoker?**	**Risk Factor**
N	M	Y	.18
N	M	N	.01
N	F	Y	.14
N	F	N	.005
Y	M	Y	.32
Y	M	N	.03
Y	F	Y	.24
Y	F	N	.02

Figure 7.3   A Three-Factor Decision in Chart and Decision Table Form.

The chart at the top and the decision table at the bottom both depict a decision based on three factors. The three factors can each take on two different values, leading to $2^3 = 8$ possible risk values as output. I implemented the logic for this decision-making using an IF/ELSE in Figure 7.4. In Figure 7.11 (page 136) I show you a much better way of coding it with VS COBOL II's new EVALUATE verb. (This example first appeared in *Commercial Software Engineering* by James Janossy, published by John Wiley & Sons in 1985.)

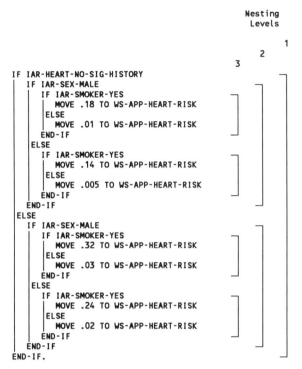

Figure 7.4   How You Can Use END-IF.

END/IF lets you add clarity to large nested IF/ELSE logic structures. This logic actually implements the decision-making required by the chart and decision table shown in Figure 7.3. But even with END-IF this logic will be difficult to maintain. See Figure 7.11 (page 136) for a much clearer way to code this using the new EVALUATE verb.

The explicit scope delimiters beside these allow you to put statements like ADD, CALL, COMPUTE, DELETE, UNSTRING, EVALUATE, SUBTRACT, MULTIPLY, PERFORM, READ, RETURN, REWRITE, IF, START, STRING, SEARCH, DIVIDE, and WRITE *within* conditional statements.

7.7   END- : MAKING A CONDITIONAL STATEMENT INTO IMPERATIVE

An important feature of an imperative ("doing") statement is that it can be embedded within another statement, whereas a conditional statement cannot be embedded:

```
IF WS-EOF-FLAG NOT = 'E'
    READ INPUT-DATA FILE
      | AT END
      | IF WS-INPUT-REC-COUNT = 0
      |   | PERFORM 8000-FINISH-EMPTY
      |   | ELSE
      |   | PERFORM 8500-FINISH-WITH-RECS
      | END-IF
    END-READ
ELSE
    PERFORM 8900-PROCESS-NO-READ.
```

You could not code an IF (a conditional statement) within an AT END within an IF under VS COBOL because the period that ended the inner IF/ELSE would end the outer IF/ELSE too. END-READ marks the end of the READ verb in the way that only a period formerly marked.

Your use of the END-xxx scope delimiters such as END-IF and END-READ has something to do with functionality but much to do with style. Is it really a good idea to build logic such as that shown above? No requirement exists for you to use any END- scope delimiters except END-PERFORM, and END-PERFORM is required only with in-line PER-FORMs.

7.8   NEXT SENTENCE AND CONTINUE

VS COBOL II still supports NEXT SENTENCE, which lets you "jump out" of an IF/ELSE. You can still use NEXT SENTENCE to use positive logic instead of negative logic. For instance, both of these statements are equivalent, but you may prefer the first since it doesn't involve a NOT:

```
IF WS-STATE-ABBREV-OK
    NEXT SENTENCE
ELSE
    PERFORM 3000-STATE-ERROR
END-IF
```

does the same thing as:

```
IF NOT WS-STATE-ABBREV-OK
    PERFORM 3000-STATE-ERROR
END-IF
```

VS COBOL II also provides a new null statement—CONTINUE. You can use CONTINUE in an IF/ELSE, but it was really created for use with the EVALUATE verb. Unlike NEXT SENTENCE, CONTINUE has little relevance to a simple IF statement like that above. NEXT SENTENCE branches to a point after the next period. CONTINUE branches to after the next END-IF.

You can use CONTINUE in a nested IF/ELSE, but its effect will be very confusing. Practically speaking no good use exists for CONTINUE in an IF/ELSE statement.

7.9 IF/ELSE TRIVIA

VS COBOL II conforms to standard structured programming syntax in the use of the noise word "THEN". You can now include this extra word after the IF in an IF/ELSE to provide what some people would consider a prettier IF ... THEN/ELSE structure. For example, either of these codings is correct in VS COBOL II:

```
IF PORRIDGE-TOO-COLD
    PERFORM 1000-MOVE-TO-NEXT-BOWL
  ELSE
IF PORRIDGE-TOO-HOT
    PERFORM . . .
```

or

```
IF PORRIDGE-TOO-COLD
  THEN
    PERFORM 1000-MOVE-TO-NEXT-BOWL
  ELSE
IF PORRIDGE-TOO-HOT
  THEN
    PERFORM . . .
```

The extra word "THEN" does not affect processing; the same processing takes place with or without it. Relegate THEN to a very low priority of attention.

The reserved word OTHERWISE, which was permitted in VS COBOL, is no longer supported. You must use ELSE instead of OTHERWISE in VS COBOL II.

7.10 COMPARING EVALUATE AND IF/ELSE

EVALUATE gives you an improved way to code "case-type" logic. In the past you would have used serial IF/ELSEs to do this. You can continue to use IF/ELSE as before, but you might want to explore how EVALUATE can make some of your decision coding easier. The easiest way to understand what EVALUATE can do is to see how an older serial case-type IF/ELSE can be converted to the new coding.

Look at program E1OLDIF in Figure 7.5. This program uses serial (case-type) IF/ELSE logic to decide what interpretation to give each letter grade:

A   Excellent work!
B   Very good!
C   Ok, but you can do better.
D   Much room for improvement!
F   Failed—try again.

Letter grades other than these are invalid and the program identifies them as ?? UNKNOWN GRADE ??. Look at the output of E1OLDIF listed at the end of the program to see how it works.

EVALUATE replaces a serial IF/ELSE with more compact code as shown in program E1EVAL in Figure 7.6. Here is the EVALUATE statement in that program:

```
EVALUATE WS-LETTER-GRADE(WS-SUB)                    Selection subject
   WHEN 'A'
      DISPLAY 'EXCELLENT WORK!'
   WHEN 'B'
      DISPLAY 'VERY GOOD!'
   WHEN 'C'                                          Selection
      DISPLAY 'OK, BUT YOU CAN DO BETTER'            objects
   WHEN 'D'                                          at WHENs
      DISPLAY 'MUCH ROOM FOR IMPROVEMENT!'
   WHEN 'F'
      DISPLAY 'FAILED -- TRY AGAIN'
   WHEN OTHER
      DISPLAY '?? UNKNOWN GRADE ??'.
```

```
000100 IDENTIFICATION DIVISION.
000200 PROGRAM-ID.      E1OLDIF.
000300 AUTHOR.          J. JANOSSY.
000400*
000500*REMARKS.         IF/ELSE EXAMPLE FOR CONVERSION TO EVALUATE.
000600*                 ROWS ARE TAKEN FROM TABLE TO SIMULATE
000700*                 RECORDS BEING READ IN A SIMPLE WAY.
000800*
000900 ENVIRONMENT DIVISION.
001000*
001100 DATA DIVISION.
001200 WORKING-STORAGE SECTION.
001300 01  WS-SUB              PIC 9(1)  VALUE 0.
001400 01  WS-DATA-TABLE-SETUP.
001500     05  FILLER          PIC X(7)  VALUE 'STEVE B'.
001600     05  FILLER          PIC X(7)  VALUE 'JON   F'.
001700     05  FILLER          PIC X(7)  VALUE 'DAVID A'.
001800     05  FILLER          PIC X(7)  VALUE 'SARAH X'.
001900     05  FILLER          PIC X(7)  VALUE 'MICAH D'.
002000     05  FILLER          PIC X(7)  VALUE 'JUDY  C'.
002100 01  WS-DATA-TABLE REDEFINES  WS-DATA-TABLE-SETUP.
002200     05  WS-DATA-ELEMENT  OCCURS 6 TIMES.
002300         10  WS-NAME          PIC X(5).
002400         10  FILLER           PIC X(1).
002500         10  WS-LETTER-GRADE  PIC X(1).
002600/
002700 PROCEDURE DIVISION.
002800 0000-MAINLINE.
002900     DISPLAY 'E1OLDIF PROGRAM STARTING'.
003000     PERFORM 1000-GRADE-RATING
003100         VARYING WS-SUB FROM 1 BY 1
003200             UNTIL WS-SUB > 6.
003300     STOP RUN.
003400*
003500 1000-GRADE-RATING.
003600     DISPLAY '--------------------------------------------'.
003700     DISPLAY WS-NAME(WS-SUB), ' ' WS-LETTER-GRADE(WS-SUB).
003800*
003900     IF WS-LETTER-GRADE(WS-SUB) = 'A'
004000         DISPLAY 'EXCELLENT WORK!'
004100     ELSE
004200     IF WS-LETTER-GRADE(WS-SUB) = 'B'
004300         DISPLAY 'VERY GOOD!'
004400     ELSE
004500     IF WS-LETTER-GRADE(WS-SUB) = 'C'
004600         DISPLAY 'OK, BUT YOU CAN DO BETTER'
004700     ELSE
004800     IF WS-LETTER-GRADE(WS-SUB) = 'D'
004900         DISPLAY 'MUCH ROOM FOR IMPROVEMENT!'
005000     ELSE
005100     IF WS-LETTER-GRADE(WS-SUB) = 'F'
005200         DISPLAY 'FAILED -- TRY AGAIN'
005300     ELSE
005400         DISPLAY '?? UNKNOWN GRADE ??'.
```

Output:

```
E1OLDIF PROGRAM STARTING
----------------------------------------
STEVE  B
VERY GOOD!
----------------------------------------
JON    F
FAILED -- TRY AGAIN
----------------------------------------
DAVID  A
EXCELLENT WORK!
----------------------------------------
SARAH  X
?? UNKNOWN GRADE ??
----------------------------------------
MICAH  D
MUCH ROOM FOR IMPROVEMENT!
----------------------------------------
JUDY   C
OK, BUT YOU CAN DO BETTER
```

Figure 7.5   Case-Type IF/ELSE Logic.

This program "pulls" data from a hardcoded table to simulate records being read and processed. It provides a simple "test bed" to confirm that the serial IF/ELSE in lines 3900 through 5400 properly interpret each letter grade and associate the correct message with it. The output listed at the bottom confirms that this IF/ELSE is working properly. How could you use EVALUATE to make these decisions more compactly? See Figure 7.6!

```
000100 IDENTIFICATION DIVISION.
000200 PROGRAM-ID.     E1EVAL.
000300 AUTHOR.         J. JANOSSY.
000400*
000500*REMARKS.        HOW TO USE EVALUATE INSTEAD OF IF/ELSE.
000600*                ROWS ARE TAKEN FROM TABLE TO SIMULATE
000700*                RECORDS BEING READ IN A SIMPLE WAY.
000800*
000900 ENVIRONMENT DIVISION.
001000*
001100 DATA DIVISION.
001200 WORKING-STORAGE SECTION.
001300 01  WS-SUB                 PIC 9(1)  VALUE 0.
001400 01  WS-DATA-TABLE-SETUP.
001500     05 FILLER              PIC X(7)  VALUE 'STEVE B'.
001600     05 FILLER              PIC X(7)  VALUE 'JON   F'.
001700     05 FILLER              PIC X(7)  VALUE 'DAVID A'.
001800     05 FILLER              PIC X(7)  VALUE 'SARAH X'.
001900     05 FILLER              PIC X(7)  VALUE 'MICAH D'.
002000     05 FILLER              PIC X(7)  VALUE 'JUDY  C'.
002100 01  WS-DATA-TABLE REDEFINES WS-DATA-TABLE-SETUP.
002200     05 WS-DATA-ELEMENT  OCCURS 6 TIMES.
002300         10 WS-NAME            PIC X(5).
002400         10 FILLER             PIC X(1).
002500         10 WS-LETTER-GRADE    PIC X(1).
002600/
002700 PROCEDURE DIVISION.
002800 0000-MAINLINE.
002900     DISPLAY 'E1EVAL PROGRAM STARTING'.
003000     PERFORM 1000-GRADE-RATING
003100         VARYING WS-SUB FROM 1 BY 1
003200             UNTIL WS-SUB > 6.
003300     STOP RUN.
003400*
003500 1000-GRADE-RATING.
003600     DISPLAY '----------------------------------------'.
003700     DISPLAY WS-NAME(WS-SUB), ' ' WS-LETTER-GRADE(WS-SUB).
003800*
003900     EVALUATE WS-LETTER-GRADE(WS-SUB)
004000         WHEN 'A'
004100             DISPLAY 'EXCELLENT WORK!'
004200         WHEN 'B'
004300             DISPLAY 'VERY GOOD!'
004400         WHEN 'C'
004500             DISPLAY 'OK, BUT YOU CAN DO BETTER'
004600         WHEN 'D'
004700             DISPLAY 'MUCH ROOM FOR IMPROVEMENT!'
004800         WHEN 'F'
004900             DISPLAY 'FAILED -- TRY AGAIN'
005000         WHEN OTHER
005100             DISPLAY '?? UNKNOWN GRADE ??'.
```

ⓐ ⓑ ⓒ

Output:

```
E1EVAL PROGRAM STARTING
----------------------------------------
STEVE  B
VERY GOOD!
----------------------------------------
JON    F
FAILED -- TRY AGAIN
----------------------------------------
DAVID  A
EXCELLENT WORK!
----------------------------------------
SARAH  X
?? UNKNOWN GRADE ??
----------------------------------------
MICAH  D
MUCH ROOM FOR IMPROVEMENT!
----------------------------------------
JUDY   C
OK, BUT YOU CAN DO BETTER
```

Figure 7.6 How You Can Use the EVALUATE Verb.

This program replaces a long serial (case-type) IF/ELSE with an EVALUATE verb in lines 3900 through 5100.

a. Data simulating input records to process is coded as rows in a table just to simplify this program.

b. Six records of test data will be processed, pulled out of the table with PER-FORM . . . VARYING and a subscript.

c. This EVALUATE interprets the letter grade in simulated data records being processed and associates the correct phrase with each. WS-LETTER-GRADE(WS-SUB) is the *selection subject*. The literal values at each WHEN are the *selection objects*.

7.11 SYNTAX REFERENCE FOR EVALUATE VARIATIONS

Here are some syntax rules you have to follow when you use the EVAL-UATE statement:

- When you code a data name as the selection subject, you have to code the selection objects (WHENs) as literal values, ranges of literal values, or other data names.
- When you code TRUE or FALSE as the selection subject, you can code relation tests at the selection objects (WHENs) or use 88-level names there.

Based on my experience, you need concise, clear examples to keep these rules straight! Figure 7.7 provides an EVALUATE syntax reference chart you will find handy.

7.12 EVALUATE WITH TRUE AND RELATION CODING

You can code EVALUATE so that the selection subject (the item that comes after the word "evaluate") is a truth condition such as TRUE rather than a data-name. To do this you must make the selection subjects either relation conditions (onething = otherthing) or 88-level condition names. This often requires more code and can cause VS COBOL II to generate a less efficient machine language load module:

```
EVALUATE TRUE
    WHEN WS-LETTER-GRADE(WS-SUB) = 'A'
        DISPLAY 'EXCELLENT WORK!'
    WHEN WS-LETTER-GRADE(WS-SUB) = 'B'
        DISPLAY 'VERY GOOD!'
    WHEN WS-LETTER-GRADE(WS-SUB) = 'C'
        DISPLAY 'OK, BUT YOU CAN DO BETTER'
    WHEN WS-LETTER-GRADE(WS-SUB) = 'D'
        DISPLAY 'MUCH ROOM FOR IMPROVEMENT!'
    WHEN WS-LETTER-GRADE(WS-SUB) = 'F'
        DISPLAY 'FAILED -- TRY AGAIN'
    WHEN OTHER
        DISPLAY '?? UNKNOWN GRADE ??'.
```

7.13 EVALUATE WITH TRUE AND 88-LEVEL CONDITION NAMES

You can code EVALUATE using 88-level condition names as the selection object (the item that appears after each WHEN). To do this you must code the selection subject (after "evaluate") as TRUE or FALSE:

```
01 STUDENT-INPUT-REC.
      05 SR-NAME              PIC X(5).
      05 FILLER              PIC X(1).
      05 SR-LETTER-GRADE     PIC X(1).
          88 SR-EXCELLENT             VALUE 'A'.
          88 SR-GOOD                  VALUE 'B'.
          88 SR-OK                    VALUE 'C'.
          88 SR-NEED-IMPROV           VALUE 'D'.
          88 SR-FAIL                  VALUE 'F'.
/
PROCEDURE DIVISION.
      -
      -
      EVALUATE TRUE
          WHEN SR-EXCELLENT
             DISPLAY 'EXCELLENT WORK!'
          WHEN SR-GOOD
             DISPLAY 'VERY GOOD!'
          WHEN SR-OK
          -
          -
```

7.14 A COMMON EVALUATE MISTAKE

EVALUATE gives you so much flexibility that it's easy to make mistakes and mix object and selection types. Here are the matching rules illustrated in Figure 7.7:

- If you code a data-name or expression after the word "EVALUATE" you have to code the WHENs as data values, data names, or literal data ranges. You *cannot* code the WHENs as 88-level condition names relations or relations with = or > or <.
- If you code the WHENs as relations involving = or > or < or 88-level names, the word after EVALUATE has to be TRUE or FALSE.

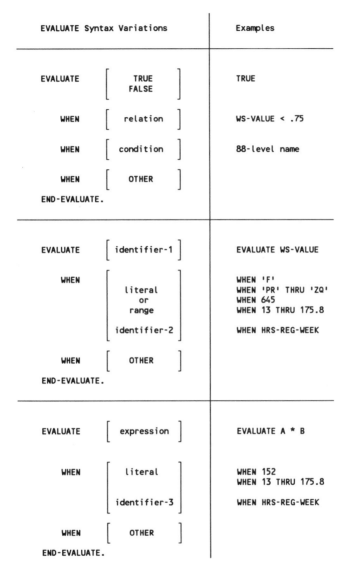

EVALUATE Syntax Variations	Examples

EVALUATE   [TRUE / FALSE]   TRUE

WHEN   [relation]   WS-VALUE < .75

WHEN   [condition]   88-level name

WHEN   [OTHER]

END-EVALUATE.

EVALUATE   [identifier-1]   EVALUATE WS-VALUE

WHEN   [literal / or / range / identifier-2]   WHEN 'F'
                                                          WHEN 'PR' THRU 'ZQ'
                                                          WHEN 645
                                                          WHEN 13 THRU 175.8
                                                          WHEN HRS-REG-WEEK

WHEN   [OTHER]

END-EVALUATE.

EVALUATE   [expression]   EVALUATE A * B

WHEN   [literal / identifier-3]   WHEN 152
                                             WHEN 13 THRU 175.8
                                             WHEN HRS-REG-WEEK

WHEN   [OTHER]

END-EVALUATE.

Figure 7.7 Syntax Reference: How to Use the EVALUATE Verb.

When you use EVALUATE you have to make sure that the selection subject (the item after EVALUATE) and the selection objects (the items after the WHENs) are matched according to this chart. If the selection subject is a data name or expression, you can't use a relation test such as $<$, $=$, or $>$ after the WHENs!

The following example is wrong! It mismatches the form of selection subject with the form of the selection objects:

```
05 SR-LETTER-GRADE       PIC X(1).
   88 SR-EXCELLENT                VALUE 'A'.
   88 SR-GOOD                     VALUE 'B'.
   88 SR-OK                       VALUE 'C'.
   88 SR-NEED-IMPROV              VALUE 'D'.
   88 SR-FAIL                     VALUE 'F'.
   -
   -
```

```
PROCEDURE DIVISION.
    -
    EVALUATE SR-LETTER-GRADE
       WHEN SR-EXCELLENT
           DISPLAY 'EXCELLENT WORK!'
       WHEN SR-GOOD
           DISPLAY 'VERY GOOD!'
       WHEN SR-OK
       -
```

> Wrong! You need TRUE or FALSE after EVALUATE for these WHENs

```
    EVALUATE SR-LETTER-GRADE
       WHEN > 'B'
           DISPLAY 'EXCELLENT WORK!'
       WHEN > 'C'
           DISPLAY 'VERY GOOD!'
       -
       -
       -
       -
       -
```

> Wrong! You need literal values, data names, or WHEN ranges when a data name is at EVALUATE

This example is correct:

```
    EVALUATE SR-LETTER-GRADE
       WHEN 'A'
           DISPLAY 'EXCELLENT WORK!'
       WHEN 'B'
           DISPLAY 'VERY GOOD!'
       -
       -
```

> Correct: data-name with a value

This example is also correct:

```
EVALUATE SR-LETTER-GRADE
    WHEN 'A' THRU 'F'
        DISPLAY 'VALID GRADE'
    WHEN OTHER
        DISPLAY 'GRADE NOT VALID'
    -
    -
```

> Correct:
> data-name
> with a
> range

7.15 *TRY IT!* REPLACING IF/ELSE WITH EVALUATE

EVALUATE gives you a way to code decision statements in a compact form. From the foregoing discussion you might think EVALUATE is a snap to use. It can be once you get the hang of it. But interestingly enough, over 50% of the people who try the E2OLDIF conversion exercise (below) in corporate classes I conduct make a mistake on it when they first use EVALUATE! E2OLDIF "reads" data like this from an internal table:

```
JOSE CANSECO       OAKLAND      .307
HANK AARON         BREWERS      .427
TONY FERNANDEZ     BLUE JAYS    .302
INDY PITZ          ??????       .049
JOHNNY RAY         ANGELS       .289
WRATHER B. HOME    ??????       .103
GREGG JEFFRIES     METS         .258
GARY SHEFFIELD     BREWERS      .247
WILL B. GONE       ??????       .160
DWIGHT SMITH       CUBS         .324
```

The fields in each row are baseball player name, team, and batting average (a number from .000 to .999 that indicates how many times the player hits the ball as a percentage of the total number of times the ball is pitched to him). The program interprets each player's batting average using a serial IF/ELSE to associate each batting average with a phrase:

```
IF PR-BATTING-AVG < .050
    DISPLAY 'CHOOSE ANOTHER CAREER'
 ELSE
IF PR-BATTING-AVG < .150
    DISPLAY 'BACK TO THE MINOR LEAGUES?'
 ELSE
IF PR-BATTING-AVG < .200 ...
```

The output from E2OLDIF is listed after it in Figure 7.8. Your task: replace the IF/ELSE in E2OLDIF with an EVALUATE statement, renaming the program E2EVAL. Use a data name after the word EVALUATE. *Try it!*

```
000100 IDENTIFICATION DIVISION.
000200 PROGRAM-ID.     E2OLDIF.
000300 AUTHOR.         J. JANOSSY.
000400*
000500*REMARKS.        IF/ELSE EXAMPLE FOR YOU TO CONVERT TO EVALUATE.
000600*                ROWS ARE TAKEN FROM A TABLE TO SIMULATE
000700*                RECORDS BEING READ IN A SIMPLE WAY.
000800*
000900 ENVIRONMENT DIVISION.
001000*
001100 DATA DIVISION.
001200 WORKING-STORAGE SECTION.
001300 01  WS-SUB               PIC 9(2)   VALUE 0.
001400 01  WS-DATA-TABLE-SETUP.
001500     05 FILLER  PIC X(29)  VALUE 'JOSE CANSECO    OAKLAND   307'.
001600     05 FILLER  PIC X(29)  VALUE 'HANK AARON      BREWERS   427'.
001700     05 FILLER  PIC X(29)  VALUE 'TONY FERNANDEZ  BLUE JAYS 302'.
001800     05 FILLER  PIC X(29)  VALUE 'INDY PITZ       ??????    049'.
001900     05 FILLER  PIC X(29)  VALUE 'JOHNNY RAY      ANGELS    289'.
002000     05 FILLER  PIC X(29)  VALUE 'WRATHER B. HOME ??????    103'.
002100     05 FILLER  PIC X(29)  VALUE 'GREGG JEFFRIES  METS      258'.
002200     05 FILLER  PIC X(29)  VALUE 'GARY SHEFFIELD  BREWERS   247'.
002300     05 FILLER  PIC X(29)  VALUE 'WILL B. GONE    ??????    160'.
002400     05 FILLER  PIC X(29)  VALUE 'DWIGHT SMITH    CUBS      324'.
002500 01  WS-DATA-TABLE  REDEFINES  WS-DATA-TABLE-SETUP.
002600     05 WS-DATA-ROW  OCCURS 10 TIMES.
002700        10 WS-NAME-AND-TEAM         PIC X(26).
002800        10 WS-BATTING-AVG           PIC V999.
002900 01  PLAYER-RECORD.
003000     05 PR-NAME-AND-TEAM            PIC X(26).
003100     05 PR-BATTING-AVG              PIC .999.
003200 01  BATTING-AVG-9                  PIC V999.
003300/
003400 PROCEDURE DIVISION.
003500 0000-MAINLINE.
003600     DISPLAY 'DAVE''S PLAYER RATING PROGRAM STARTING'.
003700     PERFORM 1000-PLAYER-RATING
003800        VARYING WS-SUB FROM 1 BY 1
003900           UNTIL WS-SUB > 10.
004000     STOP RUN.
004100*
004200 1000-PLAYER-RATING.
004300     MOVE WS-NAME-AND-TEAM(WS-SUB)  TO PR-NAME-AND-TEAM.
004400     MOVE WS-BATTING-AVG(WS-SUB)    TO PR-BATTING-AVG
004500                                       BATTING-AVG-9.
004600     DISPLAY '-------------------------------------------'.
004700     DISPLAY PLAYER-RECORD.
004800*
004900     IF BATTING-AVG-9 < .050
005000        DISPLAY 'CHOOSE ANOTHER CAREER'
005100     ELSE
005200     IF BATTING-AVG-9 < .150
005300        DISPLAY 'BACK TO THE MINOR LEAGUES?'
005400     ELSE
005500     IF BATTING-AVG-9 < .200
005600        DISPLAY 'VERY SHAKY FUTURE'
005700     ELSE
005800     IF BATTING-AVG-9 < .250
005900        DISPLAY 'POSSIBLE TRADE IN THE NEAR FUTURE?'
006000     ELSE
006100     IF BATTING-AVG-9 < .270
006200        DISPLAY 'AVERAGE BATTER'
006300     ELSE
006400     IF BATTING-AVG-9 < .299
006500        DISPLAY 'A PROMISING FUTURE !'
006600     ELSE
006700     IF BATTING-AVG-9 < .349
006800        DISPLAY 'ALL STAR !!'
006900     ELSE
007000        DISPLAY 'SUPER HOT STUFF !!!!'.
```

Figure 7.8 *Try It!* Replace the IF/ELSE With an EVALUATE.

Output:

```
DAVE'S PLAYER RATING PROGRAM STARTING
-------------------------------------------
JOSE CANSECO    OAKLAND   .307
ALL STAR !!
-------------------------------------------
HANK AARON      BREWERS   .427
SUPER HOT STUFF !!!
-------------------------------------------
TONY FERNANDEZ  BLUE JAYS .302
ALL STAR !!
-------------------------------------------
INDY PITZ       ??????    .049
CHOOSE ANOTHER CAREER
-------------------------------------------
JOHNNY RAY      ANGELS    .289
A PROMISING FUTURE !
-------------------------------------------
WRATHER B. HOME ??????    .103
BACK TO THE MINOR LEAGUES?
-------------------------------------------
GREGG JEFFRIES  METS      .258
AVERAGE BATTER
-------------------------------------------
GARY SHEFFIELD  BREWERS   .247
POSSIBLE TRADE IN THE NEAR FUTURE?
-------------------------------------------
WILL B. GONE    ??????    .160
VERY SHAKY FUTURE
-------------------------------------------
DWIGHT SMITH    CUBS      .324
ALL STAR !!
```

Figure 7.8 *Continued*

This program uses a serial IF/ELSE to interpret batting averages and associate a phrase with each. The "data records" to be processed are stored in a table for convenience and pulled out row-by-row with a PERFORM . . . VARYING and a subscript. EVALUATE is not hard to use. But over 50% of the personnel in corporate training classes I conduct make a mistake using it the first time, because of the variations possible! Consult the syntax reference chart in Figure 7.7 when you try to convert the IF/ELSE in lines 4900 thru 7000 to an EVALUATE!

7.16 *TRY IT!* EVALUATE WITH COMPOUND CONDITIONS

EVALUATE supports compound condition testing with the word ALSO. To see how this is used, picture a simple two-condition situation involving a word processing workstation that can be either a microcomputer (a PC manufactured by anybody) or a "dedicated" console made by the XYZ Word Processor Company. You are a manager and must decide whether to buy spell checking software for the machine (and if so, where) or to dispose of the machine if it's broken.

Figure 7.9 depicts the cases involved in your decision about PCs and word processing software. Figure 7.10, which lists the source code for program E3EVAL, shows you how you could code an EVALUATE to do the necessary decision-making. As with a single-condition EVALUATE, only one of the WHEN outcomes will receive control. If none of the WHEN outcomes is appropriate, none of the actions is taken—but this is not regarded as an error by VS COBOL II.

If you code compound conditions in an EVALUATE, the number of selection objects in each WHEN has to match the number selection subjects after the word "evaluate." You need a corresponding ALSO for every ALSO in the EVALUATE except for WHEN OTHER.

EVALUATE gives you a powerful new tool for decision-making! You can use it with multiple conditions to literally encode decision tables in a compact and reliable way. I've included a *"Try It!"* exercise for you in Figure 7.11 that demonstrates how to program the decision table of Figure 7.3 using EVALUATE. The decision table itself is in the program listing as comments so you don't have to refer back to earlier pages.

In Figure 7.11 I showed you some of the output of E4EVAL, but not all of it. Are you curious about how EVALUATE works with three factors? Run E4EVAL and try it!

	W	B
PC	Buy software from store	Sell it to a fix-it shop
XYZ	Buy software from maker	Send machine to the maker

Figure 7.9   Decision Based on Two Factors.

This chart shows how the manager of an information center might deal with various equipment and software upgrade requirements. Used microcomputers (PCs) can be sold to repair shops if broken (B), or upgraded to word processing workstations by buying appropriate software at any computer store if working (w). Dedicated word processing equipment has to be repaired by its manufacturer if broken or upgraded software has to be acquired only from that manufacturer. The program in Figure 7.10 shows you how to implement this two-factor decision-making using the EVALUATE verb.

```
000100 IDENTIFICATION DIVISION.
000200 PROGRAM-ID.      E3EVAL.
000300 AUTHOR.          J. JANOSSY.
000400*
000500*REMARKS.        DEMONSTRATE EVALUATE WITH COMPOUND CONDITIONS
000600*
000700 ENVIRONMENT DIVISION.
000800*
000900 DATA DIVISION.
001000 WORKING-STORAGE SECTION.
001100 01  WS-SUB                  PIC 9(1)   VALUE 0.
001200 01  WS-DATA-TABLE-SETUP.
001300     05 FILLER               PIC X(5)   VALUE 'PC  W'.
001400     05 FILLER               PIC X(5)   VALUE 'PC  B'.
001500     05 FILLER               PIC X(5)   VALUE 'XYZ W'.
001600     05 FILLER               PIC X(5)   VALUE 'XX  B'.
001700     05 FILLER               PIC X(5)   VALUE 'XYZ B'.
001800     05 FILLER               PIC X(5)   VALUE 'XYZ Q'.
001900     05 FILLER               PIC X(5)   VALUE 'RIP Q'.
002000 01  WS-DATA-TABLE  REDEFINES  WS-DATA-TABLE-SETUP.
002100     05 WS-DATA-ROW  OCCURS 7 TIMES.
002200         10 DATA-TYPE             PIC X(3).
002300         10 FILLER                PIC X(1).
002400         10 DATA-STATUS           PIC X(1).
002500*
002600 01  MACHINE-RECORD.
002700     05 MACHINE-TYPE             PIC X(3).
002800     05 FILLER                   PIC X(1).
002900     05 MACHINE-STATUS           PIC X(1).
003000/
003100 PROCEDURE DIVISION.
003200 0000-MAINLINE.
003300     DISPLAY 'PROGRAM E3EVAL STARTING'.
003400     PERFORM 1000-DECISION
003500         VARYING WS-SUB FROM 1 BY 1
003600             UNTIL WS-SUB > 7.
003700     STOP RUN.
003800*
003900 1000-DECISION.
004000     DISPLAY '-------------------------------------'.
004100     MOVE WS-DATA-ROW(WS-SUB) TO MACHINE-RECORD.
004200     DISPLAY MACHINE-RECORD.
004300*
004400     EVALUATE MACHINE-TYPE  ALSO MACHINE-STATUS
004500         WHEN 'PC'           ALSO 'W'
004600             DISPLAY 'BUY SOFTWARE FROM STORE'
004700         WHEN 'PC'           ALSO 'B'
004800             DISPLAY 'SELL MACHINE TO FIX-IT SHOP'
004900         WHEN 'XYZ'          ALSO 'W'
005000             DISPLAY 'BUY SOFTWARE FROM MAKER'
005100         WHEN 'XYZ'          ALSO 'B'
005200             DISPLAY 'RETURN MACHINE TO MAKER'
005300         WHEN OTHER
005400             DISPLAY 'INVALID MACHINE OR STATUS CODE'
005500     END-EVALUATE.
```

Output:

```
PROGRAM E3EVAL STARTING
---------------------------------------
PC  W
BUY SOFTWARE FROM STORE
---------------------------------------
PC  B
SELL MACHINE TO FIX-IT SHOP
---------------------------------------
XYZ W
BUY SOFTWARE FROM MAKER
---------------------------------------
XX  B
INVALID MACHINE OR STATUS CODE
---------------------------------------
XYZ B
RETURN MACHINE TO MAKER
---------------------------------------
XYZ Q
INVALID MACHINE OR STATUS CODE
---------------------------------------
RIP Q
INVALID MACHINE OR STATUS CODE
```

Figure 7.10 EVALUATE With Two Decision Factors.

I coded the EVALUATE at lines 4400 through 5500 in this program using ALSO to deal with two decision factors (two selection subjects). When you code EVALUATE this way, every WHEN except for OTHER needs to have two selection objects joined by ALSO. Is the output of this program accurate?

```
000100 IDENTIFICATION DIVISION.
000200 PROGRAM-ID.    E4EVAL.
000300 AUTHOR.        J. JANOSSY.
000400*
000500*REMARKS.        DO COMPOUND DECISION WITH 3 FACTORS
000600*                WITH EVALUATE; IMPLEMENT DECISION TABLE:
000700*
000800*    Family history of                          Risk
000900*    heart disease?      Sex        Smoker?      Factor
001000*         N              M             Y           .18
001100*         N              M             N           .01
001200*-------------------------------------------------------
001300*         N              F             Y           .14
001400*         N              F             N           .005
001500*-------------------------------------------------------
001600*         Y              M             Y           .32
001700*         Y              M             N           .03
001800*-------------------------------------------------------
001900*         Y              F             Y           .24
002000*         Y              F             N           .02
002100*
002200 ENVIRONMENT DIVISION.
002300*
002400 DATA DIVISION.
002500 WORKING-STORAGE SECTION.
002600 01  WS-SUB              PIC 9(2) VALUE 0.
002700 01  WS-RISK             PIC Z.999.
002800 01  WS-DATA-TABLE-SETUP.
002900     05 FILLER           PIC X(3)  VALUE 'NMY'.
003000     05 FILLER           PIC X(3)  VALUE 'NMN'.
003100     05 FILLER           PIC X(3)  VALUE '***'.
003200     05 FILLER           PIC X(3)  VALUE 'NFY'.
003300     05 FILLER           PIC X(3)  VALUE 'NFN'.
003400     05 FILLER           PIC X(3)  VALUE 'NM*'.
003500     05 FILLER           PIC X(3)  VALUE 'YMY'.
003600     05 FILLER           PIC X(3)  VALUE 'YMN'.
003700     05 FILLER           PIC X(3)  VALUE 'N*Y'.
003800     05 FILLER           PIC X(3)  VALUE 'YFY'.
003900     05 FILLER           PIC X(3)  VALUE 'YFN'.
004000     05 FILLER           PIC X(3)  VALUE '*MY'.
004100 01  WS-DATA-TABLE  REDEFINES  WS-DATA-TABLE-SETUP.
004200     05 WS-DATA-ROW  OCCURS 12 TIMES.
004300        10 WS-HISTORY          PIC X(1).
004400        10 WS-SEX              PIC X(1).
004500        10 WS-SMOKER           PIC X(1).
004600*
004700 01  IN-DATA.
004800     10 ID-HISTORY             PIC X(1).
004900     10 ID-SEX                 PIC X(1).
005000     10 ID-SMOKER              PIC X(1).
005100/
005200 PROCEDURE DIVISION.
005300 0000-MAINLINE.
005400     DISPLAY 'PROGRAM E4EVAL STARTING'.
005500     PERFORM 1000-DECISION
005600         VARYING WS-SUB FROM 1 BY 1
005700             UNTIL WS-SUB > 12.
005800     STOP RUN.
005900*
006000 1000-DECISION.
006100     DISPLAY '---------------------------------------'.
006200     MOVE WS-DATA-ROW(WS-SUB) TO IN-DATA.
006300     DISPLAY IN-DATA(1:1) ' ' IN-DATA(2:1) ' ' IN-DATA(3:1).
006400*
006500*    This EVALUATE directly implements the decision table.
006600*    Invalid values are given risk 9.999 but could be
006700*    better identified in a data validation process:
006800*
006900     EVALUATE  ID-HISTORY  ALSO ID-SEX  ALSO ID-SMOKER
007000         WHEN 'N'          ALSO 'M'     ALSO 'Y'
007100             MOVE .18 TO WS-RISK
007200         WHEN 'N'          ALSO 'M'     ALSO 'N'
007300             MOVE .01 TO WS-RISK
007400         WHEN 'N'          ALSO 'F'     ALSO 'Y'
007500             MOVE .14 TO WS-RISK
007600         WHEN 'N'          ALSO 'F'     ALSO 'N'
007700             MOVE .005 TO WS-RISK
007800         WHEN 'Y'          ALSO 'M'     ALSO 'Y'
007900             MOVE .32 TO WS-RISK
008000         WHEN 'Y'          ALSO 'M'     ALSO 'N'
008100             MOVE .03 TO WS-RISK
008200         WHEN 'Y'          ALSO 'F'     ALSO 'Y'
008300             MOVE .24 TO WS-RISK
008400         WHEN 'Y'          ALSO 'F'     ALSO 'N'
008500             MOVE .02 TO WS-RISK
008600         WHEN OTHER
008700             MOVE 9.999 TO WS-RISK
008800     END-EVALUATE.
008900*
009000     DISPLAY 'RISK FACTOR IS ', WS-RISK.
```

(a)

(b)

(c)

(d)

Figure 7.11   *(see legend next page)*

Output

```
PROGRAM E4EVAL STARTING
----------------------------------------
N M Y
RISK FACTOR IS  .180
----------------------------------------
N M N
RISK FACTOR IS  .010
----------------------------------------
* * *
RISK FACTOR IS 9.999
----------------------------------------
■
■
■
```

Does it really work?
To find out,

Try It!

Figure 7.11   EVALUATE With Three Decision Factors.

This program uses EVALUATE at lines 6900 through 8800 with two ALSOs to deal with three decision factors. Compare this EVALUATE to the much larger IF/ELSE shown in Figure 7.3, which does the same thing. The coding in the EVALUATE is a literal interpretation of the decision table shown in Figure 7.2 and included as documentation here.

a. I put the decision table into the program as comments for documentation and to save you the bother of referring back to Figure 7.2.

b. The rows of this table represent test data records. The three codes in each "record" represent all combinations of valid and invalid data.

c. This DISPLAY makes use of *reference modification*, a new technique offered by VS COBOL II to reference parts of character fields. I'll show you how to use more reference modification features in Chapter 11.

d. You can code an EVALUATE with three factors literally from a decision table (a). This can tremendously speed your coding while actually improving the reliability and accuracy of your coding! This aspect of EVALUATE is one of the most productivity-boosting features of VS COBOL II.

7.17   CONTINUE AND OTHER IN EVALUATE STATEMENTS

VS COBOL II provides you with two elements of syntax for dealing with special cases. You can code the word CONTINUE at any selection object when you don't want to do anything at that case. You can code OTHER as the "catch all" final case which receives controls if none of the selection objects has been satisfied.

Suppose you have to examine letter grades assigned to students and take special action for only A, B, or F grades. C and D are legitimate grade codes, but let's say that you do not have to take any special action for them. Any character other than A, B, C, D, and F is invalid and requires that you issue an error message. Here is how you could handle this logic requirement using CONTINUE and OTHER in an EVALUATE statement:

```
05 WS-LETTER-GRADE      PIC X(1).
-------------------------------------------
EVALUATE WS-LETTER-GRADE
   WHEN 'A'
     DISPLAY 'EXCELLENT WORK!'
   WHEN 'B'
     DISPLAY 'VERY GOOD!'
   WHEN 'C'
     CONTINUE
   WHEN 'D'
     CONTINUE
   WHEN 'F'
     DISPLAY 'FAILED-TRY AGAIN'
   WHEN OTHER
     DISPLAY '?? UNKNOWN GRADE ??'
END-EVALUATE
```

CONTINUE is similar to NEXT SENTENCE. The difference between CONTINUE and NEXT SENTENCE is easy to remember. CONTINUE branches to the point after the next END- scope delimiter (in this case, END-EVALUATE). NEXT SENTENCE branches to the point after the next period.

You can code OTHER only as the last of your list of selection objects. You always code only one word OTHER, even if you have multiple selection objects in the EVALUATE statement, as I've illustrated in Figures 7.10 and 7.11.

7.18   SYNTAX REFERENCE FOR 88-LEVELS

88-levels are called condition names. Support for 88-levels has not changed from VS COBOL to VS COBOL II but they assume greater significance now because of the capabilities of EVALUATE:

```
01  WS-EOF-FLAG                PIC X(1).
      88 END-OF-FILE                      VALUE 'E'.
      88 MORE-RECORDS-IN-FILE             VALUE 'M'.
```

A condition name becomes "true" when the value associated with it is contained in the field. If you MOVEed 'E' to WS-EOF-FLAG, then END-OF-FILE becomes true:

```
IF WS-EOF-FLAG = 'E'
   PERFORM . . .
```

or

```
IF END-OF-FILE
   PERFORM . . .
```

You can associate more than one value with a given 88-level name. When you do this the 88-level name becomes true when any one of its data values is contained in the field:

```
01  WS-GREGORIAN-DATE.
    05 WS-GDATE-MONTH         PIC X(2).
       88 MONTH-WITH-31-DAYS  VALUES
          '01'  '03'  '05'  '07'  '08'  '10'  '12'.
       88 MONTH-WITH-30-DAYS  VALUES '04' '06' '09' '11'.
       88 MONTH-OF-FEB        VALUE  '02'.
       88 MONTH-VALID         VALUES '01' THRU '12'.
```

With VS COBOL II you must specify 88-level values as numeric if the field they are defined for is numeric, and vice-versa:

```
01  WS-GREGORIAN-DATE-9.
    05 WS-GDATE-MONTH-9       PIC 9(2).
       88 MONTH-WITH-31-DAYS  VALUES  1  3  5  7  8  10  12.
       88 MONTH-WITH-30-DAYS  VALUES  4  6  9  11.
       88 MONTH-OF-FEB        VALUE   2.
       88 MONTH-VALID         VALUES  1 THRU 12.
```

Ranges (with THRU) process more efficiently than lists of values because COBOL uses only two logic tests for a range but constructs a list for discrete values.

7.19 *TRY IT!* USE SET TO CONTROL 88-LEVEL NAMES

In VS COBOL the SET verb controls indexes: it's how you change the value of an index:

```
SET DT-IX TO 1.


SET DT-IX UP BY 1.
```

Under VS COBOL II, SET still manipulates indexes. But now you can also use SET to control the TRUE/FALSE status of 88-level condition names.

Defined below are two typical 88-level condition names. The flag field under which they are defined controls the processing loop in a batch program. You typically affect the value of this flag within the paragraph that does file reading:

```
01  WS-EOF-FLAG             PIC X(1)    VALUE 'M'.
    88 MORE-RECORDS-TO-READ             VALUE 'M'.
    88 END-OF-FILE                      VALUE 'E'.
    -
    PROCEDURE DIVISION.
    -
        READ INPUT-FILE
            AT END
                MOVE 'E' TO WS-EOF-FLAG.
```

With the enhancement of SET provided by VS COBOL II you can now take this action:

```
        READ INPUT-FILE
            AT END
                SET END-OF-FILE TO TRUE.
```

This SET automatically moves the value that makes END-OF-FILE true to the field involved, WS-EOF-FLAG. It leaves 'E' in WS-EOF-FLAG in this case, as shown in Figure 7.12.

SET for 88-level condition names is very significant! This type of SET finally provides the "other half" of syntax that has been missing in 88-level condition name coding. Using this capability you can concentrate on what your logic in the PROCEDURE DIVISION is actually trying to do with flags, rather than on literal code values. This type of coding makes program maintenance much easier and more reliable. It becomes unnecessary for you or another programmer to look back to WORKING-STORAGE when you are trying to follow the logic of a program.

```
000100 IDENTIFICATION DIVISION.
000200 PROGRAM-ID.      E5SET.
000300 AUTHOR.          J. JANOSSY.
000400*
000500*REMARKS.        DEMONSTRATE SET FOR AN 88-LEVEL CONDITION NAME
000600*
000700 ENVIRONMENT DIVISION.
000800*
000900 DATA DIVISION.
001000 WORKING-STORAGE SECTION.
001100 01  WS-EOF-FLAG           PIC X(1)  VALUE 'M'.
001200     88 MORE-RECORDS-TO-READ        VALUE 'M'.
001300     88 END-OF-FILE                 VALUE 'E'.
001400/
001500 PROCEDURE DIVISION.
001600 0000-MAINLINE.
001700     DISPLAY 'PROGRAM E5SET STARTING'.
001800     DISPLAY '----------------------------------'.
001900     DISPLAY 'FLAG VALUE BEFORE SET         = ', WS-EOF-FLAG.
002000     SET END-OF-FILE TO TRUE.
002100     DISPLAY '----------------------------------'.
002200     DISPLAY 'FLAG VALUE AFTER "SET TO TRUE" = ', WS-EOF-FLAG.
002300     DISPLAY '----------------------------------'.
002400     DISPLAY 'PROGRAM ENDING'.
002500     STOP RUN.
```

Output:

```
PROGRAM E5SET STARTING
----------------------------------
FLAG VALUE BEFORE SET         = M
----------------------------------
FLAG VALUE AFTER "SET TO TRUE" = E
----------------------------------
PROGRAM ENDING
```

Figure 7.12 Using SET With 88-Level Condition Names.

You can now use SET as in line 2000 of this program to set the true/false status of a condition name. For example, SET END-OF-FILE TO TRUE automatically moves 'E' to WS-EOF-FLAG. This is much more reliable than having to MOVE a literal value itself. Begin using SET in this way. It can significantly ease and speed program maintenance. Want to make sure this program works? Run it and *Try It!*

If the 88-level condition name has multiple values assigned to it, SET assigns the first of the multiple values to the controlling field. For example, in this case the SET statement causes WS-GDATE-MONTH-9 to assume a value of 4:

```
01  WS-GREGORIAN-DATE-9.
05  WS-GDATE-MONTH-9      PIC 9(2).
        88 MONTH-WITH-31-DAYS   VALUES  1  3  5  7  8  10  12.
        88 MONTH-WITH-30-DAYS   VALUES  4  6  9  11.
        88 MONTH-OF-FEB         VALUE   2.
        88 MONTH-VALID          VALUES  1 THRU 12.
        -
PROCEDURE DIVISION
        -
    SET MONTH-WITH-30-DAYS TO TRUE.
```

8

Tables and Syntax Improvements

VS COBOL II allows you to code much larger programs accessing much larger variables and tables because it supports 31-bit addressing. But VS COBOL II also provides several other significant improvements in table definition and handling. I'll show you all of these in this chapter.

8.1 TABLE SIZE LIMITS EXPANDED

Under VS COBOL a hard-coded table like this could contain at the most 131,070 bytes:

```
01  CODE-TABLE-SETUP.
    05 FILLER    PIC X(12)  VALUE  'F FRESHMAN  '.
    05 FILLER    PIC X(12)  VALUE  'S SOPHOMORE '.
    05 FILLER    PIC X(12)  VALUE  'J JUNIOR    '.
    05 FILLER    PIC X(12)  VALUE  'R SENIOR    '.
    05 FILLER    PIC X(12)  VALUE   G GRADUATE  '.
*
01  CODE-TABLE  REDEFINES  CODE-TABLE-SETUP.
    05 CT-ROW  OCCURS 5 TIMES  INDEXED BY CT-IX.
       10 CT-CODE       PIC X(1).
       10 FILLER        PIC X(1).
       10 CT-NAME       PIC X(10).
```

A hard-coded table is a table in which the contents are coded within the program. The row length (12 here) times the number of rows (nnn) tells

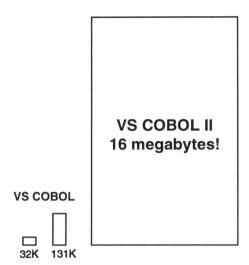

Figure 8.1   Difference in VS COBOL and VS COBOL II Table Support.

VS COBOL II allows all tables to be as large as 16 megabytes. VS COBOL could support only "hard-coded" tables of 131K bytes or less and allowed tables to be only a maximum of 32K bytes if you used the "OCCURS DEPENDING ON" ("ODO") option as in runtime-loaded tables.

how many bytes the table contains. This table contains only 5 x 12 = 60 bytes.

   The "opposite" of a hard-coded table is a runtime-loaded table. In a runtime-loaded table you don't code the contents in FILLER lines in your source code, so your table definition does not REDEFINE anything. Instead, you read in the rows of the table from a file when the program starts running. You keep track of how many rows you have loaded using a field such as WS-COUNT. This is a runtime-loaded table:

```
01  WS-COUNT          PIC S9(4)  COMP  VALUE +0.
01  CODE-TABLE.
    05 CT-ROW  OCCURS 1 TO 5 TIMES
               DEPENDING ON WS-COUNT
               INDEXED BY CT-IX.
       10 CT-CODE      PIC X(1).
       10 FILLER       PIC X(1).
       10 CT-NAME      PIC X(10).
```

Runtime-loading gives you more flexibility since many programs can use the same table data. You can house the table rows as records in a file that can be updated on-line. But under VS COBOL a runtime-loaded table (also sometimes called a "variable length table" or a dynamically-loaded table) was limited to only 32,767 bytes of data content.

As Figure 8.1 shows, the size limit of tables with VS COBOL II is huge by comparison to VS COBOL. Both hardcoded (OCCURS nnn TIMES) and variable length (OCCURS 1 TO nnn TIMES DEPENDING ON . . .) tables can now contain as much as 16,777,215 bytes! A maximum size table would typically exist like this:

```
01  WS-ROW-COUNT           PIC S9(4)  COMP   VALUE +0.
01  CODE-TABLE-SETUP.
    05 FILLER   PIC X(12)  VALUE  'F FRESHMAN  '.
    05 FILLER   PIC X(12)  VALUE  'S SOPHOMORE '.
    05 FILLER   PIC X(12)  VALUE  'J JUNIOR    '.
    -
    -
*
01  CODE-TABLE  REDEFINES  CODE-TABLE-SETUP.
    05 CT-ROW  OCCURS 1 TO 1398101 TIMES
            DEPENDING ON WS-ROW-COUNT
            INDEXED BY CT-IX.
       10 CT-CODE     PIC X(1).
       10 FILLER      PIC X(1).
       10 CT-NAME     PIC X(10).
```

The value nnn in the OCCURS nnn TIMES in a fixed-length table can be as large as 16,777,215. This means that at one extreme a table like this is possible:

```
01  WS-VALUE  OCCURS 16777215 TIMES  PIC X(1).
```

The expanded table size limits are one of the most important improvements of VS COBOL II. They free you from the tricky coding that you had to do in VS COBOL to split large tables into parts.

8.2 YOU CAN NOW USE VALUE ON A TABLE DEFINITION

VS COBOL does not let you code VALUE on any field that has an OCCURS clause or on any field under it. VS COBOL II does let you do this:

```
01  DATA-TABLE.
    05 DATA-ROW   OCCURS 1 TO 10000 TIMES
                     DEPENDING ON WS-ROW-COUNT
                     INDEXED BY DR-IX.
        10 DATA-ALPHA          PIC X(3)   VALUE 'ABC'
        10 DATA-NUMERIC        PIC 9(4)   VALUE 9870.
        10 FILLER             PIC X(1)   VALUE SPACE.
        10 DATA-NO-VALUE       PIC 9(7).
```

When you code VALUE on a field within a table, all occurrences of it are given the value. In the coding above, all 10,000 occurrences of DATA-ALPHA carry the value 'AAA' due to the VALUE 'AAA' clause on it. To get this result under VS COBOL you had to code a loop:

```
PROCEDURE DIVISION.
    -
    MOVE SPACES TO DATA-TABLE.
    PERFORM 1000-TABLE-INIT
        VARYING DR-IX FROM 1 BY 1
           UNTIL DR-IX > 10000.
*
    1000-TABLE-INIT.
       MOVE 'AAA' TO DATA-ALPHA(DR-IX).
       MOVE 9870 TO DATA-NUMERIC(DR-IX).
```

Using a loop like this now is unnecessary and inefficient. When you use the VALUE approach the compiler does all of the work (once) in establishing and loading the table. But initializing with a loop consumes resources every time the program runs, and there's a chance you or someone doing program maintenance may make a mistake in doing it!

8.3 *TRY IT!* VALUE AND RELATIVE SUBSCRIPTING/INDEXING

VS COBOL II supports access to fields with a variation on literal and nonliteral subscripting and indexing. Here is a simple table:

```
WORKING-STORAGE SECTION.
01  WS-SUB        PIC S9(4)  COMP VALUE +0.
01  CODE-TABLE-SETUP.
    05 FILLER     PIC X(12)  VALUE 'F FRESHMAN  '.
    05 FILLER     PIC X(12)  VALUE 'S SOPHOMORE '.
    05 FILLER     PIC X(12)  VALUE 'J JUNIOR    '.
    05 FILLER     PIC X(12)  VALUE 'R SENIOR    '.
    05 FILLER     PIC X(12)  VALUE 'G GRADUATE  '.
*
01  CODE-TABLE  REDEFINES  CODE-TABLE-SETUP.
    05 CT-ROW  OCCURS 5 TIMES  INDEXED BY CT-IX.
       10 CT-CODE  PIC X(1).
       10 FILLER   PIC X(1).
       10 CT-NAME  PIC X(10).
```

These are all legitimate ways to access rows in this table:

```
PROCEDURE DIVISION
    -
    MOVE +2 TO WS-SUB.
    MOVE CT-NAME(2) TO . . .              Literal subscripting
    MOVE CT-NAME(WS-SUB) TO . . .         Nonliteral subscripting
    MOVE CT-NAME(WS-SUB + 1) TO . . .     Relative subscripting
    -
    SET CT-IX TO 2.
    MOVE CT-NAME(CT-IX) TO . . .          Ordinary indexing
    MOVE CT-NAME(CT-IX + 1) TO . . .      Relative indexing
```

Relative subscripting and relative indexing act as if a computation had been done before the statement where you use it. The subscript or index is *not* changed in value. The subscript or index value that results from your relative reference has to be within the bounds of the table or it may cause an abend.

Figure 8.2 shows you the complete source code for a small program named F1TABLE. You can actually enter F1TABLE into your system and run it to demonstrate for yourself how VS COBOL II handles very large tables, allows VALUE under an OCCURS clause, and permits relative subscripting and indexing. (If you have acquired the version of this book provided with a diskette, you can upload F1TABLE and try it without the bother of entering source code manually.)

8.4 LOOKUP TABLES

Figure 8.3 (page 151) shows you a sketch of a cruise ship operated by the Miracle Pleasure Cruise Company. ("If you like the cruise, it's a Miracle.") I'm going to use this as a focal point to explain differences between VS COBOL and VS COBOL II in table lookup.

A passenger ship has several decks. Each of these decks has a common name. When a ship is used to transport tourists, the cost of the ticket is usually based on the deck on which the tourist's cabin is located. The higher the deck the more desirable it is since higher decks are farther away from the noise of the ship's engines.

Let's suppose a program needs to process data about tickets purchased for passage on a ship. Each ticket could carry information such as this:

```
01  TICKET-RECORD.
    05 TR-KEY          PIC X(5).        A unique identifier
    05 TR-NAME         PIC X(25).       Passenger name
    05 TR-CRUISE-DATE  PIC X(6).        Date the ship leaves
    05 TR-DECK-CODE    PIC X(2).        Deck of the passenger's room
    05 . . . other information
```

When reports are to be produced, a table is needed to look up ship's deck codes and supply the name and cost factor for each deck. Some decks have discounted cost factors relative to deck C (the main deck), which is rated at 100% of the quoted cost of passage. Other higher decks carry a premium over the deck C price:

```
01  DECK-TABLE-SETUP.
    05 FILLER PIC X(37) VALUE 'B  BRIDGE DECK    400'.
    05 FILLER PIC X(37) VALUE 'B1 BOAT DECK      330'.
    05 FILLER PIC X(37) VALUE 'B2 PROMENADE DECK 285'.
    05 FILLER PIC X(37) VALUE 'S  SHELTER DECK   215'.
```

```
000001  000100 IDENTIFICATION DIVISION.
000002  000200 PROGRAM-ID.    F1TABLE.
000003  000300 AUTHOR.        J. JANOSSY.
000004  000400*
000005  000500*REMARKS.       DEMONSTRATE MAJOR VS COBOL II TABLE SIZE
000006  000600*               AND SYNTAX IMPROVEMENTS
000007  000700*
000008  000800 ENVIRONMENT DIVISION.
000009  000900*
000010  001000 DATA DIVISION.
000011  001100 WORKING-STORAGE SECTION.
000012  001200 01  WS-SUB          PIC 9(5)    VALUE 0.
000013  001300 01  WS-ROW-COUNT    PIC 9(5)    VALUE 0.
000014  001400*
000015  001500*      Here is table that consumes 180,000 bytes of memory.
000016  001600*      VS COBOL would gag on this table; Try it! But
000017  001700*      VS COBOL II accepts this table and even microcomputer
000018  001800*      1985 COBOL compilers easily handle it!
000019  001900*
000020  002000 01  DATA-TABLE.
000021  002100 05  DATA-ROW    OCCURS 1 TO 10000 TIMES                     13
000022  002200              DEPENDING ON WS-ROW-COUNT
000023  002300              INDEXED BY DR-IX.
000024  002400      10  DATA-ALPHA      PIC X(3)    VALUE 'XYZ'.
000025  002500      10  DATA-NUMERIC    PIC 9(4)    VALUE 1234.
000026  002600      10  FILLER          PIC X(1)    VALUE SPACE.
000027  002700      10  DATA-NO-VALUE   PIC 9(11).
000028  002800/
000029  002900 PROCEDURE DIVISION.
000030  003000 0000-MAINLINE.                                              IMP
000031  003100      DISPLAY 'PROGRAM F1TABLE STARTING'.
000032  003200      DISPLAY 'SOME TABLE CONTENTS BEFORE LOOP INITIALIZATION:'.
000033  003300      DISPLAY 'ROW 00001 = ', DATA-ROW(1).                   21
000034  003400      MOVE 4400 TO WS-SUB.                                   12
000035  003500      DISPLAY 'ROW 04400 = ', DATA-ROW(WS-SUB).              21  12
000036  003600      DISPLAY 'ROW + 82 = ', DATA-ROW(WS-SUB + 82).          21  12
000037  003700      DISPLAY 'ROW 09000 = ', DATA-ROW(9000).                21
000038  003800      DISPLAY 'ROW 10000 = ', DATA-ROW(10000).               21
000039  003900*
000040  004000      PERFORM                                               23
000041  004100          VARYING DR-IX FROM 1 BY 1                          23
000042  004200 1        UNTIL DR-IX > 10000                                27  23  23
000043  004300              SET DATA-NO-VALUE(DR-IX) TO DR-IX
000044  004400      END-PERFORM.
000045  004500*
000046  004600      DISPLAY 'SOME TABLE CONTENTS AFTER LOOP INITIALIZATION:'.
000047  004700      SET WS-ROW-COUNT TO DR-IX.                             13  23
000048  004800      DISPLAY 'WS-ROW-COUNT = ', WS-ROW-COUNT.               13
```

a

b

148

```
000049        004900     DISPLAY 'ROW 00001 = ', DATA-ROW(1).
000050        005000     MOVE 4400 TO WS-SUB.
000051        005100     DISPLAY 'ROW 04400 = ', DATA-ROW(WS-SUB).
000052        005200     DISPLAY 'ROW  + 82 = ', DATA-ROW(WS-SUB + 82).
000053        005300     DISPLAY 'ROW 09000 = ', DATA-ROW(9000).
000054        005400     DISPLAY 'ROW 10000 = ', DATA-ROW(10000).
000055        005500     DISPLAY 'PROGRAM ENDING'.
000056        005600     STOP RUN.
   . .
```

Output:

```
PROGRAM F1TABLE STARTING
SOME TABLE CONTENTS BEFORE LOOP INITIALIZATION:
ROW 00001 = XYZ1234
ROW 04400 = XYZ1234
ROW  + 82 = XYZ1234
ROW 09000 = XYZ1234
ROW 10000 = XYZ1234
SOME TABLE CONTENTS AFTER LOOP INITIALIZATION:
WS-ROW-COUNT = 10001
ROW 00001 = XYZ1234  00000000001
ROW 04400 = XYZ1234  00000004400
ROW  + 82 = XYZ1234  00000004482
ROW 09000 = XYZ1234  00000009000
ROW 10000 = XYZ1234  00000010000
PROGRAM ENDING
```

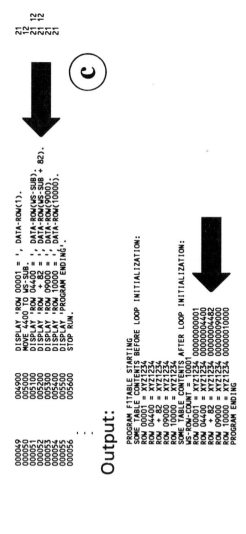

Figure 8.2 *Try It!* Demonstrating VS COBOL II Table Features.

Program F1TABLE defines a table 190K in size with the OCCURS DEPENDING ON option. You can see here how to use several important VS COBOL II table handling features.

a. You can now code VALUE on field definitions listed under an OCCURS clause. This is a much more efficient way than a loop to initialize all occurrences of a field. All 10,000 occurrences of DATA-NUMERIC automatically assume the value 1234 due to VALUE 1234 on its definition.

b. This loop accomplishes an initialization not possible with VALUE. It puts the row number of each table row into each DATA-NO-VALUE field. This field will be different in each table row.

c. Line 005200 shows you an example of *relative subscripting*. The subscript value 4482 is computed and temporarily stored to be used in accessing the table. But the value of WS-SUB does not change due to the reference (WS-SUB + 82). You can also do *relative indexing* in the same way.

149

```
05 FILLER PIC X(37) VALUE 'S1 FREEBOARD DECK 155'.
05 FILLER PIC X(37) VALUE 'C  MAIN DECK       100'.
05 FILLER PIC X(37) VALUE 'C1 LOWER DECK      085'.
05 FILLER PIC X(37) VALUE 'C2 ORLOP DECK      076'.
*
01 DECK-TABLE REDEFINES DECK-TABLE-SETUP.
   05 DECK-TABLE-ROW   OCCURS 8 TIMES
                       INDEXED BY DT-IX.
      10 DT-DECK-CODE      PIC X(2).
      10 FILLER            PIC X(1)
      10 DT-DECK-NAME      PIC X(14).
      10 FILLER            PIC X(1).
      10 DT-FACTOR         PIC 9V99.
```

8.5 VS COBOL II SEARCH AND SEARCH ALL

The discussion above covers a table named DECK-TABLE. We created it to be able to look up ship deck codes and find the corresponding deck name and cost factor. To do a table lookup, VS COBOL II still provides the SEARCH and SEARCH ALL verbs. SEARCH still performs sequential access while SEARCH ALL still does a binary search, as illustrated in Figure 8.4.

Let's assume that WS-COST-FACTOR and WS-DECK-NAME are two fields in memory into which we want to put the appropriate factor and name looked up in the table. The SEARCH verb provides a sequential search. It starts with the row at which the index is positioned and moves downward row-by-row from there. To get a complete search, you SET the index to 1 beforehand:

```
SET DT-IX TO 1.
SEARCH DECK-TABLE-ROW
   AT END
      MOVE 0     TO WS-COST-FACTOR
      MOVE ALL '*' TO WS-DECK-NAME
   WHEN TR-DECK-CODE = DT-DECK-CODE(DT-IX)
      MOVE DT-DECK-NAME(DT-IX) TO WS-DECK-NAME
      MOVE DT-FACTOR(DT-IX) TO WS-COST-FACTOR.
```

In VS COBOL II as in VS COBOL, SEARCH can manipulate only one dimension of a table. You code the name after SEARCH that carries the OCCURS you want SEARCH to manipulate. But SEARCH is now the

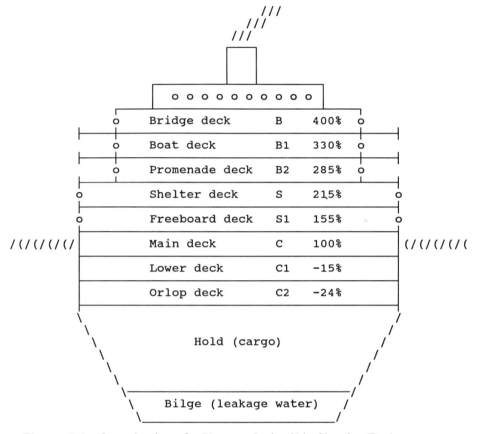

Figure 8.3 Cross Section of a Pleasure Cruise Ship Showing Decks.

The different decks of a pleasure cruise ship have unique names, identifying codes, and pricing factors. In this example the rate for the main deck is used as a base. Passage on decks above it cost a premium to occupy, while passage on decks below it is sold at a discount. Miracle Pleasure Cruise Company, is hypothetical ("If you like the cruise, it's a Miracle") but the need for a lookup table in a situation like this is real.

preferred way to access a table with up to *70 rows*. Up to this limit it is more cost-effective than SEARCH ALL.

SEARCH ALL conducts a binary search of a table. This means that it does not start with the row that the index currently points to but instead starts with the row at the midpoint of the table. SEARCH ALL is faster for large tables but it requires more in table setup coding, using the

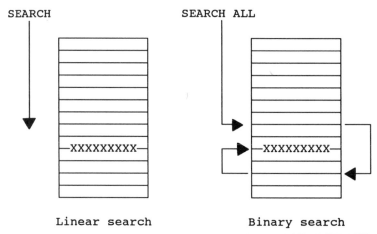

SEARCH   SEARCH ALL

Linear search   Binary search

Figure 8.4   Difference in Action Between SEARCH and SEARCH ALL.

The SEARCH verb begins accessing a table at the first row (if you SET the index to 1 before the SEARCH). SEARCH ALL does a binary search in which it starts in the middle. It quickly "homes in" on the row you seek by repeating this "cut in half" action until it finds the row you seek or it confirms that the row is not present. In VS COBOL II you should use SEARCH for tables with 70 rows or less, and SEARCH ALL for tables larger than 70 rows.

ASCENDING KEY IS clause. The rows of the table have to be in ascending or descending order of "search key." If rows are not in this order, the binary search is "fooled" and some values searched for will not be found, even if they are present in the table.

In VS COBOL II you define a table to be binary searched as in VS COBOL. It is still your responsibility to ensure that the rows actually are in correct sorted sequence, and you must still document what field is the search key:

```
01  DECK-TABLE REDEFINES DECK-TABLE-SETUP.
    05 DECK-TABLE-ROW   OCCURS 8 TIMES
                        INDEXED BY DT-IX
                        ASCENDING KEY IS DT-DECK-CODE.
        10 DT-DECK-CODE    PIC X(2).
        10 FILLER          PIC X(1)
        10 DT-DECK-NAME    PIC X(14).
        10 FILLER          PIC X(1).
        10 DT-FACTOR       PIC 9V99.
```

You still code SEARCH ALL without SETting the index to 1 beforehand, since the binary search will decide for itself to start at the midpoint of the table. But the SEARCH ALL verb now follows an ANSI coding convention. You must now, in all cases, list the field name in the table *first* after WHEN:

```
SET DT-IX TO 1.
SEARCH DECK-TABLE-ROW
    AT END
        MOVE 0       TO WS-COST-FACTOR
        MOVE ALL '*' TO WS-DECK-NAME
    WHEN DT-DECK-CODE(DT-IX) = TR-DECK-CODE    ◄───────
        MOVE DT-DECK-NAME(DT-IX) TO WS-DECK-NAME
        MOVE DT-FACTOR(DT-IX) TO WS-COST-FACTOR.
```

You can code the indexed name first with SEARCH also and it's a good idea to do that. Then if you have to change a SEARCH to a SEARCH ALL, you can save the almost inevitable recompile you'd need to rediscover this data-name placement requirement.

SEARCH ALL always requires VS COBOL II to access a runtime library. This means extra I/O during program execution. This overhead is greater than using a simple SEARCH when a table has less than 70 rows. SEARCH ALL is much more efficient for tables larger than 70 rows.

8.6   TABLE DIMENSIONS

The number of dimensions corresponds to the number of OCCURS clauses in the table definition. The number of dimensions dictates how many subscripts or indexes you need to code within parentheses to access a row or field. Here is an example of a single dimension table:

```
WORKING-STORAGE SECTION.
01  WS-SUB        PIC S9(4)  COMP VALUE +0.
01  CODE-TABLE-SETUP.
        05 FILLER    PIC X(12)  VALUE 'F FRESHMAN  '.
        05 FILLER    PIC X(12)  VALUE 'S SOPHOMORE '.
        05 FILLER    PIC X(12)  VALUE 'J JUNIOR    '.
        05 FILLER    PIC X(12)  VALUE 'R SENIOR    '.
        05 FILLER    PIC X(12)  VALUE 'G GRADUATE  '.
    *
    01  CODE-TABLE REDEFINES CODE-TABLE-SETUP.
        05 CT-ROW  OCCURS 5 TIMES INDEXED BY CT-IX.
            10 CT-CODE            PIC X(1).
            10 FILLER             PIC X(1).
            10 CT-NAME            PIC X(10).
```

Table row ─────────── 05 CT-ROW OCCURS 5 TIMES INDEXED BY CT-IX.

Fields in the table row

This definition carries one OCCURS clause so it has one dimension. (It's easy to mistakenly think of it as two-dimensional since you picture the coding as rows and columns, but the columns are really fields in rows.) Accessing either one entire table row or one field within the row requires the use of one subscript or index:

```
MOVE CT-ROW(3) TO . . .        moves 12 bytes
MOVE CT-CODE(3) TO . . .       moves 1 byte
MOVE CT-NAME(3) TO . . .       moves 10 bytes
```

A table definition with two OCCURS clauses (one nested within the other) is a two-dimension table. Figure 8.5 illustrates such a table.

VS COBOL supports tables of up to three dimensions. VS COBOL II supports tables with up to *seven* dimensions. Here is an example of the definition for a maximum-dimension table:

```
01  COMPLEX-TABLE.
    05 CT-MAIN OCCURS 4 TIMES.
       10 CT-ONE-DOWN OCCURS 10 TIMES.
          15 CT-TWO-DOWN OCCURS 5 TIMES.
             20 CT-THREE-DOWN OCCURS 7 TIMES.
                25 CT-FOUR-DOWN OCCURS 9 TIMES.
                   30 CT-FIVE-DOWN OCCURS 6 TIMES.
                      35 CT-SIX-DOWN OCCURS 8 TIMES.
                         40 CT-DATA-CODE PIC X(2).
                         40 CT-DATA-VALUE PIC 9(5).
```

To access a given data value in such a complex table, you need to code a corresponding number of subscripts or indexes:

```
MOVE CT-DATA-VALUE(1,2,3,4,5,6,7) TO . . .
```

You will probably never experience a need for such a large quantity of table dimensions. Even tables of two dimensions cause problems in program maintenance.

8.7 *TRY IT!* SUBSCRIPT/INDEX VALIDITY CHECKING WITH SSRANGE

The VS COBOL II compiler is smart enough to produce an error message and a return code of 0008 for literal subscripts of negative or zero value. But it can't check nonliteral (data name) subscript or index values until you run a program, because nonliteral subscripts and indexes don't re-

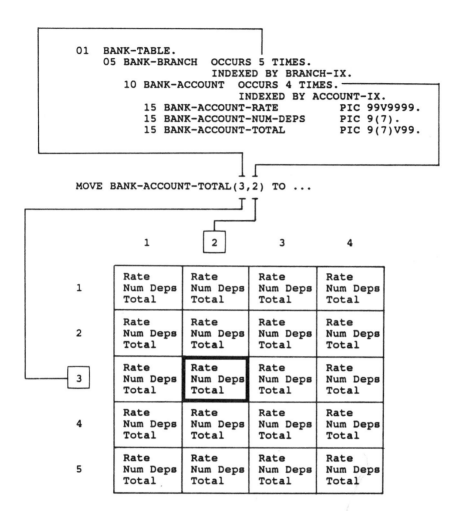

```
01  BANK-TABLE.
    05 BANK-BRANCH  OCCURS 5 TIMES.
                    INDEXED BY BRANCH-IX.
       10 BANK-ACCOUNT   OCCURS 4 TIMES.
                         INDEXED BY ACCOUNT-IX.
          15 BANK-ACCOUNT-RATE        PIC 99V9999.
          15 BANK-ACCOUNT-NUM-DEPS    PIC 9(7).
          15 BANK-ACCOUNT-TOTAL       PIC 9(7)V99.
```

MOVE BANK-ACCOUNT-TOTAL(3,2) TO ...

MOVE BANK-ACCOUNT-TOTAL(3,2) TO ...

Figure 8.5   A Two-Dimension Table in VS COBOL II.

VS COBOL II supports tables of up to seven dimensions. A table has as many dimensions as its definition has OCCURS clauses. The first OCCURS defines the row and the second OCCURS defines the column. Beyond three dimensions it becomes difficult to imagine a physical representation of a table, but high-dimension tables are valid mathematically. You need as many subscripts or indexes to access a field as you have OCCURS clauses above it.

ceive values until runtime. If a subscript or index carries a value out-of-bounds of the table, you may successfully access "garbage" within the memory address of your program. Or you may stray outside of the memory addresses assigned to your program and abend with an OC4 system completion code. What do you think will happen with this example?

```
01  WS-SUB                  PIC 9(2).
01  DATA-TABLE.
    05 DATA-ROW  OCCURS 10 TIMES
              INDEXED BY DR-IX.
       10 DR-CHARACTERS      PIC X(2)  VALUE '*'.
       10 DR-ALPHA           PIC X(1)  VALUE '*'.
     -
     -
PROCEDURE DIVISION.
     -
    MOVE 0 TO WS-SUB.
    DISPLAY 'TABLE ROW 0  = ', DATA-ROW(WS-SUB).
    DISPLAY 'TABLE ROW 2  = ', DATA-ROW(2).
    MOVE 39 TO WS-SUB.
    DISPLAY 'TABLE ROW 39 = ', DATA-ROW(WS-SUB).
```

With VS COBOL II you can request and receive subscript and index error checking at runtime by using the SSRANGE compile option. You can code SSRANGE on a PROCESS statement before the IDENTIFICATION DIVISION or make it active using the JCL that executes your compile and link procs.

If you compile with the SSRANGE option, subscript and index range checking will occur when the compiled program executes. If the program tries to access a table with a subscript or index value that is out-of-bounds (out of the address range of the table), the run will terminate with an error message.

I wrote program F2TABLE so that you could experiment with the SSRANGE option. Figure 8.6 lists the source code and run results for F2TABLE, which actually tries to do an out-of-bounds table access. I did not use SSRANGE for this run, and it did not fail. Instead, you see garbage DISPLAYed for non-existent rows 0 and 39!

Figure 8.7 shows you how the same program F2TABLE is processed with the SSRANGE option. You now get another new user abend code, U1006, and a message buried in your system print as shown in the top part of Figure 8.7.

Try It! Copy (or upload) and run program F2TABLE yourself to duplicate the results shown in Figures 8.6 and 8.7. Then change the code so that you set DR-IX to zero, or to 39, and change lines 3400 and 3700 to SET DR-IX instead of WS-SUB. Run your modified F2TABLE a third and fourth time with and without SSRANGE.

8.8 WHY SSRANGE DOESN'T ALWAYS WORK

SSRANGE can help you in debugging a program. If you get a 0C4 error, you can recompile the program with this option and see if the compiler can help you pinpoint the problem. But SSRANGE produces best results with tables of one dimension.

SSRANGE only checks to see if the address computed from a set of subscripts is within the address range of the entire table. If a table has two dimensions, SSRANGE doesn't do adequate checking. In the two-dimension table that follows, for example, you should only access rows with subscripts no greater than (5,4):

```
01  BANK-TABLE.
    05 BANK-BRANCH OCCURS 5 TIMES.
        10 BANK-ACCOUNT OCCURS 4 TIMES PIC 9(7)V99
    -
    -
PROCEDURE DIVISION.
    -
    MOVE BANK-ACCOUNT(5,4) TO . . .
```

Here the BANK-BRANCH subscript should not exceed 5 and the BANK-ACCOUNT subscript should not exceed 4. The final data address computed by VS COBOL II in this case is $5 \times 4 = 20$, which is in the address range of the table. But if you coded this it would represent a logical error:

```
01  WS-SUB1        PIC 9(2).
01  WS-SUB2        PIC 9(2).
-
PROCEDURE DIVISION.
-
-
    MOVE 1 TO WS-SUB1.
    MOVE 10 TO WS-SUB2.
    MOVE BANK-ACCOUNT(1,10) TO . . .
```

Yet the address computed here by VS COBOL II is $1 \times 10 = 10$. This is within the address range of the table but it is not correct. The program will not fail but you will access the wrong row in the table. *SSRANGE will not catch this kind of problem!*

```
EDIT ---- A1092JJ.LIB.JCL(F2TABLE) - 01.00 ---------------- COLUMNS 001 072
COMMAND ===>                                                SCROLL ===> PAGE
****** *********************************** TOP OF DATA *******************************
000001 //A1092JJA JOB (1092,COB2),'JANOSSY',CLASS=A,MSGCLASS=X,
000002 //          NOTIFY=A1092JJ
000003 //*
000004 //*   THIS JCL = A1092JJ.LIB.JCL(F2TABLE)
000005 //*
000006 //STEPA    EXEC COB2UCLG,
000007 //PARM.COB2=('NOADV',
000008 //          'NOCMPR2',
000009 //          'DATA(31)',
000010 //          'DYN',
000011 //          'FASTSRT',
000012 //          'LANGUAGE(UE)',
000013 //          'NUMPROC(PFD)',
000014 //          'NOMAP',
000015 //          'FDUMP',
000016 //          'NOSSRANGE',       <=== SSRANGE is not to be active
000017 //          'NOVBREF')
000018 //COB2.SYSIN DD DSN=A1092JJ.LIB.COBOL(F2TABLE),DISP=SHR
000019 //GO.SYSOUT DD SYSOUT=*
000020 //
```

```
J E S 2   J O B   L O G  --  S Y S T E M   G I S A  --  N O D E   G I S A N J E

19.32.05 JOB 2610 IEF097I A1092JJA - USER A1092JJ ASSIGNED
19.32.06 JOB 2610 IEF677I WARNING MESSAGE(S) FOR JOB A1092JJA ISSUED
19.32.06 JOB 2610 $HASP373 A1092JJA STARTED - INIT 2 - CLASS A - SYS GISA - DATE 92126
19.32.16 JOB 2610 IEF403I A1092JJA - STARTED - TIME=19.32.06
19.32.16 JOB 2610
```

| | | | | | TIMINGS | | | SERV | PG | PAGING COUNTS | | | |
-JOBNAME	STEPNAME	PROCSTEP	RC	EXCP	CPU	SRB	CLOCK			PAGE	SWAP	VIO	SWAPS
-A1092JJA	STEPA	COB2	04	390	.30	.03	.1	7668	1	0	0	0	1
-A1092JJA	STEPA	LKED	00	180	.10	.02	.1	2758	1	0	0	0	2
-A1092JJA	STEPA	GO	00	13	.03	.00	.0	537	1	0	0	0	0

```
19.32.16 JOB 2610
19.32.23 JOB 2610
19.32.24 JOB 2610
19.32.24 JOB 2610 IEF404I A1092JJA - ENDED
19.32.24 JOB 2610 -A1092JJA ENDED.  NAME-JANOSSY      TOTAL CPU TIME=    .43  TOTAL ELAPSED TIME=   .3
19.32.24 JOB 2610 $HASP395 A1092JJA ENDED

----- JES2 JOB STATISTICS -----
05 MAY 92 JOB EXECUTION DATE
     20 CARDS READ
    347 SYSOUT PRINT RECORDS
      0 SYSOUT PUNCH RECORDS
     20 SYSOUT SPOOL KBYTES
   0.31 MINUTES EXECUTION TIME
```

(a)

(b)

```
000001 000100 IDENTIFICATION DIVISION.
000002 000200 PROGRAM-ID.    F2TABLE.
000003 000300 AUTHOR.        J. JANOSSY.
000004 000400*
000005 000500*REMARKS.       DEMONSTRATE TABLE OUT-OF-BOUNDS PROBLEM
000006 000600*               WITH AND WITHOUT VS COBOL II SSRANGE OPTION
000007 000700*
000008 000800 ENVIRONMENT DIVISION.
000009 000900*
000010 001000 DATA DIVISION.
000011 001100 WORKING-STORAGE SECTION.
000012 001200 01  WS-SUB                          PIC 9(2).
000013 001300 01  DATA-TABLE.
000014 001400   05  DATA-ROW   OCCURS 10 TIMES
000015 001500                    INDEXED BY DR-IX.
000016 001600     10  DR-CHARACTERS        PIC X(2)  VALUE ' *'.
000017 001700     10  DR-NUMBER            PIC 9(3)  VALUE 0.
000018 001800/
000019 001900 PROCEDURE DIVISION.
000020 002000 0000-MAINLINE.
000021 002100   DISPLAY 'PROGRAM F2TABLE STARTING'.
000022 002200   DISPLAY ' '.
000023 002300   DISPLAY 'TABLE AT START  = ', DATA-TABLE.          13
000024 002400*
000025 002500   PERFORM
000026 002600     VARYING DR-IX FROM 1 BY 1                        15
000027 002700     UNTIL DR-IX > 10                                 15
000028 002800   1 SET DR-NUMBER(DR-IX) TO DR-IX                    17 15 15
000029 002900   END-PERFORM.
000030 003000*
000031 003100   DISPLAY 'TABLE AFTER LOAD = ', DATA-TABLE.         13
000032 003200   DISPLAY 'TABLE ROW 6  = ', DATA-ROW(6).            14
000033 003300   DISPLAY 'TABLE ROW 2  = ', DATA-ROW(2).            14
000034 003400   MOVE 0 TO WS-SUB.                                  12
000035 003500   DISPLAY 'TABLE ROW 0  = ', DATA-ROW(WS-SUB).       14 12
000036 003600   DISPLAY 'TABLE ROW 8  = ', DATA-ROW(8).            14
000037 003700   MOVE 39 TO WS-SUB.                                 12
000038 003800   DISPLAY 'TABLE ROW 39 = ', DATA-ROW(WS-SUB).       14 12
000039 003900   DISPLAY ' '.
000040 004000   DISPLAY 'PROGRAM ENDING'.
000041 004100   STOP RUN.
. . .
```

Figure 8.6 (see legend on page 161)

PROGRAM F2TABLE STARTING

TABLE AT START   = *000 *000 *000 *000 *000 *000 *000 *000 *000 *000
TABLE AFTER LOAD = *001 *002 *003 *004 *005 *006 *007 *008 *009 *010
TABLE ROW 6 = *006
TABLE ROW 2 = *002
TABLE ROW 0 = *....
TABLE ROW 8 = *008
TABLE ROW 39 = *.....

PROGRAM ENDING

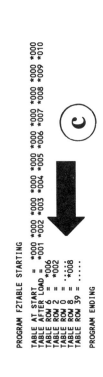

Output when viewed in hexadecimal with SDSF "set hex on" command:

```
SDSF OUTPUT DISPLAY A1092JUA JOB 2610  DSID  102 LINE 24   COLUMNS 02- 81
COMMAND INPUT ===>  set hex on                             SCROLL ===> PAGE
-------------------------------------------------------------------------------
PROGRAM F2TABLE STARTING
DDDCDD4CFECCDC4EECDECDC44444444444444444444444444444444444444444444444444
79679140623123502319595700000000000000000000000000000000000000000000

TABLE AT START   = *000 *000 *000 *000 *000 *000 *000 *000 *000 *000
ECCDC4CE4EECDE4447445FFF45FFF45FFF45FFF45FFF45FFF45FFF45FFF44444444444444
3123501302319300E00C0000C000C000C000C000C000C000C000C000C0100000000000000

TABLE AFTER LOAD = *001 *002 *003 *004 *005 *006 *007 *008 *009 *010
ECCDC4CCED4DDCC47445FFF45FFF45FFF45FFF45FFF45FFF45FFF45FFF44444444444444
3123501635903614 0E00C0010C0020C0030C0040C0050C0060C0070C0080C0090C0100

TABLE ROW 6  = *006
ECCDC4DDE4F4447445FFF4444444444444444444444444444444444444444444444444444
3123509660600600E00C006000000000000000000000000000000000000000000000

TABLE ROW 2  = *002
ECCDC4DDE4F4447445FFF4444444444444444444444444444444444444444444444444444
3123509660200E00C002000000000000000000000000000000000000000000000000

TABLE ROW 0  = *008
ECCDC4DDE4F4474D0000[    ]44444444444444444444444444444444444444444444444
3123509660000E0[    ]00000000000000000000000000000000000000000000000

TABLE ROW 8  = *008
ECCDC4DDE4F4447445FFF4444444444444444444444444444444444444444444444444444
3123509660800800E00C008000000000000000000000000000000000000000000000

TABLE ROW 39 = *.....
ECCDC4DDE4F4F45F2400444444444444444444444444444444444444444444444444444444
3123509660390E0C206000000000000000000000000000000000000000000000000000

PROGRAM ENDING
DDDCDD4CDCDC44444444444444444444444444444444444444444444444444444444444444
79679140554957000000000000000000000000000000000000000000000000000000
-------------------------------------------------------------------------------
```

F2TABLE when compiled and run under Micro Focus COBOL (note: no abend!):

```
PROGRAM F2TABLE STARTING

TABLE AT START    =   *000 *000 *000 *000 *000 *000 *000 *000 *000 *000
TABLE AFTER LOAD  =   *001 *002 *003 *004 *005 *006 *007 *008 *009 *010
TABLE ROW 6  =  *006
TABLE ROW 2  =  *002
TABLE ROW 0  =
TABLE ROW 8  =  *008
TABLE ROW 39 = AFTER          (Note: The out-of-bound table access happens to get some literals from line 31!)

PROGRAM ENDING
```

F2TABLE when compiled and run under Ryan McFarland RM/COBOL-85 (it abends):

```
PROGRAM F2TABLE STARTING

TABLE AT START    =   *000 *000 *000 *000 *000 *000 *000 *000 *000 *000
TABLE AFTER LOAD  =   *001 *002 *003 *004 *005 *006 *007 *008 *009 *010
TABLE ROW 6  =  *006
TABLE ROW 2  =  *002
COBOL data reference error 104 at line 35 in F2TABLE (C:\RMCOB85\F2TABLE.COB)
compiled 92/05/05 20:05:12
```

Figure 8.6 Out-of-Bounds Table Access Doesn't Always Produce an 0C4!

Program F2TABLE intentionally tries to access row 0 and row 39 in a table that has only 10 rows.

a. I didn't activate the SSRANGE option for this compile of F2TABLE. NOSSRANGE is the default on this system I used.

b. F2TABLE executes with a condition code of 0000. Since its out-of-bounds access was not far enough to address memory outside that allocated to the program, the operating system did not "see" a memory violation.

c. The output produced by F2TABLE shows garbage accessed at row 0 and row 39.

d. Turn hexadecimal display on in SDSF with the SET HEX ON command (ordinary HEX ON does not work in SDSF!).

e. If you compile and run program F2TABLE with the Micro Focus microcomputer compiler you get this result.

f. If you compile and run program F2TABLE with the Ryan McFarland RM/COBOL-85 microcomputer compiler you get this.

161

Panel (a):

```
EDIT ---- A1092JJ.LIB.JCL(F2TABLE) - 01.01 ---------------- COLUMNS 001 072
COMMAND ===>                                                 SCROLL ===> PAGE
****** **************************** TOP OF DATA ****************************
000001 //A1092JA  JOB (1092,COB2),'JANOSSY',CLASS=A,MSGCLASS=X,
000002 //         NOTIFY=A1092JJ
000003 //*
000004 //*      THIS JCL = A1092JJ.LIB.JCL(F2TABLE)
000005 //*
000006 //STEPA    EXEC COB2UCLG,
000007 //  PARM.COB2=('NOADV',
000008 //         'NOCMPR2',
000009 //         'DATA(31)',
000010 //         'DYN',
000011 //         'FASTSRT',
000012 //         'LANGUAGE(UE)',
000013 //         'NUMPROC(PFD)',
000014 //         'NOMAP',
000015 //         'FDUMP',
000016 //         'SSRANGE',      <=== Now uncommented, so SSRANGE is on!
000017 //         'NOVBREF')',
000018 //*
000019 //COB2.SYSIN  DD  DSN=A1092JJ.LIB.COBOL(F2TABLE),DISP=SHR
000020 //GO.SYSOUT   DD  SYSOUT=*
```

Panel (b):

```
          J E S 2   J O B   L O G  --  S Y S T E M   G I S A  --  N O D E   G I S A N J E

19.32.28  JOB 2623  IEF097I A1092JJA - USER A1092JJ ASSIGNED
19.32.28  JOB 2623  IEF677I WARNING MESSAGE(S) FOR JOB A1092JJA ISSUED
19.32.29  JOB 2623  $HASP373 A1092JJA STARTED - INIT 2 - CLASS A - SYS GISA - DATE 92126
19.32.29  JOB 2623  IEF403I A1092JJA - STARTED - TIME=19.32.29
                                                 --- TIMINGS ---           --- PAGING COUNTS ---
19.32.39  JOB 2623  -JOBNAME STEPNAME PROCSTEP  RC  EXCP  CPU  SRB  CLOCK  SERV  PG  PAGE  SWAP  VIO  SWAPS
19.32.39  JOB 2623  -A1092JJA STEPA   COB2      04  398   .32  .03   .1    7920  0   0     0     0    1
19.32.39  JOB 2623
19.32.44  JOB 2623  -A1092JJA STEPA   LKED      00  185   .10  .02   .0    2831  1   0     0     0    0
19.32.44  JOB 2623  +IGZ006I The reference to table 'DATA-ROW' by verb number '01' on line
19.32.44  JOB 2623  +        '000035' addressed an area outside the region of the table.
19.32.44  JOB 2623  IEA995I SYMPTOM DUMP OUTPUT
                      USER COMPLETION CODE=1006
                      TIME=19.32.43 SEQ=07598 CPU=0000 ASID=0019
                      PSW AT TIME OF ERROR  078D1000  80029286  ILC 2  INTC 0D
                        ACTIVE LOAD MODULE=IGZCPCO   ADDRESS=00029058  OFFSET=0000022E
                        DATA AT PSW  00029280 - 00181610  0A0D47F0  C0EC4820
                        GPR 0-3   80000000  800003EE  000003EE  000441A4
                        GPR 4-7   00043DF8  80014A6C  800441B0  FFFFFFFB
                        GPR 8-11  80006E14  80014A6C  0002E2EC  0002E878
                        GPR 12-15 80029280  000430B0  8002920A  8001B1A0
                      END OF SYMPTOM DUMP
19.32.50  JOB 2623  +IGZ057I An ABEND was intercepted by the COBOL execution time ABEND
19.32.50  JOB 2623  +        handler.  It is described by a corresponding IEA995I message.
19.32.50  JOB 2623  IEF450I A1092JJA GO STEPA - ABEND=S000 U1006 REASON=00000000
19.32.50  JOB 2623  -        TIME=19.32.50
19.32.50  JOB 2623  -A1092JJA STEPA   GO        U1006  62  .22  .01   .1    4324  1   0     0     0    1
19.32.51  JOB 2623  IEF404I A1092JJA - ENDED - TIME=19.32.51
19.32.51  JOB 2623  -A1092JJA ENDED.  NAME-JANOSSY       TOTAL CPU TIME=   .64  TOTAL ELAPSED TIME=   .3
```

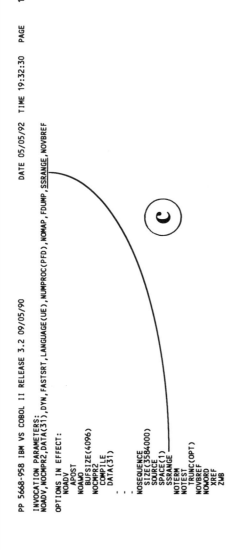

```
PP 5668-958 IBM VS COBOL II RELEASE 3.2 09/05/90          DATE 05/05/92  TIME 19:32:30   PAGE   1

INVOCATION PARAMETERS:
NOADV,NOCMPR2,DATA(31),DYN,FASTSRT,LANGUAGE(UE),NUMPROC(PFD),NOMAP,FDUMP,SSRANGE,NOVBREF

OPTIONS IN EFFECT:
    NOADV
        APOST
    NOAWO
        BUFSIZE(4096)
    NOCMPR2
        COMPILE
        DATA(31)
    -
    -
    NOSEQUENCE
        SIZE(5584000)
        SOURCE
        SPACE(1)
        SSRANGE
    NOTERM
    NOTEST
        TRUNC(OPT)
    NOVBREF
        XREF
        ZWB
```

c

Figure 8.7 Out-of-Bounds Table Access Caught by SSRANGE.
When program F2TABLE is compiled with the SSRANGE option it can detect out-of-bounds accesses.

a. I have activated the SSRANGE option via my compile/link/go execution JCL. You can also activate SSRANGE by using a PROCESS statement at the beginning of the program.

b. Execution of F2TABLE produces an abend with user abend code U1006. Notice that buried in the job log is the text of the message related to this code, IGZ006I, related to the abend code by the last three digits of the code. The message points to LINEID 35 (not the COBOL line number, which is 003500 here) as the point of abend.

c. OPTIONS IN EFFECT confirms that the SSRANGE option is active.

163

```
000001 000100 IDENTIFICATION DIVISION.
000002 000200 PROGRAM-ID.    F2TABLE.
000003 000300 AUTHOR.        J. JANOSSY.
000004 000400*
000005 000500*REMARKS.       DEMONSTRATE TABLE OUT-OF-BOUNDS PROBLEM
000006 000600*               WITH AND WITHOUT VS COBOL II SSRANGE OPTION
000007 000700*
000008 000800 ENVIRONMENT DIVISION.
000009 000900*
000010 001000 DATA DIVISION.
000011 001100 WORKING-STORAGE SECTION.
000012 001200 01 WS-SUB                      PIC 9(2).
000013 001300 01 DATA-TABLE.
000014 001400    05 DATA-ROW  OCCURS 10 TIMES
000015 001500               INDEXED BY DR-IX.
000016 001600       10 DR-CHARACTERS         PIC X(2)  VALUE ' *'.
000017 001700       10 DR-NUMBER             PIC 9(3)  VALUE 0.
000018 001800/
000019 001900 PROCEDURE DIVISION.
000020 002000 0000-MAINLINE.
000021 002100    DISPLAY 'PROGRAM F2TABLE STARTING'.
000022 002200    DISPLAY ' '.
000023 002300    DISPLAY 'TABLE AT START = ', DATA-TABLE.                13
000024 002400*
000025 002500    PERFORM
000026 002600       VARYING DR-IX FROM 1 BY 1                            15
000027 002700       UNTIL DR-IX > 10                                    15
000028 002800       SET DR-NUMBER(DR-IX) TO DR-IX                    17 15 15
000029 002900    END-PERFORM.
000030 003000*
000031 003100    DISPLAY 'TABLE AFTER LOAD = ', DATA-TABLE.             13
000032 003200    DISPLAY 'TABLE ROW 6 = ', DATA-ROW(6).                 14
000033 003300    DISPLAY 'TABLE ROW 2 = ', DATA-ROW(2).                 14
000034 003400    MOVE 0 TO WS-SUB.                                      12
000035 003500    DISPLAY 'TABLE ROW 0 = ', DATA-ROW(WS-SUB).         14 12
000036 003600    DISPLAY 'TABLE ROW 8 = ', DATA-ROW(8).                 14
000037 003700    MOVE 39 TO WS-SUB.                                  12 12
000038 003800    DISPLAY 'TABLE ROW 39 = ', DATA-ROW(WS-SUB).        14 12
000039 003900    DISPLAY 'PROGRAM ENDING'.
000040 004000    STOP RUN.
000041 004100
```

d

164

--- VS COBOL II ABEND Information ---

Program = 'F2TABLE' compiled on '05/05/92' at '19:32:30'
  TGT = '03103028'

No files were used in this program.

Contents of base locators for working storage are:
  0-00043E88

Contents of base locators for the linkage section are:
  0-00000000

No variably located areas were used in this program.

No EXTERNAL data was used in this program.

Contents of indexes are:
  1-00000032

--- End of VS COBOL II ABEND Information ---

(e)

--- VS COBOL II Formatted Dump at ABEND ---

```
Program = 'F2TABLE'
Completion code = 'U1006'
```

PSW at ABEND = '078D100080029286'

The ABEND address was outside of mainline COBOL code.

Optimization was in effect for this program.

The relative address of the next instruction to be executed:

'FCF284C6'

```
The GP registers at entry to ABEND were
  Regs 0 - 3  : '80000000  800003EE  000003EE  00441A4'
  Regs 4 - 7  : '0004430F8  80014A6C  000441B0  FFFFFFB'
  Regs 8 - 11 : '80006E14  80014A6C  000052EC  0002E878'
  Regs 12 - 15: '800291AA  00043080  8002920A  8001B1A0'
```

(f)

Figure 8.7 *Continued*

d. LINEID 35 is the first place I try to do an out-of-bounds access, to table row zero; no such row exists.

e. The out-of-bounds access detected by SSRANGE causes a "user abend" and I get this ABEND information.

f. FDUMP "formatted dump" information includes the repetition of the user abend code, U1006.

165

```
Data Division dump of 'F2TABLE'
000012 01 F2TABLE.WS-SUB 99
         DISP ===>00

000013 01 F2TABLE.DATA-TABLE AN-GR
000014 02 F2TABLE.DATA-ROW AN-GR
000015 00 F2TABLE.DR-IX IX
              ===>11
000016 03 F2TABLE.DR-CHARACTERS XX
              SUB(1)
         DISP ===>*
              SUB(2)
         DISP ===>*
              SUB(3)
         DISP ===>*
              SUB(4)
         DISP ===>*
              SUB(5)
         DISP ===>*
              SUB(6)
         DISP ===>*
              SUB(7)
         DISP ===>*
000017 03 F2TABLE.DR-NUMBER 999
              SUB(1)
         DISP ===>001
              SUB(2)
         DISP ===>002
              SUB(3)
         DISP ===>003
              SUB(4)
         DISP ===>004
              SUB(5)
         DISP ===>005
              SUB(6)
         DISP ===>006
              SUB(7)
--- End of VS COBOL II Formatted Dump at ABEND ---
```

```
PROGRAM F2TABLE STARTING

TABLE AT START  = *000 *000 *000 *000 *000 *000 *000 *000 *000 *000
TABLE AFTER LOAD = *001 *002 *003 *004 *005 *006 *007 *008 *009 *010
TABLE ROW 6 = *006
TABLE ROW 2 = *002
```

Figure 8.7 *Continued*

g. FDUMP "formatted dump" information includes the contents of each field in each row of the table.

h. Only partial output is produced by program F2TABLE. The last line of output here was produced just before the abend.

8.9 SSRANGE, NOSSRANGE, AND EFFICIENCY

SSRANGE makes the compiler produce a program that runs much more slowly than it would without the option. It works by CALLing a library routine for each subscript or index check at runtime. This can create a very large amount of extra I/O when a program is run.

You can shut off SSRANGE at the time you run a program by passing it what is known as a "runtime" PARM. You specify a runtime PARM on the EXEC statement that invokes a program. For example, a program named ABCD1234 is normally executed this way using MVS JCL:

```
//STEP010 EXEC PGM=ABCD1234
```

To shut off a runtime option like SSRANGE (assuming you had compiled the program with the option on) you code execute it:

```
//STEP010 EXEC PGM=ABCD1234,PARM='/NOSSRANGE'
```

If program ABCD1234 was coded to expect a user PARM value, the slash separates the user PARM from the runtime PARM. For example, suppose ABCD1234 had a LINKAGE SECTION that expected to receive a Gregorian date from the EXEC statement. You could code your JCL EXEC like this to pass user PARM '091591' to the program as well as pass VS COBOL II runtime PARM 'NOSSRANGE' to the runtime environment:

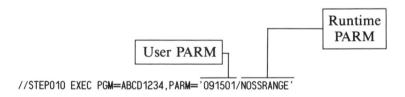

```
//STEP010 EXEC PGM=ABCD1234,PARM='091501/NOSSRANGE'
```

Since / separates user and runtime PARMs you can never use the slash itself as part of a user PARM value.

You can't turn on an option like SSRANGE that was off at compile time. You can't, for example, turn on SSRANGE at compile time to help debug a production program that was not compiled with SSRANGE.

9

Numeric Handling Differences

VS COBOL II gives you new numeric capabilities including the de-editing of formatted numbers (numbers as printed) into computable form. But it also perpetuates some of the weaknesses of arithmetic imprecision that plagued VS COBOL. And under the guise of flexibility, VS COBOL II also introduces some complexity into the treatment of number representation. I show you the important aspects of these changes here.

9.1 NEW WAYS TO CODE COMP-3 AND COMP

In Chapter 5, I showed you a new way to code packed decimal numbers. These two definitions now accomplish the same thing:

```
01  WS-MONEY-VAL      PIC S9(5)V99  COMP-3  VALUE +0.
```

or

```
01  WS-MONEY-VAL      PIC S9(5)V99  PACKED-DECIMAL  VALUE +0.
```

They define a seven digit number with an implied decimal point, stored in four bytes of memory. Each digit requires four bits, and the sign of the number requires four bits. Packed decimal remains the best way to store and work with dollars and cents and most other numeric values because it economizes on memory, disk, and tape space:

This is how VS COBOL II stores a PIC S9(5)V99 number when it
contains positive 98,765.32 (each box represents one byte of
memory):

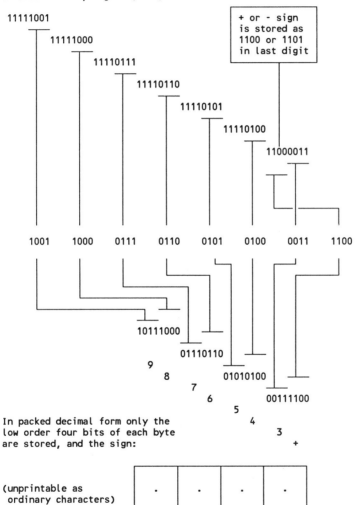

In actual binary digits (bits):

In packed decimal form only the
low order four bits of each byte
are stored, and the sign:

(unprintable as
 ordinary characters)

Packed decimal also continues to be the way that the System/390 and ES-9000 machines actually do arithmetic. If you define numbers as PIC 9(nn) or PIC S9(nn) without making them packed decimal, the system has to do more work to convert them to packed decimal before doing computations with them.

You can now define pure binary fields in either of these ways:

```
01 WS-COUNT          PIC S9(4) COMP VALUE +0.
```

or

```
01 WS-COUNT          PIC S9(4) BINARY VALUE +0.
```

Binary fields continue to be useful only for subscripts or other integer values. They are very efficient but still require alignment on a "word boundary," which occurs every four bytes. 01 levels always start on a word boundary. At other levels you should code SYNC to synchronize a binary field on a word boundary:

```
01 WS-COUNTS.
    05 WS-COUNT-1   PIC S9(4) BINARY  SYNC  VALUE +0.
    05 WS-COUNT-2   PIC S9(4) BINARY  SYNC  VALUE +0.
    05 WS-COUNT-3   PIC S9(4) BINARY  SYNC  VALUE +0.
```

Binary fields store numbers in "base 2" form. This can accurately represent whole numbers (integers). *But binary storage cannot accurately represent numbers to the right of a decimal point.* This coding is possible but you should never use it:

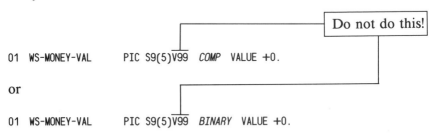

```
                                            Do not do this!

01  WS-MONEY-VAL     PIC S9(5)V99 COMP  VALUE +0.

or

01  WS-MONEY-VAL     PIC S9(5)V99 BINARY VALUE +0.
```

9.2   SPEEDING UP YOUR CALCULATIONS

To make your number handling as efficient as possible in VS COBOL II, define your internal (WORKING-STORAGE) fields as PACKED-DECIMAL. Design your files so that packed decimal fields are used to store number values. You'll also enhance efficiency if you understand and abide by a few other simple factors.

VS COBOL II calculations are faster on fields that have an equal quantity of digits to the right of the decimal point. To the extent that you can arrange it, code fields to make this situation occur.

Some VS COBOL II arithmetic operations are slower than others. Addition and subtraction (+ −) are the fastest operations. Then comes multiplication (*), then division (/), and lastly exponentiation (**). Don't let the concern for processing efficiency dominate your thinking to the point where you implement calculations unclearly. But where you have a choice, keep the efficiency of operations in mind. For example, to double a number, addition is much better:

```
ADD WS-FIELD TO WS-FIELD              Best
COMPUTE WS-FIELD = WS-FIELD * 2       Inefficient
```

To compute the square of a number, multiplication is much better than exponentiation:

```
COMPUTE WS-FIELD = WS-FIELD * WS-FIELD     Best
COMPUTE WS-FIELD = WS-FIELD ** 2           Terrible!
```

Exponentiation in VS COBOL II is particularly slow because it requires loading of a library routine. Avoid it if you can!

9.3   DE-EDITING DURING MOVE

Here is a piece of coding that will shock a programmer accustomed to working in VS COBOL:

```
WORKING-STORAGE SECTION.
01  WS-NUM                  PIC S9(7)V99  COMP-3.
01  WS-NUM-EDITED           PIC Z,ZZ9.99-.
    -
    -
PROCEDURE DIVISION.
    -
    MOVE -1234.56 TO WS-NUM-EDITED.
    MOVE WS-NUM-EDITED TO WS-NUM.
```

How can you move an edited field such as WS-NUM-EDITED, which carries a PIC Z,ZZ9.99- involving leading zero suppression, comma, real period for decimal point, and potentially a hyphen, to a pure number field such as WS-NUM?

This coding is permitted by VS COBOL II Release 3. It's called "de-editing." Editing is the process of making a pure number printable. De-editing is the opposite process: it makes a number already formatted for printing back into a pure number you can compute with. The process even preserves a negative sign if it is present in the edited field.

How can you find de-editing useful? I can think of a few ways:

- Pick apart what is ordinarily print output from a vendor's reporting package to get the data back into machine-readable form. You can take an edited print field from a printline stored as a record and move it to a numeric field. This way, you can do whatever you like with the data—perform further computations, report it differently, and so forth.

- Use de-editing to take data uploaded from a microcomputer database or spreadsheet and change it into a form that can be further processed on the mainframe.

You might also think of using the de-editing feature if you work with CICS and lack a de-editing routine for numeric data entry fields. But your use of de-editing here with CICS will be impractical. De-edit blows up if you give it "bad" data, as I'll show you!

9.4 *TRY IT!* DE-EDITING IN VS COBOL II

Program G1DEEDIT, listed in Figure 9.1, uses the de-editing feature to move a field named WS-NUM-FORMATTED to two numeric receiving fields named WS-NUM and WS-NUM-PACKED. The first such de-editing move is at line 2900 and works fine. The value $12,345.67 is de-edited into both signed and packed receiving fields (although you can't see the contents of the packed decimal receiving field directly in the figure).

The second de-editing move in G1DEEDIT occurs at line 3600, after I have moved the characters 'ABCEDFGHIJK' to the memory occupied by WS-NUM-FORMATTED. (I did this move using a REDEFINES field, since I could not move these contents to a data-name with a numeric edited PIC.)

The second de-editing move causes an abend! Read the legends in Figure 9.1 to see how the user abend messages associated with this abend appear. Unfortunately there is no data class such as "NUMERIC-

EDITED" for you to use to validate the contents of a formatted numeric field before you use a de-editing MOVE in VS COBOL II.

You will be much better off using de-editing MOVEs on microcomputer-based compilers. Both RM/COBOL-85 and Micro Focus COBOL compilers support de-editing, but neither causes an abend when invalid data is present in the numeric formatted field. Programs compiled with RM/COBOL-85 or Micro Focus COBOL and run on a microcomputer simply produce zero as the result in the numeric receiving fields when the formatted field being MOVEd contains invalid data. Here are two reasons why this is important for you to know:

- If you prepare and test a program that uses a de-editing MOVE on a microcomputer, it won't abend with bad data. If you upload the program for compiling and running on your mainframe using VS COBOL II, you *can* abend with bad data!
- As a practical matter, if you need to de-edit microcomputer-produced data and you have access to either RM/COBOL-85 or Micro Focus COBOL, you can do your actual processing on the microcomputer. Then upload the de-edited data to the mainframe.

IBM may enhance support for de-editing in subsequent releases of VS COBOL II so that it does not produce abends for "non de-editable" data. It would be very desirable to see IBM do this!

9.5 COMPUTATIONAL PRECISION AND ACCURACY: NO IMPROVEMENT!

Intermediate fields in a computation have an effect on the accuracy of results. To implement the following simple COMPUTE, the compiler constructs an unseen intermediate field to house the result of the division. It then multiplies this intermediate field by 100:

```
COMPUTE WS-ERROR-PERCENTAGE =
   (WS-RECORDS-WITH-ERROR / WS-TOTAL-RECORDS) * 100.
```

Unfortunately, VS COBOL II still relies on many esoteric rules to figure out how big and how precise intermediate fields should be.

The sad fact is that minicomputer and microcomputer COBOL compilers have for a long time done a much cleaner job in this area. IBM manuals cite the rules to determine how COMPUTE will construct intermediate fields, but these rules are complex and ultimately still leave

(text continues on page 178)

```
10.20.36  JOB 3531   IEF097I A1092JJA - USER A1092JJ ASSIGNED
10.20.37  JOB 3531   IEF677I WARNING MESSAGE(S) FOR JOB A1092JJA ISSUED
10.20.37  JOB 3531   $HASP373 A1092JJA STARTED - INIT 2 - CLASS A - SYS GISA - DATE 92126
10.20.37  JOB 3531   IEF403I A1092JJA STARTED - TIME=10.20.37
10.20.54  JOB 3531
10.20.54  JOB 3531   -                                        --- TIMINGS ---        --- PAGING COUNTS ---
10.20.54  JOB 3531   -JOBNAME STEPNAME PROCSTEP   RC  EXCP   CPU  SRB CLOCK  SERV  PG  PAGE SWAP VIO SWAPS
10.20.54  JOB 3531   -A1092JJA STEPA   COB2       04   375  .30  .04    .2   7465   1     0    0   0     1
10.20.57  JOB 3531
10.20.57  JOB 3531   -A1092JJA STEPA   LKED       00    80  .08  .01    .0   1738   1     0    0   0     0
10.20.59  JOB 3531
10.20.59  JOB 3531
10.20.59  JOB 3531
```

```
+IGZ063I An invalid sign was detected in a numeric edited sending field
+        in 'G1DEDIT' on line number '36'.
IEA995I SYMPTOM DUMP OUTPUT
 USER COMPLETION CODE=1063
 TIME=10.20.59 SEQ=00446 CPU=0000 ASID=0020
 PSW AT TIME OF ERROR  U78DT0DD  80029286  ILC 2  INTC UD
 ACTIVE LOAD MODULE=IGZCPCO   ADDRESS=0029058 OFFSET=0000022E
 DATA AT PSW  00029280 - 00181610 0A0D47F0 C0EC4820
 GPR 0-3   80000000 00000427 00000427 000441BC
 GPR 4-7   000430F8 80014B50 000441C8 FFFFFFE2
 GPR 8-11  80006E14 80014B50 000052EC 0002E878
 GPR 12-15 800291AA 000430B0 8002920A 8001B1A0
END OF SYMPTOM DUMP
```

```
10.21.02  JOB 3531   +IGZ057I An ABEND was intercepted by the COBOL execution time ABEND
10.21.03  JOB 3531   +        handler. It is described by a corresponding IEA995I message.
10.21.03  JOB 3531   IEF450I A1092JJA GO STEPA - ABEND=S000 U1063 REASON=00000000
10.21.03  JOB 3531            TIME=10.21.03
10.21.03  JOB 3531   -A1092JJA STEPA   GO      U1063   97  .24  .01    .0   4843   0     0    0   0     0
10.21.03  JOB 3531
10.21.04  JOB 3531   IEF404I A1092JJA - ENDED - TIME=10.21.04
10.21.04  JOB 3531   -A1092JJA ENDED.  NAME-JANOSSY      TOTAL CPU TIME=   .62  TOTAL ELAPSED TIME=  .4
10.21.04  JOB 3531   $HASP395 A1092JJA ENDED - DATE 92126
10.21.04  JOB 3531
------ JES2 JOB STATISTICS ------
```

```
PP 5668-958 IBM VS COBOL II RELEASE 3.2 09/05/90                  GIDEDIT  DATE 05/05/92  TIME 10:20:39  PAGE  2
LINEID PL SL  ----+*A-1-B--+----2----+----3----+----4----+----5----+----6----+----7-|--+----8  MAP AND CROSS REFERENCE

000001 000100 IDENTIFICATION DIVISION.
000002 000200 PROGRAM-ID.    GIDEDIT.
000003 000300 AUTHOR.        J. JANOSSY.
000004 000400*
000005 000500*REMARKS.       DEMONSTRATE VS COBOL II DE-EDITING
000006 000600*
000007 000700 ENVIRONMENT DIVISION.
000008 000800*
000009 000900 DATA DIVISION.
000010 001000 WORKING-STORAGE SECTION.
000011 001100 01 WS-DISPLAY-LINE.
000012 001200    05 FILLER          PIC X(51) VALUE
000013 001300      'RECEIVING FIELDS AFTER DE-EDIT DURING MOVE: SIGNED:'.
000014 001400    05 WS-NUM          PIC S9(5)V99.
000015 001500    05 FILLER          PIC X(10) VALUE ' PACKED:'.
000016 001600    05 WS-NUM-PACKED   PIC S9(5)V99 PACKED-DECIMAL.
000017 001700*
000018 001800 01 WS-ALPHANUM        PIC X(11).                                          18
000019 001900 01 WS-NUM-FORMATTED   REDEFINES WS-ALPHANUM  PIC $ZZ,ZZZ.99-.
000020 002000/
000021 002100 PROCEDURE DIVISION.
000022 002200 0000-MAINLINE.
000023 002300    DISPLAY 'PROGRAM GIDEDIT STARTING'.
000024 002400*
000025 002500    DISPLAY '----------------------------------------------'.
000026 002600    DISPLAY 'DE-EDIT OF $12,345.67 WORKS:'.
000027 002700    MOVE -12345.67 TO WS-NUM-FORMATTED.                                     19
000028 002800    DISPLAY 'WS-NUM-FORMATTED = ', WS-NUM-FORMATTED.                         19
000029 002900    MOVE WS-NUM-FORMATTED TO  WS-NUM  WS-NUM-PACKED.                         19 14 16
000030 003000    DISPLAY WS-DISPLAY-LINE.                                                 11
000031 003100*
000032 003200    DISPLAY '----------------------------------------------'.
000033 003300    DISPLAY 'DE-EDIT OF "ABCEDFGHIJK" ABENDS:'.
000034 003400    MOVE 'ABCEDFGHIJK' TO WS-ALPHANUM.                                       18
000035 003500    DISPLAY 'WS-NUM-FORMATTED = ', WS-NUM-FORMATTED.                         19
000036 003600    MOVE WS-NUM-FORMATTED TO  WS-NUM  WS-NUM-PACKED.                         19 14 16
000037 003700    DISPLAY WS-DISPLAY-LINE.                                                 11
000038 003800*
000039 003900    DISPLAY '----------------------------------------------'.
000040 004000    DISPLAY 'PROGRAM ENDED NORMALLY'.
000041 004100    STOP RUN.
```

Figure 9.1 *(see legend page 177)*

--- VS COBOL II ABEND Information ---

Program = 'G1DEEDIT' compiled on '05/05/92' at '10:20:39'
    TGT = '03101028'

No files were used in this program.

Contents of base locators for working storage are:
0-00043E88

Contents of base locators for the linkage section are:
0-00000000

No variably located areas were used in this program.

No EXTERNAL data was used in this program.

No indexes were used in this program.

--- End of VS COBOL II ABEND Information ---

This is the result under VS COBOL II (abends; output stops at line 35):

```
PROGRAM G1DEEDIT STARTING
---------------------------------------
DE-EDIT OF $12,345.67- WORKS:
WS-NUM-FORMATTED = $12,345.67-
RECEIVING FIELDS AFTER DE-EDIT DURING MOVE: SIGNED:123456P    PACKED:....
---------------------------------------
DE-EDIT OF "ABCEDFGHIJK"
WS-NUM-FORMATTED = ABCEDFGHIJK
```


As compiled and run under Micro Focus COBOL (does not abend):

```
PROGRAM G1DEEDIT STARTING
---------------------------------------
DE-EDIT OF $12,345.67- WORKS:
WS-NUM-FORMATTED = $12,345.67-
RECEIVING FIELDS AFTER DE-EDIT DURING MOVE: SIGNED:123456W    PACKED:.4V}
---------------------------------------
DE-EDIT OF "ABCEDFGHIJK" ABENDS:
WS-NUM-FORMATTED = ABCEDFGHIJK
RECEIVING FIELDS AFTER DE-EDIT DURING MOVE: SIGNED:0000000    PACKED:....
---------------------------------------
PROGRAM ENDED NORMALLY
```

As compiled and run under Ryan McFarland RM/COBOL-85 (does not abend):

```
PROGRAM G1DEEDIT STARTING
-----------------------------------
DE-EDIT OF $12,345.67- WORKS:
WS-NUM-FORMATTED = $12,345.67-
RECEIVING FIELDS AFTER DE-EDIT DURING MOVE: SIGNED:123456P    PACKED:.4V}

DE-EDIT OF "ABCDEFGHIJK"
WS-NUM-FORMATTED = ABCDEFGHIJK
RECEIVING FIELDS AFTER DE-EDIT DURING MOVE: SIGNED:000000(    PACKED:.....

PROGRAM ENDED NORMALLY
```

Figure 9.1 De-editing in VS COBOL II Abends With Bad Data!

VS COBOL II gives you the ability to de-edit formatted numbers and turn them back into pure computable numbers. The feature works fine, but abends if the formatted field contains invalid characters. Microcomputer COBOL 1985 compilers such as RM/COBOL-85 and Micro Focus do not abend under these conditions and simply produce zero in the receiving field.

a. (Page 174) The de-editing abend produces a message associated with the user return code U1063. The last three digits of this return code point to VS COBOL II runtime error message IGZ063I.

b. (Page 174) Although the abend resulting from trying to de-edit invalid numeric formatted data causes your program to stop, it is not reported with a system completion code but rather with a user return code generated automatically.

c. (Page 175) WS-NUM and WS-NUM-PACKED are two receiving fields. I put them under a group name so I could DISPLAY and see their contents as-is, without any interpretation.

d. (Page 175) The MOVE at line 2900 causes de-editing of WS-NUM-FORMATTED into the numeric receiving fields WS-NUM and WS-NUM-PACKED. If you view the output of this program using TSO/ISPF, you can turn on the "hex" option to see the contents of the packed field, which do not appear in this printer-produced image.

e. (Page 175) The program abends at line 3600 when I try to do a second de-edit. The sending field, WS-NUM-FORMATTED, contains invalid characters since I MOVEd 'ABCDEFGHIJK' to the memory it occupies. This same condition will not cause a program compiled using RM/COBOL-85 or Micro Focus COBOL to abend.

you responsible for the correctness of computations. Even with VS COBOL II you can still be "burned" by the way COMPUTE allocates intermediate fields!

9.6 *TRY IT!* COMPUTE PRECISION PROBLEMS AND SOLUTION

Figure 9.2 lists G2MATH, a simple demonstration of a computation. The program computes a percentage by dividing two numbers and multiplying the result by 100. If you compile, link, and run this program as is using VS COBOL II, it will tell you that the result of this calculation is 20%:

(248 / 1000) * 100 = 20.00 | Result is not correct! |

But the correct answer is 24.8. The program will give you the correct answer *as is* if you compile it using RM/COBOL-85 or Micro Focus COBOL on a microcomputer. Try it with VS COBOL II. You may be shocked!

The presence of low-precision fields like integers on the right side of the equal sign can cause VS COBOL II's COMPUTE verb to develop intermediate fields of too little precision. This can cause a loss of information. This is the same way VS COBOL worked. I had hoped that IBM would correct this situation in producing VS COBOL II. Perhaps IBM will correct this in a future release.

How do you correct this problem using VS COBOL II on the mainframe? You correct it in the same way that was necessary in VS COBOL. As a rule of thumb you should overspecify the precision of the receiving field in any computation that involves integers, such as the one above. Making WS-ERROR-PERCENTAGE have PIC 99V999 instead of PIC 99V9 will do it. If you then want lesser precision, you can compute with rounding as shown in the revised version of G2MATH named G3MATH in Figure 9.3, which also shows you how you should consider using ROUNDING in general.

9.7 VS COBOL II ROUNDING PROBLEMS

VS COBOL II provides the ROUNDED option for COMPUTE and the older ADD, SUBTRACT, MULTIPLY and DIVIDE math verbs. ROUNDING rounds a result up to the next significant digit:

(text continues on page 182)

```
PP 5668-958 IBM VS COBOL II RELEASE 3.2 09/05/90          G2MATH   DATE 05/05/92  TIME 13:09:08  PAGE   2
LINEID PL SL ----+*A-1-B-+----2----+----3----+----4----+----5----+----6----+----7-|--+----8 MAP AND CROSS REFERENCE

000001       000100 IDENTIFICATION DIVISION.
000002       000200 PROGRAM-ID.   G2MATH.
000003       000300 AUTHOR.       J JANOSSY.
000004       000400*
000005       000500*REMARKS.           SHOW PROBLEM IN VS COBOL II COMPUTE PRECISION
000006       000600*
000007       000700*                   THIS PROGRAM WORKS FINE WITH RM/COBOL-85 AND
000008       000800*                   MICRO FOCUS COBOL BUT GIVES THE WRONG ANSWER
000009       000900*                   IN VS COBOL II|
000010       001000*
000011       001100 ENVIRONMENT DIVISION.
000012       001200*
000013       001300 DATA DIVISION.
000014       001400 WORKING-STORAGE SECTION.
000015       001500 01  WS-RECORDS-WITH-ERROR      PIC 9(4).        VALUE 248.
000016       001600 01  WS-TOTAL-RECORDS           PIC 9(4).        VALUE 1000.
000017       001700 01  WS-ERROR-PERCENTAGE        PIC 9(3)V9.
000018       001800 01  OUTPUT-LINE.
000019       001900     05  OL-RECORDS-WITH-ERROR  PIC 9999.                        IMP
000020       002000     05  FILLER                 PIC X(2) VALUE SPACES.
000021       002100     05  OL-TOTAL-RECORDS       PIC 9999.                        IMP
000022       002200     05  FILLER                 PIC X(7) VALUE SPACES.
000023       002300     05  OL-ERROR-PERCENTAGE    PIC ZZ9.99.
000024       002400/
000025       002500 PROCEDURE DIVISION.
000026       002600 0000-MAINLINE.
000027       002700     DISPLAY 'PROGRAM G2MATH STARTING'.
000028       002800     DISPLAY 'ERR TOTAL  Err/Total %'.
000029       002900*
000030       003000     COMPUTE WS-ERROR-PERCENTAGE =                               17
000031       003100        (WS-RECORDS-WITH-ERROR / WS-TOTAL-RECORDS) * 100.        15 16
000032       003200*
000033       003300     MOVE WS-RECORDS-WITH-ERROR  TO  OL-RECORDS-WITH-ERROR.      15 19
000034       003400     MOVE WS-TOTAL-RECORDS       TO  OL-TOTAL-RECORDS.           16 21
000035       003500     MOVE WS-ERROR-PERCENTAGE    TO  OL-ERROR-PERCENTAGE.        17 23
000036       003600*
000037       003700     DISPLAY OUTPUT-LINE.                                        18
000038       003800     STOP RUN.
```

Figure 9.2 *(see legend on page 180)*

179

When compiled and run under VS COBOL II as shown above (result is not accurate!):

```
PROGRAM G2MATH STARTING
ERR  TOTAL  Err/Total %
0248 1000         20.00
```

When compiled and run under Micro Focus COBOL (gives correct result):

```
PROGRAM G2MATH STARTING
ERR  TOTAL  Err/Total %
0248 1000         24.80
```

When compiled and run under Ryan McFarland RM/COBOL-85 (gives correct result):

```
PROGRAM G2MATH STARTING
ERR  TOTAL  Err/Total %
0248 1000         24.80
```

9.2 COMPUTE Continues to Lack Precision in VS COBOL II!

The computation in this program is (248/1000) * 100 but it produces an incorrect result of 20.00 due to the way the VS COBOL II COMPUTE verb creates intermediate fields. In this regard VS COBOL II is no better than VS COBOL. Yet microcomputer compilers like RM/COBOL-85 and Micro Focus COBOL both produce correct results with this code. *If you develop programs on a microcomputer for source code uploading and running on the mainframe, you will have to retest thoroughly on the mainframe!*

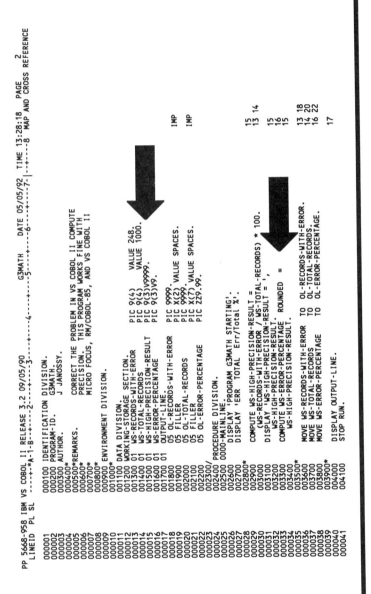

```
000001   000100 IDENTIFICATION DIVISION.
000002   000200 PROGRAM-ID.    G3MATH.
000003   000300 AUTHOR.        J JANOSSY.
000004   000400*
000005   000500*REMARKS.       CORRECT THE PROBLEM IN VS COBOL II COMPUTE
000006   000600*               PRECISION.  THIS PROGRAM WORKS FINE WITH
000007   000700*               MICRO FOCUS, RM/COBOL-85, AND VS COBOL II
000008   000800*
000009   000900 ENVIRONMENT DIVISION.
000010   001000*
000011   001100 DATA DIVISION.
000012   001200 WORKING-STORAGE SECTION.
000013   001300 01  WS-RECORDS-WITH-ERROR        PIC 9(4)     VALUE 248.
000014   001400 01  WS-TOTAL-RECORDS             PIC 9(4)     VALUE 1000.
000015   001500 01  WS-HIGH-PRECISION-RESULT     PIC 9(3)V9999.
000016   001600 01  WS-ERROR-PERCENTAGE          PIC 9(3)V9.
000017   001700 01  OUTPUT-LINE.
000018   001800    05  OL-RECORDS-WITH-ERROR     PIC 9999.                 IMP
000019   001900    05  FILLER                    PIC X(2) VALUE SPACES.
000020   002000    05  OL-TOTAL-RECORDS          PIC 9999.                 IMP
000021   002100    05  FILLER                    PIC X(7) VALUE SPACES.
000022   002200    05  OL-ERROR-PERCENTAGE       PIC ZZ9.99.
000023   002300/
000024   002400 PROCEDURE DIVISION.
000025   002500 0000-MAINLINE.
000026   002600    DISPLAY 'PROGRAM G3MATH STARTING'.
000027   002700    DISPLAY 'ERR TOTAL  Err/Total %'.
000028   002800*
000029   002900    COMPUTE WS-HIGH-PRECISION-RESULT =                      15
000030   003000       (WS-RECORDS-WITH-ERROR / WS-TOTAL-RECORDS) * 100.    13 14
000031   003100    DISPLAY 'WS-HIGH-PRECISION-RESULT = ',                  15
000032   003200    WS-HIGH-PRECISION-RESULT.                               16
000033   003300    COMPUTE WS-ERROR-PERCENTAGE  ROUNDED =                  15
000034   003400    WS-HIGH-PRECISION-RESULT.                               16
000035   003500*
000036   003600    MOVE WS-RECORDS-WITH-ERROR     TO  OL-RECORDS-WITH-ERROR.   13 18
000037   003700    MOVE WS-TOTAL-RECORDS          TO  OL-TOTAL-RECORDS.        14 20
000038   003800    MOVE WS-ERROR-PERCENTAGE       TO  OL-ERROR-PERCENTAGE.     16 22
000039   003900*
000040   004000    DISPLAY OUTPUT-LINE.                                        17
000041   004100    STOP RUN.
```

```
PROGRAM G3MATH STARTING
ERR TOTAL  Err/Total %
WS-HIGH-PRECISION-RESULT = 0248000
0248 1000     24.80
```

Overspecifying precision in the receiving field forces VS COBOL II to do accurate math:

Figure 9.3 How to Code COMPUTE For Accurate Precision and Rounding.

```
01  WS-RESULT                    PIC 999V9.
    -
    -
PROCEDURE DIVISION
    -
   COMPUTE WS-RESULT ROUNDED =
     (WS-VALUE - WS-RATE) / (WS-FACTOR * WS-ADJ).
```

ROUNDED causes the computation to be carried out to one more digit of precision than needed to satisfy the accuracy of the receiving field. If the extra digit is 5 or greater, the last digit is increased by 1.

But what about intermediate fields? COMPUTE will actually generate them and use them for a calculation like that just shown. It has to do this since it must first compute the two separate parts of the expression:

WS-VALUE - WS-RATE   and   WS-FACTOR * WS-ADJ

then do the division of these intermediate results. Does ROUNDED apply to those intermediate fields too?

It is shocking, but it's true. ***In VS COBOL II/ROUNDED causes intermediate fields to be rounded as the computation progresses!*** You might think that ROUNDED applies only to a final result but this is not the case. When a COMPUTE involves many intermediate fields and you specify ROUNDED, all of the intermediate results receive rounding. This is not the way you would do things manually and not the way to achieve accurate results.

You should apply rounding only to the final result in a series of computations so that errors in rounding are minimized. To do this correctly in VS COBOL II you have to do extra work yourself. The most reliable way to avoid problems with a computation that requires rounding of the final result is to:

1. Overspecify precision of the receiving field to force COMPUTE to give you greater intermediate field precision. Don't code ROUNDED on this COMPUTE statement. This will avoid rounding on all the intermediate fields.

2. Round your final result by doing a COMPUTE using ROUNDED:

```
01  WS-FINAL-RESULT          PIC 999V9.
01  WS-MY-RECEIVING FIELD     PIC 999V999.
```

```
   -
   -
PROCEDURE DIVISION.
   -
   COMPUTE WS-MY-RECEIVING-FIELD =
      (WS-VALUE-WS-RATE) / (WS-FACTOR * WS-ADJ).
   COMPUTE WS-FINAL-RESULT ROUNDED =
      WS-MY-RECEIVING-FIELD.
```

You might think that the second COMPUTE is odd since it seems to do something that MOVE could do. But you can't do rounding with MOVE. This is the only convenient way VS COBOL II gives you to get an accurate rounded value into WS-FINAL-RESULT. I have used this technique in Figure 9.3.

You don't need to use this technique when all you are doing is adding up values to compute a sum. But you need to use this technique if you are doing a calculation involving division or multiplication by decimal values.

Incorrect results due to the way VS COBOL II does rounding can seriously damage your credibility. I strongly suggest that you review your current use of ROUNDED and keep VS COBOL II's blanket application of rounding to intermediate fields in mind. If you were inclined to code ROUNDED on a result, use the technique shown here instead!

9.8 CHANGES IN ON SIZE ERROR

The ON SIZE ERROR clause is available for computations to detect if the final result cannot fit into the receiving field:

```
COMPUTE WS-RESULT  =  (WS-VALUE-WS-RATE) / (WS-FACTOR * WS-ADJ)
   ON SIZE ERROR
      PERFORM 3000-PROBLEM.
```

If the result is larger to the left of the decimal point than the receiving field can hold, control will go to 3000-PROBLEM.

VS COBOL II differs from VS COBOL in the way ON SIZE ERROR is applied to MULTIPLY and DIVIDE statements. This difference in operation can lead to different results. If you coded ON SIZE ERROR for MULTIPLY or DIVIDE, VS COBOL always applied error checking to intermediate fields that it generated to handle the computation. VS COBOL II does not apply ON SIZE ERROR to intermediate fields for MULTIPLY and DIVIDE. Its protection is not as complete as that of VS COBOL!

If you have been accustomed to coding ON SIZE ERROR, you should begin to think a bit more about calculating appropriately large field sizes instead. You also need to think about the possibility of inadequate intermediate field sizes and overspecify the precision of the final result field to force intermediate fields to be of adequate size.

ON SIZE ERROR detection works only for high order (left of decimal point) digit loss. If the computation gives you a result that needs to be rounded to fit into the receiving field, your lack of specifying ROUNDED will not cause an ON SIZE ERROR. Without the ROUNDED option, you may chop off (truncate) digits to the right that cannot fit into the receiving field.

9.9 NUMPROC COMPILER OPTION

VS COBOL II produces different machine language instructions to do arithmetic than VS COBOL did. You need to understand what the new NUMPROC option does since it controls arithmetic processing. NUM-PROC also tells the compiler what bit patterns should be regarded as valid signs in a numeric field. This option was called PFDSGN in Release 2 of VS COBOL II and IBM changed its name in Release 3.

9.9.1 NUMPROC(PFD)

NUMPROC(PFD) is the most efficient setting. You should use it for new programs that *do not* process data created by FORTRAN or PL/I programs.

NUMPROC(PFD) indicates that your signed numbers have valid "preferred" numeric signs. These are hexadecimal 'F' for unsigned fields and 'C' (+) or 'D' (−) for signed fields. Signed zero always contains 'C' for a sign. For example, hex '00000F' in a PIC S9(3) PACKED-DECIMAL field is regarded as non-numeric because as a signed field the value of zero should be hex '00000C'.

Unlike the other settings of NUMPROC, PFD never causes instructions to "repair" signs in your data. If a field such as WS-A in Figure 9.4 contains invalid data but you MOVE it to a numeric field, NUMPROC(PFD) does not alter the data. But as you can see in Figure 9.4, other settings of NUMPROC will actually change non-preferred number field signs to preferred signs, repairing your data in ways that you perhaps did not intend!

NUMPROC(PFD) is the most strict setting and has the greatest chance of causing an 0C7 unless you do adequate numeric data class testing with

			Contents in hex
WORKING-STORAGE SECTION.			
01 WS-A	PIC X(3)	VALUE '12X'.	F1F2E7
01 WS-B	PIC 9(3).		
01 WS-C	PIC S9(3)	VALUE -008.	F0F0D8

The way VS COBOL would do it:

1	MOVE WS-C TO WS-B.	WS-B becomes 008	F0F0F8
	MOVE WS-A TO WS-B.	WS-B becomes 127	F1F2F7

VS COBOL II with NUMPROC(PFD):

2	MOVE WS-C TO WS-B.	WS-B becomes 008	F0F0F8
	MOVE WS-A TO WS-B.	WS-B remains 12X	F1F2E7

VS COBOL II with NUMPROC(NOPFD):

3	MOVE WS-C TO WS-B.	WS-B becomes 008	F0F0F8
	MOVE WS-A TO WS-B.	WS-B becomes 127	F1F2F7

VS COBOL II with NUMPROC(MIG):

4	MOVE WS-C TO WS-B.	WS-B becomes 008	F0F0F8
	MOVE WS-A TO WS-B.	WS-B becomes 127	F1F2F7

Figure 9.4 NUMPROC(PFD) Option Is Preferred for New Programs.

The NUMPROC compiler option controls arithmetic logic and recognition of sign bits in numeric fields. VS COBOL would sometimes change sign bits during a MOVE or IF compare, making "non-preferred" signs such as hex 'E' into legitimate numeric signs (turning letters into numbers!). NUMPROC(PFD) overcomes this and generates arithmetic-handling instructions different from VS COBOL—use it for new programs. NUMPROC(NOPFD) generates new arithmetic-handling instructions but accommodates and changes signs as did VS COBOL; I don't recommend that you use it. NUMPROC(MIG) forces VS COBOL II to do exactly the same sign handling and generate the same instructions as VS COBOL. Use (MIG) for program conversions. (The PROCESS statement is handy for setting this type of program-specific compiler PARM option.)

IF ... NUMERIC. NUMPROC(PFD) causes accurate arithmetic processing, but does generate different machine language instructions than VS COBOL did.

9.9.2 NUMPROC(NOPFD)

The NOPFD setting for NUMPROC has the least chance of producing an 0C7 but its processing also differs from that of VS COBOL. NUMPROD(NOPFD) has the greatest potential to cause the sign of a number to be changed from an invalid value to a valid one if the field is involved in a comparison or computation. This can make letters inputted in the last byte of a numeric entry field appear to be numbers. This setting is recommended for reading data produced by FORTRAN or PL/I programs..

NOPFD indicates that your signed numbers may have a sign of 'F' or 'D' or 'C', not just 'C' or 'D'. For example, hex '00000F' in a PIC S9(3) PACKED-DECIMAL field is regarded as valid numeric data by this option. This option repairs the sign bits of a number to make them valid. As you can see in Figure 9.4, hex 'F1F2E7' representing '12X' is changed to hex 'F1F2F7' representing '127' by NUMPROC(NOPFD).

9.9.3 NUMPROC(MIG)

For program conversions, this is your safest option. The MIG setting for NUMPROC allows the same signs as NOPFD and it also generates exactly the same machine language instructions to process numbers as did VS COBOL.

The MIG option may cause the sign of a number to be changed from an invalid value to a valid one if the field is involved in a comparison or computation, just as NOPFD and just as did VS COBOL. For example, X'00000F' in a PIC S9(3) PACKED-DECIMAL field is regarded as numeric by this option. As you can see in Figure 9.4, hex 'F1F2E7' representing '12X' is changed to hex 'F1F2F7' representing '127' by a MOVE when you use the NUMPROC(MIG) setting.

10

User-Defined Data Classes

One of the most significant enhancements of VS COBOL II is the ability to define data classes. Data classes are similar to 88-level condition names and they are optional. But unlike 88-level names, which relate to one field only, a data class relates to all data in the program. Creating a data class is like setting up a universal one-byte 88-level name. Only it's even better, as I'll show you in this chapter!

10.1 ESTABLISHING A USER-DEFINED DATA CLASS

You establish user-defined data classes at the SPECIAL-NAMES paragraph in the CONFIGURATION SECTION of the ENVIRONMENT DIVISION. Once established, a given data class applies to the entire program.

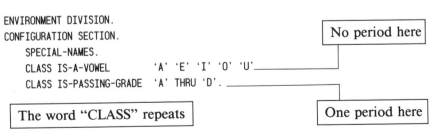

```
ENVIRONMENT DIVISION.
CONFIGURATION SECTION.                    No period here
    SPECIAL-NAMES.
    CLASS IS-A-VOWEL        'A' 'E' 'I' 'O' 'U'
    CLASS IS-PASSING-GRADE  'A' THRU 'D'.

    The word "CLASS" repeats              One period here
```

Notice that the coding to define multiple data classes is a little unusual. The coding forms one COBOL sentence. The word CLASS is repeated when you start coding each new data class within this single sentence.

10.2 ACCESSING A USER-DEFINED DATA CLASS

User-defined data classes can reduce the bulk of your coding of IF/ELSE or EVALUATE statements for data validation tasks. They can also reduce the amount of 88-level name definitions you have to code. User-defined data classes make it unnecessary to move data to a field just to access an 88-level name you have coded at it.

You can access a user-defined data class as you would any condition name:

```
WORKING-STORAGE SECTION.
01  WS-LINE-OF-A        PIC X(12) VALUE 'AAAAAAAAAAAA'.
01  WS-LINE-OF-AEIOU    PIC X(12) VALUE 'AEIOUEAUOIEA'.
01  WS-LINE-OF-OTHER    PIC X(12) VALUE 'ABCDABCDABCD'.
    -
PROCEDURE DIVISION.
    -
    IF  WS-LINE-OF-OTHER  IS-A-VOWEL
       DISPLAY 'ALL VOWELS'
      ELSE
       DISPLAY 'NOT ALL VOWELS'.
```

or

```
    EVALUATE TRUE
       WHEN  WS-LINE-OF-OTHER  IS-A-VOWEL
          DISPLAY 'ALL VOWELS'
       WHEN  WS-LINE-OF-OTHER  NOT IS-A-VOWEL
          DISPLAY 'NOT ALL VOWELS'
    END-EVALUATE.
```

A data class test is much more powerful than you might think at first. It checks each byte of the character string to see if it is one of the characters in the data class. The test above will indicate that WS-LINE-OF-OTHER is not in the data class IS-A-VOWEL (the B, C, and D in it are not vowels). But the following test identifies that WS-LINE-OF-OTHER meets the requirements of the PASSING-GRADE data class:

```
IF WS-LINE-OF-OTHER  IS-PASSING-GRADE
   DISPLAY 'ALL PASSING GRADES'
  ELSE
   DISPLAY 'NOT ALL PASSING GRADES'
```

10.3 *TRY IT!* SEE HOW A USER-DEFINED DATA CLASS WORKS

Once defined, a data class can be used to validate the contents of any field in the program. H1USER, listed in Figure 10.1, uses the two data classes I defined above in two ways. First, it scans a line of text to see if each position contains a vowel. This produces the first lines of output in Figure 10.1.

Next, H1USER uses the two data classes IS-A-VOWEL and IS-PASS-ING-GRADE to see if the entire contents of three different fields meet the requirements of either data class.

10.4 *TRY IT!* CREATING USER-DEFINED DATA CLASSES

Invalid customer data has been entering an order-entry system. H2USER, a data validation program listed for you in Figure 10.2 (pages 192–93), is intended to pinpoint records in which the customer name or the address street direction is incorrect. For testing, the program contains some test data housed within it in a table:

```
05 FILLER PIC X(30) VALUE '7-11 STORE    00145 N MAIN    '.
05 FILLER PIC X(30) VALUE 'ARMADILLO     23117 W FORD    '.
05 FILLER PIC X(30) VALUE 'THE BOAT SHOP 11620 E TOUHY   '.
05 FILLER PIC X(30) VALUE 'HAIR-DUES     00333 WABASH    '.
05 FILLER PIC X(30) VALUE 'MAD HATTER!   00001 L PLAZA   '.
05 FILLER PIC X(30) VALUE 'JOE SCHMO     00145 X ARCHER  '.
05 FILLER PIC X(30) VALUE 'MR. SMYTH     09215 S CENTRAL '.
```

Program H2USER will pull rows out of this table as if they were records and feed them through data validation logic. The program is all set to go—except that you need to supply the user-defined data classes to do the validation! Here are the validation criteria:

- Customer name can be capital letters A through Z and can contain spaces, hyphens, or periods. These are the only values that are considered valid.
- Address street direction can be north (N), south (S), east (E), or west (W), or be missing (space). These are the only values that are considered valid.

Put in the needed user-defined data classes and compile, linkage edit, and run the program using VS COBOL II. Compare your results with the correct output, which is shown at the bottom of Figure 10.2.

```
000100 IDENTIFICATION DIVISION.
000200 PROGRAM-ID.      H1USER.
000300 AUTHOR.          J. JANOSSY.
000400******************************************************************
000500*        DEMONSTRATE TWO USER-DEFINED DATA CLASSES             *
000600******************************************************************
000700 ENVIRONMENT DIVISION.
000800 CONFIGURATION SECTION.
000900 SPECIAL-NAMES.
001000     CLASS   IS-A-VOWEL          'A' 'E' 'I' 'O' 'U'
001100     CLASS   IS-PASSING-GRADE  'A' THRU 'D'.
001200*
001300 DATA DIVISION.
001400 WORKING-STORAGE SECTION.
001500 01  WS-SUB            PIC 9(2)   VALUE 0.
001600 01  WS-VOWEL-COUNT    PIC 9(2)   VALUE 0.
001700 01  WS-DATA-SETUP     PIC X(54)  VALUE
001800     'YOU CAN LEARN ABOUT VS COBOL II EASIER WITH THIS BOOK!'.
001900 01  WS-DATA  REDEFINES  WS-DATA-SETUP.
002000     05 WS-LETTER    OCCURS 54 TIMES PIC X(1).
002100*
002200 01  WS-STAR-LINE.
002300     05 WS-STAR      OCCURS 54 TIMES PIC X(1).
002400*
002500 01  WS-LINE-OF-A       PIC X(12) VALUE 'AAAAAAAAAAAA'.
002600 01  WS-LINE-OF-AEIOU   PIC X(12) VALUE 'AEIOUEAUOIEA'.
002700 01  WS-LINE-OF-OTHER   PIC X(12) VALUE 'ABCDABCDABCD'.
002800/
002900 PROCEDURE DIVISION.
003000 0000-MAINLINE.
003100     DISPLAY 'H1USER STARTING'.
003200     DISPLAY 'A STAR UNDER A LETTER MEANS IT''S A VOWEL '.
003300     DISPLAY '-------------------------------------------'.
003400     DISPLAY WS-DATA-SETUP.
003500     MOVE SPACES TO WS-STAR-LINE.
003600     PERFORM
003700        VARYING WS-SUB FROM 1 BY 1
003800        UNTIL WS-SUB > 54
003900           IF WS-LETTER(WS-SUB) IS-A-VOWEL
004000              MOVE '*' TO WS-STAR(WS-SUB)
004100           ADD 1 TO WS-VOWEL-COUNT
004200           END-IF
004300     END-PERFORM.
004400     DISPLAY WS-STAR-LINE.
004500     DISPLAY 'VOWELS = ', WS-VOWEL-COUNT.
004600*
004700     DISPLAY '-------------------------------------------'.
004800     DISPLAY WS-LINE-OF-A.
004900     IF WS-LINE-OF-A  IS-A-VOWEL
005000        DISPLAY 'ALL VOWELS'
005100      ELSE
005200        DISPLAY 'NOT ALL VOWELS'.
005300*
005400     IF  WS-LINE-OF-A  IS-PASSING-GRADE
005500        DISPLAY 'ALL PASSING GRADES'
005600      ELSE
005700        DISPLAY 'NOT ALL PASSING GRADES'.
005800*
005900     DISPLAY '-------------------------------------------'.
006000     DISPLAY WS-LINE-OF-AEIOU.
006100     IF  WS-LINE-OF-AEIOU  IS-A-VOWEL
006200        DISPLAY 'ALL VOWELS'
006300      ELSE
006400        DISPLAY 'NOT ALL VOWELS'.
006500*
006600     IF  WS-LINE-OF-AEIOU  IS-PASSING-GRADE
006700        DISPLAY 'ALL PASSING GRADES'
006800      ELSE
006900        DISPLAY 'NOT ALL PASSING GRADES'.
007000*
007100     DISPLAY '-------------------------------------------'.
007200     DISPLAY WS-LINE-OF-OTHER.
007300     IF  WS-LINE-OF-OTHER  IS-A-VOWEL
007400        DISPLAY 'ALL VOWELS'
007500      ELSE
007600        DISPLAY 'NOT ALL VOWELS'.
007700*
007800     IF  WS-LINE-OF-OTHER  IS-PASSING-GRADE
007900        DISPLAY 'ALL PASSING GRADES'
008000      ELSE
008100        DISPLAY 'NOT ALL PASSING GRADES'.
008200*
008300     STOP RUN.
```

(a)

(b)

(c)

Figure 10.1 *(see legend on page 191)*

Output:

```
H1USER STARTING
A STAR UNDER A LETTER MEANS IT'S A VOWEL
-----------------------------------------------
YOU CAN LEARN ABOUT VS COBOL II EASIER WITH THIS BOOK!
 ** *  **   * **    * * ** ** **   *    *   **
VOWELS = 20
-----------------------------------------------
AAAAAAAAAAAA
ALL VOWELS
ALL PASSING GRADES
-----------------------------------------------
AEIOUEAUOIEA
ALL VOWELS
NOT ALL PASSING GRADES
-----------------------------------------------
ABCDABCDABCD
NOT ALL VOWELS
ALL PASSING GRADES
```

Figure 10.1 Two User-Defined Data Classes: A Demonstration.

User-defined data classes let you create program-wide "88-level" names associated with one or more literal data values or ranges of values. This program shows you how to define data classes and then access them.

a. You define data classes at SPECIAL-NAMES. Although the word CLASS repeats for each data class, the set of definitions is only one COBOL sentence. Put a period only after your last data class definition.

b. This loop examines the bytes in WS-DATA-SETUP one-by-one and uses the IS-A-VOWEL data class to see if each byte meets the requirements of the data class. The only reason to use a loop like this is if you want to take some special action for each byte, such as putting an asterisk under it, as I do here. See (d) in the output produced by this loop.

c. You can use a user-defined data class in an IF statement just like an 88-level condition name and just like the predefined data classes NUMERIC and ALPHABETIC.

d. The loop at (b) produces this print where I have put an asterisk under each vowel in the sentence shown. The last three parts of the output show you how the IF statements using data classes properly identify the nature of each of the three data lines analyzed in this run.

```
000100 IDENTIFICATION DIVISION.
000200 PROGRAM-ID.      H2USER.
000300 AUTHOR.          J. JANOSSY.
000400****************************************************************
000500*       Try It!  User-Defined Data Class Program Shell      *
000600****************************************************************
000700 ENVIRONMENT DIVISION.
000800 ?
000900 ?     You need to code the appropriate user-defined
001000 ?     data classes here!
001100 ?
001200*
001300 DATA DIVISION.
001400 WORKING-STORAGE SECTION.
001500 01  WS-FLAG            PIC X(4).
001600 01  WS-SUB            PIC 9(2)  VALUE 0.
001700 01  WS-DATA-TABLE-SETUP.
001800     05 FILLER PIC X(30) VALUE '7-11 STORE     00145 N MAIN    '.
001900     05 FILLER PIC X(30) VALUE 'ARMADILLO      23117 W FORD    '.
002000     05 FILLER PIC X(30) VALUE 'THE BOAT SHOP 11620 E TOUHY    '.
002100     05 FILLER PIC X(30) VALUE 'HAIR-DUES      00333   WABASH  '.
002200     05 FILLER PIC X(30) VALUE 'MAD HATTER!   00001 L PLAZA    '.
002300     05 FILLER PIC X(30) VALUE 'JOE SCHMO      00145 X ARCHER  '.
002400     05 FILLER PIC X(30) VALUE 'MR. SMYTH      09215 S CENTRAL '.
002500 01  WS-DATA-TABLE   REDEFINES WS-DATA-TABLE-SETUP.
002600     05 WS-DATA-ROW   OCCURS 7 TIMES.
002700        10 DATA-ROW-NAME       PIC X(14).
002800        10 DATA-ROW-HOUSE-NUM   PIC X(5).
002900        10 FILLER             PIC X(1).
003000        10 DATA-ROW-DIRECTION   PIC X(1).
003100        10 FILLER             PIC X(1).
003200        10 DATA-ROW-STREET     PIC X(8).
003300*
003400 01  CUSTOMER-RECORD.
003500     05 CUST-NAME            PIC X(14).
003600     05 CUST-HOUSE-NUM        PIC X(5).
003700     05 FILLER             PIC X(1).
003800     05 CUST-DIRECTION        PIC X(1).
003900     05 FILLER             PIC X(1).
004000     05 CUST-STREET          PIC X(8).
004100/
004200 PROCEDURE DIVISION.
004300 0000-MAINLINE.
004400     DISPLAY 'H2USER STARTING'.
004500     PERFORM 1000-CHECK-IT
004600        VARYING WS-SUB FROM 1 BY 1
004700           UNTIL WS-SUB > 7.
004800     STOP RUN.
004900*
005000 1000-CHECK-IT.
005100     DISPLAY '----------------------------------------------'.
005200     MOVE WS-DATA-ROW(WS-SUB) TO CUSTOMER-RECORD.
005300     DISPLAY CUSTOMER-RECORD.
005400     MOVE 'GOOD' TO WS-FLAG.
005500*
005600     IF CUST-NAME IS NOT A-Z-HYP-DOT
005700        MOVE 'BAD' TO WS-FLAG
005800        DISPLAY 'CUSTOMER NAME INVALID'.
005900*
006000     IF CUST-DIRECTION IS NOT NEWS-N-SPACE
006100        MOVE 'BAD' TO WS-FLAG
006200        DISPLAY 'CUSTOMER DIRECTION INVALID'.
006300*
006400     IF WS-FLAG = 'GOOD'
006500        DISPLAY 'OK'
006600     ELSE
006700        DISPLAY 'RECORD HAS ERRORS!'.
```

Figure 10.2 *(see legend on page 193)*

Output:
```
H2USER STARTING
-------------------------------------------------
7-11 STORE    00145 N MAIN
CUSTOMER NAME INVALID
RECORD HAS ERRORS!
-------------------------------------------------
ARMADILLO     23117 W FORD
OK
-------------------------------------------------
THE BOAT SHOP 11620 E TOUHY
OK
-------------------------------------------------
HAIR-DUES     00333    WABASH
OK
-------------------------------------------------
MAD HATTER!   00001 L PLAZA
CUSTOMER NAME INVALID
CUSTOMER DIRECTION INVALID
RECORD HAS ERRORS!
-------------------------------------------------
JOE SCHMO     00145 X ARCHER
CUSTOMER DIRECTION INVALID
RECORD HAS ERRORS!
-------------------------------------------------
MR. SMYTH     09215 S CENTRAL
OK
```

(e)

Figure 10.2 *Try It!* Can You Code User-Defined Data Classes?

This is a program shell. I wrote the program and ran it, producing the output above. Then I eliminated the definitions of the user defined data classes. See if you understand how to employ user-defined data classes by putting the correct definitions in near the top!

a. Your coding for user-defined data classes should go here. Hint: the right code will take four lines.

b. The table at lines 1700 through 3200 has seven rows. Each row is like a data record. The loop at (c) pulls rows out of this table one-by-one to simulate the processing of data. This makes this training program easier to handle than if it had to read data records from a file.

c. This loop takes one row at a time out of WS-DATA-TABLE as if data records were being read from a file.

d. I use one data class to validate the contents of the name field, and a second data class to check the contents of the address direction field. The data classes make these validations very concise and reliable.

e. The output of the validation program clearly tells which records have errors and what those errors are. If your output from this program does not look like this, you have more work to do on your user-defined data class definitions.

```
000100 IDENTIFICATION DIVISION.
000200 PROGRAM-ID.     H3USER.
000300 AUTHOR.         J. JANOSSY.
000400******************************************************************
000500*    DEMONSTRATE HEX VALUES IN USER-DEFINED DATA CLASSES      *
000600******************************************************************
000700 ENVIRONMENT DIVISION.
000800 CONFIGURATION SECTION.
000900 SPECIAL-NAMES.
001000     CLASS PC-BORDER  X'B3' X'BF' X'C0' X'C4' X'D9' X'DA'.
001100*
001200 DATA DIVISION.
001300 WORKING-STORAGE SECTION.
001400 01  WS-SUB              PIC 9(2)    VALUE 0.
001500*
001600 01  WS-DATA-SETUP        PIC X(52)   VALUE
001700     '┌ A ┐ P ┘ 7 └ | B | ─ | S ONCE UPON A TIME ┌ ─ └ WAS'.
001800*
001900 01  WS-DATA  REDEFINES  WS-DATA-SETUP.
002000     05  WS-BYTE      OCCURS 52 TIMES  PIC X(1).
002100*
002200 01  WS-STAR-LINE.
002300     05  WS-STAR      OCCURS 52 TIMES  PIC X(1).
002400/
002500 PROCEDURE DIVISION.
002600 0000-MAINLINE.
002700     DISPLAY 'PROGRAM H3USER STARTING'.
002800     DISPLAY 'STARS ARE UNDER BYTES IN THE DATA CLASS'.
002900     DISPLAY WS-DATA-SETUP.
003000     MOVE SPACES TO WS-STAR-LINE.
003100     PERFORM
003200         VARYING WS-SUB FROM 1 BY 1
003300         UNTIL WS-SUB > 52
003400             IF WS-BYTE(WS-SUB) IS  PC-BORDER
003500                 MOVE '*' TO WS-STAR(WS-SUB)
003600             END-IF
003700     END-PERFORM.
003800     DISPLAY WS-STAR-LINE.
003900     STOP RUN.
```

(a)

(b)

Output:

```
PROGRAM H3USER STARTING
STARS ARE UNDER BYTES IN THE DATA CLASS
┌ A ┐ P ┘ 7 └ | B | ─ | S ONCE UPON A TIME ┌ ─ └ WAS
*   *   *   * *   * * *                    * * *
```

Figure 10.3   Hexadecimal Literals in User-Defined Data Classes.

You can code user-defined data classes with ordinary literals, figurative constants such as SPACES and LOW-VALUES, and also with hexadecimal literals. In this example (run on a microcomputer) I have identified the graphic symbols for borders and box corners on a PC. You can make any bit pattern part of a user-defined data class as long as you know its hex representation.

a. The coding for a user-defined data class can include X'00' where "00" is any valid hexadecimal value. If you work on a PC, make sure you realize that PCs use the ASCII bits-to-meaning scheme and represent characters differently than mainframes, which encode with EBCDIC.

b. The loop at lines 3100 through 3700 examines each byte of WS-DATA-SETUP and uses the PC-BORDER data class to see if it is one of the six graphic symbols in the data class. If it is, I put an asterisk under that byte in WS-STAR-LINE.

10.5 HEXADECIMAL CODING IN USER-DEFINED DATA CLASSES

You can code figurative constants such as SPACES and LOW-VALUES as part of a user-defined data class definition. You can also code hexadecimal literals in defining a data class. This gives you ready access to non-printable values as single values, multiple values, or ranges.

Hex literals work on the mainframe and on microcomputers. Figure 10.3 lists a short program named H3USER that shows you how to code hex literals in a data class. Since I wrote this demonstration program on a microcomputer, I thought it would be interesting to have the data class identify graphic symbols for borders that are accessible on a PC. Its output is shown at the bottom of Figure 10.3.

On an IBM PC or compatible microcomputer the hexadecimal values B3, BF, C0, C4, D9, and DA define the bit patterns that form graphic horizontal and vertical lines and the four corners of a square. These were the handiest unusual values I could think of to demonstrate how hexadecimal literals work. I put some of these symbols in the WS-DATA-SETUP line. You can see how the logic, using the data class, properly identifies these values in the output of my H3USER program.

Keep user-defined data classes and hex literals in mind if you encounter a need to analyze control characters in data transmissions. You can use them to identify unusual values in records received on non-standard tapes or in uploaded data sets.

10.6 USER-DEFINED DATA CLASS DEFINITIONS IN COPY LIBRARIES

User-defined data classes can save coding and time. You might consider establishing standard data classes for a project or application. Every program that has to validate data fields or make decisions based on field content can benefit from the definitions you create.

Consider housing project-specific user-defined data class definitions in a copy library member. One COPY compiler directive can bring in all your standard user-defined data classes, ensuring that all programs have access to them.

11

Character Handling Changes and Enhancements

VS COBOL II eliminates the EXAMINE and TRANSFORM verbs but lets you do the same things by expanding the syntax of the INSPECT verb. In addition, you get capabilities you never before had with the new REPLACE compiler directive, and a way to "pick apart" character substrings with reference modification. COPY can now exist in copy library members themselves. The Double Byte Character Set (DBCS) for graphics and Japanese (KANJI) symbols are now supported. And last (and very least) you get the ability to distinguish lowercase letters with the data class ALPHABETIC-LOWER. I'll show you these character handling changes in this chapter.

11.1 INSPECT REPLACES EXAMINE

The EXAMINE and TRANSFORM verbs do not exist in VS COBOL II. Instead, you can use INSPECT to do everything that these two verbs formerly did. In most cases substituting the new verb for the old is sufficient:

Old `EXAMINE WS-FIELD REPLACING LEADING SPACES BY ZEROS.`

New `INSPECT WS-FIELD REPLACING LEADING SPACES BY ZEROS.`

If you used the TALLY register with EXAMINE to count byte positions within a character string, you'll now need to remember to initialize it to zero yourself. EXAMINE used TALLY automatically; INSPECT requires you to name it:

Old   `EXAMINE WS-FIELD TALLYING UNTIL FIRST '*'.`

```
          MOVE 0 TO TALLY.
New       INSPECT WS-FIELD TALLYING TALLY
              FOR CHARACTERS BEFORE FIRST '*'.
```

11.2 *TRY IT!* SEEING HOW INSPECT WITH CONVERTING WORKS

The TRANSFORM statement of VS COBOL acted similarly to INSPECT but was more powerful. TRANSFORM acted on a field you specified to replace characters in it. It allowed you to define two lists of characters. Characters in the second list replaced characters in corresponding positions in the first list. INSPECT with the newly added CONVERTING clause replaces TRANSFORM. Here is how it works:

Old   `TRANSFORM WS-FIELD CHARACTERS FROM 'IJKL' TO 'WXYZ'.`

New   `INSPECT WS-FIELD CONVERTING 'IJKL' TO 'WXYZ'.`

With this code, 'W' will replace any 'I' in WS-FIELD, 'X' will replace any 'J', 'Y' will replace any 'K', and 'Z' will replace any 'L'. The best way to understand how this works is to demonstrate it.

J1CHAR, listed in Figure 11.1, does some very simple character string substitution using INSPECT and CONVERTING. It converts capital letters "AEIOU" to lowercase letters "aeiou" in the character string "THE TIME HAS COME, THE WALRUS SAID, TO SPEAK OF MANY THINGS" using this statement:

```
INSPECT WS-FIELD CONVERTING 'AEIOU' TO 'aeiou'.
```

Enter or upload J1CHAR to your system and compile, linkage edit, and run it. Your output should be identical to that at the bottom of Figure 11.1.

INSPECT with CONVERTING gives you an excellent way to convert mixed-case character strings (containing lowercase and uppercase letters) to uppercase. I need to do this in the microcomputer source code re-

```
000100 IDENTIFICATION DIVISION.
000200 PROGRAM-ID.    J1CHAR.
000300 AUTHOR.        J. JANOSSY.
000400**************************************************************
000500*        DEMONSTRATE HOW INSPECT/CONVERTING WORKS          *
000600**************************************************************
000700 ENVIRONMENT DIVISION.
000800*
000900 DATA DIVISION.
001000 WORKING-STORAGE SECTION.
001100 01  WS-FIELD.
001200     05 FILLER    PIC X(19)  VALUE 'THE TIME HAS COME, '.
001300     05 FILLER    PIC X(17)  VALUE 'THE WALRUS SAID, '.
001400     05 FILLER    PIC X(25)  VALUE 'TO SPEAK OF MANY THINGS.'.
001500 PROCEDURE DIVISION.
001600 0000-MAINLINE.
001700     DISPLAY 'PROGRAM J1CHAR STARTING'.
001800     DISPLAY WS-FIELD.
001900     INSPECT WS-FIELD CONVERTING 'AEIOU' TO 'aeiou'.
002000     DISPLAY WS-FIELD.
002100     STOP RUN.
```

Output:

```
PROGRAM J1CHAR STARTING
THE TIME HAS COME, THE WALRUS SAID, TO SPEAK OF MANY THINGS.
THe TiMe HaS CoMe, THe WaLRuS SaiD, To SPeaK oF MaNY THiNGS.
```

Figure 11.1   INSPECT With CONVERTING Replaces TRANSFORM.

VS COBOL II does not support the TRANSFORM verb of VS COBOL. Instead, INSPECT is given new capabilities with the new clause CONVERTING. As you can see in this example, the characters in the second list "aeiou" are used to replace the corresponding characters in the first list as these characters occur in the field being processed. INSPECT with CONVERTING does a lot more work than its syntax reveals. It processes each position of WS-FIELD one by one.

numbering utility I show you in Figure E.1 in Appendix E. Here are the relevant source code lines in it:

```
01  WS-FILE-IN                 PIC X(25)  VALUE SPACES.
01  WS-LOWER  PIC X(26)  VALUE 'abcdefghijklmnopqrstuvwxyz'.
01  WS-UPPER  PIC X(26)  VALUE 'ABCDEFGHIJKLMNOPQRSTUVWXYZ'.
       -
       -
PROCEDURE DIVISION.
       -
    INSPECT WS-FILE-IN CONVERTING WS-LOWER  TO  WS-UPPER.
```

11.3 *TRY IT!* CHARACTER REPLACEMENT
FOR ENCRYPTION

Program J1CHAR shows you how INSPECT/CONVERTING works. Program J2CHAR, in Figure 11.2, does something much more interesting. J2CHAR uses data-names for the "before" and "after" character lists

```
000100 IDENTIFICATION DIVISION.
000200 PROGRAM-ID.    J2CHAR.
000300 AUTHOR.        J. JANOSSY.
000400**********************************************************
000500*      DEMONSTRATE ENCRYPTION USING INSPECT/CONVERTING    *
000600**********************************************************
000700 ENVIRONMENT DIVISION.
000800*
000900 DATA DIVISION.
001000 WORKING-STORAGE SECTION.
001100 01  WS-FIELD.
001200     05 FILLER    PIC X(19)  VALUE 'THE TIME HAS COME, '.
001300     05 FILLER    PIC X(17)  VALUE 'THE WALRUS SAID, '.
001400     05 FILLER    PIC X(25)  VALUE 'TO SPEAK OF MANY THINGS.'.
001500 01  WS-PLAIN-TEXT    PIC X(28)  VALUE
001600     'ABCDEFGHIJKLMNOPQRSTUVWXYZ ,'.
001700 01  WS-CODED-TEXT    PIC X(28)  VALUE
001800     '+ )(*&^%$#@!=-0987654321><?H'.
001900 01  WS-HYPHENS       PIC X(61)  VALUE ALL '-'.
002000/
002100 PROCEDURE DIVISION.
002200 0000-MAINLINE.
002300     DISPLAY 'PROGRAM J2CHAR STARTING'.
002400     DISPLAY WS-HYPHENS.
002500     DISPLAY 'Here is a character string:'.
002600     DISPLAY WS-FIELD.
002700     DISPLAY WS-HYPHENS.
002800*
002900     INSPECT WS-FIELD CONVERTING WS-PLAIN-TEXT TO WS-CODED-TEXT.
003000     DISPLAY 'Here is the string in coded form:'.
003100     DISPLAY WS-FIELD.
003200     DISPLAY WS-HYPHENS.
003300*
003400     INSPECT WS-FIELD CONVERTING WS-CODED-TEXT TO WS-PLAIN-TEXT.
003500     DISPLAY 'Here is the string after decoding:'.
003600     DISPLAY WS-FIELD.
003700     STOP RUN.
```

(a)

(b)

(c)

Output:

```
PROGRAM J2CHAR STARTING
-------------------------------------------------------------
Here is a character string:
THE TIME HAS COME, THE WALRUS SAID, TO SPEAK OF MANY THINGS.
-------------------------------------------------------------
Here is the string in coded form:
5%*?5$=*?%+6?)0=*H?5%*?2+!746?6+$(H?50?69*+@?0&?=+->?5%$-^6.?
-------------------------------------------------------------
Here is the string after decoding:
THE TIME HAS COME, THE WALRUS SAID, TO SPEAK OF MANY THINGS.
```

(d)

Figure 11.2   INSPECT With CONVERTING Can Encrypt Field Contents.

a. WS-PLAIN-TEXT and WS-CODED-TEXT are data names that contain the "before" and "after" character lists. Characters from the second list will be substituted for characters in the corresponding positions in the first list.

b. The INSPECT at line 2900 encodes WS-FIELD by substituting characters from WS-CODED-TEXT for the characters in the field. The DISPLAY shows you the field after it is encoded, at (d). Note that the lists of characters in the CONVERTING clause can be data names as shown here.

c. The INSPECT at line 3400 reverses the character substitution process and decodes the contents of WS-FIELD.

d. The contents of WS-FIELD after encoding look like gibberish. A person familiar with encryption techniques could quickly deduce that a simple character substitution cipher had been used, but it's highly unlikely that anyone else would be able to interpret the contents of the field.

for INSPECT with CONVERTING. This allows the character replacement lists to be quite long. The program functions like a simple encryption routine to replace each character in a field with a different character. The program shows you what the encrypted field looks like in coded form. Then, using the same character lists with another INSPECT, J2CHAR turns the encrypted field back into plain (raw) text.

Compile, link, and run J2CHAR and experiment with the replacement character list. You'll see that as long as you use the same lists, you can encode and decode a field just by reversing the position of the "before" and "after" character lists in the INSPECT verb.

J2CHAR isn't good enough for a real security purpose, but it demonstrates how VS COBOL II extends the capabilities of INSPECT. With appropriately coded lists you can translate lowercase letters to uppercase and vice versa or turn unprintable hexadecimal values into other values that could be printed. You can code the list fields such as WS-PLAIN-TEXT and WS-CODED-TEXT with hexadecimal VALUE literals.

11.4 THE NEW REPLACE FEATURE

The REPLACE statement is new to VS COBOL II. REPLACE is a compiler directive, not a verb. It causes a string of text that you identify to be replaced with another string of text during the compilation process.

REPLACE is unusual in that it uses double equal signs to delimit text:

```
REPLACE ==THIS-TEST-STRING==   BY ==WHAT-A-FINE-DAY==


        ==ZIP-A-DEE-DOO-DAH==  BY ==ONE-MEAT-BALL==.
```

You can code multiple text string replacements in one REPLACE sentence. You can put this statement anywhere in a program and it is effective until you issue the statement REPLACE OFF. You can code another REPLACE statement at any point in a program but REPLACE statements are not cumulative. A subsequent REPLACE completely undoes the one in effect, setting up all new replace specifications.

REPLACE is not the same as REPLACING used with the COPY directive for copy libraries. REPLACING acts only on a copy library member. *REPLACE acts on the entire program.*

The most important thing about REPLACE is that it acts on the program *after* the compiler has brought in all copy library members. This is after the compiler has processed all COPY statements, and the material brought in by the COPY statements is present. This means that you can very easily make mass changes in source code supplied by copy library members. In program conversion you can also overcome the use of words as data names and paragraph names that are now reserved words in VS COBOL II.

11.5 *TRY IT!* A REPLACE DEMONSTRATION

REPLACE allows you to tell the compiler to do global text-string replacement in a program just before it begins to compile. This is the most comprehensive text string replacement possible. REPLACE lets you overcome some problems with new reserved words that conflict with prior usage of the same words.

Program J3REPL, listed in Figure 11.3, contains a simple table and just uses a loop to print out its contents by varying a subscript. Compile, linkage edit, and run it.

Does J3REPL work? As is, no! DAY-OF-WEEK is now a reserved word (it gives you a number from 1 to 7 indicating the current day of the week, with 1 as Monday). But if you look in Figure 11.4 you'll see J4REPL. This version of the program works. It is the same as J3REPL except for a REPLACE statement at lines 1000 through 1500. I used REPLACE to change DAY-OF-WEEK to HOWDY-DOODY, and included two other replacements to show you what REPLACE does and does not do.

The source code listing produced by the compiler does not show the "before" condition of the statements affected by REPLACE. It reflects all of the changes caused by REPLACE as if the program had been coded with the replaced character strings. To see what the code looked like before the replacing action, you have to look at your raw source code.

You can see in Figure 11.4 that VS COBOL II is very considerate in processing the REPLACE statement. The compiler makes replacements *except* within literal values and does not change the format of each source code line any more than is necessary. "SUNDAY" is not changed to "A-DAY-OFF" in line 2100 because it is a literal value, part of table contents.

Other 1985 COBOL compilers besides VS COBOL II support REPLACE, but modify the source code differently. Figure 11.5 shows you how the source code listing of J4REPL looks after processing by the Micro Focus COBOL compiler. The program executes identically with Micro Focus as with VS COBOL II. But the Micro Focus compiler takes great liberties in changing the format of source code lines involved in REPLACEments, and it causes the program to have more lines.

11.6 REPLACE CAN CURE NEW RESERVED WORD PROBLEMS

VS COBOL II makes use of about 100 more reserved words than did VS COBOL. For example, all of the END-xxx scope delimiters grab new

```
000001 000100 IDENTIFICATION DIVISION.
000002 000200 PROGRAM-ID.   J3REPL.
000003 000300 AUTHOR.       J. JANOSSY.
000004 000400********************************************
000005 000500*    DEMONSTRATE NEED FOR "REPLACE" FEATURE *
000006 000600********************************************
000007 000700 ENVIRONMENT DIVISION.
000008 000800 DATA DIVISION.
000009 000900 WORKING-STORAGE SECTION.
000010 001000 01 DAY-OF-WEEK      PIC 9(1).

==000010==> IGYDS1089-S "DAY-OF-WEEK" WAS INVALID.  SKIPPED TO THE NEXT AREA "A" ITEM,
            LEVEL-NUMBER, OR THE START OF THE NEXT CLAUSE.

000011 001100 01 DAY-TABLE-SETUP.
000012 001200    05 DAY-ROW OCCURS 7 TIMES.
000013 001300       10 FILLER    PIC X(9)  VALUE 'SUNDAY   '.
000014 001400       10 FILLER    PIC X(9)  VALUE 'MONDAY   '.
000015 001500       10 FILLER    PIC X(9)  VALUE 'TUESDAY  '.
000016 001600       10 FILLER    PIC X(9)  VALUE 'WEDNESDAY'.
000017 001700       10 FILLER    PIC X(9)  VALUE 'THURSDAY '.
000018 001800       10 FILLER    PIC X(9)  VALUE 'FRIDAY   '.
000019 001900       10 FILLER    PIC X(9)  VALUE 'SATURDAY '.
000020 002000 01 DAY-TABLE REDEFINES DAY-TABLE-SETUP.
000021 002100    05 DAY-NAME OCCURS 7 TIMES PIC X(9).               11
000022 002200/
000023 002300 PROCEDURE DIVISION.
000024 002400 0000-MAINLINE.
000025 002500     DISPLAY 'PROGRAM J3REPL STARTING'.
000026 002600     PERFORM 1000-SHOW-DAY                             32
000027 002700         VARYING DAY-OF-WEEK FROM 1 BY 1

==000027==> IGYPS2000-S EXPECTED A DATA-NAME, BUT FOUND "DAY-OF-WEEK".  THE "PERFORM" STATEMENT
            WAS DISCARDED.

000028 002800         UNTIL DAY-OF-WEEK > 7.
000029 002900     DISPLAY 'PROGRAM ENDING'.
000030 003000     STOP RUN.
000031 003100*
000032 003200 1000-SHOW-DAY.
000033 003300     DISPLAY DAY-OF-WEEK, ' ' DAY-NAME(DAY-OF-WEEK).

==000033==> IGYPS0028-S EXPECTED A DATA-NAME OR A LITERAL, BUT FOUND "DAY-OF-WEEK".  THE
            STATEMENT WAS DISCARDED.
```

Figure 11.3 This program would work in VS COBOL but fails to compile successfully using VS COBOL II because DAY-OF-WEEK is now a reserved word. Since DAY-OF-WEEK is coded at three places in the program, three error messages are generated.

territory and claim such words as END-READ that a programmer might have used in the old days for a paragraph name. DAY-OF-WEEK never was a reserved word, but it is now. And a few words, such as ALPHABETIC, have been changed to other words, in this case ALPHABETIC-UPPER.

You can use a general REPLACE statement near the beginning of a program to mass-change all of the common "problem" words to new ones if they exist in a program:

```
REPLACE==ALPHABETIC==   BY   ==ALPHABETIC-UPPER==
        ==DAY-OF-WEEK==  BY   ==WEEK-DAY==
        ==INITIALIZE==   BY   ==INITIALIZE-TOTALS==
        ==OTHER==        BY   ==OTHER-CONDITION==
        ==TRUE==         BY   ==TRUE-STATUS==
        ==END-READ==     BY   ==END-OF-READ==.
```

Since REPLACE statements don't accumulate, but rather replace one another, you must code this statement as one sentence. All of the words listed in the left column have become reserved words. Existing VS COBOL programs may contain them as data names. This REPLACE changes them to different values to avoid conflict when you convert existing programs to VS COBOL II.

Consider putting the general REPLACE statement shown above in a copy library member. You can then include it in any program you are converting, using a COPY statement. Try this variation with J4REPL and use COPY to bring the statement into the program.

When you use REPLACE you have to specify the LIB compile option. When LIB is on, the compiler seeks and opens a source code copy library (partitioned data set) at its DDname //SYSLIB.

11.7 *TRY IT!* REFERENCE MODIFICATION

Reference modification becomes available to you in VS COBOL II Release 3. You may not find much use for this unusual character string manipulation facility. But it's interesting that substrings have finally come to mainframe COBOL.

Reference modification just means being able to code an alphanumeric data-name followed by parentheses and two numbers. The numbers define a starting location and length, representing a piece of the data-name.

Suppose we had a mannequin named after one of our old western heros and we had to disassemble it for storage. We could use reference modification statements such as this:

(text continues on page 207)

```
PP 5668-958 IBM VS COBOL II RELEASE 3.2 09/05/90          J4REPL   DATE 05/05/92  TIME 09:29:07  PAGE    2
LINEID  PL SL    ----*A-1-B-+----2----+----3----+----4----+----5----+----6----+----7-|--+----8 MAP AND CROSS REFERENCE

000001  000100 IDENTIFICATION DIVISION.
000002  000200 PROGRAM-ID.    J4REPL.
000003  000300 AUTHOR.        J. JANOSSY.
000004  000400*
000005  000500*     DEMONSTRATE HOW TO USE THE "REPLACE" FEATURE
000006  000600*
000007  000700 ENVIRONMENT DIVISION.
000008  000800 DATA DIVISION.
000009  000900*
000010  001000******************************************************
000011  001100*             GLOBAL REPLACE STATEMENT               *
000012  001200******************************************************
000013  001300 REPLACE ==DAY-OF-WEEK==    BY ==HOWDY-DOODY==
000014  001400         ==SUNDAY==         BY ==ADAYOFF==
000015  001500         ==DAY-NAME==       BY ==THE-DAY-OF-THE-WEEK==.
000016  001600*
000017  001700 WORKING-STORAGE SECTION.
000018  001800 01  HOWDY-DOODY              PIC 9(1).
000019  001900 01  DAY-TABLE-SETUP.
000020  002000     05 DAY-ROW OCCURS 7 TIMES.
000021  002100        10 FILLER    PIC X(9)    VALUE 'SUNDAY   '.
000022  002200        10 FILLER    PIC X(9)    VALUE 'MONDAY   '.
000023  002300        10 FILLER    PIC X(9)    VALUE 'TUESDAY  '.
000024  002400        10 FILLER    PIC X(9)    VALUE 'WEDNESDAY'.
000025  002500        10 FILLER    PIC X(9)    VALUE 'THURSDAY '.
000026  002600        10 FILLER    PIC X(9)    VALUE 'FRIDAY   '.
000027  002700        10 FILLER    PIC X(9)    VALUE 'SATURDAY '.
000028  002800 01  DAY-TABLE REDEFINES DAY-TABLE-SETUP.
000029  002900     05 THE-DAY-OF-THE-WEEK OCCURS 7 TIMES   PIC X(9).
000030  003000/
000031  003100 PROCEDURE DIVISION.
000032  003200 0000-MAINLINE.
000033  003300     DISPLAY 'PROGRAM J4REPL STARTING'.
000034  003400     PERFORM 1000-SHOW-DAY
000035  003500         VARYING HOWDY-DOODY FROM 1 BY 1
000036  003600         UNTIL HOWDY-DOODY > 7.
000037  003700     DISPLAY 'PROGRAM ENDING'.
000038  003800     STOP RUN.
000039  003900*
000040  004000 1000-SHOW-DAY.
000041  004100     DISPLAY HOWDY-DOODY, ' ' THE-DAY-OF-THE-WEEK(HOWDY-DOODY).
```

(a)

(b)

(c)

19

40
18
18

18 29 18

204

Output:

```
PROGRAM J4REPL STARTING
1  SUNDAY
2  MONDAY
3  TUESDAY
4  WEDNESDAY
5  THURSDAY
6  FRIDAY
7  SATURDAY
PROGRAM ENDING
```

Figure 11.4   REPLACE Does Global Character String Substitution.

You can use the REPLACE statement to make global character string substitutions to cure conflicts with new reserved names in programs you are converting. Since REPLACE functions *after* COPY processing, it works on material copied-in from libraries, and source code management systems such as Panvalet and Librarian.

a. I used a global REPLACE at the beginning of J4REPL to change all occurrences of the now-reserved word DAY-OF-WEEK to HOWDY-DOODY. REPLACE uses an unusual double equal sign instead of apostrophes to frame character strings.

b. The source code shows only the "after substitution" version of source code. From line 1800 you can't see that HOWDY-DOODY was actually coded as DAY-OF-WEEK in the program. VS COBOL II processing of character string substitutions is sophisticated and does not generate additional lines of code, unlike other compilers such as Micro Focus (compare this with Figure 11.5). Notice that SUNDAY in line 2100 was not changed by the REPLACE statement since it is a literal value.

c. Map and cross-reference line numbers correctly identify the lines where the newly-named data items are defined.

d. The correct output is produced by program; inserting the REPLACE has cured the problem without requiring source code itself to be altered!

205

```
 1 IDENTIFICATION DIVISION.
 2 PROGRAM-ID.     J4REPL.
 3 AUTHOR.         J. JANOSSY.
 4*
 5*      DEMONSTRATE HOW TO USE THE "REPLACE" FEATURE
 6*
 7 ENVIRONMENT DIVISION.
 8 DATA DIVISION.
 9*
10***************************************************************
11*                 GLOBAL REPLACE STATEMENT                   *
12***************************************************************
13 REPLACE ==DAY-OF-WEEK==      BY ==HOWDY-DOODY==
14            ==SUNDAY==        BY ==ADAYOFF==
15            ==DAY-NAME==      BY ==THE-DAY-OF-THE-WEEK==.
16*
17 WORKING-STORAGE SECTION.
18 01
19                                     HOWDY-DOODY
20                       PIC 9(1).
21 01  DAY-TABLE-SETUP.
22     05 DAY-ROW   OCCURS 7 TIMES.
23           10 FILLER        PIC X(9)   VALUE 'SUNDAY   '.
24           10 FILLER        PIC X(9)   VALUE 'MONDAY   '.
25           10 FILLER        PIC X(9)   VALUE 'TUESDAY  '.
26           10 FILLER        PIC X(9)   VALUE 'WEDNESDAY'.
27           10 FILLER        PIC X(9)   VALUE 'THURSDAY '.
28           10 FILLER        PIC X(9)   VALUE 'FRIDAY   '.
29           10 FILLER        PIC X(9)   VALUE 'SATURDAY '.
30 01  DAY-TABLE   REDEFINES  DAY-TABLE-SETUP.
31     05
32                                     THE-DAY-OF-THE-WEEK
33                   OCCURS 7 TIMES PIC X(9).
34/
35 PROCEDURE DIVISION.
36 0000-MAINLINE.
37     DISPLAY 'PROGRAM J4REPL STARTING'.
38     PERFORM 1000-SHOW-DAY
39         VARYING
40                                     HOWDY-DOODY
41                         FROM 1 BY 1
42         UNTIL
43                                     HOWDY-DOODY
44                       > 7.
45     DISPLAY 'PROGRAM ENDING'.
46     STOP RUN.
47*
48 1000-SHOW-DAY.
49     DISPLAY
50                                     HOWDY-DOODY
51                  ' '
52                     THE-DAY-OF-THE-WEEK
53                        (
54                     HOWDY-DOODY
55                                        ).
```

Figure 11.5 Micro Focus COBOL Handles REPLACE But Reformats Source Code.

The same J4REPL source code fed to the Micro Focus COBOL compiler looks different after REPLACE processing. This figure shows the .LST source code listing file produced by the compiler.

a. I used the same REPLACE here as in Figure 11.4. In fact, the whole program was downloaded to a microcomputer and fed directly into Micro Focus.

b. The reformatted code has compiled properly as shown by the source listing. Substituted character strings are housed on new lines inserted into the program. The actual data names used in the program have been blanked out of the original lines. This does not produce a problem, but you may not recognize your source code in the listing!

```
01  HOPPALONG-CASSIDY         PIC X(25) VALUE
    'HEADSHOULDERSKNEESANDTOES'.
*
01  WS-STATUARY-DEPT          PIC X(20).
01  WS-LEG-DEPT               PIC X(20).
01  WS-PODIATRIST             PIC X(20).
    -
    -
PROCEDURE DIVISION.
    -
    MOVE HOPPALONG-CASSIDY(1:13) TO WS-STATUARY-DEPT.
    MOVE HOPPALONG-CASSIDY(14:5) TO WS-LEG-DEPT.
    MOVE HOPPALONG-CASSIDY(22:4) TO WS-PODIATRIST.
```

Starting position of the substring		Length of the substring

The statements above would cause the receiving fields to have these contents:

WS-STATUARY-DEPT	= 'HEADSHOULDERS	'
WS-LEG-DEPT	= 'KNEES	'
WS-PODIATRIST	= 'TOES	'

Figure 11.6 lists program J5REFMOD that demonstrates a number of reference modification features. Enter or upload this program and try it out!

11.8 GUIDELINES FOR REFERENCE MODIFICATION

Reference modification complements the STRING, UNSTRING, and INSPECT verbs in allowing manipulation of character strings. You are probably (as I was) initially curious about reference modification and whether you can use it with subscripted data names, whether you can use it on the right side of the equal sign, and so forth. Manuals make it difficult to get answers to these kinds of questions since they fragment the information in different areas. I decided to save you the grief of tracking down that information and have consolidated it all here:

- The data-name that you act upon with reference modification should be PIC X(nn) or PIC 9(nn) in format. If it's not, it is treated as if it was PIC X(nn) anyway. Reference modification doesn't unpack COMP-3 or binary numbers!
- The data-name you work on can be subscripted or indexed. This produces coding with an unusual but legal appearance:

text continues on page 209)

```
000100 IDENTIFICATION DIVISION.
000200 PROGRAM-ID.    J5REFMOD.
000300 AUTHOR.        J. JANOSSY.
000400******************************************************************
000500*          DEMONSTRATE REFERENCE MODIFICATION              *
000600******************************************************************
000700 ENVIRONMENT DIVISION.
000800*
000900 DATA DIVISION.
001000 WORKING-STORAGE SECTION.
001100 01  HOPPALONG-CASSIDY          PIC X(25) VALUE
001200     'HEADSHOULDERSKNEESANDTOES'.
001300 01  WS-DATE                    PIC X(6).
001400 01  WS-HEADING-DATE            PIC X(8).
001500/
001600 PROCEDURE DIVISION.
001700 0000-MAINLINE.
001800     DISPLAY 'PROGRAM J5REFMOD STARTING'.
001900*
002000     DISPLAY HOPPALONG-CASSIDY.
002100     DISPLAY '(1:13) = ', HOPPALONG-CASSIDY(1:13).
002200     DISPLAY '(14:5) = ', HOPPALONG-CASSIDY(14:5).
002300     DISPLAY '(22: ) = ', HOPPALONG-CASSIDY(22: ).
002400*
002500* Here is how you can use reference modification to build
002600* the CURRENT-DATE of the form MM/DD/YY from the data you
002700* get from DATE as YYMMDD (but see chapter 2 for a simpler
002800* way with STRING):
002900*
003000     ACCEPT WS-DATE FROM DATE.
003100     DISPLAY 'Here is what DATE gives you: ', WS-DATE.
003200     MOVE WS-DATE(3:2) TO WS-HEADING-DATE(1:2).
003300     MOVE '/'          TO WS-HEADING-DATE(3:1).
003400     MOVE WS-DATE(5:2) TO WS-HEADING-DATE(4:2).
003500     MOVE '/'          TO WS-HEADING-DATE(6:1).
003600     MOVE WS-DATE(1:2) TO WS-HEADING-DATE(7:2).
003700     DISPLAY 'It takes 5 MOVES to make it: ', WS-HEADING-DATE.
003800     STOP RUN.
```

(a)

(b)

Output:

(c)

```
PROGRAM J5REFMOD STARTING
HEADSHOULDERSKNEESANDTOES
(1:13) = HEADSHOULDERS
(14:5) = KNEES
(22: ) = TOES
Here is what DATE gives you:  920507
It takes 5 MOVES to make it:  05/07/92
```

Figure 11.6 Simple Demonstration of Reference Modification.

You can access parts of character strings by putting the starting location and length of a substring in parentheses after a data name. This works on both the left side and the right side of the TO in a MOVE statement.

a. The statements at 2100 through 2300 "pick apart" the field HOPPALONG-CASSIDY into three mutually exclusive parts and cause the top part of the output DISPLAYed at the bottom.

b. My five MOVEs at lines 3200 through 3600 take parts of the data obtained from DATE (YYMMDD) and move them to parts of the field named WS-HEADING-DATE. I also "poke" two slashes into positions 3 and 6 of this field to construct an equivalent of the now-unsupported CURRENT-DATE value. This is a handy example of reference modification but I showed you an easier way to form the current date using STRING in Chapter 2.

c. The output shows you that I dissected HOPPALONG-CASSIDY into his constituent parts, and formed the current date using reference modification.

```
MOVE WEEK-DAY(3) (1:4) TO . . .
```

- Reference modification can be used on a receiving field as well as on a sending field. For example the following code uses reference modification to poke pieces of WS-DATE into WS-HEADING-DATE. This is a way to build up a formatted Gregorian date such as 05/07/92 from the 920507 that DATE gives you:

```
01  WS-DATE              PIC X(6).
01  WS-HEADING-DATE      PIC X(8).
    -
    -
PROCEDURE DIVISION.
    -
    ACCEPT WS-DATE FROM DATE.
    MOVE WS-DATE(1:2) TO WS-HEADING-DATE(1:2).
    MOVE '/'          TO WS-HEADING-DATE(3:1).
    MOVE WS-DATE(3:2) TO WS-HEADING-DATE(4:2).
    MOVE '/'          TO WS-HEADING-DATE(6:1).
    MOVE WS-DATE(5:2) TO WS-HEADING-DATE(7:2).
```

- Starting position and length can be expressed as data-names or arithmetic expressions. These must result in positive integers within the valid range of character positions for the data item or you'll get an error and possibly abend.
- You can leave off the "length" number in coding reference modification: WS-FIELD(3:). If you do this it is as if you coded a length from the starting position you indicated (3 here) to the *end* of the field.
- The SSRANGE compiler option will check the literal values you code in reference modification statements at compile time, and the computed values before access when the program runs. If you are using SSRANGE you'll get an error message (and program termination) rather than an abend if your position field is greater than the length of the field. You'll also get an error with SSRANGE if your length specification extends beyond the end of the field.

11.9 *TRY IT!* YOU CAN OVERDO REFERENCE MODIFICATION

Reference modification is more flexible than simple examples indicate. You can use reference modification with subscripted variables. You can also use it for the receiving field in a MOVE statement. If you make overly heavy use of these capabilities you can write programs that are too hard for others to maintain. I want to give you a negative example so you can see why shop standards for reference modification need to be established.

Program J6REFMOD, listed in Figure 11.7, uses reference modification within a PERFORM ... VARYING loop to pull off the first three characters of each row in a table and string them together to build a new character string. This requires reference modification in both the sending and receiving fields. Compile, linkage edit, and run J6REFMOD to see what it does.

J6REFMOD actually loops through the DAY-TABLE two times. The first loop through the table (annotation b, lines 3400 through 4000) shows you how an *indexed* field can be accessed using reference modification (this may really appear strange to you!). This loop produces a listing of the rows in the table showing only the first three characters of each row. This loop is not a problem.

The second loop through the table in J6REFMOD (annotation c, in lines 4300 through 4800) is a problem. It sweeps through DAY-TABLE like this:

```
PERFORM
    VARYING WEEK-DAY FROM 1 BY 1
    UNTIL WEEK-DAY > 7
        MOVE DAY-NAME(WEEK-DAY) (1:3) TO
            WS-NEWFIELD( (((WEEK-DAY-1) * 3) + 1):3 )
END-PERFORM.
```

Whoa! The manipulation of WS-NEWFIELD involves a computation within reference modification. It is very powerful. As the loop progresses this computes the values 1, 4, 7, 10, 13, and so forth for the substring starting position. This extracts the first three bytes from each row of the table and puts it into the next successive three-byte position in WS-NEWFIELD, concatenating the extracted parts within it. As the loop executes, this is the actual effect on the receiving field:

```
Iteration #
    1      WS-NEWFIELD( (1-1) * 3 + 1) : 3 ) = (1:3)
    2      WS-NEWFIELD( (2-1) * 3 + 1) : 3 ) = (4:3)
    3      WS-NEWFIELD( (3-1) * 3 + 1) : 3 ) = (5:3)
    4      WS-NEWFIELD( (4-1) * 3 + 1) : 3 ) = (10:3)
    5      WS-NEWFIELD( (5-1) * 3 + 1) : 3 ) = (13:3)
    6      WS-NEWFIELD( (6-1) * 3 + 1) : 3 ) = (16:3)
    7      WS-NEWFIELD( (7-1) * 3 + 1) : 3 ) = (19:3)
```

This produces "MONTUEWEDTHUFRISATSUN" in the receiving

```
000100 IDENTIFICATION DIVISION.
000200 PROGRAM-ID.      J6REFMOD.
000300 AUTHOR.          J. JANOSSY.
000400******************************************************************
000500*     DEMONSTRATE TOO-COMPLEX REFERENCE MODIFICATION          *
000600******************************************************************
000700 ENVIRONMENT DIVISION.
000800*
000900 DATA DIVISION.
001000 WORKING-STORAGE SECTION.
001100 01  WS-VAL1            PIC S9(3)  COMP-3.
001200 01  WS-VAL2            PIC S9(3)  COMP-3.
001300 01  WS-NEWFIELD        PIC X(30)  VALUE SPACES.
001400 01  WEEK-DAY           PIC 9(1).
001500 01  DAY-TABLE-SETUP.
001600     05  DAY-ROW  OCCURS 7 TIMES.
001700         10 FILLER      PIC X(9)   VALUE 'MONDAY   '.
001800         10 FILLER      PIC X(9)   VALUE 'TUESDAY  '.
001900         10 FILLER      PIC X(9)   VALUE 'WEDNESDAY'.
002000         10 FILLER      PIC X(9)   VALUE 'THURSDAY '.
002100         10 FILLER      PIC X(9)   VALUE 'FRIDAY   '.
002200         10 FILLER      PIC X(9)   VALUE 'SATURDAY '.
002300         10 FILLER      PIC X(9)   VALUE 'SUNDAY   '.
002400 01  DAY-TABLE  REDEFINES  DAY-TABLE-SETUP.
002500     05 DAY-NAME  PIC X(9)  OCCURS 7 TIMES  INDEXED BY DT-IX.
002600/
002700 PROCEDURE DIVISION.
002800 0000-MAINLINE.
002900     DISPLAY 'PROGRAM J6REFMOD STARTING'.
003000     MOVE +1 TO WS-VAL1.
003100     MOVE +3 TO WS-VAL2.
003200*
003300     DISPLAY 'Output of the first loop (as loop executes):'
003400     PERFORM
003500         VARYING DT-IX FROM 1 BY 1
003600         UNTIL DT-IX > 7
003700             SET WEEK-DAY TO DT-IX
003800             DISPLAY WEEK-DAY, ' ',
003900                 DAY-NAME (DT-IX) (WS-VAL1:WS-VAL2)
004000     END-PERFORM.
004100*
004200     DISPLAY 'Output of the second loop (in WS-NEWFIELD):'
004300     PERFORM
004400         VARYING WEEK-DAY FROM 1 BY 1
004500         UNTIL WEEK-DAY > 7
004600             MOVE DAY-NAME(WEEK-DAY) (1:3) TO
004700                 WS-NEWFIELD( (((WEEK-DAY - 1) * 3) + 1):3 )
004800     END-PERFORM.
004900     DISPLAY WS-NEWFIELD.
005000     DISPLAY 'PROGRAM ENDING'.
005100     STOP RUN.
```

(a)

(b)

(c)

Output:

```
PROGRAM J6REFMOD STARTING
Output of the first loop (as loop executes):
1  MON
2  TUE
3  WED
4  THU
5  FRI
6  SAT
7  SUN
Output of the second loop (in WS-NEWFIELD):
MONTUEWEDTHUFRISATSUN
PROGRAM ENDING
```

Figure 11.7 Reference Modification and Indexed Fields; Overdoing It!

a. The small hard-coded table at lines 1600 through 2500 carries an index for demonstration purposes.

b. The PERFORM ... VARYING at lines 3400 through 4000 references DAY-NAME by index and also uses reference modification to produce the output shown.

c. The PERFORM ... VARYING at lines 4300 through 4800 produce the output shown. But the computed reference modification at line 4700 is too complex to be maintained reliably.

field! This processing by the second loop in J6REFMOD is an extreme use of reference modification. This can be *very confusing.* I suggest that you not code this way (and not condone this kind of coding) because it can tremendously increase the time required for program maintenance.

11.10   YOU CAN NEST COPY DIRECTIVES

You can use the word COPY in a program to copy in a record description or other text that has been stored in a copy library. You simply put the word COPY in column 12 or beyond, followed by the member name in the copy library:

```
COPY PAYREC.
```

The compiler seeks items you want to copy into your program at the partitioned data set (library), coded at the //SYSLIB DD statement in the JCL that executes it in the compile step. The JCL can specify one copy library or you can concatenate multiple copy libraries at this DDname.

Under VS COBOL the items you obtained by COPY could not themselves contain the word COPY. With VS COBOL II you can nest the COPY directives as much as you like. The items that you obtain with COPY can also contain COPY directives, as illustrated in Figure 11.8.

11.11   DOUBLE BYTE CHARACTER SET AND KANJI

IBM developed the Double Byte Character Set to store graphic symbols and Japanese language characters in 16 bits per byte. Eight-bit bytes only have the capacity to store 256 different values while 16-bit bytes can store over 65,000 values. DBCS characters are defined with the new picture clause PIC G(nn).

Double byte character strings are unusual and must be delimited by a special control sequence. Unless you deal with exotic or foreign language operations, you will probably have no contact with PIC G(nn) items. A data-name defined as PIC G(nn) can be tested to see if it is in the KANJI data class, just as you would test ordinary numeric data to see if the contents were numeric:

```
IF WS-SPECIAL-DATA IS KANJI PERFORM . . .
```

```
000100 IDENTIFICATION DIVISION.
000200 PROGRAM-ID.    COPYDEMO.
000300*******************************************************************
000400*               EXAMPLE PROGRAM WITH NESTED "COPY"                *
000500*******************************************************************
000600 ENVIRONMENT DIVISION.
000700 DATA DIVISION.
000800 WORKING-STORAGE SECTION.
000900 COPY STUFF.
001000 PROCEDURE DIVISION.
001100 0000-MAINLINE.
001200     STOP RUN.
```

This is STUFF:
```
01  STUFF-IN-WORKING-STORAGE.
    COPY STUFF1.
```

This is STUFF1:
```
05 STUFF-LINE-1.  COPY STUFF2.
```

This is STUFF2:
```
10 STUFF-LINE-2.  COPY STUFF3.
```

This is STUFF3:
```
15 STUFF-LINE-3.  COPY STUFF4.
```

This is STUFF4:
```
20 STUFF-LINE-4.  COPY STUFF5.
```

This is STUFF5:
```
25 STUFF-LINE-5      PIC X(1).
```

```
PP 5668-958 IBM VS COBOL II RELEASE 3.2 09/05/90            COPYDEMO  DATE 05/05/92
LINEID  PL SL  ----+-*A-1-B--+----2----+----3----+----4----+----5----+----6----+----7-|
000001        000100 IDENTIFICATION DIVISION.
000002        000200 PROGRAM-ID.    COPYDEMO.
000003        000300*******************************************************************
000004        000400*               EXAMPLE PROGRAM WITH NESTED "COPY"                *
000005        000500*******************************************************************
000006        000600 ENVIRONMENT DIVISION.
000007        000700 DATA DIVISION.
000008        000800 WORKING-STORAGE SECTION.
000009        000900 COPY STUFF.
000010C              01  STUFF-IN-WORKING-STORAGE.
000011C                  COPY STUFF1.
000012C                  05 STUFF-LINE-1.
000013C                              COPY STUFF2.
000014C                  10 STUFF-LINE-2.
000015C                              COPY STUFF3.
000016C                  15 STUFF-LINE-3.
000017C                              COPY STUFF4.
000018C                  20 STUFF-LINE-4.
000019C                              COPY STUFF5.
000020C                  25 STUFF-LINE-5      PIC X(1).
000021        001000 PROCEDURE DIVISION.
000022        001100 0000-MAINLINE.
000023        001200     STOP RUN.
```

Figure 11.8 You Can Now Nest COPY Directives.

Under VS COBOL you could not use the COPY directive within a copy library member itself. With VS COBOL II you can COPY things that themselves copy other items.

```
000100 IDENTIFICATION DIVISION.
000200 PROGRAM-ID.    J7WHEN.
000300 AUTHOR.        J. JANOSSY.
000400 INSTALLATION.  DEPAUL UNIVERSITY.
000500*
000600*REMARKS.       SHOWS YOU HOW TO GET THE "WHEN COMPILED" DATE
000700*               FROM VS COBOL II AND USE REFERENCE MODIFICATION
000800*               TO FORMAT IT FOR USE IN A PAGE HEADING.  THE
000900*               WHEN COMPILED DATE IS VERY USEFUL FOR AUDIT
001000*               CONTROL SINCE IT MAKES VISIBLE THE ACTUAL COMPILE
001100*               DATE OF THE PROGRAM LOAD MODULE THAT'S RUNNING!
001200*
001300 ENVIRONMENT DIVISION.
001400*
001500 DATA DIVISION.
001600 WORKING-STORAGE SECTION.
001700 01  WS-WHEN-COMPILED            PIC X(16).
001800 01  WS-PG-HEAD-FIELD            PIC X(14).
001900*
002000 PROCEDURE DIVISION.
002100 0000-MAINLINE.
002200     DISPLAY 'PROGRAM J7WHEN STARTING'.
002300     DISPLAY '----------------------------------'.
002400     MOVE WHEN-COMPILED TO WS-WHEN-COMPILED.
002500     DISPLAY 'WS-WHEN-COMPILED = ', WS-WHEN-COMPILED.
002600     DISPLAY '----------------------------------'.
002700     STRING WS-WHEN-COMPILED(1:8)   DELIMITED BY SIZE
002800            ' '                     DELIMITED BY SIZE
002900            WS-WHEN-COMPILED(9:2)   DELIMITED BY SIZE
003000            ':'                     DELIMITED BY SIZE
003100            WS-WHEN-COMPILED(12:2)  DELIMITED BY SIZE
003200         INTO WS-PG-HEAD-FIELD.
003300     INSPECT WS-PG-HEAD-FIELD REPLACING ALL '/' BY '-'.
003400     DISPLAY 'WS-PG-HEAD-FIELD = ', WS-PG-HEAD-FIELD.
003500     DISPLAY '----------------------------------'.
003600     STOP RUN.
```

Output:

```
PROGRAM J7WHEN STARTING
-----------------------------------
WS-WHEN-COMPILED = 03/15/9219.51.13
-----------------------------------
WS-PG-HEAD-FIELD = 03-15-92 19:51
-----------------------------------
```

Figure 11.9 Using the WHEN-COMPILED register.

11.12 ALPHABETIC NOW INCLUDES LOWERCASE LETTERS

VS COBOL II Release 3 is the first IBM COBOL compiler to regard lowercase letters as ALPHABETIC. In older compilers only uppercase satisfied this test. Now, two new data classes are also defined (and ALPHABETIC still remains):

• ALPHABETIC-LOWER is true for a field only if it contains all lowercase letters or spaces (letters between a-z or space).
• ALPHABETIC-UPPER is true for a field only if it contains all uppercase letters or spaces (letters between A-Z or space). ALPHABETIC-UPPER gives you the same effect as ALPHABETIC did before.
• ALPHABETIC is now true for mixed-case field contents such as 'AaBbCcDeEe'.

VS COBOL II makes a new distinction concerning edited fields. In the past, a PIC like the following was considered alphabetic by nature since it consisted entirely of alphabetic characters separated by spaces (B). This field is now considered to be ALPHANUMERIC-EDITED:

```
PIC A(3)BA(2)BA(4)
```

11.13   WHEN-COMPILED REGISTER

You can access a special register named WHEN-COMPILED to obtain the compile date and time stored in the load module of any VS COBOL II program. You'll get this in the format shown in Figure 11.9, which is MM/DD/YYHH.MM.SS. You can use reference modification and STRING to put this information on any print output as a 14-byte character field. Why do this? It can help serve as audit trail information to end users and EDP auditors. It identifies the particular load module version that actually executed to produce the output.

12

VSAM Changes: Communication Codes and File Status

In this chapter I show you how VS COBOL II Release 3 has improved the COBOL-to-VSAM interface in two major ways:

- It provides an additional status "information pipe" that gives you VSAM's own return codes. This is called "extended VSAM status."
- It provides 16 additional File Status values (in addition to the 18 already existing) to better communicate the cause of problems.

Both improvements deal with the amount of information and error diagnosis VSAM can provide to your VS COBOL II Release 3 programs. To get the most out of these new features you need to become familiar with a consistent pattern for their use.

12.1 VSAM BACKGROUND

IBM created the MVS operating system in 1963–64. It was endowed with three file access methods:

- Sequential access method (BSAM, later QSAM): sequential files.
- Direct access method (BDAM): relative and direct files.
- Indexed sequential files (ISAM).

IBM released VSAM (Virtual Storage Access Method) in 1973 to replace BDAM and ISAM to make better use of system resources. ISAM lacked support for alternate keys. ISAM relied too much on job control language (JCL) for file specification and was becoming unwieldy. Both BDAM and ISAM required separate support for IBM's three mainframe operating system environments (MVS, DOS, and VM). VSAM overcame these limitations. Through the use of one major utility program, IDCAMS, support for VSAM was housed outside of any operating system software.

12.2 THE VSAM/PROGRAM INTERFACE

The COBOL program interface to VSAM consists of the OPEN, CLOSE, and data set access verbs READ, WRITE, REWRITE, DELETE, and START. In response to any request from a program for service using these verbs, VSAM provides back a File Status value, called the "status key" in IBM manuals, as shown in Figure 12.1. You get the File Status value into your program by documenting its WORKING-STORAGE name in your SELECT/ASSIGN statement.

12.3 VS COBOL II EXTENDED VSAM STATUS CODES

VS COBOL II gives you a second set of optional information fields in addition to File Status. You receive File Status and the extended status

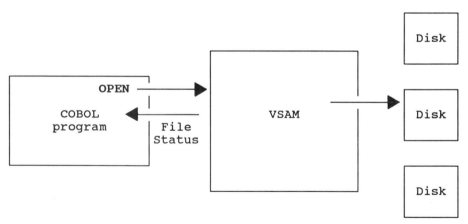

Figure 12.1   VSAM Communicates I/O Command Outcome with File Status.

Whenever you take any action with a VSAM file, you get a File Status value indicating the outcome of the action. You have to check File Status to make sure that the action succeeded, even for OPEN and CLOSE when no record is involved.

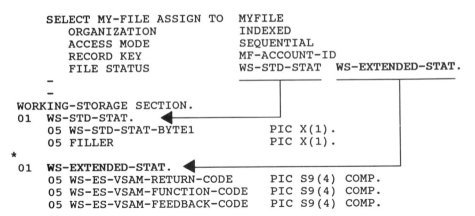

```
        SELECT MY-FILE ASSIGN TO    MYFILE
            ORGANIZATION            INDEXED
            ACCESS MODE             SEQUENTIAL
            RECORD KEY              MF-ACCOUNT-ID
            FILE STATUS             WS-STD-STAT  WS-EXTENDED-STAT.
        -
        -
    WORKING-STORAGE SECTION.
    01  WS-STD-STAT.
        05 WS-STD-STAT-BYTE1        PIC X(1).
        05 FILLER                   PIC X(1).
  *
    01  WS-EXTENDED-STAT.
        05 WS-ES-VSAM-RETURN-CODE      PIC S9(4) COMP.
        05 WS-ES-VSAM-FUNCTION-CODE    PIC S9(4) COMP.
        05 WS-ES-VSAM-FEEDBACK-CODE    PIC S9(4) COMP.
```

Figure 12.2 VS COBOL II Gives You Extended File Status Information.

If you code a second File Status field in the SELECT/ASSIGN statement for a VSAM file, you can receive three additional number codes from VSAM for each I/O action. These three binary numbers pass through information from VSAM itself. This information is meaningful only when a problem arises. It can help you resolve problems if you make it visible by DISPLAYing it. See Appendix A for a complete reference to these values!

codes as shown in Figure 12.2. These fields pass through three binary number codes directly from VSAM. They can help identify what problems exist when access to a VSAM data set fails.

The VSAM function code and the feedback code will contain meaningful values only when your attempted action is not successful. If you make these values visible outside of your program when an action fails, you are better prepared to diagnose what the problem is.

You need convenient documentation to be able to interpret the extended information codes. But IBM lists these codes in VSAM manuals, not VS COBOL II manuals. I documented the meaning of these codes (in plain language) for your ease of reference in Appendix A.

12.4 FILE STATUS REPLACES INVALID KEY

VSAM provides back a File Status value in response to any request from a program for I/O service, as shown in Figure 12.3. You need to use the File Status value to get communication about possible VSAM failure on every I/O action.

The INVALID KEY phrase is an older way to receive communication from an indexed file access method. INVALID KEY was included in VS COBOL to deal with ISAM files. For example, here is how you could do a read of an ISAM file to get a record with key value "ABCDE":

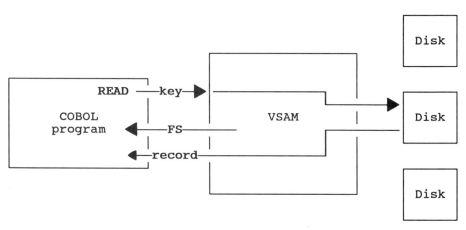

Figure 12.3 File Status Accompanies Every VSAM Record I/O Action.

When you READ a record by key from a VSAM Key-Sequenced Data Set (indexed file), you get a File Status value in return as well as (possibly) the record. The File Status value tells you whether you obtained a record or if there was no record with the key you specified. But a third possibility also exists: VSAM may have detected a file problem that your program can't deal with. Only File Status can reveal that third case to you so you must receive and handle it properly!

```
MOVE 'ABCDE' TO fd-key-field.
READ file-name
    INVALID KEY
        PERFORM 1234-action-for-key-not-found
```

VSAM File Status tells you everything that INVALID KEY tells you and much more. VS COBOL II continues to support INVALID KEY, but do you really want to perpetuate the use of the awkward INVALID KEY syntax? You have two choices: keep using INVALID KEY and test File Status within it, or abandon INVALID KEY completely and just use File Status for all access method communication. *I strongly recommend that you just use File Status!*

If you choose to perpetuate older "ISAM-style" coding within VS COBOL II, you should now do a random READ as in the top part of Figure 12.4. But since you need to check File Status anyway, why not abandon INVALID KEY and simplify things? You can now do the same random read more clearly as shown in the bottom part of Figure 12.4.

Obsolete

```
MOVE key-wanted TO fd-key-field.
READ file-name
    INVALID KEY
        if File Status not = '0' or '23'
            display File Status, perform forced abort
        else
            perform 1234-action-for-key-not-found
        end-if
    NOT INVALID KEY
        perform action for record found.
```

Modern

```
MOVE key-wanted TO fd-key-field.
READ file-name.

IF WS-File-Status-Byte1 = '0'  ◄────── Got the record
    action-for-rec-found

  ELSE

IF WS-File-Status = '23'       ◄────── Couldn't find it
    action-for-rec-not-found

  ELSE

    actions-for-forced-abort.  ◄────── VSAM failed!
```

Figure 12.4   INVALID KEY is Obsolete; Use File Status Checking.

VS COBOL II continues to support INVALID KEY as a concession to the old ISAM coding style. But you must still receive File Status and arrange to make it visible in case of a VSAM problem. The modern way to handle VSAM file I/O does not involve INVALID KEY coding. Instead, you simply take an I/O action and then interrogate File Status. This is the same pattern used by more modern system software such as DB2 (although the actual nature of the status field and value meanings differ).

12.5   THE IMPORTANCE OF FILE STATUS

You must use File Status when you access VSAM data sets! The IBM manuals and many textbooks mislead you when they say that the File Status clause is "optional." It is about as optional as bathing or washing clothes.

VS COBOL II, as did VS COBOL, has to play ball with VSAM in the way VSAM prescribes. VSAM changed the rules about data set access when it came upon the scene in 1973. Older access methods such as QSAM (which still handles ordinary sequential data sets) and BPAM (which handles partitioned data sets) cause an abend if they detect any unresolvable problem; they "blow up." For example, trying to read records from a sequential data set when you have specified an incorrect block size causes an abend with a system completion code. The value of the system completion code helps you figure out what the problem is.

Your VS COBOL II program does not abend if VSAM detects an un-resolvable problem. Instead, VSAM "tells" your program about the problem via File Status. Your program (this means you!) has the responsibility of forcing an abort when an unresolvable problem arises. Receiving and checking File Status is the only way your program can "listen" to what VSAM is saying.

You can't avoid using File Status when you use VSAM. You can perpetuate the use of INVALID KEY but you still need to check File Status for your VSAM file OPEN and CLOSE. And you still need to test File Status after every READ, WRITE, REWRITE, DELETE, and START since it is the only way that you will find out about a catastrophic VSAM failure and have any clue about its nature. Why not use File Status for all actions and abandon INVALID KEY coding? This will make your programs clearer now and more susceptible to conversion to newer versions of VS COBOL II in the future.

12.6   FILE STATUS: ANTICIPATE BEFORE ACTING!

Every time you use one of the I/O verbs with a VSAM data set:

```
OPEN   CLOSE   READ   WRITE   REWRITE   START   DELETE
```

you have to anticipate up to three possible outcomes:

- *The action is completely successful.* This can mean that the data set you were trying to OPEN did successfully open. Maybe you were trying to READ a record by key and you obtained the record. Perhaps you were trying to write a record at random and you succeeded. Maybe you deleted the record you wanted to, or your data set CLOSE worked.

- *The action is unsuccessful but the situation is program-resolvable.* Maybe you did not obtain the record you were trying to READ. Or maybe you tried to randomly WRITE a record to the data set but a record already existed with that key value. Perhaps you tried to DELETE a record that was not in the data set.

- *The action is unsuccessful but the situation is not program-resolvable.* Maybe you tried to OPEN a data set but the OPEN failed and a File Status value of 96 indicates that the JCL for the job didn't include a DD statement for the file. Perhaps you tried to OPEN a data set a second time and the OPEN failed. Maybe you tried to CLOSE a data set that wasn't open, so the CLOSE failed. Or possibly VSAM failed trying to READ, WRITE, REWRITE, or DELETE a record due entirely to reasons internal to VSAM software.

Your program logic cannot cure the third type of problem! For situations of the third kind, your program has to identify the occurrence and pass through as much information about it (such as the VSAM codes and File Status) to the outside world, then intentionally stop (abort). You can best handle this with a standard checking pattern for File Status.

12.7 STANDARD FILE STATUS CHECKING PATTERN

You need to test File Status immediately after each execution of an I/O verb (OPEN, CLOSE, READ, WRITE, REWRITE, DELETE, START). The pattern of File Status testing is easy to understand. It takes the form shown in Figure 12.5. Follow the top part of Figure 12.5 if you want to report only the File Status value when a problem arises. Follow the bottom part of Figure 12.5 if you also want to make the VSAM extended communication codes visible (a good idea).

Code File Status as a group name with two one-byte fields under it is shown in Figure 12.6. The designers of the ANSI-standard File Status actually had in mind that you would test the first byte of File Status for summary information about status, not the entire two-byte field! Make the appropriate two or three tests of File Status in an IF/ELSE statement following your I/O action:

Complete Success?

- '0' (first byte) or '97' (both bytes) for OPEN
- '0' alone for all other actions

The reason you can't just test for '00' to determine if the action was successful is that VSAM uses the second byte of File Status to give you additional information about a few actions even when they are completely successful. For example, you get '02' for a successful READ under certain conditions. And for some reason IBM didn't follow the ANSI convention for OPEN and you might get either '0' or '97' when your VSAM file OPEN is successful.

File Status only:

```
SELECT MAST-FILE              ASSIGN TO MAST
    ORGANIZATION  IS INDEXED
    ACCESS MODE   IS RANDOM
    RECORD KEY    IS MF-KEY
    ALTERNATE RECORD KEY  IS MF-SALES-AGENT
        WITH DUPLICATES
    FILE STATUS   IS WS-MF-STAT.


WORKING-STORAGE SECTION.
01  WS-MF-STAT.
    05 WS-MF-STAT-B1              PIC X(1).
    05 FILLER                     PIC X(1).
        -
PROCEDURE DIVISION.
        -
    MOVE '31573' TO MF-KEY.
    READ MAST-FILE.
    IF WS-MF-STAT-B1 = '0'
        PERFORM 4000-UPDATE-IT
    ELSE
    IF WS-MF-STAT = '23'
        PERFORM 4200-KEY-NOT-ON-FILE
    ELSE
        DISPLAY '*****************************'
        DISPLAY 'FS AT READ = ', WS-MF-STAT
        DISPLAY 'FORCED ABORT DUE TO FILE ERROR'
        DISPLAY '*****************************'
        STOP RUN.
```

Extended File Status:

```
SELECT MAST-FILE              ASSIGN TO MAST
    ORGANIZATION  IS INDEXED
    ACCESS MODE   IS RANDOM
    RECORD KEY    IS MF-KEY
    ALTERNATE RECORD KEY  IS MF-SALES-AGENT
        WITH DUPLICATES
    FILE STATUS   IS WS-MF-STAT  WS-EXTENDED-STAT.      ⬅


WORKING-STORAGE SECTION.
01  WS-MF-STAT.
    05 WS-MF-STAT-B1              PIC X(1).
    05 FILLER                     PIC X(1).
*
01  WS-EXTENDED-STAT.
    05 WS-ES-VSAM-RETURN-CODE     PIC S9(4) COMP.
    05 WS-ES-VSAM-FUNCTION-CODE   PIC S9(4) COMP.       ⬅
    05 WS-ES-VSAM-FEEDBACK-CODE   PIC S9(4) COMP.
01  WS-RETURN-CODE                PIC 9(4).
01  WS-FUNCTION-CODE              PIC 9(4).
01  WS-FEEDBACK-CODE              PIC 9(4).
        -
PROCEDURE DIVISION.
        -
    MOVE '31573' TO MF-KEY.
    READ MAST-FILE.
    IF WS-MF-STAT-B1 = '0'
        PERFORM 4000-UPDATE-IT
    ELSE
    IF WS-MF-STAT = '23'
        PERFORM 4200-KEY-NOT-ON-FILE
    ELSE
        MOVE WS-ES-VSAM-RETURN-CODE    TO WS-RETURN-CODE
        MOVE WS-ES-VSAM-FUNCTION-CODE  TO WS-FUNCTION-CODE
        MOVE WS-ES-VSAM-FEEDBACK-CODE  TO WS-FEEDBACK-CODE
        DISPLAY '*****************************'
        DISPLAY 'FS AT READ = ', WS-MF-STAT
        DISPLAY 'VSAM RETURN CODE   = ', WS-RETURN-CODE      ⬅
        DISPLAY 'VSAM FUNCTION CODE = ', WS-FUNCTION-CODE
        DISPLAY 'VSAM FEEDBACK CODE = ', WS-FEEDBACK-CODE
        DISPLAY 'FORCED ABORT DUE TO FILE ERROR'
        DISPLAY '*****************************'
        STOP RUN.
```

Figure 12.5   File Status Checking Source Code: A Standard Pattern.

Program-Resolvable Lack of Success?

- '1' (first-byte) for sequential processing; it means end of file.
- '21' or '22' applies to WRITE or REWRITE; you're trying to write records out of sequence (sequential processing) or you are trying to add a record to a data set with a key that already exists in the data set.
- '23' means "key not found" and applies to READ, DELETE, and START, but not to WRITE!

First byte	This means:	Your response
0	The action was successful	Continue
1	AT END, sequential processing	End of job?
2	INVALID KEY detected	Trans key bad?
3	I/O error	Force abend, fix
4	Logic error	Force abend, fix
9	Implementation error	Force abend, fix

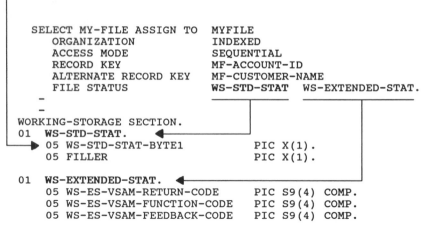

```
SELECT MY-FILE ASSIGN TO    MYFILE
       ORGANIZATION         INDEXED
       ACCESS MODE          SEQUENTIAL
       RECORD KEY           MF-ACCOUNT-ID
       ALTERNATE RECORD KEY MF-CUSTOMER-NAME
       FILE STATUS          WS-STD-STAT   WS-EXTENDED-STAT.
    -
    -
WORKING-STORAGE SECTION.
01  WS-STD-STAT.
    05 WS-STD-STAT-BYTE1         PIC X(1).
    05 FILLER                    PIC X(1).

01  WS-EXTENDED-STAT.
    05 WS-ES-VSAM-RETURN-CODE    PIC S9(4) COMP.
    05 WS-ES-VSAM-FUNCTION-CODE  PIC S9(4) COMP.
    05 WS-ES-VSAM-FEEDBACK-CODE  PIC S9(4) COMP.
```

Figure 12.6 Interpretation of File Status Values (First Byte).

VS COBOL II follows the ANSI-standard coding scheme for File Status values. The first byte of File Status reveals the outcome of your attempted I/O action. You test this first byte for '0' to see if the action was successful. Depending on the specific action you are attempting you then test either the first byte alone for another value, or the full two-byte value, to see if a program-resolvable error situation exists. It's incorrect to test the two-byte field for '00' as a measure of success. Some successful I/O outcomes produce '0' in the first byte but a non-zero value in the second byte!

Unresolvable Error?

In this third category your program can't cure the problem so it doesn't need to test further to find out the specific File Status value. What it does need to do is DISPLAY or otherwise output the File Status value and extended VSAM codes, record keys, and location/action in the program where the situation developed. The program then needs to stop (abort) in a very visible way.

Figure 12.7 shows you how the standard File Status checking pattern tells you about a program-unresolvable error. This resulted from a program that was being processed with a compile/link/go proc, and you'll recognize the linkage editor messages immediately above the program-generated abend information. File Status '96' deals with an OPEN problem. Check Appendix B and see if you can figure out what error was detected with the OPEN.

```
        SELECT MAST-FILE          ASSIGN TO MAST
            ORGANIZATION  IS INDEXED
            ACCESS MODE   IS RANDOM
            RECORD KEY    IS MF-KEY
            ALTERNATE RECORD KEY  IS MF-SALES-AGENT
                WITH DUPLICATES
            FILE STATUS   IS WS-MF-STAT.
        -
        -
    WORKING-STORAGE SECTION.
    01  WS-MF-STAT.
        05 WS-MF-STAT-B1           PIC X(1).
        05 FILLER                  PIC X(1).
        -
        -
    PROCEDURE DIVISION
        -
        -
        OPEN  I-O  MAST-FILE.
        IF WS-MF-STAT-B1 = '0'
           OR WS-MF-STAT = '97'
              NEXT SENTENCE
           ELSE
              DISPLAY '******************************'
              DISPLAY 'FS AT OPEN = ', WS-MF-STAT
              DISPLAY 'FORCED ABORT DUE TO FILE ERROR'
              DISPLAY '******************************'
              STOP RUN.
```

```
** MAIN       DID NOT PREVIOUSLY EXIST BUT WAS ADDED AND HAS AMODE 31
** LOAD MODULE HAS RMODE ANY
** AUTHORIZATION CODE IS        0.


******************************
FS AT OPEN = 96
FORCED ABORT DUE TO FILE ERROR
******************************
```

Figure 12.7 Output of Standard File Status Checking for an Error.

This DISPLAYed output was produced by the standard File Status checking pattern for a VSAM key-sequence data set OPEN. Use Appendix B in this book to find out what problem is indicated. To create production-caliber VS COBOL II programs, you need to provide standard logic to output File Status values like this.

12.8 VS COBOL II EXPANDS THE SET OF FILE STATUS VALUES!

Prior to the introduction of VS COBOL II Release 3, only 18 File Status code values existed. This lumped many problems under a catch all value such as '92', which was given the vague definition "program logic error." The 18 File Status values did not help programmers as much as was desirable in solving some types of problems.

With VS COBOL Release 3, IBM expanded the number of File Status values to a total of 34. You can now receive much more precise information about catastrophic problems. Figure 12.8 shows you the File Status values in the various versions of IBM's COBOL. Your programs need to be able to pass them through to the outside world when problems occur. I have listed the meaning of each of the File Status values (the original 18 and the 16 new ones) for you in Appendix B.

12.9 YOU LOSE IF YOU EMULATE RELEASE 2 WITH CMPR2

VS COBOL II provides a compiler option named CMPR2. CMPR2 stands for "CoMPatibility with Release 2." If you use the CMPR2 option, VS COBOL II Release 3 works as if it were Release 2. You can select this option either by using it on the EXEC statement PARM line for the compiler or by including it in a PROCESS statement at the start of your program (see Chapter 3).

VS COBOL VS COBOL-II Release 1,2 The existing codes:	VS COBOL-II Release 3 Now these also exist:
00 02 10 20 21 22 23 24 30 34 90 91 92 93 94 95 96 97	04 05 07 14 35 37 38 39 41 42 43 44 46 47 48 49

Figure 12.8 Summary of VS COBOL II Expanded File Status Values.

VS COBOL II adds the 16 File Status values shown on the right to the traditional 18 values produced by VS COBOL. This gives you much more specific diagnostic help for program-unresolvable error situations. See Appendix B; it tells you the meaning of all 34 File Status values!

You may be tempted to process programs already converted to VS COBOL II Release 2, or programs originated in it, with the CMPR2 option instead of converting them to Release 3. When you use the CMPR2 option of VS COBOL II Release 3, your program will receive only the original 18 File Status values. To receive the full VS COBOL II 34 File Status values you must compile your program *without* the CMPR2 option.

Watch out! Your installation may have set CMPR2 as the default. Check your list of PARM options from a VS COBOL II compile (see Figure 3.3). If CMPR2 is in effect by default, make sure you override it with NOCMPR2 in your compile JCL or with a PROCESS statement in your programs!

12.10 *TRY IT!* SEEING VSAM EXTENDED COMMUNICATION CODES

The best way to become familiar with new VS COBOL II VSAM features is to try out a program and experiment with it. This takes a little preparation, however, since you need to establish a VSAM file for a program to deal with. I have documented for you here a complete "environment" including test data, file definition JCL and IDCAMS coding, and a demonstration program to make your try-out of the new features as easy as possible.

Figure 12.9 shows you some data intended to be housed in a VSAM key-sequenced data set (IBM's term for an indexed file). You may recognize the relationship of this data to the discussion of the Miracle Pleasure Cruise company in Chapter 8 (see Figure 8.3). Each record in this file documents a purchase of passage on a cruise. The key of a record is in the first five bytes and is unique. A nonunique alternate key field named SALES-AGENT exists in positions 46 through 68. The DECK-CODE field carries a code matching the table in Figure 8.3.

Figure 12.10 provides complete MVS JCL and IDCAMS control statement coding to define a key-sequenced data set to house passenger ticket records. This JCL is named VSAMJCL. You can follow this as a pattern but you will have to provide installation-specific information about disk volume serial number and data set names in order to use it. I suggest (here is admittedly a plug) that you consult *Practical VSAM For Today's Programmers* (Janossy and Guzik, John Wiley and Sons, Inc., 1988) if you need a refresher on the composition of this IDCAMS coding.

I have listed program VSAMDEMO in Figure 12.11. This program uses the standard File Status checking pattern I described earlier. The program illustrates how you can code a modern OPEN for update, random READ, REWRITE, DELETE, and CLOSE. The program updates the VSAM-stored passenger records shown in Figure 12.9 and produces only simple DISPLAY messages as shown after the source code listing.

Figure 12.12 provides you with the JCL I used to compile, linkage edit, and run VSAMDEMO. I named this VSAMRUN. I put an IDCAMs print of data set contents before and after the run to be able to compare data set contents. You need the two "GO." references to MAST and MAST1. MAST is coded in the SELECT/ASSIGN statement of VSAM-DEMO. VS COBOL II automatically generates a reference to MAST1 by appending a "1" to my DDname because the SELECT/ASSIGN mentions an alternate record key. Your JCL has to point this generated DDname to the alternate index path name. I did this in line 30 of Figure 12.12. (See section 12.14 for more discussion about this phenomenon.)

MF-KEY	Passenger Name		Cruise Date	Ticket Qty	Deck Code	SALES AGENT	Date Bought	Filler
	Last	First						
X(5)	X(14)	X(15)	X(6)	9(3)	X(2)	X(23)	X(6)	X(6)
1　　5	6　　19	20　　34	35　　40	41　　43	44　　45	46　　68	69　　74	75　　80
0						45		

```
BROWSE - CSCJGJ.CSC.CNTL(TICKDATA) - 01.01 ----------- LINE 000000 COL 001 080
COMMAND ===>                                              SCROLL ===> PAGE
******************************** TOP OF DATA ********************-CAPS ON-**
   31256NILLY        WILLIE       900216002S1HOBBIT INTERNATIONAL   890718
   31257IPPI         MRS.         900216001B2JACK SPRAT TRAVEL      890817
   31260MALLOW       MARSHA       900216001B HOLIDAY TOURS, INC.    890805
   31307WARE         DELLA        900216004B1WORLD TRAVEL, INC.     890909
   31310SHAW         ARKAN        900216007S1HOLIDAY TOURS, INC.    890911
   31573WALLBANGER   HARVEY       900216002B HOBBIT INTERNATIONAL   891214
   31574AH           GEORGE       900216001S1HOBBIT INTERNATIONAL   900103
   31668ZOORI        MOE          900216004S1FOX VALLEY TRAVEL      900103
   31778SLEEPING     R. U.        900216001B1UWANNAGO TRAVEL, INC.  900107
   31779HEAD         M. T.        900216002C KOOK'S TOURS           900113
   35112CABOOSE      LUCE         900331001B2HOBBIT INTERNATIONAL   900121
   35189HOE          IDA          900331002S HOBBIT INTERNATIONAL   890603
******************************* BOTTOM OF DATA ********************-CAPS ON-**
```

Figure 12.9 The Miracle Pleasure Cruise Company Passenger Ticket File.

The 80-byte records shown here are housed in a sequential data set that can be loaded to a VSAM key-sequenced data set to serve as a master file. Each record documents the passages arranged by a person for a pleasure cruise. The unique key field of each record is MF-KEY. SALES-AGENT is a nonunique alternate key. The DECK-CODE field indicates the deck of the ship on which passage has been arranged. See Figure 8.3 in Chapter 8 for a sketch of the cross section of the pleasure cruise ship. The JCL in Figure 12.10 loads these records to a VSAM file so you can experiment with the programs in this chapter.

```
EDIT --- CSCJGJ.CSC.CNTL(VSAMJCL) - 01.01 ------------------ COLUMNS 001 072
COMMAND ===>                                               SCROLL ===> PAGE
****** ************************** TOP OF DATA ******************************
000001 //CSCJGJA    JOB 1,'BIN 7 JANOSSY',MSGLEVEL=(1,1),MSGCLASS=X,
000002 //  NOTIFY=CSCJGJ
000003 //*
000004 //*   CSCJGJ.CSC.CNTL(VSAMJCL)
000005 //*   CREATE VSAM MIRACLE TOURS TICKET MASTER FILE
000006 //*   WITH ALTERNATE KEY FOR SALES AGENT
000007 //*
000008 //******************************************************************
000009 //*                                                                *
000010 //*   DEFINE AND LOAD THE CUSTOMER KSDS                            *
000011 //*                                                                *
000012 //******************************************************************
000013 //STEPA     EXEC  PGM=IDCAMS
000014 //SYSPRINT  DD    SYSOUT=*
000015 //MASTIN    DD    DSN=CSCJGJ.CSC.CNTL(TICKDATA),
000016 //  DISP=SHR
000017 //*
000018 //WORKSRT1  DD    DSN=CSCJGJ.CSC.IDCUT1,
000019 //  UNIT=SYSDA,
000020 //  DISP=OLD,
000021 //  AMP='AMORG',
000022 //  VOL=SER=ACSCAC
000023 //*
000024 //WORKSRT2  DD    DSN=CSCJGJ.CSC.IDCUT2,
000025 //  UNIT=SYSDA,
000026 //  DISP=OLD,
000027 //  AMP='AMORG',
000028 //  VOL=SER=ACSCAC
000029 //*
000030 //SYSIN     DD    *
000031                                        /* HOUSEKEEPING DELETES */
000032
000033     DELETE      CSCJGJ.CSC.TICKMST2 -
000034                 CLUSTER
000035
000036     DELETE      CSCJGJ.CSC.IDCUT1 -
000037                 CLUSTER
000038
000039     DELETE      CSCJGJ.CSC.IDCUT2 -
000040                 CLUSTER
000041
000042     SET LASTCC=0                       /* MAY NOT BE FOUND; GET */
000043     SET MAXCC=0                        /* RID OF COND CODE 8    */
000044
000045     /* - - - - - - - - - - - CREATE BASE CLUSTER - - - - -*/
000046
000047     DEFINE -
000048         CLUSTER    (   NAME(CSCJGJ.CSC.TICKMST2) -
000049                        VOLUMES(ACSCAC) -
000050                        RECORDSIZE(80 80) -
000051                        KEYS(5 0) -
000052                        TRACKS(1 1) -
000053                        SHAREOPTIONS(2 3) -
000054                        SPEED -
000055                        IMBED                        ) -
000056                 -
000057         DATA       (   NAME(CSCJGJ.CSC.TICKMST2.DATA) -
000058                        CONTROLINTERVALSIZE(4096) -
000059                        FREESPACE(6 1)               ) -
000060                 -
000061         INDEX      (   NAME(CSCJGJ.CSC.TICKMST2.INDEX)    )
000062
000063     /* - - - - - - - - - - - IF CREATE OKAY, LOAD IT - - -*/
000064
000065     IF LASTCC = 0 -
000066     THEN -
000067         REPRO      INFILE(MASTIN) -
000068                    OUTDATASET(CSCJGJ.CSC.TICKMST2)
000069
000070     /* - - - - - - - - - - - DEFINE THE ALTERNATE INDEX - */
000071
000072     DEFINE -
000073         AIX        (   NAME(CSCJGJ.CSC.TICKMST2.SALEAIX) -
000074                        RELATE(CSCJGJ.CSC.TICKMST2) -
000075                        VOLUMES(ACSCAC) -
000076                        RECORDSIZE(33 523) -
000077                        KEYS(23 45) -
000078                        NONUNIQUEKEY -
000079                        TRACKS(1 1) -
000080                        SHAREOPTIONS(2 3) -
000081                        UNIQUE -
000082                        UPGRADE -
000083                        SPEED -
000084                        IMBED                        ) -
000085                 -
000086         DATA       (   NAME(CSCJGJ.CSC.TICKMST2.SALEAIX.DATA) -
000087                        CONTROLINTERVALSIZE(4096) -
000088                        FREESPACE(2 1)               ) -
000089                 -
000090         INDEX      (   NAME(CSCJGJ.CSC.TICKMST2.SALEAIX.INDEX) )
000091
000092     BLDINDEX    INDATASET(CSCJGJ.CSC.TICKMST2) -
000093                 OUTDATASET(CSCJGJ.CSC.TICKMST2.SALEAIX) -
000094                 WORKFILES(WORKSRT1 WORKSRT2) -
000095                 EXTERNALSORT
```

(a)

(b)

(c)

(d)

(e)

Figure 12.10 *(see legend on page 230)*

```
000096
000097     DEFINE -
000098        PATH      (    NAME(CSCJGJ.CSC.TICKMST2.SALEAIX.PATH) -
000099                       PATHENTRY(CSCJGJ.CSC.TICKMST2.SALEAIX) )
000100
000101     /* - - - - - - - - - - - LIST CATALOG TO SEE INFO  - -*/
000102
000103     LISTCAT -
000104        ENTRIES   ( CSCJGJ.CSC.TICKMST2 -
000105                    CSCJGJ.CSC.TICKMST2.SALEAIX ) -
000106                  ALL
000107
000108     /* - - - - - - - - - - PRINT IT IN PRIMARY KEY SEQ  - -*/
000109
000110     PRINT        INDATASET(CSCJGJ.CSC.TICKMST2) -
000111                  COUNT(50) -
000112                  CHARACTER
000113
000114     /* - - - - - - - - - - NOW PRINT IT IN ALT KEY SEQ  - -*/
000115
000116     PRINT        INDATASET(CSCJGJ.CSC.TICKMST2.SALEAIX.PATH) -
000117                  COUNT(50) -
000118                  CHARACTER
000119
000120     /* - - - - - - - - - - THIS PRINTS THE AIX RECORDS  - -*/
000121
000122     PRINT        INDATASET(CSCJGJ.CSC.TICKMST2.SALEAIX) -
000123                  COUNT(50) -
000124                  CHARACTER
000125  /*
000126  //
```

Figure 12.10   JCL and IDCAMS Control Statements to Create a VSAM KSDS.

This MVS JCL will execute the IDCAMS utility to define and load a VSAM key-sequenced data set housing the passenger records illustrated in Figure 12.9.

a. (page 229) IDCAMS DELETE statements eliminate existing copies of the data set to be created and any copies of work files used by the BLDINDEX command at (e). You may not have to code lines 36 through 40 or use lines 94 and 95, depending on how your installation supports BLDINDEX.

b. (page 229) The DEFINE places the information in the system catalog necessary to create a VSAM data set. The coding of these specifications is tied to the primary key length and offset from the beginning of the record, and contains installation-dependent items such as disk volume serial number.

c. (page 229) REPRO copies the records in the sequential data set to the newly-defined VSAM data set.

d. (page 229) DEFINE AIX defines the alternate index in the system catalog. KEYS here mentions the length and offset of the alternate key field in each record. NONUNIQUEKEY tells VSAM that the same sales agent name may exist in more than one data record.

e. (page 229) The BLDINDEX command reads the newly loaded VSAM data set, "picks off" primary and alternate key field information, and builds the alternate index records. It sorts them into ascending sequence of alternate key and houses them in a key-sequenced data set of its own. The PATH command establishes a name for access via the alternate index.

f. (page 230) LISTCAT tells IDCAMS to produce a formatted listing of catalog-stored information about the VSAM data set and the alternate index.

g. (page 230) The three PRINT commands at the end of the job stream tell IDCAMS to print the data records in primary key sequence, then in alternate key sequence via the alternate index, and finally to print the alternate index records themselves.

```
000100 IDENTIFICATION DIVISION.
000200 PROGRAM-ID.    VSAMDEMO.
000300 AUTHOR.        J JANOSSY
000400 INSTALLATION.  DEPAUL UNIVERSITY.
000500 DATE-WRITTEN.  SEPT 1991.
000600 DATE-COMPILED.
000700*REMARKS.        DEMONSTRATION OF RANDOM ACCESS READ, REWRITE,
000800*                AND DELETE. THIS IS NOT A MODEL FOR REAL
000900*                UPDATE LOGIC, IT ONLY DEMONSTRATES THE SYNTAX
001000*                OF VSAM I/O CODING AND VERBS.
001100*
001200 ENVIRONMENT DIVISION.
001300 INPUT-OUTPUT SECTION.
001400 FILE-CONTROL.
001500     SELECT MAST-FILE          ASSIGN TO MAST
001600         ORGANIZATION  IS INDEXED
001700         ACCESS MODE   IS RANDOM
001800         RECORD KEY    IS MF-KEY
001900         ALTERNATE RECORD KEY  IS MF-SALES-AGENT
002000             WITH DUPLICATES
002100         FILE STATUS   IS WS-MF-STAT.
002200*
002300 DATA DIVISION.
002400 FILE SECTION.
002500*
002600* Note: No "BLOCK CONTAINS" clause is used for a VSAM file:
002700*
002800 FD  MAST-FILE
002900     LABEL RECORDS ARE STANDARD
003000     RECORD CONTAINS 80 CHARACTERS.
003100 01  MAST-RECORD.
003200     05 MF-KEY                  PIC X(5).
003300     05 MF-LAST-NAME            PIC X(14).
003400     05 MF-FIRST-NAME           PIC X(15).
003500     05 MF-CRUISE-DATE          PIC X(6).
003600     05 MF-TICKET-QTY           PIC 9(3).
003700     05 MF-DECK-CODE            PIC X(2).
003800     05 MF-SALES-AGENT          PIC X(23).
003900     05 MF-DATE-BOUGHT          PIC X(6).
004000     05 FILLER                  PIC X(6).
004100/
004200 WORKING-STORAGE SECTION.
004300 01  WS-MF-STAT.
004400     05 WS-MF-STAT-B1           PIC X(1).
004500     05 FILLER                  PIC X(1).
004600/
004700 PROCEDURE DIVISION.
004800 0000-MAINLINE.
004900     PERFORM 1000-BOJ.
005000     PERFORM 2000-PROCESS.
005100     PERFORM 3000-EOJ.
005200     STOP RUN.
005300*
005400 1000-BOJ.
005500*-------------------------------------------------------------
005600* Demonstrating how to OPEN a VSAM file for update:
005700*-------------------------------------------------------------
005800     OPEN I-O  MAST-FILE.
005900     IF WS-MF-STAT-B1 = '0'
006000        OR WS-MF-STAT = '97'
006100           NEXT SENTENCE
006200     ELSE
006300         DISPLAY '********************************'
006400         DISPLAY 'FS AT OPEN = ', WS-MF-STAT
006500         DISPLAY 'FORCED ABORT DUE TO FILE ERROR'
006600         DISPLAY '********************************'
006700         STOP RUN.
006800*
006900* If you have any sequential files OPEN them here after you
007000* have confirmed that the VSAM file opened successfully.
007100/
007200 2000-PROCESS.
007300*-------------------------------------------------------------
007400* Demonstrating the random access READ (key on file):
007500*-------------------------------------------------------------
007600     MOVE '31668' TO MF-KEY.
007700     READ MAST-FILE.
007800     IF WS-MF-STAT-B1 = '0'
007900        DISPLAY MAST-RECORD
008000     ELSE
008100     IF WS-MF-STAT = '23'
008200        DISPLAY MF-KEY, '  KEY NOT FOUND ON VSAM FILE'
008300        ELSE
008400         DISPLAY '********************************'
008500         DISPLAY 'FS AT READ = ', WS-MF-STAT
008600         DISPLAY 'FORCED ABORT DUE TO FILE ERROR'
008700         DISPLAY '********************************'
008800         STOP RUN.
008900*-------------------------------------------------------------
009000* Demonstrating the random access READ (key not on file):
009100*-------------------------------------------------------------
009200     MOVE 'ABCDE' TO MF-KEY.
009300     READ MAST-FILE.
009400     IF WS-MF-STAT-B1 = '0'
009500        DISPLAY MAST-RECORD
```

(a)

(b)

(c)

(d)

(e)

Figure 12.11 *(see legend page 233)*

```
009600         ELSE
009700         IF WS-MF-STAT = '23'
009800             DISPLAY MF-KEY, '  KEY NOT FOUND ON VSAM FILE'
009900         ELSE
010000             DISPLAY '*******************************'
010100             DISPLAY 'FS AT READ = ', WS-MF-STAT
010200             DISPLAY 'FORCED ABORT DUE TO FILE ERROR'
010300             DISPLAY '*******************************'
010400             STOP RUN.
010500*--------------------------------------------------------------
010600* Demonstrating the random access READ (key on file) followed
010700* by a change to the record and REWRITE of the record:
010800*--------------------------------------------------------------
010900         MOVE '31573' TO MF-KEY.
011000         READ MAST-FILE.
011100         IF WS-MF-STAT-B1 = '0'
011200             DISPLAY 'BEFORE UPDATE= ', MAST-RECORD
011300             PERFORM 4000-UPDATE-IT
011400         ELSE
011500         IF WS-MF-STAT = '23'
011600             DISPLAY MF-KEY, '  KEY NOT FOUND ON VSAM FILE'
011700         ELSE
011800             DISPLAY '*******************************'
011900             DISPLAY 'FS AT READ = ', WS-MF-STAT
012000             DISPLAY 'FORCED ABORT DUE TO FILE ERROR'
012100             DISPLAY '*******************************'
012200             STOP RUN.
012300*--------------------------------------------------------------
012400* Demonstrating the random access READ (key on file) followed
012500* by DELETE of the record:
012600*--------------------------------------------------------------
012700         MOVE '31260' TO MF-KEY.
012800         READ MAST-FILE.
012900         IF WS-MF-STAT-B1 = '0'
013000             DISPLAY 'BEFORE DELETE = ', MAST-RECORD
013100             PERFORM 5000-DELETE-IT
013200         ELSE
013300         IF WS-MF-STAT = '23'
013400             DISPLAY MF-KEY, '  KEY NOT FOUND ON VSAM FILE'
013500         ELSE
013600             DISPLAY '*******************************'
013700             DISPLAY 'FS AT READ = ', WS-MF-STAT
013800             DISPLAY 'FORCED ABORT DUE TO FILE ERROR'
013900             DISPLAY '*******************************'
014000             STOP RUN.
014100*==============================================================
014200 3000-EOJ.
014300         CLOSE MAST-FILE.
014400         IF WS-MF-STAT-B1 = '0'
014500             NEXT SENTENCE
014600         ELSE
014700             DISPLAY '*******************************'
014800             DISPLAY 'FS AT CLOSE = ', WS-MF-STAT
014900             DISPLAY 'FORCED ABORT DUE TO FILE ERROR'
015000             DISPLAY '*******************************'
015100             STOP RUN.
015200*==============================================================
015300 4000-UPDATE-IT.
015400         MOVE 'WANDA' TO MF-FIRST-NAME.
015500         DISPLAY 'AFTER UPDATE = ', MAST-RECORD
015600         REWRITE MAST-RECORD.
015700         IF WS-MF-STAT-B1 = '0'
015800             NEXT SENTENCE
015900         ELSE
016000             DISPLAY '*******************************'
016100             DISPLAY 'FS AT REWRITE =', WS-MF-STAT
016200             DISPLAY 'FORCED ABORT DUE TO FILE ERROR'
016300             DISPLAY '*******************************'
016400             STOP RUN.
016500*
016600 5000-DELETE-IT.
016700         DELETE MAST-FILE.
016800         IF WS-MF-STAT-B1 = '0'
016900             DISPLAY 'RECORD DELETED'
017000         ELSE
017100             DISPLAY '*******************************'
017200             DISPLAY 'FS AT DELETE =', WS-MF-STAT
017300             DISPLAY 'FORCED ABORT DUE TO FILE ERROR'
017400             DISPLAY '*******************************'
017500             STOP RUN.
```

(f)

(g)

(h)

(i)

(j)

Output

```
31668ZOORI        MOE             900216004S1FOX VALLEY TRAVEL        900103

ABCDE  KEY NOT FOUND ON VSAM FILE

BEFORE UPDATE = 31573WALLBANGER    HARVEY      900216002B HOBBIT INTERNATIONAL
AFTER UPDATE  = 31573WALLBANGER    WANDA       900216002B HOBBIT INTERNATIONAL

BEFORE DELETE = 31260MALLOW        MARSHA      900216001B HOLIDAY TOURS, INC.
RECORD DELETED
```

Figure 12.11 *Continued*

Figure 12.11 VSAMDEMO Program Illustrates VS COBOL II VSAM Code.

This program shows you how to code a VS COBOL II program for random access update to a VSAM key-sequenced data set. This coding is also compatible with VS COBOL, so you can begin conversion even before you fully install VS COBOL II!

a. (page 231) The SELECT/ASSIGN statement indicates ACCESS MODE IS RANDOM to allow direct read by key. I did not code the extended VSAM communication codes (the second File Status field) but you can add this when your shop is fully converted to VS COBOL II. The coding here does get you the complete set of expanded File Status values (34 in all).

b. (page 231) Your FD must contain the primary key and any alternate keys correctly positioned. I have coded the whole record layout in the FD rather than in WORKING-STORAGE to make this program as simple as possible.

c. (page 231) Define File Status as two one-byte fields under a group name, and code the group name in the SELECT/ASSIGN statement. This way you can test just the first byte of File Status for '0' for successful outcome (except for OPEN, where you also have to test for '97').

d. (page 231) Standard File Status checking pattern for VSAM data set OPEN for input/output, I-O. This OPEN allows you to use the READ, WRITE, REWRITE, and DELETE verbs with the data set. (See also Figure 12.7 for OPEN information.)

e. (page 231) Standard File Status checking pattern for a random READ for inquiry purposes. This and the READ at lines 9200 through 10400 produce the first and second line of output at the bottom of the listing.

f. (page 232) (See next page.) Standard logic and File Status checking pattern for random access READ leading to potential record update (REWRITE). This READ produces the third line of output.

g. (page 232) Standard logic and File Status checking pattern for random access READ leading to potential record deletion (DELETE). This logic produces the fifth line of output.

h. (page 232) Standard File Status checking pattern for VSAM data set CLOSE.

i. (page 232) Standard logic and File Status checking pattern for REWRITE (update) after successful READ. There is no program-resolvable error case here because you read and obtained the record to be rewritten immediately before this REWRITE; see (f). This logic produces the fourth line of output.

j. (page 232) Standard logic and File Status checking pattern for DELETE after successful READ. There is no program-resolvable error case here because you read and obtained the record to be DELETEd immediately before this action; see (g). This logic produces the sixth line of output.

```
EDIT --- CSCJGJ.CSC.CNTL(VSAMRUN) - 01.03 ----------------- COLUMNS 001 072
COMMAND ===>                                                  SCROLL ===> PAGE
****** *************************** TOP OF DATA ********************************
000001 //CSCJGJA  JOB 1,'BIN 7 JANOSSY',MSGCLASS=X,MSGLEVEL=(1,1),
000002 //  NOTIFY=CSCJGJ
000003 //*
000004 //*    CSCJGJ.CSC.CNTL(VSAMRUN)
000005 //*    RUN VSAMDEMO PROGRAM TO ILLUSTRATE VSAM I/O VERBS
000006 //*    ** NOTE: THIS USES A COMPILE/LINK/GO AT //STEP020
000007 //*
000008 //*****************************************************************
000009 //*                                                               *
000010 //*    LIST THE MASTER FILE BEFORE UPDATE                         *
000011 //*                                                               *
000012 //*****************************************************************
000013 //STEP010  EXEC  PGM=IDCAMS
000014 //SYSPRINT   DD   SYSOUT=*
000015 //SYSIN      DD   *
000016      PRINT           INDATASET( CSCJGJ.CSC.TICKMST2 ) -
000017                      COUNT(100) -
000018                      CHARACTER
000019 /*
000020 //*
000021 //*****************************************************************
000022 //*                                                               *
000023 //*    COMPILE, LINK, AND RUN THE VSAMDEMO UPDATE PROGRAM         *
000024 //*                                                               *
000025 //*****************************************************************
000026 //STEP020 EXEC  PROC=CLINKGO,
000027 //          PDS='CSCJGJ.CSC.COBOL',
000028 //     MEMBER='VSAMDEMO'
000029 //GO.MAST    DD  DSN=CSCJGJ.CSC.TICKMST2,DISP=SHR
000030 //GO.MAST1   DD  DSN=CSCJGJ.CSC.TICKMST2.SALEAIX.PATH,DISP=SHR
000031 //*
000032 //*****************************************************************
000033 //*                                                               *
000034 //*    LIST THE MASTER FILE AFTER UPDATE                          *
000035 //*                                                               *
000036 //*****************************************************************
000037 //STEP030   EXEC  PGM=IDCAMS,COND=(5,LT)
000038 //SYSPRINT   DD   SYSOUT=*
000039 //SYSIN      DD   *
000040      PRINT           INDATASET( CSCJGJ.CSC.TICKMST2 ) -
000041                      COUNT(100) -
000042                      CHARACTER
000043 /*
000044 //
```

Figure 12.12   MVS JCL to Execute a VS COBOL II VSAM KSDS Update.

The first and third steps of this job stream just use IDCAMS to print the contents of the passenger file before and after the VSAMDEMO update. The second step does a compile/link/go of VSAMDEMO using CLINKGO, a proc I use for teaching purposes. CLINKGO is similar to IBM's proc COB2UCLG. GO.MAST and GO.MAST1 are DD statements for the passenger KSDS base cluster and its alternate index path name (see Section 12.14).

12.11 *TRY IT!* INTERPRETING EXPANDED FILE STATUS VALUES

Once you have created your VSAM passenger file and run VSAMDEMO, you can experiment with it in several ways. First of all, try installing extended VSAM File Status values and reporting by following the pattern in the lower part of Figure 12.5. Submit VSAMJCL to delete and recreate the passenger file, then submit VSAMRUN. You'll see the extended VSAM communication codes. But they will not be meaningful because your program will not experience a program-unresolvable problem.

I have listed here three program-unresolvable problems you can introduce in VSAMDEMO to see how File Status and the extended VSAM codes work. Introduce these problems one by one. Using Appendix B, look up the File Status value you receive for each problem. Correct each problem before you try the next one:

1. Code a PIC X(1) field between lines 3100 and 3200 in VSAM-DEMO. Change line 4000 to PIC X(5) rather than PIC X(6). These changes make the key positions you indicate in the FD inconsistent with the way the file is actually defined. VSAM will complain about this when you try to OPEN the passenger file. Of course, its complaint will be expressed in an interesting File Status value!

2. Correct problem 1. Then repeat lines 5800 through 6700 so that you try to OPEN the file twice. The result will be interesting—VSAM will complain. You will notice that the new File Status value you receive for this in the 40s range will be a lot more specific than the old 90/92 value you would get for this with VS COBOL!

3. Correct problem 2. Comment out the DD statement for the alternate index path (line 30) in the VSAMRUNCL. You will get quite a specific File Status value, which my Appendix B will help you interpret.

File Status values and extended VSAM codes provide the means to diagnose problems in VSAM file access. This is why you have to make them visible when your program detects that an action has not been handled successfully and the program cannot handle the situation.

12.12 FILE STATUS FOR QSAM (SEQUENTIAL) FILES

File Status is usually associated with VSAM files. But File Status is a part of the ANSI standard for COBOL in connection with all types of files. VS COBOL II expands the range of File Status values and lends much better support to solving file-related problems. You can code File Status with ordinary QSAM (sequential) files too:

```
SELECT MY-FILE ASSIGN TO DATA-FILE
    FILE STATUS IS WS-DF-STAT.
    -
    -
WORKING-STORAGE SECTION.
01  WS-DF-STAT.
    05 WS-DF-STAT-BYTE1        PIC X(1).
    05 FILLER                  PIC X(1).
```

Only VSAM provides extended communication codes, so you don't code a name or fields to receive them when you use a QSAM file.

You'll get the most benefit from recognizing File Status for QSAM files at OPEN time since File Status values '04', '05', and '07' can tell you about potential error conditions. File Status values in the 30s and 40s ranges will also be very helpful for QSAM files since many of these expand on the old catch-all File Status '92' ("program logic error") value you might already have seen in connection with QSAM abends.

12.13 OPTIONAL FILES: NEW FOR VS COBOL II RELEASE 3

You can now code the word OPTIONAL on a SELECT/ASSIGN statement to specify that the file does not have to be available to the program when it runs. You can code any type of file, including QSAM and VSAM files, as OPTIONAL:

```
QSAM:    SELECT OPTIONAL LOG-FILE ASSIGN TO LOGFILE.

VSAM:    SELECT OPTIONAL LOG-FILE ASSIGN TO LOGFILE
              ORGANIZATION IS INDEXED
              ACCESS MODE  IS SEQUENTIAL
              RECORD KEY   IS LF-FRAME-ID
              FILE STATUS  IS WS-LF-STAT  WS-LF-EX-STAT.
```

A QSAM file is "available" if a DD statement (or TSO CLIST allocate) exists for it. Otherwise, a QSAM file is unavailable. If you use an optional QSAM file for input and the file is not available to the program, the program "sees" it as an empty file. You can even omit a DD statement for it. If an optional QSAM file is used by a program for output but is unavailable, VS COBOL II allocates it dynamically using default attributes. These are usually RECFM = U, LRECL = 0, BLKSIZE = 32760. This is not a recommended practice.

A VSAM file is available if:

1. A DD statement exists for it, and
2. it has been defined using IDCAMS, and
3. it has previously contained at least one record.

A VSAM file is "unavailable" if criteria 1 and 2 are met but not criteria 3. If you use an optional, unavailable VSAM file for output, VS COBOL II automatically writes a dummy record to it, then deletes the record, preparing the file for use. This saves you from having to take this action yourself. You may find this slightly useful albeit a bit confusing.

12.14 ALTERNATE INDEX SELECT/ASSIGN CODING AND JCL

You can define and create up to 253 alternate indexes for a key-sequenced data set. But for performance reasons you would want to define only one or perhaps (rarely) two alternate indexes. For example, you might want to be able to access customer information by account number (primary key) or by customer name (nonunique alternate key):

```
SELECT MY-FILE ASSIGN TO  MYFILE
    ORGANIZATION          INDEXED
    ACCESS MODE           SEQUENTIAL
    RECORD KEY            MR-ACCOUNT-ID
    ALTERNATE RECORD KEY  MR-CUSTOMER-NAME
    FILE STATUS           WS-STAT  WS-EX-STAT.
```

You have to define both MF-ACCOUNT-ID and MF-CUSTOMER-NAME in the FD for the file:

```
FD  MY-FILE
    RECORD CONTAINS 250 CHARACTERS.
01  MY-RECORD.
    05 MR-CUSTOMER-NAME     PIC X(25).
    05 MR-ACCOUNT-ID        PIC X(8).
    05 MR-CUSTOMER-ADDRESS  PIC X(30).
     -
     -

//MYFILE    DD  DSN=CSCJGJ.CSC.CUSTMAST,DISP=SHR
//MYFILE1   DD  DSN=CSCJGJ.CSC.CUSTMAST.AIX.PATH,DISP=SHR
```

The JCL for this file would need two DD statements. You must point the second (compiler-generated DDname) DD statement to the alternate index path.

VS COBOL II generates a DDname for each ALTERNATE RECORD KEY IS clause. It creates these by modifying the original DDname. A "1" is either appended to the name or used to overlay the eighth character in the name if the name is eight characters long. A "2" is used for a second alternate key, a "3" for a third alternate key, and so forth.

You will get File Status '96' when you try to open the file if you forget to code the DD statements that match the generated DDnames.

12.15 READ . . . NEXT AND DYNAMIC ACCESS

The SELECT/ASSIGN statement gives you three choices for ACCESS MODE:

```
SELECT MY-FILE ASSIGN TO  MYFILE
    ORGANIZATION          INDEXED

                          ⎡SEQUENTIAL⎤
    ACCESS MODE            RANDOM
                          ⎣DYNAMIC   ⎦

    RECORD KEY            MR-ACCOUNT-ID
    ALTERNATE RECORD KEY  MR-CUSTOMER-NAME
    FILE STATUS           WS-STAT  WS-EX-STAT.
```

SEQUENTIAL gives you access to the file as if it were an ordinary sequential data set. You will receive the records in ascending key sequence, either by primary key or by an alternate key. The READ verb gives you one record after another and eventually hits end-of-file (First-byte File Status '1'). You cannot accomplish direct access by record key with ACCESS MODE IS SEQUENTIAL and READ. Some File Status values apply only to sequential mode.

RANDOM lets you specify the key of the record you want when you do a READ. You will get only the record you want, or File Status '23' indicating that no such record exists. A random-mode READ will never hit end-of-file.

DYNAMIC gives you both sequential and random access capabilities. But note this very important difference in READ verb operation when you code DYNAMIC:

- READ will act as it does for RANDOM: direct access.
- READ filename NEXT accomplishes sequential reading.

You can use the START verb only when you have coded SEQUENTIAL or DYNAMIC modes.

12.16 CURRENT RECORD POINTER AND KEY OF REFERENCE

VSAM maintains two hidden values called the Current Record Pointer and the Key of Reference. While the READ and WRITE verbs can affect these, the most common way to control them is with the START verb. VS COBOL II enhances START verb coding. You can code the START verb to accomplish one or both of these actions:

- Position the **Current Record Pointer** (CRP) to a given location in an indexed file. The CRP is a behind-the-scenes value maintained by

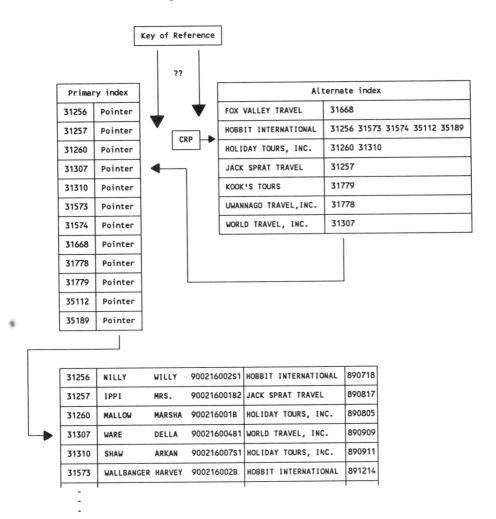

Figure 12.13   Key of Reference (KOR) and Current Record Pointer (CRP).

The Key of Reference is a hidden value maintained by VSAM. It guides VSAM to access either the primary index or the alternate index for sequential access. The Current Record Pointer is another hidden value that points to the next record to be obtained by READ (in SEQUENTIAL access mode) or READ . . . NEXT (in DYNAMIC access mode). You can change the value of the Key of Reference and Current Record Pointer using a single START verb as shown in Figure 12.15 item (e).

VSAM as a program accesses a data set. It points to the record that will be obtained by the next sequential READ or READ . . . NEXT.

- Set the **Key of Reference** (KOR). The KOR is a behind-the-scenes value maintained by VSAM as you access a data set. It is a flag that indicates which path of access you are using: either the primary key or an alternate key. When you first OPEN a KSDS, the KOR points to the primary index. The KOR has work to do only if you have defined and created at least one alternate index for a file. With only a primary index, the KOR automatically points to it at OPEN and afterwards.

Figure 12.13 shows you how you can picture the CRP and KOR for the passenger file (Figure 12.9) accessed by VSAMDEMO. The alternate index (SALES-AGENT) is nonunique, so you can see that some alternate index records point to more than one data record. If the KOR is the primary key, you can read the data records sequentially in primary key sequence. If the KOR is set to the alternate key, your sequential reading will obtain the data records as if they were stored in SALES-AGENT order because VSAM will follow the "list" presented by the alternate index.

12.17 USING THE START VERB

You use the START verb expecting to test File Status immediately afterwards. File Status will tell you with '0' in the first byte if the START succeeded. A File Status of '23' means the START did not succeed.

To code the START verb you put a desired value in the primary key field or an alternate key field. You then involve that field, by its FD name, with the START verb:

```
SELECT MAST-FILE           ASSIGN TO MAST
     ORGANIZATION  IS INDEXED
     ACCESS MODE   IS SEQUENTIAL
     RECORD KEY    IS MF-KEY
     ALTERNATE RECORD KEY  IS MF-SALES-AGENT
        WITH DUPLICATES
     FILE STATUS IS WS-MF-STAT.
-------------------------------------------------

FD  MAST-FILE
    LABEL RECORDS ARE STANDARD
    RECORD CONTAINS 80 CHARACTERS.
01  MAST-RECORD.
    05 MF-KEY                  PIC X(5).
```

```
05 MF-LAST-NAME        PIC X(14).
05 MF-FIRST-NAME       PIC X(15).
05 MF-CRUISE-DATE      PIC X(6).
05 MF-TICKET-QTY       PIC 9(3).
05 MF-DECK-CODE        PIC X(2).
05 MF-SALES-AGENT      PIC X(23).
05 MF-DATE-BOUGHT      PIC X(6).
05 FILLER              PIC X(6).
-   -
```

Start at or beyond a given MF-KEY (sets KOR to primary index and CRP to 31307 or the next higher record key):

```
MOVE '31307' TO MF-KEY.
START MY-FILE
   KEY >= MF-KEY.
IF WS-STAT-BYTE1 = '0' . . .
```

Start at or beyond a given sales-agent name (sets CRP to the alternate index and sales-agent to HOLIDAY TOURS, INC.):

```
MOVE 'HOL' TO MF-SALES-AGENT.
START MY-FILE
   KEY >= MF-SALES-AGENT.
IF WS-STAT-BYTE1 = '0' . . .
```

12.18 RELATIONAL CONDITIONS AVAILABLE WITH START

VS COBOL II gives you much clearer START verb syntax than VS COBOL did. Figure 12.14 illustrates the operators you can now use. The most commonly useful operator is >= ("equal to or greater than"). This test almost always positions the Current Record Pointer successfully because it is satisfied by a record with the key value you coded or by the next record in sequence. The only time it fails is if no records exist beyond the key value in the START relation operator (end of file).

VS COBOL forced you to code >= as "NOT LESS THAN." Both of these codings are supported by VS COBOL II to accomplish the same thing:

```
MOVE value TO fd-key.
START filename
```

KEY	EQUAL TO GREATER THAN NOT LESS THAN GREATER THAN OR EQUAL TO = > NOT < >=	fd-key.

```
IF file-status-byte1 = '0' ...
```

Figure 12.14 VS COBOL II Syntax For the START Verb.

VS COBOL II expands the ways you can code the relation condition in the START verb. The most significant improvement is that you can now code $>=$ for "equal to or greater than" to begin a browsing action or read a key sequenced data set sequentially by its alternate key. See Figure 12.15 (e) for an example of this coding.

VS COBOL

```
MOVE LOW-VALUES TO MF-SALES-AGENT.
START MAST-FILE
    KEY NOT < MF-SALES-AGENT.
IF WS-STAT-BYTE1 = '0' ...
```

VS COBOL II

```
MOVE 'LOW-VALUES' TO MF-SALES-AGENT.
START MAST-FILE
    KEY >= MF-SALES-AGENT.
IF WS-STAT-BYTE1 = '0' ...
```

12.19 READING A VSAM KSDS SEQUENTIALLY VIA ALTERNATE KEY

Figure 12.15 shows you the source code for program VSAMLIST, while Figure 12.16 shows the JCL I used to run it. This program reads records sequentially from the passenger file in alternate key sequence and uses a simple DISPLAY to output them to paper. Its output is shown at the end of the source code listing.

To read sequentially by alternate key, you have to change the Key of Reference to the alternate key. You can use START in beginning of job to do this for the whole run. Since it's impossible to predict the value of the first alternate key, you use a starting value as low as possible (LOW-VALUES) and code START with a $>=$ or NOT $<$ condition. You then involve the alternate key field name in the START, as program VSAM-LIST does in its lines 7600 through 8900:

```
MOVE LOW-VALUES TO MF-SALES-AGENT.
START MAST-FILE
   KEY NOT LESS THAN MF-SALES-AGENT.
IF WS-MF-STAT-B1 = '0'
   NEXT SENTENCE
 ELSE
IF WS-MF-STAT = '23'
   DISPLAY MF-SALES-AGENT, '  START FAILED ON ALT KEY'
 ELSE
   DISPLAY '****************************'
   DISPLAY 'FS AT READ =  ', WS-MF-STAT
   DISPLAY 'FORCED ABORT DUE TO FILE ERROR'
   DISPLAY '****************************'
   STOP RUN.
```

This START does two things: it sets the Key of Reference to the alternate key and positions it to the first record whose alternate key is equal to or greater than LOW-VALUES. This is, of course, the first alternate index record. The only way this START can fail is if the file being accessed is empty or if VSAM encounters an internal problem. But it's still necessary to do File Status checking!

12.20 *TRY IT!* EXPERIMENTING WITH START AND ALTERNATE KEYS

The beauty of a live model like program VSAMLIST is that you can learn from experimenting with it. I have listed here some actions you can take with the START verb in VSAMLIST to produce interesting results. Do each action separately. You can leave code from step 1 in place for all of the other actions.

1. Change line 9500 so that it DISPLAYs not only the record obtained from the file, but also the present File Status value:

   ```
   009500    DISPLAY MAST-RECORD, '  FS  =  ', WS-MF-STAT.
   ```

   You may be surprised at the fact that a successful READ does not always produce a File Status value of '00'!
2. Change LOW-VALUES at line 7600 to put 'J' in the MF-SALES-AGENT field and see what happens when you run the program.

(text continues on page 246)

```
000100 IDENTIFICATION DIVISION.
000200 PROGRAM-ID.     VSAMLIST.
000300 AUTHOR.         J JANOSSY
000400 INSTALLATION.   DEPAUL UNIVERSITY.
000500 DATE-WRITTEN.   SEPT 1991.
000600 DATE-COMPILED.
000700*REMARKS.        DEMONSTRATION OF SEQUENTIAL READING OF VSAM
000800*                FILE IN ALTERNATE KEY SEQUENCE
000900*
001000 ENVIRONMENT DIVISION.
001100 INPUT-OUTPUT SECTION.
001200 FILE-CONTROL.
001300     SELECT MAST-FILE            ASSIGN TO MAST
001400         ORGANIZATION  IS INDEXED
001500         ACCESS MODE   IS SEQUENTIAL
001600         RECORD KEY    IS MF-KEY
001700         ALTERNATE RECORD KEY  IS MF-SALES-AGENT
001800             WITH DUPLICATES
001900         FILE STATUS   IS WS-MF-STAT.
002000*
002100 DATA DIVISION.
002200 FILE SECTION.
002300*
002400*  Note: No "BLOCK CONTAINS" clause is used for a VSAM file:
002500*
002600 FD  MAST-FILE
002700     LABEL RECORDS ARE STANDARD
002800     RECORD CONTAINS 80 CHARACTERS.
002900 01  MAST-RECORD.
003000     05 MF-KEY               PIC X(5).
003100     05 MF-LAST-NAME         PIC X(14).
003200     05 MF-FIRST-NAME        PIC X(15).
003300     05 MF-CRUISE-DATE       PIC X(6).
003400     05 MF-TICKET-QTY        PIC 9(3).
003500     05 MF-DECK-CODE         PIC X(2).
003600     05 MF-SALES-AGENT       PIC X(23).
003700     05 MF-DATE-BOUGHT       PIC X(6).
003800     05 FILLER               PIC X(6).
003900/
004000 WORKING-STORAGE SECTION.
004100 01  WS-MF-STAT.
004200     05 WS-MF-STAT-B1        PIC X(1).
004300     05 FILLER               PIC X(1).
004400 01  WS-RECORD-COUNT         PIC 9(5)  VALUE 0.
004500/
004600 PROCEDURE DIVISION.
004700 0000-MAINLINE.
004800     PERFORM 1000-BOJ.
004900     PERFORM 2000-PROCESS
005000         UNTIL WS-MF-STAT-B1 = '1'.
005100     PERFORM 3000-EOJ.
005200     STOP RUN.
005300*
005400 1000-BOJ.
005500*------------------------------------------------------------
005600*  Demonstrating how to OPEN a VSAM file for sequential reading:
005700*------------------------------------------------------------
005800     OPEN  INPUT  MAST-FILE.
005900     IF WS-MF-STAT-B1 = '0'
006000        OR WS-MF-STAT = '97'
006100           NEXT SENTENCE
006200        ELSE
006300           DISPLAY '*******************************'
006400           DISPLAY 'FS AT OPEN = ', WS-MF-STAT
006500           DISPLAY 'FORCED ABORT DUE TO FILE ERROR'
006600           DISPLAY '*******************************'
006700           STOP RUN.
006800*
006900* This START sets the Key of Reference (KOR) to the alternate
007000* key and positions the Current Record Pointer (CRP) to the start
007100* of the alternate index.  If you comment out this START and
007200* the File Status checking after it you'll get the records in
007300* key sequence.  With this code you get the records in alternate
007400* key sequence.
007500*
007600     MOVE LOW-VALUES TO MF-SALES-AGENT.
007700     START MAST-FILE
007800         KEY NOT LESS THAN MF-SALES-AGENT.
007900     IF WS-MF-STAT-B1 = '0'
008000        NEXT SENTENCE
008100        ELSE
008200     IF WS-MF-STAT = '23'
008300        DISPLAY MF-SALES-AGENT, '  START FAILED ON ALT KEY'
008400        ELSE
008500           DISPLAY '*******************************'
008600           DISPLAY 'FS AT START = ', WS-MF-STAT
008700           DISPLAY 'FORCED ABORT DUE TO FILE ERROR'
008800           DISPLAY '*******************************'
008900           STOP RUN.
009000*
009100 2000-PROCESS.
009200*------------------------------------------------------------
009300* This does a sequential READ; use READ...NEXT in DYNAMIC mode:
009400*------------------------------------------------------------
009500     DISPLAY MAST-RECORD.
009600     READ MAST-FILE.
```

Figure 12.15 *(see legend on page 245)*

```
009700        IF WS-MF-STAT-B1 = '0'
009800            ADD +1 TO WS-RECORD-COUNT
009900        ELSE
010000        IF WS-MF-STAT-B1 = '1'
010100            NEXT SENTENCE
010200        ELSE
010300            DISPLAY '********************************'
010400            DISPLAY 'FS AT READ = ', WS-MF-STAT
010500            DISPLAY 'FORCED ABORT DUE TO FILE ERROR'
010600            DISPLAY '********************************'
010700            STOP RUN.
010800*
010900 3000-EOJ.
011000        CLOSE MAST-FILE.
011100        DISPLAY 'RECORDS LISTED = ', WS-RECORD-COUNT.
011200        IF WS-MF-STAT-B1 = '0'
011300            NEXT SENTENCE
011400        ELSE
011500            DISPLAY '********************************'
011600            DISPLAY 'FS AT CLOSE = ', WS-MF-STAT
011700            DISPLAY 'FORCED ABORT DUE TO FILE ERROR'
011800            DISPLAY '********************************'
011900            STOP RUN.
```

f

g

Output

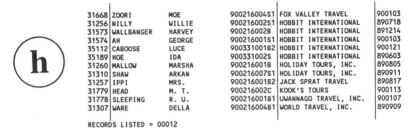

```
31668 ZOORI        MOE       900216004S1 FOX VALLEY TRAVEL        900103
31256 NILLY        WILLIE    900216002S1 HOBBIT INTERNATIONAL     890718
31573 WALLBANGER   HARVEY    900216002B  HOBBIT INTERNATIONAL     891214
31574 AH           GEORGE    900216001S1 HOBBIT INTERNATIONAL     900103
35112 CABOOSE      LUCE      900331001B2 HOBBIT INTERNATIONAL     900121
35189 HOE          IDA       900331002S  HOBBIT INTERNATIONAL     890603
31260 MALLOW       MARSHA    900216001B  HOLIDAY TOURS, INC.      890805
31310 SHAW         ARKAN     900216007S1 HOLIDAY TOURS, INC.      890911
31257 IPPI         MRS.      900216001B2 JACK SPRAT TRAVEL        890817
31779 HEAD         M. T.     900216002C  KOOK'S TOURS             900113
31778 SLEEPING     R. U.     900216001B1 UWANNAGO TRAVEL, INC.    900107
31307 WARE         DELLA     900216004B1 WORLD TRAVEL, INC.       890909

RECORDS LISTED = 00012
```

h

Figure 12.15   How to Read a KSDS Sequentially by Alternate Key.

a. The SELECT/ASSIGN statement specifies ACCESS MODE IS SEQUEN-
TIAL. I could also have used DYNAMIC access mode in which case I would
have to use the READ . . . NEXT verb for sequential reading.

b. You must describe the primary and alternate key fields in correct position in
the File Description (FD).

c. I defined File Status as two one-byte fields so I could check just the first byte
for '0' (action OK) or '1' (end-of-file) conditions.

d. I use the standard pattern for File Status checking at the OPEN.

e. You can use the START verb to change the Key of Reference by involving
the FD alternate key field name with the START. Since this START will also
position the Current Record Pointer it's appropriate to move LOW-VALUES
to the alternate key field. This way the relation condition NOT LESS THAN
(equivalent to the "equal to or greater than" symbol >=) is satisfied by
positioning the CRP at the beginning of the alternate index.

f. I use File Status to detect end-of-file. '0' means I obtained a record, '1' means
end-of-file, and any other value at the sequential READ means a program-
unresolvable VSAM problem. Notice that at line 005000 the first byte of File
Status serves as my end-of-file flag. This is why I can code NEXT SENTENCE
at line 010100.

g. I use the standard pattern for File Status checking at CLOSE.

h. VSAMLIST provides the records in alternate key sequence. Compare this
output to the contents of the alternate index in Figure 12.13.

```
EDIT --- CSCJGJ.CSC.CNTL(VSAMLIST) - 01.00 ----------------- COLUMNS 001 072
COMMAND ===>                                                 SCROLL ===> PAGE
****** ************************** TOP OF DATA ******************************
000001 //CSCJGJA  JOB 1,'BIN 7 JANOSSY',MSGCLASS=X,MSGLEVEL=(1,1),
000002 //  NOTIFY=CSCJGJ
000003 //*
000004 //*     CSCJGJ.CSC.CNTL(VSAMLIST)
000005 //*     RUN VSAMLIST PROGRAM TO ILLUSTRATE VSAM ALT KEY START
000006 //*
000007 //STEP010 EXEC  PROC=CLINKGO,
000008 //      PDS='CSCJGJ.CSC.COBOL',
000009 //  MEMBER='VSAMLIST'
000010 //GO.MAST    DD  DSN=CSCJGJ.CSC.TICKMST2,DISP=SHR
000011 //GO.MAST1   DD  DSN=CSCJGJ.CSC.TICKMST2.SALEAIX.PATH,DISP=SHR
000012 //GO.SYSOUT  DD  SYSOUT=*
000013 //
```

Figure 12.16 MVS JCL to Run Program VSAMLIST.

This JCL invokes my CLINKGO compile/link/go proc (similar to IBM's proc COB2UCLG) to run VSAMLIST. The DD statement GO.MAST points to the VSAM data set base cluster and GO.MAST1 points to the alternate index path. VS COBOL II "makes up" the MAST1 DDname because the SELECT/ASSIGN statement for MAST1 refers to an alternate key.

3. Change LOW-VALUES at line 7600 to put ALL 'Z' in the MF-SALES-AGENT field and see what happens when you run the program.

4. Leave action 3 in place (ALL 'Z' to MF-SALES-AGENT) but comment out lines 7900 through 8900. This will mean that you do not react to the problem situation the ALL 'Z' will cause. The program will attempt to read anyway. Will you then get a problem File Status value for the next READ?

5. Change line 7600 so that LOW-VALUES is moved to MF-SALES-AGENT, as was originally the case. Change line 005000 so that it is:

```
PERFORM 2000-PROCESS
   UNTIL WS-MF-STAT-B1 = '5'.
```

This condition will never be satisfied and you will read past the end of the file. How will VSAM tell you this?

13

Changes for CICS, IMS, and IMS/DC

VS COBOL II maintains restrictions in coding that you have become familiar with in your previous CICS and IMS work. For example, you still cannot issue operating system I/O commands in programs that use CICS or IMS/DC. In this chapter I will explain the changes that do occur in CICS, IMS, and IMS/DC programming when you convert to VS COBOL II.

13.1 CICS CODE RESTRICTIONS FOR VS COBOL II

As illustrated in Figure 13.1, programs (even VS COBOL II programs) operating under CICS are really treated as subprograms since CICS acts as an operating system within the operating system. You still need to follow the "chain of command" and avoid using COBOL verbs that communicate directly with the operating system:

ACCEPT	REWRITE
DISPLAY	DELETE
OPEN	START
CLOSE	RERUN
READ	SORT
WRITE	MERGE

These verbs either do file access (such as READ, WRITE, and so forth) or request MVS services (such as ACCEPT and DISPLAY). CICS handles all such communication. In VS COBOL II, as in VS COBOL, you still go through CICS to perform these functions. VS COBOL II does not support macro level CICS coding.

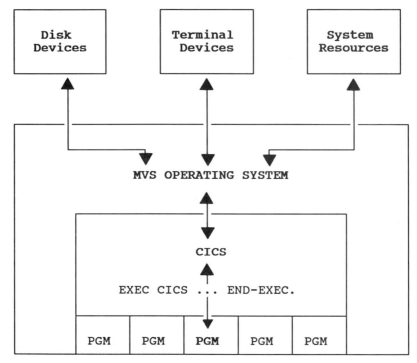

Figure 13.1 CICS Programs Are Really Subprograms.

All locally-written CICS programs are really subprograms to CICS, the always-executing teleprocessing monitor. CICS is the only program "seen" by the MVS operating system. Since CICS deals with MVS you violate the chain of command if you use verbs like ACCEPT, DISPLAY, or file I/O verbs. Those verbs deal directly with MVS. In VS COBOL II you must still request CICS to perform I/O services for you.

13.2 NEW STOP RUN, EXIT PROGRAM, GOBACK USAGE

Many changes exist in CICS coding with VS COBOL II. In some cases these changes make familiar verbs and commands act differently than they had in the past. For example, you can now code STOP RUN in your CICS programs. It is treated as EXEC CICS RETURN. This is a major improvement. It prevents CICS from being brought down by a misplaced STOP RUN statement. It also makes it unnecessary to hide a STOP RUN in an unreachable place in the program just to please the compiler and avoid a "no stop run" warning (and 0004 compiler return code).

You can code GOBACK in a program if the program receives control with LINK, XCTL, or CALL. In these cases GOBACK acts like CICS RETURN.

You can code EXIT PROGRAM in a program that receives control from a CALL, and it acts as CICS RETURN. It is ignored if the program receives control with LINK or XCTL.

The difference between GOBACK and EXIT PROGRAM means that you should abandon EXIT PROGRAM and use GOBACK instead, in CICS programs that receive control with LINK, XCTL, or CALL. GOBACK always acts the same no matter where it is coded, but the treatment of EXIT PROGRAM varies.

13.3 CICS GETS THE CALL VERB!

Your legal use of the CALL verb in CICS programs was restricted under VS COBOL because CALL could cause abends due to program/CICS conflict for CPU registers. This possibility has now been eliminated.

You can use the CALL statement in a VS COBOL II CICS program to call a subprogram written in VS COBOL II or assembler language. But a VS COBOL program cannot CALL a VS COBOL II subprogram, or vice versa. For VS COBOL/VS COBOL II program mixtures, you must continue to use the CICS LINK command.

You can use any CICS commands in the VS COBOL II subprogram that are permitted in a VS COBOL II CALLing (main) program including READ/WRITE DATASET. Letting you use the CALL statement legally is a big improvement:

- CALL makes it possible for you to modularize functions and standardize them in subprograms without concern that IBM would later enforce VS COBOL restrictions against use of CALL.
- You do not need to request systems programmers to make a Processing Program Table (PPT) entry for a subprogram, as you must for a program you plan to access with EXEC CICS LINK.

Starting with CICS Release 2.1, subprograms that you CALL can be either static ("hard-linked") or dynamically accessed. Hard-linked CALLs execute much more efficiently than the CICS LINK command.

13.4 USING CALL IN CICS PROGRAMS

If you make subprogram CALLs in your CICS programs, you need to be aware of a few details. For one thing, even if the CALLed program (the subprogram) does not use CICS commands you should still process it with the CICS translator. Using the CICS compile proc will ensure that you use the appropriate compiler and linkage editor options.

You share data with a subprogram by coding a LINKAGE SECTION within it. As with any CICS program, you need to code the first item in the LINKAGE SECTION as your DFHCOMMAREA. The translator will automatically insert code for DFHEIBLK (the execution interface block) in the LINKAGE SECTION of the subprogram in front of DFHCOM-MAREA.

When you compile the subprogram with the CICS proc you code its PROCEDURE DIVISION heading with USING and just the ordinary data fields you intend pass to it. The translator will automatically recode the subprogram PROCEDURE DIVISION heading to cite DFHEIBLK and DFHCOMMAREA first after USING. To match this you need to state DFHEIBLK and DFHCOMMAREA first in any CALL to the subprogram:

```
CALL 'HANDYSUB' USING DFHEIBLK
                      DFHCOMMAREA
                      (...other shared fields).
```

This passes the addresses of the execution interface block and your common area to the subprogram as its PROCEDURE DIVISION heading expects.

Compile the subprogram using the RENT and RES compiler options. Linkage edit the subprograms and main program using the RENT linkage editor option.

13.5 USE LOCATE MODE WITHOUT CODING BLL CELLS!

It's advantageous to minimize the size of WORKING-STORAGE of a CICS program to make the program load module as small as possible. A technique for doing this is "locate mode" coding. With locate mode coding you establish definitions for major data items in the LINKAGE SECTION rather than in WORKING-STORAGE. Definitions coded in the LINKAGE SECTION do not "own" memory and are not reflected in the program's load module size.

But LINKAGE SECTION coding doesn't carry memory addresses known to the program when it is compiled; the address of LINKAGE SECTION fields becomes known only when this memory is assigned as the program executes. To establish addressability to LINKAGE SEC-TION memory used for a program's own data, VS COBOL requires you to code BLL cells (base locator for linkage cells). Each BLL cell is a number field capable of holding a 24-bit memory address (a number up to 16,777,216, in other words, an 8-digit number).

One BLL cell can point to the start of 4,096 bytes of data. If the data area you define in the LINKAGE SECTION is longer than 4,096 bytes, additional BLL cells are needed in VS COBOL programs to house each successive address used for the rest of the data in increments of 4,096 bytes.

VS COBOL II lets you use locate mode techniques but it simplifies BLL cell management. It forces you to change existing VS COBOL CICS programs when you upgrade them to the new compiler:

- You have to remove any code for BLL cells from VS COBOL programs to convert them to VS COBOL II.
- With the elimination of BLL cell coding you do not need to code SERVICE RELOAD statements to initialize the BLL cells. If you continue to code SERVICE RELOAD it is now treated as a comment.

Figures 13.2 and 13.3 show you VS COBOL and VS COBOL II locate mode coding so that you can compare them.

13.6 LENGTH OF REGISTER SIMPLIFIES CICS I/O

VS COBOL II makes it easier for you to code CICS I/O commands such as READ DATASET ... INTO and WRITE DATASET ... FROM. The LENGTH OF special register now exists for each item defined in WORKING-STORAGE or the LINKAGE SECTION. You can obtain the length of any data field using LENGTH OF:

```
01  TR-RECORD.
    05  TR-KEY              PIC X(5).
    05  TR-NAME             PIC X(20).
    -
    -
    -
01  TR-REC-LENGTH           PIC S9(9) COMP.
    -
    -
PROCEDURE DIVISION.
    -
    MOVE LENGTH OF TR-RECORD TO TR-REC-LENGTH.
```

But the real benefit of the LENGTH OF register is that it is used *automatically* by CICS commands that require a memory area length to be specified. In VS COBOL many CICS commands required you to state the length of the area to be affected by I/O at the LENGTH specification:

```
EXEC CICS REWRITE DATASET('STOCK1')
        FROM(MYTABLE-IN-LS)
        LENGTH(402)    END-EXEC.
```

Under VS COBOL II these commands are simplified since CICS automatically accesses the LENGTH OF register for the item itself:

```
EXEC CICS REWRITE DATASET('STOCK1')
        FROM(MYTABLE-IN-LS)         END-EXEC.
```

You can continue to code LENGTH(nn) or LENGTH(data-name) to override the length known by the LENGTH OF register.

13.7 POINTER FIELDS AND ADDRESS OF

You can define a new type of field (in WORKING-STORAGE or the LINKAGE SECTION) to house a memory storage address. It's called a pointer field:

```
01  WS-POINTERS.
    12 WS-TABLE-A-PTR    USAGE IS POINTER VALUE NULL.
    12 WS-FIELD-B-PTR    USAGE IS POINTER.
    -
```

or, more briefly:

```
01  WS-POINTERS.
    12 WS-TABLE-A-PTR    POINTER VALUE NULL.
    12 WS-FIELD-B-PTR    POINTER.
    -
```

Pointer fields are implicitly defined by the compiler as PIC S9(9). NULL is a nonnumeric zero, not LOW-VALUES (X'00'). It initializes a pointer field to a known invalid value.

You can now use ADDRESS OF to obtain the actual storage address of a 77 or 01 level field and put it into a POINTER field:

```
SET WS-TABLE-A-PTR  TO  ADDRESS OF WS-TABLE-A.
```

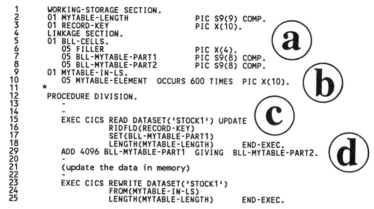

```
 1    WORKING-STORAGE SECTION.
 2    01 MYTABLE-LENGTH              PIC S9(9) COMP.
 3    01 RECORD-KEY                  PIC X(10).
 4    LINKAGE SECTION.
 5    01 BLL-CELLS.
 6       05 FILLER                   PIC X(4).
 7       05 BLL-MYTABLE-PART1        PIC S9(8) COMP.
 8       05 BLL-MYTABLE-PART2        PIC S9(8) COMP.
 9    01 MYTABLE-IN-LS.
10       05 MYTABLE-ELEMENT  OCCURS 600 TIMES  PIC X(10).
11    *
12    PROCEDURE DIVISION.
13       -
14       -
15    EXEC CICS READ DATASET('STOCK1') UPDATE
16              RIDFLD(RECORD-KEY)
17              SET(BLL-MYTABLE-PART1)
18              LENGTH(MYTABLE-LENGTH)      END-EXEC.
29    ADD 4096 BLL-MYTABLE-PART1  GIVING  BLL-MYTABLE-PART2.
20       -
21    (update the data in memory)
22       -
23    EXEC CICS REWRITE DATASET('STOCK1')
24              FROM(MYTABLE-IN-LS)
25              LENGTH(MYTABLE-LENGTH)      END-EXEC.
```

Figure 13.2   VS COBOL "Locate Mode" BLL Cell Coding.

The LINKAGE SECTION provides pictures of memory not owned by a program. By putting memory definitions in it (and not in WORKING-STORAGE) you keep the size of your CICS program load modules smaller. But your program does not know the address of LINKAGE SECTION fields until memory is assigned when the program is given control. VS COBOL forces you to code Base Locator for Linkage (BLL) cells to serve as address pointers for each 4,096 block of LINKAGE SECTION memory you use.

a. Each BLL cell is a PIC S9(8) COMP number. This is a 32-bit binary which takes 4 bytes of memory. The system creates and uses the first BLL cell to address the LINKAGE SECTION itself. Each successive BLL cell you define can address another 4,096 bytes of memory.

b. MYTABLE-IN-LS is longer than 4,096 bytes so it requires two BLL cells to address it. The first BLL cell points to the start of this data. The second BLL cell points to the location of byte 4,097 of the data.

c. The SET clause in CICS READ DATASET puts the address at which the data was stored into the first user-defined BLL cell, BLL-MYTABLE-PART1. The LENGTH clause puts the length of the stored data in the field MYTABLE-LENGTH in WORKING-STORAGE so it can be used in the following REWRITE command.

d. The ADD at line 19 set the second user-defined BLL cell to point to byte 4,097 of MYTABLE-IN-LS. This completes processing to gain addressability to the entire 6,000 bytes of MYTABLE-IN-LS housed in LINKAGE SECTION memory borrowed from CICS.

Pointers and the ADDRESS OF registers associated with each LINKAGE SECTION field make it possible to pass addressability between VS COBOL II programs. Figure 13.4 shows how a program defines two pointers and sets them to the address of the TCTUA and to memory obtained for a large data item. This program then does a LINK to a subprogram and passes the pointers to it.

```
1    WORKING-STORAGE SECTION.
2    01 RECORD-KEY                    PIC X(10).
3    LINKAGE SECTION.
4    01 MYTABLE-IN-LS.
5        05 MYTABLE-ELEMENT  OCCURS 600 TIMES  PIC X(10).
6  *
7    PROCEDURE DIVISION.
8          -
9          -
10         EXEC CICS READ DATASET('STOCK1') UPDATE
11                   RIDFLD(RECORD-KEY)
12                   SET(ADDRESS OF MYTABLE-IN-LS) END-EXEC.
13         -
14         (update the data in memory)
15
16         EXEC CICS REWRITE DATASET('STOCK1')
17                   FROM(MYTABLE-IN-LS)            END-EXEC.
```

(a)

(b)

Figure 13.3 VS COBOL II "Locate Mode" Coding Without BLL Cells.

In VS COBOL II you no longer code BLL cells yourself when you use locate mode. Instead, the compiler manages BLL cells itself, making your life easier.

a. The SET clause at line 12 in the CICS READ DATASET command stores the address assigned to MYTABLE-IN-LS in the hidden ADDRESS register for it, using the ADDRESS OF feature. BLL cells are still used by the compiler but it manages them for you now and you don't code them. The length of the stored data is automatically recorded in the hidden LENGTH register maintained by the compiler.

b. You don't code the LENGTH clause in the CICS REWRITE DATASET command at line 16 because the length of the item being rewritten is automatically supplied by the LENGTH register.

13.8 CICS PROGRAM TRANSLATION, COMPILE AND LINKAGE EDIT

VS COBOL II can be used with CICS releases 1.6 onward and it gives you many advantages. But you need to use the CICS translator option *COBOL2* when you use VS COBOL II. If you use advanced VS COBOL II Release 3 features, such as nested programs, reference modification, and lowercase characters in code, you also have to specify the ANSI85 option in running the CICS Release 2.1 translator.

VS COBOL II programs can reside above the 16-megabyte line, freeing up 24-bit address space for software that is limited to it. Some factors affect this, however. Linkage editing a program with the linkage editor option RMODE(ANY) makes it operate above the 16-megabyte line (using 31-bit addressing) which is highly desirable. But if the module named DFHECI is inadvertently linkage edited by the systems programming staff with RMODE(24), all advantages of 31-bit addressing are lost to all CICS programs. You may recognize DFHECI as the program invoked by translator-generated CALLs.

In the VS COBOL II main program:

```
 1      IDENTIFICATION DIVISION.
 2      PROGRAM-ID.   MAINPGM.
 3      DATA DIVISION.
 4      WORKING-STORAGE SECTION.
 5      01 PASSED-ADDRESS-POINTERS.
 6          05 TCTUA-PNT                 POINTER.
 7          05 MY-DATA-ITEM-PNT          POINTER.
 8      LINKAGE SECTION.
 9      01 MY-DATA-ITEM                  PIC X(6500).
10      *
11      PROCEDURE DIVISION.
12          EXEC CICS ADDRESS TCTUA(TCTUA-PNT) END-EXEC.
13          EXEC CICS GETMAIN
14              SET(MY-DATA-ITEM-PNT)
15              LENGTH(LENGTH OF MY-DATA-ITEM) END-EXEC.
16          SET ADDRESS OF MY-DATA-ITEM TO MY-DATA-ITEM-PNT.
17          MOVE some-data TO MY-DATA-ITEM.
18          EXEC CICS LINK PROGRAM('SUBPGM')
19              COMMAREA(PASSED-ADDRESS-POINTERS) END-EXEC.
```

(a) (b) (c) (d) (e)

In the VS COBOL II subprogram LINK-ed to by the main program:

```
 1      IDENTIFICATION DIVISION.
 2      PROGRAM-ID.    SUBPGM.
 3      DATA DIVISION.
 4      LINKAGE SECTION.
 5      01 PASSED-ADDRESS-POINTERS.
 6          12 TCTUA-PNT                 POINTER.
 7          12 MY-DATA-ITEM-PNT          POINTER.
 8      01 TCTUA-AREA                    PIC X(90).
 9      01 MY-DATA-ITEM                  PIC X(6500).
10      *
11      PROCEDURE DIVISION.
12          SET ADDRESS OF TCTUA-AREA TO TCTUA-PNT.
13          SET ADDRESS OF MY-DATA-ITEM TO MY-DATA-ITEM-PNT.
        -
        -
```

(f) (g)

Figure 13.4 Passing Addressability to a LINKed-to Subprogram.

a. Code POINTER fields in your WORKING-STORAGE to receive the addresses involved. Here I have coded pointer fields to the address of the Task Control Terminal User Area (TCTUA) and a data item named MY-DATA-ITEM which I have defined in the LINKAGE SECTION.

b. MY-DATA-ITEM is in the LINKAGE SECTION, not in WORKING-STORAGE, to borrow memory to house it from CICS.

c. The CICS ADDRESS command at line 12 puts the memory address of the TCTUA into its pointer field.

d. The SET command at line 15 points the description of my MY-DATA-ITEM to the address of the memory I acquired with GETMAIN.

e. The CICS LINK at line 18 passes the memory addresses of the TCTUA and MY-DATA-ITEM to SUBPGM.

f. When LINKed-to, SUBPGM receives PASSED-ADDRESS-POINTERS but its ADDRESS registers do not contain the addresses.

g. The SET commands put the addresses in the passed pointer fields into the ADDRESS registers for TCTUA-AREA and MY-DATA-ITEM.

13.9 TOOLS FOR DEBUGGING VS COBOL II CICS PROGRAMS

You can use the VS COBOL II compiler batch TEST option with a CICS program. To do this you use the CECI transaction. You put your debugging commands into the temporary storage queue named CSCOxxxx where xxxx is the identifier of the terminal where you are working.

Many installations have found that mature interactive debugging software beyond the VS COBOL II TEST option is critical to productive CICS work. Software such as INTERTEST (On-line Software International), CA-EZTEST/CICS (Computer Associates, Inc.), and CICS dBUG-AID (Compuware Corporation) have been adapted to work with VS COBOL II. Each debugging system offers its own commands and CICS memory dump options.

The formatted dump option FDUMP is available under CICS. FDUMP results in output being written to temporary storage under the name CEBRxxxx where xxxx is the identifier of your terminal. But three major problems exist with FDUMP:

- FDUMP requires additional virtual storage to operate, which can degrade operation of the software you are testing. Don't use FDUMP in production programs!

- Temporary storage used by FDUMP is not automatically freed after its use. A programmer must remember to give commands to free it. If it is not freed, other transactions may be affected and their operation even suspended.

- If an abend occurs after a program has executed EXEC CICS HANDLE ABEND, control is passed to the statement cited in the HANDLE ABEND statement and FDUMP processing is bypassed.

13.10 IMS/DC RESTRICTIONS

As with VS COBOL programming, you can't use these verbs in IMS/DC programs:

OPEN	READ	REWRITE	START
CLOSE	WRITE	DELETE	

But the new compiler does give you some additional language capabilities beyond those of VS COBOL. You can now use these previously forbidden verbs in any VS COBOL II IMS program:

```
ACCEPT          INSPECT              STOP RUN
DISPLAY         UNSTRING
```

This gives you a little more latitude for character handling and debugging.

13.11   IMS PROGRAM COMPILING

Prior to its release, IMS 3.1 communicated with other programs below the 16-megabyte address line using 24-bit addressing. Programs making calls to IMS needed to be compiled with the DATA(24) compiler option. This forced AMODE(24), or addressing mode, for the program. With IMS 3.1 and MVS/XA this requirement no longer exists.

Regardless of your IMS release your programs themselves can execute in memory above the 16-megabyte line. This takes advantage of efficiencies possible under VS COBOL II and frees up 24-bit address space for other software that needs it. You should compile applications consisting entirely of VS COBOL II programs using IMS/DC with the RES and RENT options. This generates RMODE = ANY for the load module, which provides 31-bit addressing. What do these compile options do?

- RES makes the modules continuously resident (they won't be swapped out by MVS in pieces).
- RENT makes the modules reentrant (usable by more than one concurrent task).

If older VS COBOL programs are part of your IMS/DC application, for greatest flexibility you should compile them with the VS COBOL compiler's analogous RES and NOENDJOB options.

Load modules for IMS programs may be preloaded to memory to speed up access to them. IMS/DC load module preloading does two beneficial things. It puts your load modules (machine code) into storage before they are actually needed for your program run. It also allows load modules to remain in memory after execution so that they are already there for the next time your application calls them.

Preloading and linkage editor options are the "turf" of your systems programmers. You may not have to worry about specifying them but will gain their benefit in your standard compile and link procs.

13.12   LINKAGE EDITOR OPTIONS FOR IMS

Compiler options and linkage editor options need to be coordinated when IMS programs are processed. If the applications are composed only of VS COBOL II programs compiled with the compiler's RENT option, the RENT option of the linkage editor should also be used. This linkage editor option specifies that a single copy of the load module in memory can be used concurrently by multiple active tasks.

You can mix VS COBOL II and VS COBOL programs in linkage editing if necessary. If you do this, VS COBOL II will accept whatever linkage editor options you need to specify to run the VS COBOL program. For a mixture of VS COBOL II and VS COBOL programs, follow these guidelines:

- If the VS COBOL programs will be preloaded, you should use the linkage editor REUS option.
- If the VS COBOL programs will not be preloaded you should specify NOREUS in the linkage edit.

13.13   RUNTIME OPTIONS FOR IMS

If you operate existing VS COBOL programs in the same application as VS COBOL II programs, they will access the new VS COBOL II service routine libraries. When a program is executed under IMS using the new libraries, the VS COBOL II environment is rebuilt each time the main application program receives control. This process can introduce tremendous overhead and will degrade your processing rate.

You can speed up the processing of all programs using the VS COBOL II libraries by making them memory-resident with the LIBKEEP option governing the runtime environment. As with IMS module preloading, LIBKEEP is an option usually set by systems programmers. Systems programming personnel should specify the LIBKEEP runtime option to preload the VS COBOL II runtime libraries and keep them in memory. Keeping VS COBOL II libraries names IGZCPAC, IGZCPCO, IGZEINI, IGZEPCL, IGZEPSU, and IGZCTCO in memory will help make mixed VS COBOL/VS COBOL II and pure VS COBOL II IMS applications run faster.

14

Using SORT
Without SECTIONs

VS COBOL II lets you abandon the use of SECTIONs in your programs that use the internal SORT verb. Abandoning SECTIONs will make your programs easier to read and more reliable to maintain. In this chapter I tell you why SECTIONs came to be associated with internal sorting, and show you an example of how to simplify your internal SORT programs by abandoning the use of SECTIONs.

14.1 WHAT IS A SECTION?

A SECTION is a group of paragraphs. SECTION is an optional element of COBOL that had much more of a purpose in pre-virtual storage days (before 1973). A SECTION name looks like a paragraph name except it is coded with the freestanding word "SECTION" after the name:

```
1000-SELECT-BUILD-RELEASE   SECTION.
1100-BEGIN-INPUT.
   OPEN  INPUT INSURANCE-FILE  OUTPUT . . .
```

You code the start of the first paragraph in the SECTION immediately after the section heading. A SECTION contains one or more paragraphs. In fact, once you define a SECTION heading all of the paragraphs that follow are "in" it until you reach another SECTION heading or the end of the program.

14.2   WHY ARE SECTIONS OBSOLETE?

In the early days when a large program had to be forced to fit into a small memory allocation you could "cut up" the program into separate "overlays" that could replace each other in memory. Each overlay was a SECTION, and you coded a priority number after its name to govern its placement in memory. While overlays made it possible to run large programs in limited memory, they required very careful planning and physical placement of logic into self-contained SECTIONs.

Beginning in 1973 with the MVS operating system, you no longer had to worry about segmenting programs into overlays because the operating system did it automatically for you. In fact, under MVS, segmenting a program into SECTIONs and using priority numbers to control their placement in memory actually conflicts with operating system memory management.

As of 1973, the original purpose of SECTIONs disappeared. They still remain as a supported element in COBOL, including VS COBOL II.

14.3   RESTRICTIONS AND FEATURES OF SECTIONS

Since the SECTION originated as a program segmentation device, code in one SECTION is prohibited from performing code in another section. Code in one SECTION can never GO TO code in another SECTION. All SECTIONs, however, can access all of working storage.

Even though the original purpose of SECTIONs has long since been rendered obsolete, some programmers still use SECTIONs for these reasons:

- VS COBOL required you to house code in SECTIONs if you used the internal SORT verb.
- Some people feel that SECTIONs help organize their code since paragraph names (but not data names) in one section are isolated from other SECTIONs and can duplicate.
- When you PERFORM a SECTION name, you perform all of the paragraphs within it. This is popular as a CICS program structuring device since many CICS commands cause logic branches when you use HANDLE AID and HANDLE ABEND.

Using SECTIONs can complicate program maintenance. In the long run, the use of SECTIONs will disappear in COBOL. The first reason listed above for using SECTIONs (internal SORTing) has already disappeared with VS COBOL II since you no longer need to house SORT input and output procedures in SECTIONs.

14.4   WHY SECTIONS FOR SORT INPUT AND OUTPUT PROCEDURES?

The sort utility (IBM's DFSORT or Computer Associate's Syncsort) always has three distinct phases of operation: input data to sort work space, sorting, and output data from sort work space. You can execute the sort utility directly using JCL or from a COBOL program using the SORT verb. COBOL itself has no logic for sorting and "hooks up" with the sort utility

When you use the SORT verb with an input procedure, you assume the responsibility of supplying COBOL logic to handle the first phase of the work, which inputs data to sort work space. When you use the SORT verb with an output procedure, you assume the responsibility of supplying COBOL logic to handle the last phase of the work—data outputting from sort work space. Until VS COBOL II, you had to house the input procedure as a SECTION and the output procedure as a SECTION.

It was natural for COBOL's inventors to require housing input and output procedures in separate SECTIONs. A program using the SORT verb with input/output procedures was a natural candidate for segmentation into memory overlays using SECTIONs. When the input procedure was executing, neither the sort phase nor the outputting phase could be active. When the sort was executing, neither the input nor the output procedure needed to be in memory. And when the output procedure was executing, there was no need for the input procedure or sort logic to be in memory.

14.5   WHY YOU SHOULD ABANDON SECTIONS NOW

SECTIONs are unusual and complicate program maintenance, so it is a very good idea to abandon them now. SECTIONs physically couple together all the paragraphs following the SECTION heading. If extra code is added into or between these paragraphs, it can be executed unintentionally.

A SECTION is an awkward construct because it ends in code only when the next SECTION starts. COBOL does not provide any actual command or syntax to mark this point. You can code an EXIT paragraph at the end of a SECTION but it is really just an empty paragraph. A SECTION-EXIT paragraph usually fools people into thinking that it marks the end of a section, but it marks the end only if another SECTION starts immediately afterward.

SECTIONs are strange for another reason. There is no COBOL command that lets you end the execution of a SECTION and get out of it. *You have to execute the last instruction in a SECTION to end its execution.* The inventors of the SECTION had no concept of modern structured programming. They assumed that you would naturally be at the bottom of your section of code when you were finished executing it. This was true of flowchart-developed code but is almost never true of modern structured code that you implement with PERFORM verbs. In modern programming this quirk of SECTION operation forces you to code a GO TO to send control to the bottom of the SECTION. Since nothing inherently marks the bottom of a SECTION, you usually have to code an empty paragraph (the EXIT paragraph) at the end of the SECTION just to have a place to GO TO!

14.6 *TRY IT!* ECAR3035: A NO-SECTION INTERNAL SORT EXAMPLE

You can try out an actual internal sort program that does not use SECTIONs by entering or uploading program ECAR3035, which is listed in Figure 14.3. This is the best way to see how abandoning SECTIONs simplifies your logic!

Figure 14.1 lists data that will be read by program ECAR3035. Each record documents a car insurance claim made by a policy holder. Records get into this file as policy holders have accidents and claim reimbursement for property damage, vehicle damage, and/or medical costs.

Program ECAR3035 reads the accident claims file and produces the report shown in Figure 14.2. This selects records from the claim file that have any medical cost associated with them. For these records, the program has to compute the total cost of the claim, which is the sum of all three cost components. It then has to sort the records into descending order of total claim cost and list them as in Figure 14.2. This figure was, in fact, produced from the claims data shown in Figure 14.1. (You can see that three of the records in the file were not listed since they had a medical cost of zero.)

The source code for Program ECAR3035 is listed in Figure 14.3. The program uses an internal sort. It makes sense to use an internal sort here for a variety of reasons. Record selection is apparent: not all of the records in the input file are to be sorted. The program selects only the records with medical cost greater than zero and RELEASEs them directly to sort work space. Before releasing those records, however, the program builds the record to be sorted. It builds the record coded at the Sort Description

```
         1           2        3            4        5        6        7          8
 ----+----0-|---+----0----+----0-|---+--|--|0----|+----|0----|+----0----+----0----|-----0

75187|P67386|JEROME IZHOME    |061490|CA|00172|00054|00036|*
76152|P18707|ANNETTE LACEY    |081590|CA|00078|00029|00000|*
80013|A41183|WARREN A. WHIG   |101290|NV|00290|00834|00095|ALBERT H. SMITHSON
81550|P24878|ALICE SPRINGS    |102990|CA|01100|00376|00195|WILSON ARMSTRONG
85681|A51690|EDDIE EDWARD     |011991|OR|00325|00100|00465|GWENDOLYN MCGUIRE
85693|A50103|MARTIN SMARTIN   |021391|CA|00867|01410|04650|VANESSA R. ALLAN
86771|A92016|CAROL O'FARRELL  |030191|CA|00000|00553|00208|JOSE MARIELLA
87101|P87452|STELLA STARLITE  |030691|NV|04067|00438|01116|WEI PING CHU
87396|A13019|LUCE CANNON      |031091|AZ|02250|01763|00558|GLENN IWANAGA
87908|P65611|RAMON MARTINEZ   |031491|CA|00058|00158|00025|*
94879|A91300|MRS. IPPI        |040391|CA|00000|00400|00110|*
94946|A64997|SEYMOUR CALLAHAN |053091|OR|00375|00276|00000|*
96094|P43398|LAUREL LEAF      |072991|UT|00504|00212|00000|*
96173|A14617|MABEL LEAF       |082091|CA|01408|00655|03160|MARTHA F. SINFUEGO
97982|P54916|GEORGE E. PORGIE |101391|CA|00672|00136|00196|*
```

```
01  PAID-CLAIM-FILE.
    05  PCF-CLAIM-NO                 PIC X(5).
    05  PCF-POLICY-NO                PIC X(6).
    05  PCF-CLAIMANT-NAME            PIC X(20).
    05  PCF-CLAIM-DATE               PIC X(6).
    05  PCF-ACCIDENT-STATE           PIC X(2).
    05  PCF-SETTLEMENT-COSTS.
        10  PCF-SETTLE-PROP-DAMAGE   PIC 9(5).
        10  PCF-SETTLE-VEH-DAMAGE    PIC 9(5).
        10  PCF-SETTLE-MEDICAL-COST  PIC 9(5).
    05  PCF-INJURED-PARTY.
        10  PCF-INJURED-FIRST-CHAR   PIC X(1).
            88  PCF-NO-OTHER-INJURED-PARTY       VALUE '*'.
        10  FILLER                   PIC X(19).
```

Figure 14.1 Auto Accident Claims Data Read by Program ECAR3035.

Each record in this file documents one claim for reimbursement of costs incurred in a car accident. The record carries the insurance policy holder name and identifying information, and three components of cost: property damage (to repair what the car hit), vehicle damage (to repair the car), and medical costs (to "repair" the driver and passengers). Note that in some cases property damage or medical cost is zero.

(SD), including the computation of the total claim field which functions as a sort key. All of these actions take place in the program's sort input procedure.

Outputting of data from the sort utility is handled by ECAR3035 in an output procedure. As with the input procedure you previously had to code this as a SECTION. But in ECAR3035 you see no SECTIONs. I wrote it without SECTIONs for the input or output procedures since VS

(text continues on page 271)

CLAIMANT NAME	CLAIM DATE	CLAIM NUMBER	POLICY NUMBER	PROP DAMAGE	VEHICLE REPAIR	MEDICAL COSTS	TOTAL CLAIM PAID
MARTIN SMARTIN	02/13/91	85693	A5010	867	1,410	4,650	6,927
STELLA STARLITE	03/06/91	87101	P8745	4,067	438	1,116	5,621
MABEL LEAF	08/20/91	96173	A1461	1,408	655	3,160	5,223
LUCE CANNON	03/10/91	87396	A1301	2,250	1,763	558	4,571
ALICE SPRINGS	10/29/90	81550	P2487	1,100	376	195	1,671
WARREN A. WHIG	10/12/90	80013	A4118	290	834	95	1,219
GEORGE E. PORGIE	10/13/91	97982	P5491	672	136	196	1,004
EDDIE EDWARD	01/19/91	85681	A5169	325	100	465	890
CAROL O'FARRELL	03/01/91	86771	A9201		553	208	761
MRS. IPPI	04/03/91	94879	A9130		400	110	510
JEROME IZHOME	06/14/90	75187	P6738	172	54	36	262
RAMON MARTINEZ	03/14/91	87908	P6561	58	158	25	241
			SUMMARY TOTALS	11,209	6,877	10,814	28,900

```
*** END OF JOB
CLAIM RECORDS READ .......... 15
CLAIM RECORDS OMITTED ....... 3
RECORDS RELEASED TO SORT .... 12
RECORDS RETURNED FROM SORT .. 12
RECORDS PRINTED ............. 12
```

Figure 14.2 Report Produced by Program ECAR3035.

This report is produced by ECAR3035, which does record selection, computation of a sort key, and internal sorting. Records from the auto accident claims file having any medical cost component are listed in descending order of total claim cost (a field not present in the original records).

```
000100 IDENTIFICATION DIVISION.
000200 PROGRAM-ID.    ECAR3035.
000300 AUTHOR.        J JANOSSY.
000400********************************************************************
000500*INSTALLATION. EMPLOYERS INSURANCE CORP. SAN DIEGO, CALIF.  *
000600*REMARKS.      READS A FILE OF VEHICLE INSURANCE CLAIMS AND  *
000700*              SELECTS RECORDS FOR CLAIMS WITH ANY MEDICAL   *
000800*              COSTS. COMPUTES TOTAL SETTLEMENT AMOUNT FOR   *
000900*              SUCH CLAIMS FOR USE AS SORT KEY. FORMS SORT   *
001000*              RECORDS, SORTS ON TOTAL COST, CREATES REPORT. *
001100*                                                           *
001200*              USES VS COBOL II WITHOUT SECTIONS            *
001300********************************************************************
001400*
001500 ENVIRONMENT DIVISION.
001600 INPUT-OUTPUT SECTION.
001700 FILE-CONTROL.
001800*-----------------------------------------------------------
001900* FOR RM-COBOL ON MICROCOMPUTERS:
002000     SELECT PAID-CLAIMS-FILE   ASSIGN TO DISK 'CLAIMS.DAT'
002100         ORGANIZATION IS LINE SEQUENTIAL.
002200     SELECT REPORT1            ASSIGN TO DISK 'EC3035R1.DAT'
002300         ORGANIZATION IS LINE SEQUENTIAL.
002400     SELECT CLAIM-SD-FILE      ASSIGN TO DISK 'CUSTWORK.DAT'
002500         ORGANIZATION IS LINE SEQUENTIAL.
002600*-----------------------------------------------------------
002700* FOR IBM VS COBOL AND VS COBOL II:
002800*     SELECT PAID-CLAIMS-FILE   ASSIGN TO CLAIMS.
002900*     SELECT REPORT1            ASSIGN TO EC3035R1.
003000*     SELECT CLAIM-SD-FILE      ASSIGN TO CUSTWORK.
003100*-----------------------------------------------------------
003200 DATA DIVISION.
003300 FILE SECTION.
003400*
003500 FD  PAID-CLAIMS-FILE
003600     BLOCK CONTAINS 0 RECORDS
003700     RECORD CONTAINS 80 CHARACTERS.
003800 01  PAID-CLAIMS-FILE-REC.
003900     05 PCF-CLAIM-NO             PIC X(5).
004000     05 PCF-POLICY-NO            PIC X(6).
004100     05 PCF-CLAIMANT-NAME        PIC X(20).
004200     05 PCF-CLAIM-DATE           PIC X(6).
004300     05 PCF-ACCIDENT-STATE       PIC X(2).
004400     05 PCF-SETTLEMENT-COSTS.
004500        10 PCF-SETTLE-PROP-DAMAGE    PIC 9(5).
004600        10 PCF-SETTLE-VEH-DAMAGE     PIC 9(5).
004700        10 PCF-SETTLE-MEDICAL-COST   PIC 9(5).
004800     05 PCF-INJURED-PARTY.
004900        10 PCF-INJURED-FIRST-CHAR    PIC X(1).
005000           88 PCF-NO-OTHER-INJURED-PARTY     VALUE '*'.
005100        10 FILLER                    PIC X(25).
005200*
005300 FD  REPORT1
005400     BLOCK CONTAINS 0 RECORDS
005500     RECORD CONTAINS 132 CHARACTERS.
005600 01  REPORT1-REC                 PIC X(132).
005700*
005800 SD  CLAIM-SD-FILE
005900     RECORD CONTAINS 59 CHARACTERS.
006000 01  CLAIM-SD-REC.
006100     05 CSR-CLAIMANT-NAME        PIC X(20).
006200     05 CSR-CLAIM-DATE.
006300        10 CSR-CLAIM-DATE-MO      PIC X(2).
006400        10 CSR-CLAIM-DATE-DA      PIC X(2).
006500        10 CSR-CLAIM-DATE-YR      PIC X(2).
006600     05 CSR-CLAIM-DATE-WHOLE  REDEFINES
006700        CSR-CLAIM-DATE           PIC X(6).
006800     05 CSR-CLAIM-NO             PIC X(6).
006900     05 CSR-POLICY-NO            PIC X(5).
007000     05 CSR-SETTLE-PROP-DAMAGE   PIC 9(5).
007100     05 CSR-SETTLE-VEH-DAMAGE    PIC 9(5).
007200     05 CSR-SETTLE-MEDICAL-COST  PIC 9(5).
007300     05 CSR-COMPUTED-TOTAL-COST  PIC 9(7).
007400*
007500 WORKING-STORAGE SECTION.
007600 01  WS-FLAG-VALUES.
007700     05 FF1-INPUT-FILE-FLAG      PIC X(1)    VALUE 'M'.
007800        88 FF1-MORE-INPUT                    VALUE 'M'.
007900        88 FF1-END-OF-INPUT                  VALUE 'E'.
008000     05 FF2-SORT-FILE-FLAG       PIC X(1)    VALUE 'M'.
008100        88 FF2-MORE-SORT-RECS                VALUE 'M'.
008200        88 FF2-END-OF-SORT-RECS              VALUE 'E'.
008300     05 WS-VALIDATION-FLAG       PIC X(1).
008400 01  WS-TOTAL-PROP-DAMAGE        PIC S9(7)   COMP-3 VALUE 0.
008500 01  WS-TOTAL-VEH-DAMAGE         PIC S9(7)   COMP-3 VALUE 0.
008600 01  WS-TOTAL-MEDICAL-COSTS      PIC S9(7)   COMP-3 VALUE 0.
008700*- - - - - - - - - - - - - - - - - - - - - - - - -
008800 01  WS-COUNTER-VALUES.
008900     05 WS-CLAIM-RECS-READ       PIC S9(5)   COMP-3  VALUE +0.
009000     05 WS-CLAIM-RECS-OMITTED    PIC S9(5)   COMP-3  VALUE +0.
009100     05 WS-RECS-RELEASED         PIC S9(5)   COMP-3  VALUE +0.
009200     05 WS-RECS-RETURNED         PIC S9(5)   COMP-3  VALUE +0.
009300     05 WS-RECS-PRINTED          PIC S9(5)   COMP-3  VALUE +0.
009400 01  WS-COUNTERS-BY-SUB  REDEFINES  WS-COUNTER-VALUES.
009500     05 WS-COUNTER-VALUE  OCCURS 5 TIMES  PIC S9(5)  COMP-3.
```

a

b

Figure 14.3 *(see legend on page 269)*

```
009600*
009700 01  WS-COUNTER-LABELS.
009800     05 FILLER  PIC X(30) VALUE 'CLAIM RECORDS READ ...........'.
009900     05 FILLER  PIC X(30) VALUE 'CLAIM RECORDS OMITTED ........'.
010000     05 FILLER  PIC X(30) VALUE 'RECORDS RELEASED TO SORT .....'.
010100     05 FILLER  PIC X(30) VALUE 'RECORDS RETURNED FROM SORT ...'.
010200     05 FILLER  PIC X(30) VALUE 'RECORDS PRINTED ..............'.
010300 01  WS-COUNTER-LABELS-BY-SUB  REDEFINES  WS-COUNTER-LABELS.
010400     05 WS-COUNTER-LABEL  OCCURS 5 TIMES  PIC X(30).
010500*
010600 01  WS-SUB                    PIC S9(4)  COMP  VALUE +0.
010700*- - - - - - - - - - - - - - - - - - - - - - - - - - - - - -
010800 01  REPORT1-HOUSEKEEPING.
010900     05 R1-LINE-LIMIT          PIC S9(2)  COMP-3  VALUE +59.
011000     05 R1-LINES-REMAINING     PIC S9(2)  COMP-3.
011100     05 R1-PAGE-COUNT          PIC S9(3)  COMP-3  VALUE +0.
011200     05 R1-NORMAL-LINE-SPACING PIC S9(3)  COMP-3  VALUE +1.
011300     05 R1-WANTED-LINE-SPACING PIC S9(3)  COMP-3.
011400     05 R1-PRINT-SLOT          PIC X(133).
011500*
011600 01  R1-TOP.
011700     05 STD-HEADING-LINE1.
011800        10 FILLER  PIC X(1)   VALUE ' '.
011900        10 FILLER  PIC X(131) VALUE ALL '*'.
012000        10 FILLER  PIC X(1)   VALUE SPACE.
012100     05 STD-HEADING-LINE2.
012200        10 FILLER  PIC X(1)   VALUE ' '.
012300        10 FILLER  PIC X(22)  VALUE '*    EMPLOYERS INSURANC'.
012400        10 FILLER  PIC X(20)  VALUE 'E CORPORATION    *   '.
012500        10 SHL2-SYSTEM-NAME   PIC X(47).
012600        10 FILLER  PIC X(21)  VALUE '   *              '.
012700        10 FILLER  PIC X(22)  VALUE '        *        *  '.
012800     05 STD-HEADING-LINE3.
012900        10 FILLER  PIC X(1)   VALUE ' '.
013000        10 FILLER  PIC X(22)  VALUE '*           1000 MIRA VIS'.
013100        10 FILLER  PIC X(20)  VALUE 'TA WAY          *   '.
013200        10 SHL3-REPORT-NAME   PIC X(47).
013300        10 FILLER  PIC X(7)   VALUE '   *   '.
013400        10 SHL3-CENTERED-DATE PIC X(18).
013500        10 FILLER  PIC X(11)  VALUE '  *     PAGE '.
013600        10 SHL3-PAGE-NO       PIC ZZ9.
013700        10 FILLER  PIC X(5)   VALUE '  *  '.
013800     05 STD-HEADING-LINE4.
013900        10 FILLER  PIC X(1)   VALUE ' '.
014000        10 FILLER  PIC X(22)  VALUE '*      CORONA DEL MAR, '.
014100        10 FILLER  PIC X(22)  VALUE 'CALIFORNIA       *    '.
014200        10 FILLER  PIC X(15)  VALUE '         PROGRAM '.
014300        10 SHL4-PROGRAM-NAME  PIC X(8).
014400        10 FILLER  PIC X(9)   VALUE ' REPORT '.
014500        10 SHL4-REPORT-NO     PIC X(4).
014600        10 FILLER  PIC X(8)   VALUE SPACES.
014700        10 FILLER  PIC X(22)  VALUE '      *              '.
014800        10 FILLER  PIC X(22)  VALUE '        *        *  '.
014900*
015000 01  R1-COLUMN-HEADINGS.
015100     05 R1-COL-HDR1.
015200        10 FILLER  PIC X(1)   VALUE ' '.
015300        10 FILLER  PIC X(22)  VALUE '                      '.
015400        10 FILLER  PIC X(22)  VALUE '                      '.
015500        10 FILLER  PIC X(22)  VALUE '          CLAIM    POL'.
015600        10 FILLER  PIC X(22)  VALUE 'ICY       PROP    VEHI'.
015700        10 FILLER  PIC X(22)  VALUE 'CLE      MEDICAL      '.
015800        10 FILLER  PIC X(22)  VALUE 'TOTAL                '.
015900     05 R1-COL-HDR2.
016000        10 FILLER  PIC X(1)   VALUE ' '.
016100        10 FILLER  PIC X(22)  VALUE '                     C'.
016200        10 FILLER  PIC X(22)  VALUE 'LAIMANT NAME       CLA'.
016300        10 FILLER  PIC X(22)  VALUE 'IM DATE  NUMBER    NUM'.
016400        10 FILLER  PIC X(22)  VALUE 'BER     DAMAGE     REP'.
016500        10 FILLER  PIC X(22)  VALUE 'AIR      COSTS     CLA'.
016600        10 FILLER  PIC X(22)  VALUE 'IM PAID              '.
016700*
016800 01  R1-DETLINE.
016900     05 FILLER                 PIC X(1)  VALUE ' '.
017000     05 FILLER                 PIC X(16) VALUE SPACES.
017100     05 R1-CLAIMANT            PIC X(22).
017200     05 FILLER                 PIC X(4)  VALUE SPACES.
017300     05 R1-CLAIM-DATE          PIC XX/XX/XX.
017400     05 FILLER                 PIC X(4)  VALUE SPACES.
017500     05 R1-CLAIM-NO            PIC X(5).
017600     05 FILLER                 PIC X(4)  VALUE SPACES.
017700     05 R1-POLICY-NO           PIC X(6).
017800     05 FILLER                 PIC X(5)  VALUE SPACES.
017900     05 R1-SETTLE-PROP-DAMAGE  PIC ZZ,ZZZ.
018000     05 FILLER                 PIC X(5)  VALUE SPACES.
018100     05 R1-SETTLE-VEH-DAMAGE   PIC ZZ,ZZZ.
018200     05 FILLER                 PIC X(5)  VALUE SPACES.
018300     05 R1-SETTLE-MEDICAL-COST PIC ZZ,ZZZ.
018400     05 FILLER                 PIC X(6)  VALUE SPACES.
018500     05 R1-SETTLE-TOTAL-COST   PIC ZZZ,ZZZ.
018600     05 FILLER                 PIC X(17) VALUE SPACES.
018700*
018800 01  R1-SUM-LINE.
018900     05 FILLER                 PIC X(1)  VALUE SPACE.
019000     05 FILLER                 PIC X(54) VALUE SPACES.
019100     05 FILLER                 PIC X(17) VALUE
019200        'SUMMARY TOTALS   '.
019300     05 R1-SL-TOTAL-PROP-DAMAGE PIC Z,ZZZ,ZZZ.
019400     05 FILLER                 PIC X(2)  VALUE SPACES.
```

Figure 14.3 *Continued*

```
019500      05 R1-SL-TOTAL-VEH-DAMAGE        PIC Z,ZZZ,ZZZ.
019600      05 FILLER                        PIC X(2)  VALUE SPACES.
019700      05 R1-SL-TOTAL-MEDICAL-COSTS     PIC Z,ZZZ,ZZZ.
019800      05 FILLER                        PIC X(4)  VALUE SPACES.
019900      05 R1-SL-GRAND-TOTAL-COSTS       PIC Z,ZZZ,ZZZ.
020000      05 FILLER                        PIC X(17) VALUE SPACES.
020100*
020200 01  R1-ENDLINE.
020300      05 FILLER                        PIC X(1)  VALUE SPACE.
020400      05 R1-EL-MESSAGE                 PIC X(30).
020500      05 FILLER                        PIC X(2)  VALUE SPACES.
020600      05 R1-EL-COUNT                   PIC ZZ,ZZ9.
020700      05 FILLER                        PIC X(94) VALUE SPACES.
020800*
020900 01  WS-CENTERED-DATE                  PIC X(18).
021000/
021100 PROCEDURE DIVISION.
021200 0000-MAINLINE.
021300      SORT CLAIM-SD-FILE
021400           ON DESCENDING KEY   CSR-COMPUTED-TOTAL-COST
021500           ON ASCENDING KEY    CSR-CLAIM-DATE-YR
021600                               CSR-CLAIM-DATE-MO
021700                               CSR-CLAIM-DATE-DA
021800           INPUT PROCEDURE IS  1000-SELECT-BUILD-RELEASE
021900           OUTPUT PROCEDURE IS 2000-RETURN-AND-REPORT.
022000      STOP RUN.
022100*
022200*- - - - - - - - - - - - - - - - - - - - - - - - - - - - -
022300*
022400 1000-SELECT-BUILD-RELEASE.
022500      OPEN INPUT PAID-CLAIMS-FILE.
022600      PERFORM 1700-READ.
022700      PERFORM 1500-LOAD-SORT-SPACE
022800           UNTIL FF1-INPUT-FILE-FLAG = 'E'.
022900      CLOSE PAID-CLAIMS-FILE.
023000*
023100 1500-LOAD-SORT-SPACE.
023200      MOVE 'G' TO WS-VALIDATION-FLAG.
023300*
023400      IF PCF-SETTLE-PROP-DAMAGE NOT NUMERIC
023500         MOVE 'B' TO WS-VALIDATION-FLAG.
023600*
023700      IF PCF-SETTLE-VEH-DAMAGE NOT NUMERIC
023800         MOVE 'B' TO WS-VALIDATION-FLAG.
023900*
024000      IF PCF-SETTLE-MEDICAL-COST NOT NUMERIC
024100         MOVE 'B' TO WS-VALIDATION-FLAG.
024200*
024300      IF WS-VALIDATION-FLAG = 'G'
024400         AND PCF-SETTLE-MEDICAL-COST > 0
024500             PERFORM 1520-BUILD-RELEASE-SD
024600      ELSE
024700         ADD +1 TO WS-CLAIM-RECS-OMITTED.
024800      PERFORM 1700-READ.
024900*
025000 1520-BUILD-RELEASE-SD.
025100      MOVE PCF-CLAIMANT-NAME        TO CSR-CLAIMANT-NAME.
025200      MOVE PCF-CLAIM-DATE           TO CSR-CLAIM-DATE.
025300      MOVE PCF-CLAIM-NO             TO CSR-CLAIM-NO.
025400      MOVE PCF-POLICY-NO            TO CSR-POLICY-NO.
025500      MOVE PCF-SETTLE-PROP-DAMAGE   TO CSR-SETTLE-PROP-DAMAGE.
025600      MOVE PCF-SETTLE-VEH-DAMAGE    TO CSR-SETTLE-VEH-DAMAGE.
025700      MOVE PCF-SETTLE-MEDICAL-COST  TO CSR-SETTLE-MEDICAL-COST.
025800      COMPUTE CSR-COMPUTED-TOTAL-COST =
025900          PCF-SETTLE-PROP-DAMAGE +
026000          PCF-SETTLE-VEH-DAMAGE +
026100          PCF-SETTLE-MEDICAL-COST.
026200      RELEASE CLAIM-SD-REC.
026300      ADD +1 TO WS-RECS-RELEASED.
026400*
026500 1700-READ.
026600      READ PAID-CLAIMS-FILE
026700          AT END
026800              MOVE 'E' TO FF1-INPUT-FILE-FLAG.
026900      IF FF1-INPUT-FILE-FLAG NOT = 'E'
027000          ADD +1 TO WS-CLAIM-RECS-READ.
027100*
027200*- - - - - - - - - - - - - - - - - - - - - - - - - - - - -
027300*
027400 2000-RETURN-AND-REPORT.
027500      PERFORM 2200-BOP.
027600      PERFORM 2500-REPORT
027700           UNTIL FF2-SORT-FILE-FLAG = 'E'.
027800      PERFORM 2990-EOP.
027900*
028000 2200-BOP.
028100      PERFORM 2998-INITIALIZE.
028200      OPEN OUTPUT REPORT1.
028300      PERFORM 2900-R1-NEWPAGE.
028400      PERFORM 2700-RETURN.
028500*
028600 2500-REPORT.
028700      MOVE CSR-CLAIMANT-NAME        TO R1-CLAIMANT.
028800      MOVE CSR-CLAIM-DATE-WHOLE     TO R1-CLAIM-DATE.
028900      MOVE CSR-CLAIM-NO             TO R1-CLAIM-NO.
```

f

g

h

i

Figure 14.3   *Continued*

```
029000          MOVE CSR-POLICY-NO            TO R1-POLICY-NO.
029100          MOVE CSR-SETTLE-PROP-DAMAGE   TO R1-SETTLE-PROP-DAMAGE.
029200          MOVE CSR-SETTLE-VEH-DAMAGE    TO R1-SETTLE-VEH-DAMAGE.
029300          MOVE CSR-SETTLE-MEDICAL-COST  TO R1-SETTLE-MEDICAL-COST.
029400          MOVE CSR-COMPUTED-TOTAL-COST  TO R1-SETTLE-TOTAL-COST.
029500          MOVE R1-DETLINE              TO R1-PRINT-SLOT.
029600          MOVE R1-NORMAL-LINE-SPACING  TO R1-WANTED-LINE-SPACING.
029700          PERFORM 2800-R1-WRITE.
029800          ADD +1 TO WS-RECS-PRINTED.
029900*
030000          ADD CSR-SETTLE-PROP-DAMAGE    TO WS-TOTAL-PROP-DAMAGE.
030100          ADD CSR-SETTLE-VEH-DAMAGE     TO WS-TOTAL-VEH-DAMAGE.
030200          ADD CSR-SETTLE-MEDICAL-COST   TO WS-TOTAL-MEDICAL-COSTS.
030300*
030400          PERFORM 2700-RETURN.
030500*
030600 2700-RETURN.
030700          RETURN CLAIM-SD-FILE
030800             AT END
030900                MOVE 'E' TO FF2-SORT-FILE-FLAG.
031000          IF FF2-SORT-FILE-FLAG NOT = 'E'
031100             ADD +1 TO WS-RECS-RETURNED.
031200*
031300 2800-R1-WRITE.
031400          IF R1-LINES-REMAINING < R1-WANTED-LINE-SPACING
031500             PERFORM 2900-R1-NEWPAGE.
031600          WRITE REPORT1-REC FROM R1-PRINT-SLOT
031700             AFTER ADVANCING R1-WANTED-LINE-SPACING LINES.
031800          COMPUTE R1-LINES-REMAINING =
031900             (R1-LINES-REMAINING - R1-WANTED-LINE-SPACING).
032000*
032100 2900-R1-NEWPAGE.
032200          ADD +1                TO R1-PAGE-COUNT.
032300          MOVE R1-PAGE-COUNT  TO SHL3-PAGE-NO.
032400          WRITE REPORT1-REC FROM STD-HEADING-LINE1
032500             AFTER ADVANCING PAGE.
032600          WRITE REPORT1-REC FROM STD-HEADING-LINE2
032700             AFTER ADVANCING 1 LINES.
032800          WRITE REPORT1-REC FROM STD-HEADING-LINE3
032900             AFTER ADVANCING 1 LINES.
033000          WRITE REPORT1-REC FROM STD-HEADING-LINE4
033100             AFTER ADVANCING 1 LINES.
033200          WRITE REPORT1-REC FROM STD-HEADING-LINE1
033300             AFTER ADVANCING 1 LINES.
033400          WRITE REPORT1-REC FROM R1-COL-HDR1
033500             AFTER ADVANCING 3 LINES.
033600          WRITE REPORT1-REC FROM R1-COL-HDR2
033700             AFTER ADVANCING 1 LINES.
033800          MOVE SPACES TO REPORT1-REC.
033900          WRITE REPORT1-REC
034000             AFTER ADVANCING 2 LINES.
034100          COMPUTE R1-LINES-REMAINING = (R1-LINE-LIMIT - 11).
034200          MOVE +1 TO R1-WANTED-LINE-SPACING.
034300*
034400 2990-EOP.
034500          MOVE WS-TOTAL-PROP-DAMAGE     TO R1-SL-TOTAL-PROP-DAMAGE.
034600          MOVE WS-TOTAL-VEH-DAMAGE      TO R1-SL-TOTAL-VEH-DAMAGE.
034700          MOVE WS-TOTAL-MEDICAL-COSTS   TO R1-SL-TOTAL-MEDICAL-COSTS.
034800          COMPUTE R1-SL-GRAND-TOTAL-COSTS =
034900             WS-TOTAL-PROP-DAMAGE
035000           +  WS-TOTAL-VEH-DAMAGE
035100           +  WS-TOTAL-MEDICAL-COSTS.
035200          MOVE R1-SUM-LINE TO R1-PRINT-SLOT.
035300          MOVE +2 TO R1-WANTED-LINE-SPACING.
035400          PERFORM 2800-R1-WRITE.
035500*
035600          MOVE SPACES TO R1-ENDLINE.
035700          MOVE '*** END OF JOB   ' TO R1-EL-MESSAGE
035800          MOVE R1-ENDLINE TO R1-PRINT-SLOT.
035900          MOVE +2 TO R1-WANTED-LINE-SPACING.
036000          PERFORM 2800-R1-WRITE.
036100*
036200          MOVE +1 TO R1-WANTED-LINE-SPACING.
036300          PERFORM 2995-WRITE-COUNTS
036400             VARYING WS-SUB FROM +1 BY +1
036500                UNTIL WS-SUB > +5.
036600          CLOSE  REPORT1.
036700*
036800 2995-WRITE-COUNTS.
036900          MOVE WS-COUNTER-LABEL(WS-SUB) TO R1-EL-MESSAGE.
037000          MOVE WS-COUNTER-VALUE(WS-SUB) TO R1-EL-COUNT.
037100          MOVE R1-ENDLINE TO R1-PRINT-SLOT.
037200          PERFORM 2800-R1-WRITE.
037300*
037400 2998-INITIALIZE.
037500          MOVE '    NON-FLEET AUTOMOBILE INSURANCE SUPPORT SYSTEM'
037600             TO SHL2-SYSTEM-NAME.
037700          MOVE '    CLAIMS ANALYSIS AND AUDIT REPORTING (CARR) UNIT'
037800             TO SHL3-REPORT-NAME.
037900          MOVE 'ECAR3035' TO SHL4-PROGRAM-NAME.
038000          MOVE 'R-01'     TO SHL4-REPORT-NO.
038100          CALL 'VS2DATE' USING SHL3-CENTERED-DATE.
```

j

k

l

m

Figure 14.3 *Continued*

Figure 14.3 VS COBOL II Source Code for Program ECAR3035.

a. Microcomputer COBOL compilers and VS COBOL II use different formats of SELECT/ASSIGN statement. If you develop on a microcomputer and upload to a mainframe, I suggest you use two sets of SELECT/ASSIGN statements in your programs. Comment out the set that does not apply.

b. The Sort Description (SD) functions like the door on a washing machine; the records to be sorted, like clothes to be washed, enter and leave the sort utility (washing machine) through this door.

c. I code counters and their labels as two "parallel" tables. This makes it easy to output all counts in a loop at end-of-job.

d. I modularized report writing variable and actions in this program. REPORT1-HOUSEKEEPING is where the controlling variables for the report are. R1-PRINT-SLOT is a printline-sized place that is printed when I PERFORM 2800-R1-WRITE. I put any line I want to print in R1-PRINT-SLOT and then do this PERFORM, so I don't have to worry about page control throughout the program.

e. You can code literal printlines, such as column headings, as six lines of 22 bytes each, as I do, to simplify your source code and make it more compact.

f. The SORT verb refers to the fields in the SD to provide sort key information. It splices together the input and output procedures, which are similar to complete programs in themselves. In VS COBOL the names 1000-SELECT-BUILD-RELEASE and 2000-RETURN-AND-REPORT would be SECTION names. In this program they are ordinary paragraph names.

g. The input procedure has a mainline that controls it, just like an ordinary program. 1000-SELECT-BUILD-RELEASE is the input procedure. Since it is not a SECTION it does not end with a GO TO any "section exit."

h. The RELEASE verb sends a copy of the record I have built up in the SD directly into the disk sort work space of the sort utility.

i. The output procedure has a mainline that controls it, just like an ordinary program. 2000-RETURN-AND-REPORT is the output procedure.

j. The job of the 2800-R1-WRITE paragraph is to write whatever is in R1-PRINT-SLOT to the report with the amount of AFTER ADVANCING I have specified in R1-WANTED-LINE-SPACING. It handles checking for room on the page and generation of a new page heading if necessary. You can think of this paragraph as a function.

k. 2900-R1-NEWPAGE starts a new page, complete with page heading, whenever it is invoked. I invoke it directly once in beginning-of-job, and 2800-R1-WRITE invokes it thereafter whenever necessary.

l. I write summary counts out from a table using a loop. This way, my logic is always the same no matter how many or how few counts I have to produce.

m. I put beginning-of-job initialization actions at the end of the program because they are invoked only once. This allows the rest of the program logic to be physically closer, making operation more efficient under MVS.

```
000100 IDENTIFICATION DIVISION.
000200 PROGRAM-ID.    VS2DATE.
000300 AUTHOR.        J. JANOSSY
000400******************************************************************
000500*       VS2DATE DATE SUBPROGRAM IN LEARN VS COBOL II!         *
000600* J. Janossy, DePaul Univ. (John Wiley and Sons, Inc., 1992)  *
000700*                                                             *
000800*   This subprogram makes it easy to acquire the spelled-out  *
000900*   current date in VS COBOL II. You can customize the month  *
001000*   name table to your own language and format requirements.  *
001100*   The current date is automatically provided centered in an *
001200*   18-byte field shared by the CALLing program.              *
001300*                                                             *
001400*       Copyright 1991 J. Janossy    All rights reserved      *
001500******************************************************************
001600*
001700 ENVIRONMENT DIVISION.
001800*
001900 DATA DIVISION.
002000 WORKING-STORAGE SECTION.
002100 01  WS-DATE.
002200     12 WS-YEAR                    PIC X(2).
002300     12 WS-MONTH                   PIC 9(2).
002400     12 WS-DAY.
002500        15 WS-DAY-HIGH-ORDER       PIC X(1).
002600        15 WS-DAY-LOW-ORDER        PIC X(1).
002700*
002800 01  WS-DAY-WORKAREA               PIC X(2).
002900 01  WS-STRING-AREA.
003000     12 WS-BYTE   OCCURS 18 TIMES  PIC X(1).
003100 01  WS-SUB                        PIC S9(4) COMP.
003200 01  WS-PTR                        PIC S9(4) COMP.
003300* - - - - - - - - - - - - - - - - - - - - - - - - - - - - - - -
003400* Make the month names in this table full names or any other
003500* abbreviations you like. Make them French in Quebec, Spanish
003600* or Portuguese in South America. The stringing logic will
003700* automatically eliminate trailing blanks.
003800* - - - - - - - - - - - - - - - - - - - - - - - - - - - - - - -
003900 01  MONTH-TABLE.
004000     12 FILLER                     PIC X(10) VALUE 'JAN      '.
004100     12 FILLER                     PIC X(10) VALUE 'FEB      '.
004200     12 FILLER                     PIC X(10) VALUE 'MAR      '.
004300     12 FILLER                     PIC X(10) VALUE 'APR      '.
004400     12 FILLER                     PIC X(10) VALUE 'MAY      '.
004500     12 FILLER                     PIC X(10) VALUE 'JUN      '.
004600     12 FILLER                     PIC X(10) VALUE 'JUL      '.
004700     12 FILLER                     PIC X(10) VALUE 'AUG      '.
004800     12 FILLER                     PIC X(10) VALUE 'SEP      '.
004900     12 FILLER                     PIC X(10) VALUE 'OCT      '.
005000     12 FILLER                     PIC X(10) VALUE 'NOV      '.
005100     12 FILLER                     PIC X(10) VALUE 'DEC      '.
005200 01  MONTH-TABLE-NAME  REDEFINES  MONTH-TABLE.
005300     12 MONTH-NAME  OCCURS 12 TIMES  PIC X(10).
005400*
005500 LINKAGE SECTION.
005600 01  DATE-X18                      PIC X(18).
005700/
```

ⓐ

ⓑ

Figure 14.4   VS COBOL II Source Code for Subprogram VS2DATE
You can CALL this subprogram from any other program and share an 18-byte alphanumeric field with it. VS2DATE gets the current date from DATE and uses the month to look up month name in a small table. It formats the current date with month, day, and year, such as MAY 5, 1992, automatically centered in the 18-byte field.

a. This table supplies the month names. You can make the names into abbreviations, as I have done here, or full-length names. You can even code them in a language other than English. The date centering logic automatically handles trailing spaces.

b. The LINKAGE SECTION receives the 18-byte alphanumeric field that the CALLing program shares with VS2DATE. You have to cite the name of this area in the LINKAGE SECTION in the PROCEDURE DIVISION heading after the word USING. If you forget to code USING and this name, your subprogram will abend since it will not get the address of the shared data.

```
005800 PROCEDURE DIVISION USING DATE-X18.
005900 0000-MAINLINE.
006000     MOVE SPACES TO WS-STRING-AREA DATE-X18.
006100     ACCEPT WS-DATE FROM DATE.
006200     IF WS-DAY-HIGH-ORDER = '0'
006300        MOVE WS-DAY-LOW-ORDER TO WS-DAY-WORKAREA
006400     ELSE
006500        MOVE WS-DAY TO WS-DAY-WORKAREA.
006600*
006700     STRING MONTH-NAME(WS-MONTH) DELIMITED BY ' '
006800            ' '                  DELIMITED BY SIZE
006900            WS-DAY-WORKAREA      DELIMITED BY ' '
007000            ' 19'                DELIMITED BY SIZE
007100            WS-YEAR              DELIMITED BY SIZE
007200        INTO WS-STRING-AREA.
007300* - - - - - - - - - - - - - - - - - - - - - - - - - - -
007400* The following logic figures out where to position the string
007500* pointer WS-PTR to center the date in the DATE-X18 field. The
007600* CONTINUE statement doesn't do anything but fills the role of
007700* the imperative statement needed in a PERFORM. The PERFORM
007800* loop locates the first non-blank position from the right:
007900* - - - - - - - - - - - - - - - - - - - - - - - - - - -
008000     PERFORM
008100        VARYING WS-SUB FROM +18 BY -1
008200           UNTIL WS-SUB < +1
008300           OR WS-BYTE(WS-SUB) NOT = SPACE
008400        CONTINUE
008500     END-PERFORM.
008600     IF WS-SUB > +16
008700        MOVE +1 TO WS-PTR
008800     ELSE
008900        COMPUTE WS-PTR = ( (18 - WS-SUB) / 2 ) + 1.
009000*
009100     STRING WS-STRING-AREA DELIMITED BY SIZE
009200        INTO DATE-X18 WITH POINTER WS-PTR.
009300     GOBACK.
```

c

d

Figure 14.4 *Continued*

c. The CONTINUE in this in-line PERFORM takes the place of a statement that actually does something. There is nothing to be done in this loop. The VARYING option actually does the work of scanning backwards from the end of the field looking for the first non-space position, and the UNTIL stops the loop when this point is found.

d. STRING with the POINTER option puts the date into the 18-byte field starting at the position where it should go to appear centered. Use GOBACK instead of EXIT PROGRAM since GOBACK is simpler. If you code EXIT PROGRAM, it has to be in a paragraph by itself.

COBOL II permits this. Not using SECTIONs makes ECAR3035 simpler to code and maintain. You can use this program as a pattern and logical building block for programs you might write or maintain having internal sorts.

I wrote ECAR3035 using the RM/COBOL-85 compiler mentioned in Chapter 1. If you develop programs using a microcomputer and later upload them to a mainframe, I suggest you include two sets of SELECT/ASSIGN statements as I did in lines 1900 through 3000. Comment out the SELECT/ASSIGN statement version not suited to the compiler you are using instead of trying to change the statements as you change environments.

14.7 VS2DATE: A HANDY CALLABLE DATE SUBROUTINE FOR VS COBOL II

You'll notice at the very end of program ECAR3035 that a CALL is made to a subprogram named VS2DATE. This CALL is actually part of the beginning-of-job actions of the ECAR3035. I housed some initialization at the end of the program since they would be invoked only once. The CALL to VS2DATE in line 038100 of ECAR3035 supplies the current date formatted with month name, centered in an 18-byte field in the page heading of the report. It provided the centered MAY 5, 1992 in Figure 14.2.

Figure 14.4 (page 270) shows you the source code for VS2DATE. I've included it here because it's compact and flexible. Almost all reporting programs require the current date in a heading and the VS2DATE subprogram is an easy way to meet this need. If you put this subprogram on your mainframe system any program can acquire the current date with one simple CALL as in line 038100 of ECAR3035. The only memory the CALLing program needs to share with VS2DATE is an 18-byte field in the page heading where the current date is intended to go.

VS2DATE shows you some interesting aspects of VS COBOL II, which you can read in the figure legend for Figure 14.4. You can customize it to produce the month name in any language. The logic in VS2DATE automatically takes care of trailing spaces.

I prepared VS2DATE using the RM/COBOL-85 compiler discussed in Chapter 1. This compiler supports dynamic CALLs just as does MVS. Using it, you don't need to "hard" linkage edit a CALLing program and subprogram, so CALLs are expecially convenient and flexible. Micro Focus COBOL works in exactly the same way. Yes, hard-linked modules execute more efficiently. But when you are developing and testing code in the microcomputer environment for eventual uploading to the mainframe, convenience is much more important than execution efficiency!

15

COBTEST Batch Mode Debugging

You lose the READY TRACE and EXHIBIT verbs of VS COBOL when you move to VS COBOL II because it doesn't support these verbs. In this chapter I show you how to accomplish the same debugging actions using the new COBTEST debugger in batch mode.

15.1 WHAT IS COBTEST?

VS COBOL II gives you two ways to debug programs. Both of these ways rely on a feature called COBTEST. The word "COBTEST" is actually a marketing term, a play on words. VS COBOL provided a crude interactive debugger named TESTCOB. COBTEST is the VS COBOL II version of mainframe debugging. A software engineer at IBM displayed a minuscule amount of creativity in changing the debugger's name from TESTCOB to COBTEST. COBTEST is really a program named COBDBG.

15.2 BATCH AND INTERACTIVE DEBUGGING

Figure 15.1 shows you the customary compile, linkage edit, and "go" by which an ordinary program run takes place. You have done this many times. Your local VS COBOL II compile/link/go proc orchestrates it.

When you do a batch run to debug a program it occurs as in Figure 15.2. Notice that instead of a direct go where your program load module is loaded to memory, COBDBG is loaded instead. You give control statements to COBDBG to identify your load module so that it can control its execution. You give additional control statements to COBDBG to control debugging actions. Appendix F in this book lists most of the

(text continues on page 276)

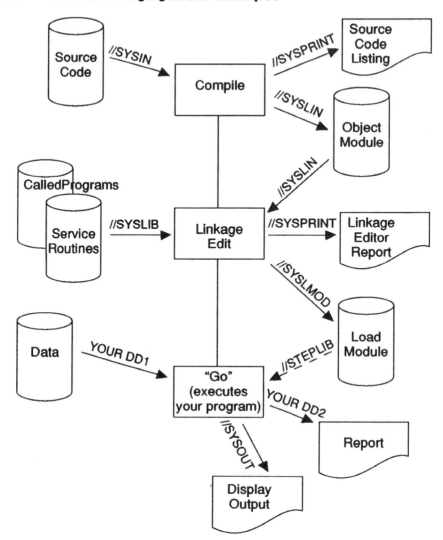

Figure 15.1 Ordinary Compile, Linkage Edit, and GO Execution.

When you process source code for a program run the compiler reads it, lists it noting any syntax errors, and creates an object module. The object module contains logic translated to machine language and references to input/output service routines (and reference to CALLed programs if you used the CALL verb). The linkage editor completes processing of the object module into an executable load module by combining input/output service routine logic (and subprogram logic) with the object module. The load module is the machine language equivalent of your program and is loaded to memory, given control, and executed. IBM supplies the COB2UCLG cataloged procedure (proc) to do this.

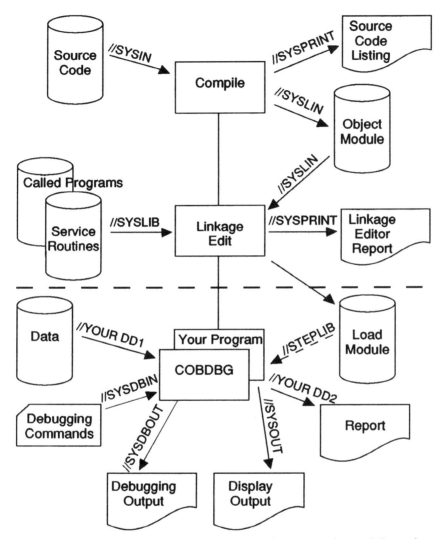

Figure 15.2 VS COBOL II COBTEST Debugging Processing and Execution.

When you process source code for a debugging run, the compile and linkage edit steps are done as in ordinary processing. But the GO step is not done as usual. Instead, you execute the program COBDBG, which actually makes up the COB-TEST feature. You give COBDBG instructions to execute your load module in debugging mode by feeding debugging control statements and commands into COBDBG at the //SYSDBIN DD statement. COBDBG learns the name of the library your load module is located in via //STEPLIB. You tell COBDBG the load module member name via the COBTEST statement. IBM supplies a cata-loged procedure (proc) named COB2UCL to accomplish the compile and linkage edit. You supply the remaining raw JCL, as in //STEP020 of Figure 15.6, to invoke COBDBG.

debugging commands. The complete reference for these commands is an IBM manual named *VS COBOL II: Application Program Debugging*, publication number SC26–4049.

You have two ways to execute COBDBG. If you execute it through JCL, as shown in Figure 15.6, the process is called "batch mode" debugging. In this mode you can use only a subset of the full range of debugging commands. You put the commands into your batch JCL as instream data. I show you how to do this in this chapter.

You can also execute COBDBG under TSO/ISPF from the TSO/ISPF "foreground" option panel (main menu selection 4). This mode is called "interactive debugging." Interactive debugging has nothing to do with CICS or IMS/DC programming; it just means debugging a batch program using COBDBG under TSO.

Using interactive debugging is entirely optional. Interactive debugging lets you enter COBDBG commands as you think about them, to interact with your program as it runs. Interactive debugging can be productive since you can stop your program, "peek" into variables, modify variables, and start the program again. I show you how to explore interactive debugging in Chapter 16.

15.3 READY TRACE NOT SUPPORTED!

Certain COBTEST batch debugging commands can give you the same results as the old READY TRACE. This is why IBM omitted support for READY TRACE from the VS COBOL II compiler. Under VS COBOL you could put READY TRACE into your program to have the system print the names of paragraphs as they executed:

```
004200 PROCEDURE DIVISION.
004300 0000-MAINLINE.
004400     READY TRACE.
          -
          -

005000     PERFORM 1000-COIN1
005100        VARYING WS-COIN1
005200           FROM 1 BY 1
005300              UNTIL WS-COIN1 > 3.
          -
          -

006600 1000-COIN1.
006700     IF WS-COIN1 = +1
006800        MOVE +.01 TO WS-VAL1
006900     ELSE
          -
          -
```

Figure 15.3 lists program K1DEBUG, from which these statements were drawn. You might recognize this as a tabulating version of B2COINS, introduced in Chapter 4. Figure 4.3 shows the original output of this program and Figure 4.4 shows the original code. Now instead of DIS-PLAYing each combination of coins possible, the program counts the occurrence of each combination in a table. It writes out the contents of the table as printlines to a report at end of job.

In VS COBOL, the READY TRACE at line 7100 of program K1DEBUG would produce the output shown in Figure 15.4. Read this compact output horizontally. It shows you the name of each paragraph as it received control and so traces program flow of control for you. Values in parentheses, such as (00000003), indicate that the last printed paragraph name received control repeatedly, in this case three times.

15.4 *TRY IT!* SIMULATING READY TRACE OUTPUT WITH COBTEST

COBTEST lets you receive output similar in function to the old READY TRACE, but more detailed. When you execute your program via COBDBG you can request a trace with the command TRACE NAME. The trace you receive will appear as in Figure 15.5. This output is vertical and so consumes a lot more paper than READY TRACE if you actually print it. It is also more detailed than the old READY TRACE. This output shows you a paragraph name when an instruction in the paragraph receives control, and also the line number and verb number within a line as each instruction receives control. For example, 82.1 means line 82, verb 1.

To receive a trace like that in Figure 15.5 you have to use JCL similar to that shown in Figure 15.6. The specific JCL you have to use may vary slightly because your systems programmers may have changed the name of the IBM compile and link proc for VS COBOL II or may have changed the names of the compile and link steps. But the control statements that produce a trace showing paragraph names will appear as in Figure 15.6.

In VS COBOL you could also put EXHIBIT NAMED into your source code to print out labeled values of data-names as the program executed. COBDBG does not give you a batch-mode equivalent of EXHIBIT NAMED. The closest you can come to EXHIBIT NAMED is the DIS-PLAY verb, which has no "smarts" to label data values with their names or conditionally display the contents of a variable.

15.5 COBTEST BATCH MODE DEBUGGING JCL

To use VS COBOL II COBTEST you need to compile and linkage edit your program with the TEST option. If you use your installation compile

(text continues on page 283)

```
000100 IDENTIFICATION DIVISION.
000200 PROGRAM-ID.      K1DEBUG.
000300 AUTHOR.          J. JANOSSY.
000400*****************************************************************
000500*    Droesselmeyer's generous coin game for nieces and   *
000600*    nephews, including logic to tabulate results by      *
000700*    loading unique values generated to a table           *
000800*****************************************************************
000900 ENVIRONMENT DIVISION.
001000 INPUT-OUTPUT SECTION.
001100 FILE-CONTROL.
001200*---------------------------------------------------------------
001300* FOR RM-COBOL ON MICROCOMPUTERS:
001400*    SELECT  TAB-OUTPUT-FILE  ASSIGN TO DISK 'TABOUT.DIS'
001500*        ORGANIZATION IS LINE SEQUENTIAL.
001600*---------------------------------------------------------------
001700* FOR IBM VS COBOL AND VS COBOL II:
001800     SELECT  TAB-OUTPUT-FILE  ASSIGN TO TABOUT.
001900*---------------------------------------------------------------
002000*
002100 DATA DIVISION.
002200 FILE SECTION.
002300 FD  TAB-OUTPUT-FILE
002400     LABEL RECORDS ARE STANDARD
002500     BLOCK CONTAINS 0 RECORDS
002600     RECORD CONTAINS 132 CHARACTERS.
002700 01  TAB-OUTPUT-RECORD.
002800     05 FILLER                 PIC X(1).
002900     05 TOF-TAB-MONEY          PIC $ZZ.99.
003000     05 FILLER                 PIC X(2).
003100     05 TOF-TAB-COUNT          PIC ZZ9-.
003200     05 FILLER                 PIC X(2).
003300     05 TOF-STARBYTE           PIC X(1)
003400                               OCCURS 25 TIMES
003500                               INDEXED BY STAR-IX.
003600     05 FILLER                 PIC X(92).
003700 01  TAB-SUMMARY-RECORD.
003800     05 TSR-MESSAGE            PIC X(37).
003900     05 TSR-VALUE              PIC ZZZ9-.
004000     05 FILLER                 PIC X(90).
004100/
004200 WORKING-STORAGE SECTION.
004300 01  WS-TAB-ROW-COUNT          PIC S9(4)  COMP  VALUE +0.
004400*
004500 01  WS-COINS.
004600     05 WS-COIN1               PIC 9(1).
004700     05 WS-COIN2               PIC 9(1).
004800     05 WS-COIN3               PIC 9(1).
004900     05 WS-COIN4               PIC 9(1).
005000*
005100 01  WS-VALUES.
005200     05 WS-VAL1                PIC S9(3)V99.
005300     05 WS-VAL2                PIC S9(3)V99.
005400     05 WS-VAL3                PIC S9(3)V99.
005500     05 WS-VAL4                PIC S9(3)V99.
005600     05 WS-TOTAL               PIC S9(3)V99.
005700*
005800*---------------------------------------------------------------
005900* This table will store one row for each unique value;
006000* allocated for 100 rows but will probably load much less
006100*---------------------------------------------------------------
006200 01  WS-TABLE-OF-VALUES.
006300     05 WS-TAB-VAL  OCCURS 1 TO 100 TIMES
006400                    DEPENDING ON WS-TAB-ROW-COUNT
006500                    INDEXED BY WS-TAB-IX.
006600         10 WS-TAB-MONEY       PIC S9(3)V99  COMP-3.
006700         10 WS-TAB-COUNT       PIC S9(3)     COMP-3.
006800/
006900 PROCEDURE DIVISION.
007000 0000-MAINLINE.
007100*    READY TRACE.
007200     PERFORM 0500-BOJ.
007300     PERFORM 1000-COIN1
007400         VARYING WS-COIN1
007500             FROM 1 BY 1
007600                 UNTIL WS-COIN1 > 3.
007700     PERFORM 9000-EOJ.
007800     STOP RUN.
```

Figure 15.3 *(see legends on page 280)*

```
007900*
008000 0500-BOJ.
008100     OPEN OUTPUT TAB-OUTPUT-FILE.
008200     MOVE 'PROGRAM K1DEBUG STARTING' TO TAB-OUTPUT-RECORD.
008300     WRITE TAB-OUTPUT-RECORD.
008400     MOVE 'VALUE   COUNT' TO TAB-OUTPUT-RECORD.
008500     WRITE TAB-OUTPUT-RECORD.
008600*------------------------------------------------------------
008700* Process choice for first cup, vary second cup
008800*------------------------------------------------------------
008900 1000-COIN1.
009000     IF WS-COIN1 = +1
009100         MOVE +.01 TO WS-VAL1
009200     ELSE
009300     IF WS-COIN1 = +2
009400         MOVE +.10 TO WS-VAL1
009500     ELSE
009600     IF WS-COIN1 = +3
009700         MOVE +1.00 TO WS-VAL1.
009800     PERFORM 2000-COIN2
009900         VARYING WS-COIN2
010000             FROM +1 BY +1
010100                 UNTIL WS-COIN2 > +3.
010200*------------------------------------------------------------
010300* Process choice for second cup, vary third cup
010400*------------------------------------------------------------
010500 2000-COIN2.
010600     IF WS-COIN2 = +1
010700         MOVE +.01 TO WS-VAL2
010800     ELSE
010900     IF WS-COIN2 = +2
011000         MOVE +.10 TO WS-VAL2
011100     ELSE
011200     IF WS-COIN2 = +3
011300         MOVE +1.00 TO WS-VAL2.
011400     PERFORM 3000-COIN3
011500         VARYING WS-COIN3
011600             FROM +1 BY +1
011700                 UNTIL WS-COIN3 > +3.
011800*------------------------------------------------------------
011900* Process choice for third cup, vary fourth cup
012000*------------------------------------------------------------
012100 3000-COIN3.
012200     IF WS-COIN3 = +1
012300         MOVE +.01 TO WS-VAL3
012400     ELSE
012500     IF WS-COIN3 = +2
012600         MOVE +.10 TO WS-VAL3
012700     ELSE
012800     IF WS-COIN3 = +3
012900         MOVE +1.00 TO WS-VAL3.
013000     PERFORM 4000-COIN4
013100         VARYING WS-COIN4
013200             FROM +1 BY +1
013300                 UNTIL WS-COIN4 > +3.
013400*------------------------------------------------------------
013500* Process choice for fourth cup; total and update table
013600* adding a new row if necessary or updating existing row
013700*------------------------------------------------------------
013800 4000-COIN4.
013900     IF WS-COIN4 = +1
014000         MOVE +.01 TO WS-VAL4
014100     ELSE
014200     IF WS-COIN4 = +2
014300         MOVE +.10 TO WS-VAL4
014400     ELSE
014500     IF WS-COIN4 = +3
014600         MOVE +1.00 TO WS-VAL4.
014700*
014800     COMPUTE WS-TOTAL =
014900         WS-VAL1 + WS-VAL2 + WS-VAL3 + WS-VAL4.
015000*
015100     SET WS-TAB-IX TO 1.
015200     SEARCH WS-TAB-VAL
015300         AT END
015400             ADD +1       TO WS-TAB-ROW-COUNT
015500             SET WS-TAB-IX TO WS-TAB-ROW-COUNT
015600             MOVE WS-TOTAL TO WS-TAB-MONEY(WS-TAB-IX)
015700             MOVE +1       TO WS-TAB-COUNT(WS-TAB-IX)
015800         WHEN WS-TOTAL = WS-TAB-MONEY(WS-TAB-IX)
```

(c)

Figure 15.3   *Continued*

```
015900              ADD +1           TO WS-TAB-COUNT(WS-TAB-IX).
016000*
016100*=======================================================
016200* End of job
016300*=======================================================
016400 9000-EOJ.
016500      PERFORM 9500-UNLOAD-A-ROW
016600          VARYING WS-TAB-IX
016700              FROM 1 BY 1
016800                  UNTIL WS-TAB-IX > WS-TAB-ROW-COUNT.
016900*
017000      MOVE WS-TAB-ROW-COUNT TO TSR-VALUE.
017100      MOVE 'TOTAL DIFFERENT COMBINATION VALUES = '
017200          TO TSR-MESSAGE.
017300      WRITE TAB-SUMMARY-RECORD.
017400      CLOSE TAB-OUTPUT-FILE.
017500*-----------------------------------------------------
017600* GENERATE ONE LINE OF FINAL PRINT EACH TIME INVOKED
017700*-----------------------------------------------------
017800 9500-UNLOAD-A-ROW.
017900      MOVE SPACES TO TAB-OUTPUT-RECORD.
018000      MOVE WS-TAB-MONEY(WS-TAB-IX) TO TOF-TAB-MONEY.
018100      MOVE WS-TAB-COUNT(WS-TAB-IX) TO TOF-TAB-COUNT.
018200      PERFORM 9510-STARMOVE
018300          VARYING STAR-IX FROM 1 BY 1
018400              UNTIL STAR-IX > WS-TAB-COUNT(WS-TAB-IX).
018500      WRITE TAB-OUTPUT-RECORD.
018600*
018700 9510-STARMOVE.
018800      MOVE '*' TO TOF-STARBYTE(STAR-IX).
```

(d)

(e)

Figure 15.3 Source Code for K1DEBUG, An Example Program for Debugging.

K1DEBUG is a revised version of B2COINS, introduced in Chapter 4 (Figures 4.3 and 4.4). My earlier versions of this program use nested loops to exercise all 81 possible combinations of a penny, dime, and dollar when a person is allowed to choose one four successive times. The earlier versions of this program DISPLAYed the actual combinations. K1DEBUG instead tabulates the value of each of the 81 combinations and builds a table in memory to see which combinations occur most. Instead of DISPLAYing the output (which would be produced at the DDname //SYSOUT) it writes the output as printlines to DDname //TABOUT. You can try out this program using VS COBOL to see how READY TRACE at line 7100 (uncomment it!) produces the output shown in Figure 15.4. Try this program with VS COBOL II and a COBTEST TRACE NAME debug to see how it produces the output shown in Figure 15.5.

a. TAB-OUTPUT-FILE has two forms of printline. TAB-OUTPUT-RECORD has a repeating field at the end to form the bar chart. TAB-SUMMARY-RECORD is the final line of the report.

b. WS-TABLE-OF-VALUES is loaded at runtime. Each row carries a money value and frequency count. At the start of the run the table is empty and WS-TAB-ROW-COUNT is zero.

c. The SEARCH loads the WS-TABLE-OF-VALUES table. If the money value just generated is not already in the table, it is put into the next available row and its count is set to 1. If the money value just generated is already in the table, the count for that row is incremented upward by 1.

d. Every iteration of this loop in end-of-job logic outputs a row of the table to paper.

e. This loop in end-of-job logic repeats for however many asterisks are to be printed in the bar for the row. The bar chart part of each printline is formed here.

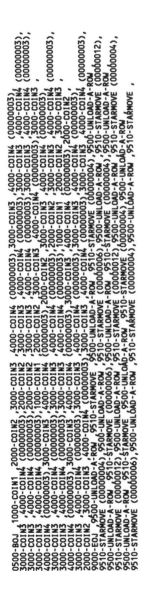

```
0500-BOJ ,1000-COIN1 ,2000-COIN2 ,3000-COIN3 ,4000-COIN4 (00000003),
3000-COIN3 ,4000-COIN4 (00000003),2000-COIN2 ,3000-COIN3 ,4000-COIN4 (00000003),
3000-COIN3 ,4000-COIN4 (00000003),1000-COIN1 ,2000-COIN2 ,3000-COIN3 ,4000-COIN4 (00000003),3000-COIN3 ,
4000-COIN4 (00000003),3000-COIN3 ,4000-COIN4 (00000003),2000-COIN2 ,3000-COIN3 ,4000-COIN4 (00000003),
3000-COIN3 ,4000-COIN4 (00000003),3000-COIN3 ,4000-COIN4 (00000003),1000-COIN1 ,2000-COIN2 ,3000-COIN3 ,
4000-COIN4 (00000003),3000-COIN3 ,4000-COIN4 (00000003),3000-COIN3 ,4000-COIN4 (00000003),2000-COIN2 ,
3000-COIN3 ,4000-COIN4 (00000003),3000-COIN3 ,4000-COIN4 (00000003),3000-COIN3 ,4000-COIN4 (00000003),
2000-COIN2 ,3000-COIN3 ,4000-COIN4 (00000003),3000-COIN3 ,4000-COIN4 (00000003),9500-UNLOAD-A-ROW (00000003),
9000-EOJ ,9500-UNLOAD-A-ROW (00000004),9500-UNLOAD-A-ROW (00000006),9510-STARMOVE (00000012),
9510-STARMOVE (00000004),9500-UNLOAD-A-ROW ,9510-STARMOVE (00000006),9500-UNLOAD-A-ROW ,
9500-UNLOAD-A-ROW ,9510-STARMOVE (00000012),9500-UNLOAD-A-ROW ,9510-STARMOVE (00000004),
9510-STARMOVE (00000012),9500-UNLOAD-A-ROW ,9510-STARMOVE (00000004),9500-UNLOAD-A-ROW ,
9500-UNLOAD-A-ROW ,9510-STARMOVE (00000004),9510-STARMOVE (00000004),9500-UNLOAD-A-ROW ,
9510-STARMOVE (00000006),9500-UNLOAD-A-ROW ,9510-STARMOVE ,
```

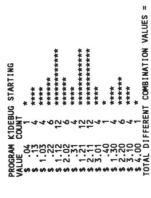

```
PROGRAM K1DEBUG STARTING
VALUE     COUNT
$   .04   1    *
$   .13   4    ****
$  1.03   4    ****
$   .22   6    ******
$  1.12   12   ************
$  2.02   6    ******
$   .31   4    ****
$  1.21   12   ************
$  2.11   12   ************
$  3.01   4    ****
$   .40   1    *
$  1.30   4    ****
$  2.20   6    ******
$  3.10   4    ****
$  4.00   1    *
TOTAL DIFFERENT COMBINATION VALUES =    15
```

Figure 15.4 Output From K1DEBUG (VS COBOL and READY TRACE).

READY TRACE produces a compact, horizontally-oriented listing of paragraph names. Each paragraph name is listed as it receives control. Values in parentheses, such as (00000003), indicate when a paragraph repeatedly receives control. The values, counts, and bar chart of frequencies at the bottom is the output produced by K1DEBUG as a report and output at DDname //TABOUT.

281

```
IGZ100I PP - 5668-958 VS COBOL II DEBUG FACILITY -- REL 3.2
IGZ102I K1DEBUG.000072.1
IGZ106I TRACING K1DEBUG
IGZ109I 000081.1 0500-BOJ
IGZ109I 000082.1
IGZ109I 000083.1
IGZ109I 000084.1
IGZ109I 000085.1
IGZ109I 000090.1 1000-COIN1
IGZ109I 000091.1
IGZ109I 000098.1
IGZ109I 000106.1 2000-COIN2
IGZ109I 000107.1
IGZ109I 000114.1
IGZ109I 000122.1 3000-COIN3
IGZ109I 000123.1
IGZ109I 000130.1
IGZ109I 000139.1 4000-COIN4
IGZ109I 000140.1
IGZ109I 000148.1
IGZ109I 000151.1
IGZ109I 000154.1
IGZ109I 000139.1 4000-COIN4
IGZ109I 000142.1
IGZ109I 000143.1
IGZ109I 000148.1
IGZ109I 000151.1
IGZ109I 000154.1
IGZ109I 000139.1 4000-COIN4
IGZ109I 000142.1
IGZ109I 000145.1
IGZ109I 000146.1
IGZ109I 000148.1
IGZ109I 000151.1
IGZ109I 000154.1
IGZ109I 000122.1 3000-COIN3
IGZ109I 000125.1
IGZ109I 000126.1
IGZ109I 000130.1
        .
        .
        .
IGZ109I 000179.1 9500-UNLOAD-A-ROW.
IGZ109I 000180.1
IGZ109I 000181.1
IGZ109I 000188.1 9510-STARMOVE
IGZ109I 000185.1 9500-UNLOAD-A-ROW
IGZ109I 000170.1 9000-EOJ
IGZ109I 000171.1
IGZ109I 000173.1
IGZ109I 000174.1
IGZ129I PROGRAM UNDER COBTEST ENDED NORMALLY
IGZ350I ******** END OF COBTEST ********
PROGRAM K1DEBUG STARTING
VALUE    COUNT
$   .04     1   *
$   .13     4   ****
$  1.03     4   ****
$   .22     6   ******
$  1.12    12   ************
$  2.02     6   ******
$   .31     4   ****
$  1.21    12   ************
$  2.11    12   ************
$  3.01     4   ****
$   .40     1   *
$  1.30     4   ****
$  2.20     6   ******
$  3.10     4   ****
$  4.00     1   *
TOTAL DIFFERENT COMBINATION VALUES =   15
```

Figure 15.5 Output From K1DEBUG (VS COBOL II COBTEST Batch Debugging).

You can use the JCL shown in Figure 15.6 to execute program K1DEBUG using the COBDBG debugger, giving the debugger the TRACE NAME command. This gives you a flow of control trace similar to the old READY TRACE. The new trace is more detailed since it shows you each statement number as it receives control in addition to each paragraph name. But since this new format of trace is vertically-oriented, your listings can be huge if you actually print them. View this type of trace using TSO/ISPF but be careful in sending this type of trace to the printer!

```
//CSCJGJA  JOB  (your locally applicable JOB statement...)
//*****************************************************
//*                                                   *
//*    USE THE COMPILE/LINK PROC TO PRODUCE LOAD MODULE *
//*                                                   *
//*****************************************************
//STEP010 EXEC COB2UCL,
//   PARM.COMP='APOST,XREF,MAP,TEST' ─────────┐ You must compile
//COMP.SYSIN DD DSN=CSCJGJ.CSC.COBOL(K1DEBUG), │ with TEST option
//   DISP=SHR                                  └─────────────
//*
//*****************************************************
//*                                                   *
//*    INVOKE THE VS COBOL II DEBUGGER COBDBG          *
//*                                                   *
//*****************************************************
//STEP020 EXEC PGM=COBDBG
//STEPLIB    DD DSN=&&GOSET,DISP=(SHR,PASS)
//           DD DSN=SYS1.COB2LIB,DISP=SHR      ┌──────────────
//TABOUT     DD SYSOUT=* ─────────────────────┤ DD statement specific
//SYSOUT     DD SYSOUT=*                        │ to my program K1DEBUG
//SYSDUMP    DD SYSOUT=*                        └──────────────
//SYSDBOUT   DD SYSOUT=*              ┌─────────────────────────
//SYSDBIN    DD *                     │ MAIN is the name of the member in
COBTEST MAIN ──────────────────────  │ the load module library.  With the
QUALIFY K1DEBUG ───────────────────  │ proc I use this is &&GOSET(MAIN)
TRACE NAME                           └─────────────────────────
/*                    ┌──────────────────────────
//                    │ K1DEBUG is the name coded in
                      │ the ID DIVISION of the program
                      └──────────────────────────
```

Figure 15.6 JCL To Do COBTEST Batch Mode Debugging.

This JCL uses the IBM-cataloged procedure COB2UCL to compile and link program K1DEBUG at //STEP010, then invokes the COBDBG debugger in //STEP020. //STEPLIB points to the load module library (&&GOSET) into which the proc has put the load module for the program, and to the VS COBOL II runtime library. The control statements tell COBDBG the load module member name of the program to be debugged and the name you coded on the program's PROGRAM-ID statement. TRACE NAME is the debugging command that requests production of the trace. Try out this JCL with K1DEBUG. You may have to adjust it slightly to suit any stepnames and DDnames in the proc locally customized by your systems programmers.

and linkage edit proc, as shown in Figure 15.6, you will need to override the entire PARM parameter of the EXEC statement for the VS COBOL II compiler. PARM.COB does this in your execution JCL. Alternatively, you can use a PROCESS statement at the start of your program to activate the compiler's TEST option. If you use a PROCESS statement, remember to remove it later when you compile the program for production execution because the TEST option makes a program execute inefficiently.

The actual running of the load module is handled by COBDBG. In Figure 15.6 you see COBDBG executed by a second step of JCL, //STEP020. At this step you need to code DD statements for the step library, COBDBG inputs and outputs, and the program being debugged! Here are the DDnames involved:

//STEPLIB—The temporary or permanent load module library where the load module of the program being debugged is stored. If you use a compile and link proc, as I did in the JCL in Figure 15.6, the load module library will be a temporary one like &&GOSET. Concatenate SYS1.COB2LIB to the load module library, since this is where VS COBOL II runtime routines are housed.

//SYSOUT, //SYSDBOUT, and //SYSDUMP—These are all places where COBDBG may want to output material intended for print.

//SYSDBIN—The place where COBDBG looks for your debugging control statements and commands. You supply statements to COBDBG that tell it the name of the program load module to be debugged, the program name, and what you want done in the debugging run.

You need to code DD statements for data sets read or written by your program at the COBDBG step of your JCL (//STEP020 in Figure 15.6) just as you would code them for normal execution of your program. I have coded //TABOUT at //STEP020 in Figure 15.6 because program K1DEBUG writes its report to this DDname.

15.6 EXPLANATION OF COBTEST AND QUALIFY CODING

The first control statement you input to COBDBG at //SYSDBIN is always the command COBTEST and the name of the load module to be run. In Figure 15.6 this is MAIN only because that's the name in the COB2UCL proc that I used. If you compile and link your program and store it as a member of a permanent load module library, you put its member name in that library on the COBTEST statement.

The first QUALIFY control statement gives the ID DIVISION name of the program you are debugging. Here you see the name K1DEBUG since that is the name of the program listed in Figure 15.3. After this QUALIFY come any commands to COBDBG. I have put only the TRACE NAME command in Figure 15.6.

If the program you are debugging CALLs any other programs, you code QUALIFY statements for each subprogram after the commands for the main (CALLing) program. After the QUALIFY for a subprogram, you code commands to control what happens in debugging as execution proceeds.

For example, suppose main program PGMA, stored as member HOT-DOG in a load module library, CALLs two subprograms SUB1 and SUB2 whose load modules are located in the same load module library. You are debugging PGMA and want a complete trace including control as it passes through the subprograms. You could code the statements:

```
COBTEST HOTDOG
QUALIFY PGMA
TRACE NAME
QUALIFY SUB1
TRACE NAME
QUALIFY SUB2
TRACE NAME
```

Debug commands don't affect any programs compiled without the TEST compile option. To get a complete trace you would have to compile SUB1 and SUB2 with the TEST option.

15.7 *TRY IT!* FREQ, LISTFREQ, AND AT DEBUGGING COMMANDS

While many of the COBDBG debugging commands are intended only for interactive use, you can try out the FREQ, LISTFREQ, and "breakpoint" AT commands, which serve a useful purpose in batch debugging:

```
COBTEST MAIN
QUALIFY K1DEBUG
FREQ ALL
TRACE NAME
AT 78 (LISTFREQ ALL)
```

FREQ ALL turns on a frequency of execution counter for each verb. The count builds up as the program executes. TRACE NAME produces the flow of control trace you have already seen. AT is a command to set a breakpoint, where the program will pause. At such pauses you can ask for actions to be taken, such as LISTFREQ, which causes the built-up verb execution counts to be printed. Line 78 is the STOP RUN statement in K1DEBUG, so the LISTFREQ I coded will be output when the program has completed all processing.

The debugger processes all your commands *before* the program to be debugged starts running. After it processes your commands it automatically issues a **GO** command which starts program execution. Some commands like TRACE cause debugging output to be generated as execution proceeds. But some commands, like FREQ ALL, just turn on a feature, such as verb execution counting. If you never do the AT command and issue a command to output accumulated information at this point, you would never see the counts that FREQ ALL caused to be accumulated. For example, if you did this you would not see any frequency counting output:

```
COBTEST MAIN
QUALIFY K1DEBUG
FREQ ALL
LISTFREQ ALL
```

Here, FREQ ALL would turn on verb frequency of execution counting but LISTFREQ ALL would output the counts immediately—before the program actually started executing!

If the debugger finds a syntax error in one of your debugging commands, it notes the error but keeps on processing. You have to look closely at the run results to see if all your debugging commands processed correctly.

15.8 BATCH DEBUGGING ADVANTAGES AND DISADVANTAGES

Batch mode debugging has a number of advantages, one of which is its familiarity and ease. In addition, batch mode debugging consumes much less in machine resources than full-screen interactive debugging does. Batch mode debugging runs can be done stand alone; you can do other work while they proceed. Interactive debugging (of course) ties up a terminal (and you). Some types of debugging output, such as TRACE NAME and FREQ ALL, are readily usable in TSO/ISPF print output viewing or on paper.

Interactive mode debugging, on the other hand, can make you productive in a different way once you surmount the learning curve associated with it.

16

Interactive COBTEST Debugging

VS COBOL II gives you the COBTEST full-screen interactive debugging environment. COBTEST is an optional feature. It operates under TSO/E and lets you exercise a program, watch the results, and look into it to see data-name values and statements as they execute. You may find that interactive debugging provides you with a convenient way to exercise a program and analyze its operation.

In this chapter I will show you how to prepare programs for interactive debugging and how to use the interactive debugger. My goal for this chapter is to get you over the bumps in setting up interactive debugging and to give you the "big picture" of what's involved in doing it. Interactive debugging relies on knowledge of TSO CLIST commands and of IBM's debugging manual, *VS COBOL II Application Programming: Debugging*, SC26–4049.

It would be a mistake for you to assume that you can learn interactive debugging within a few minutes as an expedient to solving a hot problem. In my experience it takes a person several sessions with the interactive debugger to become familiar enough with it to make it productive and comfortable tool. The investment of time and effort is warranted. But invest that time outside of any crash project to meet an impending deadline!

16.1 COBTEST MODES

You access COBTEST via the TSO/ISPF main menu. It replaces the old TESTCOB feature of VS COBOL. COBTEST offers three modes of operation:

- Batch mode (see Chapter 15)
- Interactive line-oriented mode (like VS COBOL TESTCOB; obsolescent and not covered in this book)
- Interactive full-screen mode

IBM documentation is a little difficult to follow when it discusses the interactive full-screen mode. It makes the assumption that you approach this subject with complete knowledge of interactive compiling and linkage editing and that you have several TSO "Ready" mode commands at your fingertips. My experience in training in the contemporary corporate environment indicates that many mainframe programmers don't have the background in interactive use of TSO that IBM assumes for interactive debugging. That's why I start this discussion with interactive compiling.

16.2 TSO/ISPF FOREGROUND OPERATIONS

Figure 16.1 shows you a typical TSO/ISPF main menu screen. Your local screen may vary from this in appearance because systems programmers at your installation can customize TSO/ISPF screen appearance.

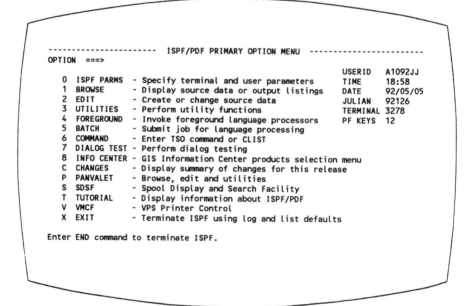

```
--------------------- ISPF/PDF PRIMARY OPTION MENU ---------------------
OPTION  ===>
                                                          USERID    A1092JJ
        0  ISPF PARMS  - Specify terminal and user parameters   TIME      18:58
        1  BROWSE      - Display source data or output listings  DATE      92/05/05
        2  EDIT        - Create or change source data            JULIAN    92126
        3  UTILITIES   - Perform utility functions               TERMINAL  3278
        4  FOREGROUND  - Invoke foreground language processors    PF KEYS   12
        5  BATCH       - Submit job for language processing
        6  COMMAND     - Enter TSO command or CLIST
        7  DIALOG TEST - Perform dialog testing
        8  INFO CENTER - GIS Information Center products selection menu
        C  CHANGES     - Display summary of changes for this release
        P  PANVALET    - Browse, edit and utilities
        S  SDSF        - Spool Display and Search Facility
        T  TUTORIAL    - Display information about ISPF/PDF
        V  VMCF        - VPS Printer Control
        X  EXIT        - Terminate ISPF using log and list defaults

Enter END command to terminate ISPF.
```

Figure 16.1 TSO/ISPF Main Menu Screen.

From the main menu, select option 4, FOREGROUND. Foreground memory is memory allocated to TSO/ISPF itself by the operating system. When you do operations "in the foreground" you use some of TSO's resources to execute software, such as the compiler, in an immediate way without JCL.

Figure 16.2 shows you the TSO/ISPF function 4 FOREGROUND selection submenu. Once again, you may see minor variations between your system and this figure. We will use options 2, 7, and 10 on this screen. Your selection numbers for the VS COBOL II compiler, linkage editor, and VS COBOL II interactive debug may differ.

16.3 TSO/ISPF FOREGROUND COMPILE AND LINK NAMING CONVENTIONS

You can use the TSO/ISPF foreground options to compile a program. When you do this the compiler acts immediately. It creates a source code listing noting any errors it finds and it produces an object file. You can invoke the linkage editor in the same immediate way to complete processing of the object file into a load module.

```
---------------------- 4  FOREGROUND SELECTION PANEL  ----------------------
OPTION  ===>

   1 - Assembler H                *7  - Linkage editor
   1A - Assembler XF               9  - SCRIPT/VS
   2 - VS COBOL II compiler      *10  - VS COBOL II interactive debug
   2A - OS/VS COBOL compiler     *10A - COBOL interactive debug
   3 - VS FORTRAN compiler       *11  - VS FORTRAN V2 interactive debug
   4 - PL/I checkout compiler     12  - Member parts list
   5 - PL/I optimizing compiler  *13  - C/370 compiler
   6 - VS PASCAL compiler

            * - No packed data support

SOURCE DATA PACKED        ===> NO      (YES or NO)
```

Figure 16.2 TSO/ISPF Function 4 Foreground Options Menu.

Compare Figure 16.3 with Figure 15.2 and you will see how the scheme of interactive debugging compares with that of batch debugging. The same software is involved (compiler, linkage editor, and COBDBG debugger), but the names created for the source code listing printlines stored as records, the object file, the linkage editor's report printlines stored as records, and the load module differ.

You have to be aware of the data set names shown on Figure 16.3. You enter some of these names as you linkage edit and run a program. The debugger also assumes that the source code listing produced by the compiler is stored with the naming convention shown in Figure 16.3. The debugger actually uses the stored source code listing to animate program operation with a visual trace.

Here is a common interactive compile and linkage edit naming convention:

Source code	`A1092JJ.TRAINING.COBOL(K2DEBUG)`
Source code listing	`A1092JJ.K2DEBUG.LIST`
Object module	`A1092JJ.TRAINING.OBJ(K2DEBUG)`
Linkage editor report	`A1092JJ.K2DEBUG.LINKLIST`
Load module	`A1092JJ.TRAINING.LOAD(K2DEBUG)`

As you do an interactive compile and link, the outputs of the compiler and linkage editor are put into data sets of the names shown. If you do not already have .OBJ and .LOAD libraries named with these conventions, the libraries are automatically created for you.

16.4   INTERACTIVE FOREGROUND VS COBOL II COMPILE

When you select function 2 from the foreground selection screen shown in Figure 16.2, you'll get the screen shown in Figure 16.4. You enter the name of the source code to be compiled at this screen at (a) as well as any compiler parameters you want to use. To make debugging possible you have to use the TEST option at (d). Read the legend for Figure 16.4 to understand how to make other entries on this screen.

When you press <Enter> after completing the screen in Figure 16.4 the VS COBOL II compiler will start operation. The screen will clear and you will receive a message from the compiler. When the compile is finished you'll get three asterisks *** from TSO/ISPF. Pressing <Enter> will automatically get you into a browse of the source code listing from the compile, stored in your LIST data set. You can print it or navigate back to foreground selection screen 4.2 (Figure 16.2).

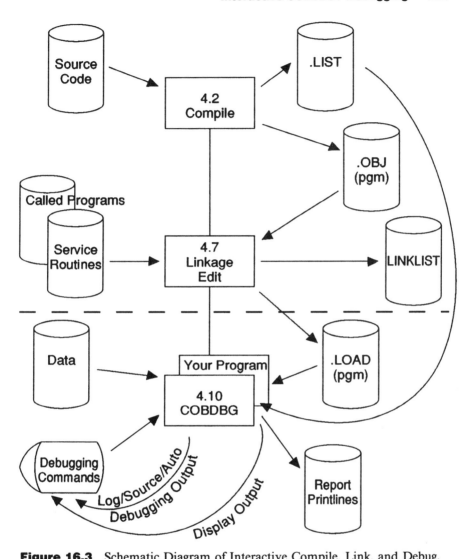

Figure 16.3 Schematic Diagram of Interactive Compile, Link, and Debug.

To do interactive debugging you have to use the TSO/ISPF function 4.2 inter-active compile followed by the TSO/ISPF function 4.7 linkage edit. The compile produces your source code listing in a data set named tsoid.pgmname.LIST. This file of printlines, which lists the source code, is used by the interactive debugger in the "source" area on the screen. The load module produced by the linkage edit is controlled by COBDBG, the debugger, to which you give control statements on the debugging screen command line.

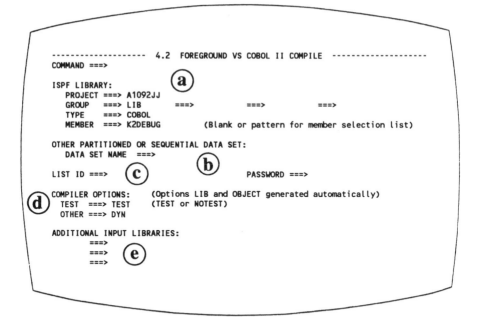

```
------------------- 4.2 FOREGROUND VS COBOL II COMPILE -------------------
COMMAND ===>

ISPF LIBRARY:          (a)
    PROJECT ===> A1092JJ
    GROUP   ===> LIB      ===>          ===>          ===>
    TYPE    ===> COBOL
    MEMBER  ===> K2DEBUG      (Blank or pattern for member selection list)

OTHER PARTITIONED OR SEQUENTIAL DATA SET:
    DATA SET NAME  ===>
                            (b)
    LIST ID ===>   (c)               PASSWORD ===>

    COMPILER OPTIONS:    (Options LIB and OBJECT generated automatically)
(d) TEST  ===> TEST      (TEST or NOTEST)
    OTHER ===> DYN

ADDITIONAL INPUT LIBRARIES:
        ===>
        ===>   (e)
        ===>
```

Figure 16.4 TSO/ISPF Function 4.2 Interactive Compile Screen.

You use this screen to initiate an interactive compile using VS COBOL II.

a. Enter the name of your source code library and member name. Leave member name blank to receive a member list.

b. You can put the name of your source code here in JCL style to override the name at the ISPF LIBRARY fields if you wish.

c. You can override the default name of the LIST data set that will contain the printlines of the source code listing produced by the compiler by putting a name here.

d. You need the TEST option of the compiler to do debugging. The second line, labeled OTHER, lets you specify other compile options if you wish.

e. You can put the names of copy libraries here if necessary.

Your object file will exist as a result of a successful compile. Once you have a successful interactive compile you can go on to do an interactive linkage edit.

If your installation has not updated the command list by which your foreground compile is invoked, that command list may not include allocate statements for all of the work files needed by the VS COBOL II compiler. This may require you to enter TSO commands on the command line for these files before you can do a foreground compile:

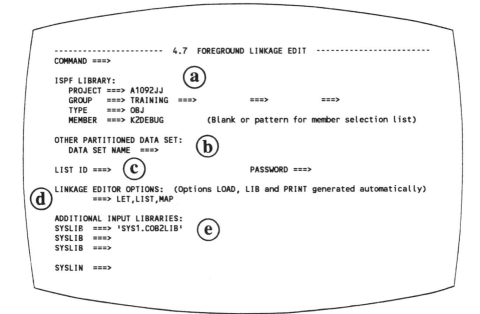

```
---------------------- 4.7  FOREGROUND LINKAGE EDIT ----------------------
COMMAND ===>

ISPF LIBRARY:                    (a)
   PROJECT ===> A1092JJ
   GROUP   ===> TRAINING  ===>          ===>          ===>
   TYPE    ===> OBJ
   MEMBER  ===> K2DEBUG        (Blank or pattern for member selection list)

OTHER PARTITIONED DATA SET:      (b)
   DATA SET NAME  ===>

LIST ID ===>   (c)                      PASSWORD ===>

    LINKAGE EDITOR OPTIONS:  (Options LOAD, LIB and PRINT generated automatically)
(d)            ===> LET,LIST,MAP

ADDITIONAL INPUT LIBRARIES:
SYSLIB  ===> 'SYS1.COB2LIB'   (e)
SYSLIB  ===>
SYSLIB  ===>

SYSLIN  ===>
```

Figure 16.5 TSO/ISPF Function 4.7 Interactive Linkage Edit Screen.

You use this screen to initiate an interactive linkage edit of the OBJ file created by your VS COBOL II interactive compile.

a. Enter the name of your OBJ file code library and member name. Leave member name blank to receive a member list.

b. You can put the name of your OBJ module here in JCL style to override the name at the ISPF LIBRARY fields if you wish.

c. You can override the default name of the LINKLIST data set that will contain the printlines of the linkage editor's status report by putting a name here.

d. You can specify options for the linkage editor here.

e. You can indicate additional service routine or CALL module libraries to be accessed by the linkage editor. You may need to specify 'SYS1.COB2LIB' as I have shown if your systems programmers have not yet concatenated this VS COBOL II library to the default libraries used in interactive linkage editing.

```
FREE FI(SYSUT6)
ALLOC FI(SYSUT6) CYLINDERS SPACE(1 1)
FREE FI(SYSUT7)
ALLOC FI(SYSUT7) CYLINDERS SPACE(1 1)
```

The TSO ALLOCATE command is like an interactive DD statement, not like the TSO/ISPF 3.2 data set allocation function. It put a DDname into your TSO session environment. Programs that you execute interactively can then hook up with DDnames to gain access to the resources they need to operate.

16.5 INTERACTIVE FOREGROUND LINKAGE EDIT

When you select function 7 from the foreground selection screen shown in Figure 16.2, you'll get the screen shown in Figure 16.5. You enter the name of the object file to be linkage edited at this screen at (a). You may also have to enter 'SYS1.COB2LIB' at (e) in order to make the appropriate VS COBOL II service routine library available to the linkage editor. Read the legend for Figure 16.5 to understand how to make the other entries on this screen.

The system response to an interactive linkage edit is similar to that for an interactive compile. You will get a message from the linkage editor. Three asterisks *** will appear when the linkage edit is finished. Press <Enter> and you will automatically branch to a browse of your LINK-LIST file, which is the status report from the linkage editor. You can print it or navigate back to the foreground selection screen 4.2 (Figure 16.2).

Your load module will exist as a result of a successful linkage edit. Once you have accomplished a successful interactive compile and linkage edit, you can go on to do interactive debugging.

16.6 INTERACTIVE DEBUGGING

To use VS COBOL II COBTEST you first compile and linkage edit your program using the Foreground Selection Panel. If you haven't done this, go back and read the first part of this chapter!

You invoke the COBTEST debugger from the TSO/ISPF function 4 panel by entering selection 10. You receive the screen shown in Figure 16.6. You use this screen to enter at (a) the name of the load module of the program you want to run interactively for debugging. If you don't complete the member name, you can choose from the load module library member list. You can enter any runtime parameters to be received by the program at (c). If you want to send EXEC PARM parameters to the program and also specify VS COBOL II runtime options, you follow the EXEC PARM data with a slash and the runtime options:

    ===> '031591/NOSSRANGE'

Read the legend for Figure 16.6 to learn about the other optional entries you can make on the interactive debug screen.

16.7 THE COBTEST FULL SCREEN

Figure 16.7 shows you the COBTEST interactive debugger screen. This screen allows you to enter debugging commands at the COMMAND = = = => line at circled letter (c). This screen shows you a log of these commands and the output they produce in a log area (g). The log is the primary output of the debugging session. It records every command you enter on the command line and the result of the command. For instance, if you enter a command to LIST the contents of a data-name, the value will print in the list. You can scroll up and down in the log using <PF7> and <PF8> keys *when the cursor is located in the log area.*

At circled letter (a) in Figure 16.7 you see the name of the program that you stated for execution. If this program CALLs a subprogram, the actual program executing during the CALL will be different from this name.

Circled letter (b) in Figure 16.7 indicates the name of the program currently executing and the statement number and verb where execution is suspended.

If you have compiled interactively and the program's source code listing exists in the LIST file, you can open a window to make the source code appear on your debugging screen. If you compiled the program using batch JCL without sending the source code listing into a file for debugger access, all you will see on your debugging screen is the log.

You can make the program execute one instruction by entering STEP 1 on the command line. If you enter GO as a command, the program will run until its end. But before you can actually do debugging you need to read the next few sections!

16.8 TSO ALLOCATE COMMANDS FOR PROGRAM FILES

You may like to try interactive debugging using the log by entering the debugging commands you used for batch debugging of program K1DEBUG in section 15.5. But here is where the debugger assumes that you have knowledge of "ready mode" TSO commands. You have to issue TSO ALLOCATE commands to service the SELECT/ASSIGN statements of the program you are debugging. K1DEBUG has only one SELECT/ASSIGN statement:

```
------------------- 4.10  VS COBOL II DEBUG INVOCATION -------------------
COMMAND ===>

ISPF LIBRARY
   PROJECT ===> A1092JJ
   GROUP   ===> TRAINING ===>          ===>         ===>
   TYPE    ===> LOAD
   MEMBER  ===> K2DEBUG  (a)  (Blank or pattern for member selection list)

OTHER PARTITIONED OR SEQUENTIAL DATA SET:
   DATA SET NAME  ===>   (b)

PASSWORD ===>                  MIXED MODE ===> NO  (YES or NO)

VS COBOL II PROGRAM PARAMETERS                    (c)
     ===>
(d)  ===>

   DDNAME  ===>           ( DDNAME TO BE ALLOCATED )
   LOG     ===> NO  (YES or NO)
   LOG DSN ===>
   RESTART ===> NO  (YES or NO)   (e)
   RESTART DSN ===>
   SYSLIN  ===>
```

Figure 16.6 TSO/ISPF Function 4.10 Interactive Debugging Screen.

You use this screen to initiate VS COBOL II interactive debugging after you have done an interactive compile and link edit.

a. Enter the name of your LOAD module library and member name. Leave member name blank to receive a member list.

b. If you wish, you can put the name of your LOAD module here in JCL style to override the name at the ISPF LIBRARY fields.

c. MIXED MODE YES means that your program uses double byte character set values. NO means that your program does not use DBCS characters.

d. You can use these fields to feed execution-time parameter values into your program load module. Feed in runtime parameters such as /NOSSRANGE by prefacing the first such parameter with a slash.

e. If you fill in a DDname it will be allocated automatically and can receive print output from your program. If you answer LOG YES your debugging log will be recorded in the data set you name at LOG DSN. If you enter RESTART YES the debugger will try to read a previous log from the data set you name at RESTART DSN and use it as a script for this debugging session.

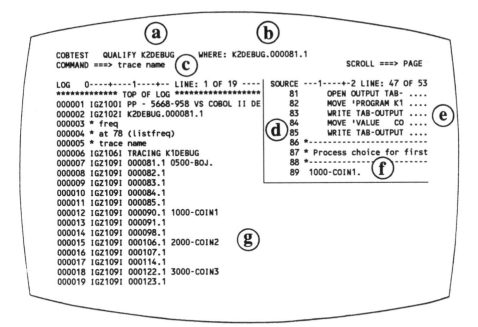

Figure 16.7   The COBTEST Interactive Debugging Screen.

This screen shows the log area as the main part of the screen, which is the default. The source window has been opened by putting the cursor at its lower left corner and pressing the PF key to which you have assigned the word SOURCE.

a. QUALIFY shows the IDENTIFICATION DIVISION name of the program being debugged.

b. WHERE shows the program name and statement number where execution has stopped. The name will be different from the name at (a) when execution is stopped within a subprogram also processed with the TEST option.

c. You enter COBTEST debugging commands on the command line.

d. If you set breakpoints with the AT line-number command, they will appear in the source code "prefix" area.

e. Some COBTEST debugging commands leave information in the source code "suffix area".

f. You can scroll the source area up and down by using <PF7> and <PF8>, the same PF keys as in TSO/ISPF.

g. The log area records the result of any LIST commands you enter as well as all of your debugging commands themselves. The asterisk in front of each command makes it a comment. If you retain the log as the LOG DSN, you can edit the log and remove the asterisk from any line. This is how you make a log into a script so you can repeat the same debugging actions in a subsequent session.

```
SELECT   TAB-OUTPUT-FILE  ASSIGN TO TABOUT.
```

To service this statement and allow K1DEBUG to send this output to a real data set, you need to issue commands such as this on the command line.

```
FREE ATTRLIST(DCB132)
ATTRIB DCB132  LRECL(132)  BLKSIZE(6204)  RECFM(F B A)  DSORG(PS)
FREE FI(TABOUT)
ALLOC FI(TABOUT)  DA(K1DEBUG.PRINT)  MOD  TRACKS  SPACE(1 1) +
   USING(DCB132)  CATALOG
```

ATTRIB DCB132 establishes "DCB132" as a list of attributes in your TSO session environment. This list of attributes is similar to the JCL you would use to take the TABOUT printlines generated by K1DEBUG and store them in a data set. ALLOC FI(TABOUT) completes the "JCL" to receive these output lines in a small cataloged data set to be named tsoid.K1DEBUG.PRINT. The FREE commands just clear your environment of any previous information associated with the names DCB132 and TABOUT before making the new assignments. You'll find it handier to enter these commands into a CLIST library and invoke them when you want to do debugging on K1DEBUG. In fact, you'll want to create "setup" commands like this specific to every program you want to debug interactively.

The pattern for TSO commands to service an output DDname, such as TABOUT in K1DEBUG are somewhat complicated. The TSO commands used to feed input from an existing file into a program that you are debugging are simpler. If a program had a SELECT/ASSIGN statement like this for a data set it would read:

```
SELECT  PAYROLL-INPUT  ASSIGN TO PAYIN.
```

These TSO commands would service the input DDname PAYIN for a debugging session, allowing the program to read data from member PAYDATA of a partitioned data set named A1092JJ.TEST.DATA:

```
FREE(PAYIN)
ALLOC F(PAYIN)  DA('A1092JJ.TEST.DATA(PAYDATA)') SHR
```

If you are inexperienced in TSO commands, you'll want to use IBM's latest TSO manuals, other reference books, or take a short course on those commands before expecting to become proficient in COBTEST interactive debugging.

16.9 TSO/ISPF PF KEY SETUP FOR INTERACTIVE DEBUGGING

To make much use of the interactive debugging screen in Figure 16.7, *you need to create some special PF key assignments.* These are not difficult to do, but IBM's documentation assumes you have already done this before making much use of the interactive debugging screen.

Put KEYS on the command line at the top of the screen. Tab down to the *<PF22>* key and change its meaning to the word VTRACE. Change the meaning of the *<PF23>* key to the word AUTO. Change the meaning of the *<PF24>* key to the word SOURCE.

16.10 SOURCE CODE WINDOW IN DEBUGGING

When you get to the interactive debugging screen shown in Figure 16.7, you will not immediately see the source code of your program on the screen. If you have stored the compiler-produced source code listing in a file accessible to the debugger (your LIST file), you can make a window with source code visible and the currently executing line highlighted as shown by the circled letter (f).

To create a source code window, assign the debugger command SOURCE to a *<PFn>* key as indicated above. (I am assuming you have assigned SOURCE to the *<PF24>* key.) Put the cursor on the screen at the point where you want the lower left corner of the source code window to be and press *<PF24>*. This will open up your source code window as shown in Figure 16.8. You can reposition the lower left corner of the window at any time by putting the cursor at the desired location and pressing *<PF24>*.

When the cursor is within your source code window, you can scroll up or down and left or right using the customary TSO/ISPF PF keys. *<PF8>* is down, *<PF7>* is up, *<PF11>* is right, *<PF10>* is left.

Circled letters (d) and (e) in the source code window of Figure 16.7 indicate where debugging "prefix" or "suffix" area commands are shown. AT is the command that establishes a breakpoint where the program will suspend operation. For example, when you enter AT 171 on the command line, you'll see a breakpoint indicated in the area of (d) in your source code window. Your commands and the contents of data-names you examine will be presented in the log.

An interesting thing to try with your source code window present is the VTRACE command. This command starts your programming running instruction-by-instruction, with a delay between each. It highlights

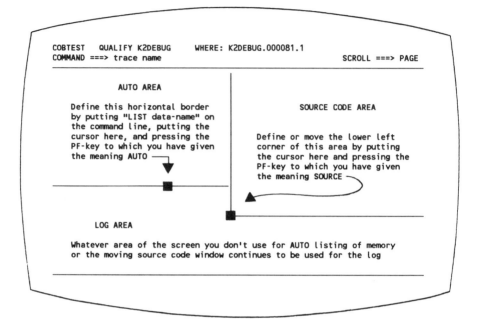

```
COBTEST   QUALIFY K2DEBUG      WHERE: K2DEBUG.000081.1
COMMAND ===> trace name                              SCROLL ===> PAGE

              AUTO AREA

   Define this horizontal border              SOURCE CODE AREA
   by putting "LIST data-name" on
   the command line, putting the
   cursor here, and pressing the        Define or move the lower left
   PF-key to which you have given       corner of this area by putting
   the meaning AUTO                     the cursor here and pressing the
                                        PF-key to which you have given
                                        the meaning SOURCE



              LOG AREA

   Whatever area of the screen you don't use for AUTO listing of memory
   or the moving source code window continues to be used for the log
```

Figure 16.8 Geography of the COBTEST Interactive Debugging Screen.

You get the LOG area by default on the debugging screen. To get the source area, you must have compiled and saved the LIST printlines in a place accessible to the debugger. You also have to assign the word SOURCE to a *<PF key>*. You put the cursor where you want the lower left corner of the SOURCE window to be and press your SOURCE *<PF Key>*. You can reposition the SOURCE window in the same way and use *<PF7>* and *<PF8>* to scroll it vertically when the cursor is inside it.

To get the AUTO area to continuously see the contents of data names, you have to assign the word AUTO to a *<PF Key>*. Then you put LIST data-name on the command line, put the cursor where you want the bottom border of the AUTO area to be, and press your AUTO *<PF Key>*. You can make the AUTO area taller or shorter in the same way and use *<PF7>* and *<PF8>* to scroll it vertically when the cursor is inside it.

each source code statement as it receives control. On a color screen the effect is very interesting. To stop a VTRACE you have to press the *<Attn>* key on the keyboard.

16.11 AUTOLIST TO SEE DATA-NAME CONTENTS

The "auto area" in Figure 16.8 shows you where the debugger displays a window with the contents of a data name that you request it to continuously monitor with the AUTOLIST command. Here is how you create this window:

1. Enter the command LIST WS-COINS on the command line. (I'm assuming you are trying out the debugger on program K1DEBUG or the simpler K2DEBUG; WS-COINS is a group data-name in these programs.)
2. Put the cursor at about the middle of the screen.
3. Press your <*PF23*> key, which I assume you have set to the meaning AUTO.

You should see the "autolist" area of your screen open up as schematically depicted in Figure 16.8. If you now do a VTRACE, you will see that the contents of this area change as the program executes, and the data-names under WS-COINS assume new values.

```
SELECTION ===>                                    VS COBOL II INTERACTIVE DEBUG

                      Main Help Menu

     1  Task menu      14  Go           27  Offwn         40  Search
     2  Tutorial       15  Help         28  Onabend       41  Set
     3  Prefix code    16  If           29  Position      42  Source
     4  Suffix code    17  Link         30  Prevdisp      43  Step
     5  At             18  List         31  Proc          44  Suffix
     6  Auto           19  Listbrks     32  Profile       45  Syscmd
     7  Color          20  Listeq       33  Printdd       46  Trace
     8  Comment        21  Listfreq     34  Qualify       47  Vtrace
     9  Drop           22  Listings     35  Quit          48  When
    10  Dump           23  Movecurs     36  Record        49  Where
    11  Equate         24  Next         37  Restart
    12  Flow           25  Norecord     38  Restore
    13  Freq           26  Off          39  Run
```

Figure 16.9 COBTEST Interactive Debugger HELP Screen.

You can see information on-line about the debugger's commands by putting HELP on the command line and going through this menu.

16.12   ON-LINE DEBUGGER COMMAND HELP

You can get information about all of the debugger commands by putting HELP on the command line and pressing *<Enter>*. Debugger help provides different tutorial help than TSO/ISPF. Figure 16.9 shows you the first screen you get when you ask for debugger HELP.

16.13   LEAVING A DEBUGGING SESSION

The interactive debugger disables the *<PF3>* key, which is usually the "End" key in TSO/ISPF. To end a debugging session you have to enter the word QUIT on the command line and press *<Enter>*.

16.14   *TRY IT!* COBTEST INTERACTIVE DEBUGGING

The best initial experience you can have with the debugger involves a program that does not have any SELECT/ASSIGN statements. This frees you from the need to allocate files using TSO commands so you can concentrate on learning the debugger itself.

Figure 16.10 shows you program K2DEBUG. This is the same as program K1DEBUG from Figure 15.3, with all references to output file TABOUT removed. I have changed the final outputting of the table in this program to use DISPLAY. To use the interactive debugger with this program you do not need to issue any TSO ALLOCATE statements.

Enter or upload K2DEBUG into your COBOL library. You can then follow these steps to experiment with VS COBOL II interactive compiling, linkage editing, and the COBTEST debugger:

1. Do an interactive compile of K2DEBUG. This will create an object file and a file containing your source code listing. Then go to the TSO/ISPF 4.7 interactive linkage edit function of TSO/ISPF. Link edit your object module from your compile of K2DEBUG. This will create a load module with .LOAD as the last part of its name. Use the TSO 3.4 function to see the names of the LIST, OBJ, LINKLIST, and LOAD data sets within your TSO account.

2. Go to the TSO/ISPF 4.10 VS COBOL II interactive debugging function. The screen will appear as in Figure 16.6. Enter the name of your load module library and the module name. Press *<Enter>* without making any other entries. You should see the screen change so that it is similar to Figure 16.7.

```
000100 IDENTIFICATION DIVISION.
000200 PROGRAM-ID.    K2DEBUG.
000300 AUTHOR.        J. JANOSSY.
000400******************************************************************
000500*    Droesselmeyer's generous coin game for nieces and  *
000600*    nephews, including logic to tabulate results by     *
000700*    loading unique values generated to a table          *
000800*                                                         *
000900*    ** WRITES changed to DISPLAY for COBTEST demo **     *
001000*    ** Do interactive debug with no TSO ALLOC commands * 
001100******************************************************************
001200 ENVIRONMENT DIVISION.
001300*
001400 DATA DIVISION.
001500 WORKING-STORAGE SECTION.
001600 01  WS-TAB-ROW-COUNT           PIC S9(4)  COMP  VALUE +0.
001700*
001800 01  WS-COINS.
001900     05 WS-COIN1                PIC 9(1).
002000     05 WS-COIN2                PIC 9(1).
002100     05 WS-COIN3                PIC 9(1).
002200     05 WS-COIN4                PIC 9(1).
002300*
002400 01  WS-VALUES.
002500     05 WS-VAL1                 PIC S9(3)V99.
002600     05 WS-VAL2                 PIC S9(3)V99.
002700     05 WS-VAL3                 PIC S9(3)V99.
002800     05 WS-VAL4                 PIC S9(3)V99.
002900     05 WS-TOTAL                PIC S9(3)V99.
003000*------------------------------------------------------------------
003100*------------------------------------------------------------------
003200* This table will store one row for each unique value;
003300* allocated for 100 rows but will probably load much less
003400*------------------------------------------------------------------
003500 01  WS-TABLE-OF-VALUES.
003600     05 WS-TAB-VAL  OCCURS 1 TO 20 TIMES
003700                        DEPENDING ON WS-TAB-ROW-COUNT
003800                        INDEXED BY WS-TAB-IX.
003900        10 WS-TAB-MONEY        PIC 9V99.
004000        10 FILLER             PIC X(1)  VALUE '/'.
004100        10 WS-TAB-COUNT        PIC 9(2).
004200        10 FILLER             PIC X(1)  VALUE SPACE.
004300/
004400 PROCEDURE DIVISION.
004500 0000-MAINLINE.
004600     PERFORM 1000-COIN1
004700         VARYING WS-COIN1
004800             FROM 1 BY 1
004900                 UNTIL WS-COIN1 > 3.
005000     DISPLAY WS-TABLE-OF-VALUES.
005100     STOP RUN.
005200*
005300*------------------------------------------------------------------
005400* Process choice for first cup, vary second cup
005500*------------------------------------------------------------------
005600 1000-COIN1.
005700     IF WS-COIN1 = +1
005800         MOVE +.01 TO WS-VAL1
005900     ELSE
006000     IF WS-COIN1 = +2
006100         MOVE +.10 TO WS-VAL1
006200     ELSE
006300     IF WS-COIN1 = +3
006400         MOVE +1.00 TO WS-VAL1.
006500     PERFORM 2000-COIN2
006600         VARYING WS-COIN2
006700             FROM +1 BY +1
006800                 UNTIL WS-COIN2 > +3.
006900*------------------------------------------------------------------
007000* Process choice for second cup, vary third cup
007100*------------------------------------------------------------------
007200 2000-COIN2.
007300     IF WS-COIN2 = +1
007400         MOVE +.01 TO WS-VAL2
007500     ELSE
007600     IF WS-COIN2 = +2
007700         MOVE +.10 TO WS-VAL2
007800     ELSE
007900     IF WS-COIN2 = +3
008000         MOVE +1.00 TO WS-VAL2.
```

Figure 16.10 *(see legend on page 304)*

```
008100      PERFORM 3000-COIN3
008200          VARYING WS-COIN3
008300              FROM +1 BY +1
008400                  UNTIL WS-COIN3 > +3.
008500*-----------------------------------------------------------
008600* Process choice for third cup, vary fourth cup
008700*-----------------------------------------------------------
008800 3000-COIN3.
008900      IF WS-COIN3 = +1
009000          MOVE +.01 TO WS-VAL3
009100      ELSE
009200      IF WS-COIN3 = +2
009300          MOVE +.10 TO WS-VAL3
009400      ELSE
009500      IF WS-COIN3 = +3
009600          MOVE +1.00 TO WS-VAL3.
009700      PERFORM 4000-COIN4
009800          VARYING WS-COIN4
009900              FROM +1 BY +1
010000                  UNTIL WS-COIN4 > +3.
010100*-----------------------------------------------------------
010200* Process choice for fourth cup; total and update table
010300* adding a new row if necessary or updating existing row
010400*-----------------------------------------------------------
010500 4000-COIN4.
010600      IF WS-COIN4 = +1
010700          MOVE +.01 TO WS-VAL4
010800      ELSE
010900      IF WS-COIN4 = +2
011000          MOVE +.10 TO WS-VAL4
011100      ELSE
011200      IF WS-COIN4 = +3
011300          MOVE +1.00 TO WS-VAL4.
011400*
011500      COMPUTE WS-TOTAL =
011600          WS-VAL1 + WS-VAL2 + WS-VAL3 + WS-VAL4.
011700*
011800      SET WS-TAB-IX TO 1.
011900      SEARCH WS-TAB-VAL
012000          AT END
012100              ADD +1          TO WS-TAB-ROW-COUNT
012200              SET WS-TAB-IX   TO WS-TAB-ROW-COUNT
012300              MOVE WS-TOTAL   TO WS-TAB-MONEY(WS-TAB-IX)
012400              MOVE +1         TO WS-TAB-COUNT(WS-TAB-IX)
012500          WHEN WS-TOTAL = WS-TAB-MONEY(WS-TAB-IX)
012600              ADD +1          TO WS-TAB-COUNT(WS-TAB-IX).
```

Output (on screen at end of run):

004/01 013/04 103/04 022/06 112/12 202/06 031/04 121/12 211/12 301/04 040/01
130/04 220/06 310/04 400/01

Figure 16.10   K2DEBUG Program for Initial Debugging Experimentation.

The K2DEBUG program does not require you to arrange any TSO ALLOC commands before you debug it, since it does not have any SELECT/ASSIGN statements. You can experiment with interactive debugging with this interesting version of the K1DEBUG program, which is used in Chapter 15 for a batch debugging demonstration.

3. Put KEYS on the command line at the top of the screen. Change the meaning of the <*PF24*> key to SOURCE. Change the meaning of the <*PF23*> key to AUTO. Change the meaning of the <*PF22*> key to VTRACE.

4. Put the cursor in the middle of the screen and press <*PF24*> (your SOURCE key). You will now see part of the source code listing for K2DEBUG appear in a window that fills the upper right corner of the screen. This is now a separate screen display area. You can scroll the material in the source screen by putting the cursor into it and pressing the up <*PF7*> and down <*PF8*> keys.

5. Enter LIST WS-COINS on the command line but don't press <*Enter*>. Instead, move the cursor about one-third down the screen at about column 15. Then press your AUTO key, <*PF23*>. You should see part of a formatted dump of the WS-COINS data items. They will contain invalid values since the program has not yet been executed. You can scroll the autolist area by putting the cursor within it and pressing <*PF7*> for up or <*PF8*> for down.

6. Press your VTRACE key <*PF22*>. The program will now start to execute, one instruction at a time. The source code listing will scroll within the source window to keep the current instruction visible. The current instruction will be highlighted or presented in a unique color. As the program executes you will see the "autolist" area containing the values of the WS-COINS fields change.

7. Press the <*Attn*> key to stop program execution. Note that the <*PF3*> "end" key does not work within the debugging function. Start the debugger again for K2DEBUG. Create source and auto list areas again. This time request to see some other variable in the autolist area. VTRACE the program again and see how the contents of this data-name change as the program runs.

8. Put HELP on the command line and explore the syntax of the AT breakpoint command. Set a breakpoint at a line containing an instruction (verb) and then do a VTRACE to see how the debugger stops at that line. Pressing the VTRACE key <*PF22*> will restart the program. Experiment with the syntax of the AT command to list data-name contents at a breakpoint. Then explore the WHEN conditional breakpoint command and how to use LIST with it.

9. Continue trying out debugging commands documented in the on-line help provided by the debugger. When you have completed trying out the debugger, press <*Attn*> to end debugging and then navigate to any other TSO/ISPF function as usual.

16.15   GOING BEYOND A COBTEST DEMONSTRATION

Manipulating and analyzing program operation using an interactive debugger is a skill that takes time and effort to develop. Perhaps the old VS COBOL TESTCOB debugger never really caught on with most programmers because it was oversold as a time-saver, when in fact it took too much time to learn for what it was able to deliver. To really get into the use of VS COBOL II COBTEST you should plan on spending several days exploring how it works and what it can do for you.

Appendix A

VSAM Return, Function, and Feedback Codes

You can receive three numeric codes from VSAM in addition to the File Status value every time you take an I/O action with a VSAM data set. These actions include opening and closing the data set. These extended VSAM codes give you information that can help you solve problems as they arise.

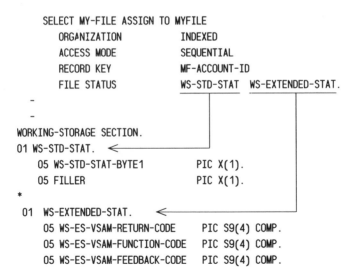

```
    SELECT MY-FILE ASSIGN TO MYFILE
        ORGANIZATION        INDEXED
        ACCESS MODE         SEQUENTIAL
        RECORD KEY          MF-ACCOUNT-ID
        FILE STATUS         WS-STD-STAT  WS-EXTENDED-STAT.
    -
    -
WORKING-STORAGE SECTION.
01 WS-STD-STAT.
    05 WS-STD-STAT-BYTE1        PIC X(1).
    05 FILLER                   PIC X(1).
*
  01  WS-EXTENDED-STAT.
      05 WS-ES-VSAM-RETURN-CODE    PIC S9(4) COMP.
      05 WS-ES-VSAM-FUNCTION-CODE  PIC S9(4) COMP.
      05 WS-ES-VSAM-FEEDBACK-CODE  PIC S9(4) COMP.
```

The extended codes consist of a return code, function code, and feedback code. The return code is important because it tells you how to interpret the feedback code for any failed action. The function code is not very helpful. The feedback code usually provides the greatest help when a failure occurs.

A.1   VSAM RETURN CODES

The VSAM return codes are the IDCAMS return codes you also get when you run IDCAMS via JCL to create or work with VSAM data sets.

0000	VSAM request successfully completed.
0004	OPEN was successful but a warning message was issued; CLOSE failed.
0008	Logical error occurred in processing the request; FUNCTION and FEEDBACK codes exist.
0012	Physical error occurred in processing the request; FUNCTION and FEEDBACK codes exist.

If the failure occurred while you were attempting an OPEN or CLOSE, look up the meaning of the feedback code associated with return code 0004. If you were attempting an action other then OPEN or CLOSE and a failure occurred, use the 0008 or 0012 return code to guide you to the proper page that follows and look up the meaning of the feedback code.

A.2   VSAM FUNCTION CODES

VSAM function codes have meaning only when the VSAM return code is not equal to 0000:

0000	Access to the base cluster was attempted; the upgrade set status is correct.
0001	The upgrade set status may be incorrect.
0002	Access to the alternate index was attempted; the upgrade set status is correct.
0003	Alternate index access attempted; upgrade set status may be incorrect.
0004	Upgrade set processing attempted; the upgrade status is correct.
0005	Upgrade set processing was attempted; the upgrade set status may be incorrect.

The VSAM function code is only slightly helpful. In the event of a failure of a processing request, it just confirms what you were trying to do. This code is less useful than the feedback code.

A.3 VSAM FEEDBACK CODES FOR OPEN/CLOSE (RC = 0004)

VSAM feedback codes are different for each type of action, such as OPEN, CLOSE, and other I/O requests. You have to interpret the feedback code in relation to the VSAM return code, and within that, by the action you are attempting.

The VSAM feedback code field may contain a value even if the VSAM return code is 0000. But the feedback code is meaningful only if the return code is greater than zero! (W) indicates a warning condition in this listing.

OPEN

0000	Data set is already open or DDname is invalid.
0100	(W) Alternate index is empty, but it is part of the upgrade set.
0104	(W) Time stamp in data set does not match catalog.
0108	Time in data component does not match index.
0116	Data set was not closed properly; implicit VERIFY failed.
0118	Data set was not closed properly; implicit VERIFY worked.
0128	DD statement for the data set is missing.
0136	Insufficient virtual memory for control blocks, work areas, and buffers.
0144	Uncorrectable I/O error reading or writing to catalog.
0168	Data set could not be opened; contention with other programs.
0180	Catalog specified (or default) does not exist; data set could not be found.
0184	Uncorrectable I/O error.
0196	Attempt to access data set via an empty path.
0232	Reset can't be used for non-empty, non-reusable data set.

CLOSE

0004	Data set is already closed.
0136	Insufficient virtual memory for control blocks, work areas, and buffers.
0144	Uncorrectable I/O error reading or writing to catalog.
0148	Error in searching VSAM catalog.
0184	Uncorrectable I/O error.

A.4 VSAM FEEDBACK CODES FOR LOGICAL ERRORS (RC = 0008)

These are the meanings of the VSAM feedback codes when the processing action you have attempted has failed with a return code of 0008:

0004	End of file during sequential processing, or the key in use is greater than the highest key in the data set.
0008	Duplicate primary key, or duplicate alternate key where alternate key has been defined as unique.
0012	Key sequence error during KSDS or RRDS processing.
0016	Record was not found.
0020	Control interval required by the program was already in use by another program.
0028	Out of space condition has occured; no space for secondary allocation or cannot increase space when SHROPT=4 and DISP=SHR.
0036	Key specified is not valid for the data set; applies only if key ranges are specified for the data set.
0040	Insufficient virtual storage to complete the request.
0068	Attempted processing was inconsistent with the way that the data set was OPENed (eg., READ when OPENed OUTPUT).
0072	Keyed access was attempted for an ESDS.
0080	Invalid attempt to delete a record from an ESDS.
0092	REWRITE or DELETE attempted without prior READ.
0096	Cannot update primary key of records in a KSDS.

0108	Invalid record length.
0112	Key length is either too large or equal to zero.
0116	Can use only WRITE with data set opened OUTPUT.
0144	Invalid pointer in alternate index; no base record.
0148	Alternate index pointer limit has been exceeded.
0152	Not enough buffers available to process request.
0156	Invalid control interval found during keyed processing.
0192	Invalid relative record number.

A.5 VSAM FEEDBACK CODES FOR PHYSICAL ERRORS (RC = 0012)

These are the meanings of the VSAM feedback codes when the processing action you have attempted has failed with a return code of 0012:

0004	Read error on data component.
0008	Read error on index set of the index component.
0012	Read error on sequence set of the index component.
0016	Write error on data component.
0020	Write error on index set of the index component.
0024	Write error on sequence set of the index component.

Physical errors are due to factors external to VSAM and your software. They include failure of a disk drive electronic circuit, detection (by the disk drive) of an unresolvable memory checking parity error, failure of the disk recording surface itself, or failures in the communication path between the disk drive, its controller, and the computer system.

You should contact your operations group to assist in resolving any physical errors. You should be prepared to recreate the VSAM data set if necessary.

Appendix B

Expanded VSAM File Status Values

This and the pages that follow provide you with a complete reference to the 34 File Status values issued by VS COBOL II. In this listing the values new in Release 3 are marked with an asterisk (*).

B.1 SUCCESSFUL CONDITIONS (00, 02, 04, 05, 07, 97)

00
The action was successful.

02
Applies only when alternate keys exist. READ was OK, next record on the file has the same alternate key; WRITE was OK, the alternate key duplicates an alternate key already on file.

04 *
READ executed successfully but the length of the record read was different than that defined for the file; the record may have been truncated.

05 *
An OPEN was successful for an "optional" file that does not exist. (OPTIONAL can be coded in the SELECT/ASSIGN statement for a file to specify that it might not exist and that no DD statement for it appears in JCL.) An optional file OPENed for input receives an end-of-file condition on the first READ. All types of VSAM files may be coded with OPTIONAL.

07 *

QSAM (non-VSAM sequential files) only; OPEN or CLOSE was coded with NO REWIND, or CLOSE was coded with FOR REMOVAL, FOR REEL, or UNIT but the file was not on tape.

97

OPEN was successful after the system itself initiated a VERIFY command to update the catalog about the file.

B.2 AT END, SEQUENTIAL PROCESSING (10, 14)

10

End of file has been reached; control will branch to the statement coded after AT END if it is present.

14 *

Sequential READ was executed for a VSAM relative record data set (RRDS), but the value placed into the relative key field by the program for the read was greater than the limit of records defined for the data set.

B.3 INVALID KEY, RANDOM PROCESSING (21, 22, 23, 24)

21

Sequence error on the primary key of a VSAM key sequenced data set (KSDS) or in a relative record data set (RRDS). This can happen if sequential access is being made and the key was changed between READ and REWRITE. Writing to a KSDS or RRDS in sequential mode requires that you write records in ascending sequence of the primary key. (This restriction and File Status value not apply when you process these files in random access mode.)

22

Duplicate key for VSAM relative record data set (RRDS) or key sequenced data set (KSDS) file in random processing. This can happen for WRITE of a duplicate key for an RRDS READ, REWRITE with duplicate primary key (KSDS), or WRITE or REWRITE for a KSDS when the primary key is unique but an alternate key that is supposed to be unique is not. *File Status 22 makes no distinction between primary and alternate key errors!*

23

Desired record not found in the VSAM RRDS or KSDS. This can happen if you do a READ with a nonexistent key, START with a relation condition that could not be satisfied, or START or random READ for an OPTIONAL file that is not present.

24

Out of space in a VSAM KSDS, or a WRITE to a VSAM RRDS with a key value greater than the limit of records defined for the file.

B.4 I/O ERRORS (30 THROUGH 39)

30

Data check or parity error on I/O device.

34

Out of space when WRITE was executed QSAM (non-VSAM sequential file) only.

35 *

OPEN with INPUT, I-O, or EXTEND specified as the SELECT/ASSIGN access mode but the file does not exist. The DD statement for the file may be missing from JCL. This error does not occur if the file is defined as OPTIONAL in the SELECT/ASSIGN statement (in that case READ actions against the file receive "end of file" or "record not found" indications).

37 *

The file being processed can't be accessed in the way that your OPEN implies. One of several reasons might exist for this. You may have specified OPEN OUTPUT or OPEN EXTEND but you can't use the WRITE verb with the file (are you trying a random WRITE on a tape?) Or you may have specified OPEN INPUT but you can't use the READ verb with the file (are you trying a random READ on a tape file?) Or you may have specified OPEN I-O but either the READ or WRITE verbs cannot be used with the file (are you trying this with a tape file?) Check your coding of the SELECT/ASSIGN statement. Have you specified ACCESS MODE IS RANDOM for a file that can't support this type of access?

38 *

You tried to OPEN a QSAM (non-VSAM sequential) file that was previously closed with the LOCK option.

39 *

OPEN failed because your file description and the catalog or label-stored characteristics of the file differ. You have coded the file organization, primary key position, alternate key position, record size, format, or block size (QSAM only) incorrectly.

B.5   LOGIC ERRORS (41 THROUGH 49)

41 *

You tried to OPEN a file that was already open.

42 *

You tried to CLOSE a file that was already closed.

43 *

You are processing a file sequentially and did not execute a READ to obtain the record you are trying to REWRITE or DELETE. To rewrite or delete records with ACCESS MODE IS SEQUENTIAL you first have to read and obtain the record.

44 *

You are processing a QSAM (non-VSAM sequential) file and have either tried to REWRITE a record that is not the same size as the one you read, or you are trying to write or rewrite a variable length record that is shorter or longer than the FD states it should be.

46 *

You are either reading past the end-of-file (sequentially) or your prior random READ failed and, as a result, the current record pointer (CRP) is undefined for the READ ... NEXT you are trying to do.

47 *

You are trying to READ from a file that you opened for OUTPUT or EXTEND.

48 *

You are trying to WRITE to a file that you opened for INPUT.

49 *

You are trying to do a DELETE or REWRITE but you did not open the file for I-O.

B.6 IMPLEMENTATION ERRORS (90 THROUGH 96)

90, 92
A program logic error has occurred. These File Status values have traditionally frustrated programmers because of their generality. You should see much less of them because many of the instances that can cause them now receive one of the File Status values numbered in the 40's.

91
The VSAM file you tried to access is password protected under VSAM's own security scheme; you have not supplied the correct password.

93
A required VSAM resource (memory or data set component) was not available.

94
The current record pointer was undefined when you attempted to do a sequential READ or READ . . . NEXT. You can only receive this under VS COBOL II Release 3 when you use the CMPR2 option to emulate the older releases of COBOL. Under "normal" Release 3 you get File Status value 46 for this condition.

95
Incomplete or invalid file information was available for the VSAM file. You will now get a File Status value of 39 instead of this value.

96
You omitted the DD statement for the file in your JCL. Note that you can get this if you forget to code the extra DD statement matching the DDname "generated" by COBOL for the alternate index path when you have an alternate key.

97
OPEN was successful after the system itself initiated a VERIFY command to update the catalog about the file; the file was closed improperly the last time it was accessed. This does not indicate a problem—your OPEN was fine! (IBM deviated from standard numbering convention here; this should have been in the "0n" series. It does not indicate any error.)

Appendix C

CALL by Content
or Reference

VS COBOL supported only CALLs by reference but VS COBOL supports CALLS by reference or by content. The distinction between these uses of the CALL verb lies in what kind of access the CALLed program has to the values (memory) shared with it by the main (CALLing) program.

C.1 CALL BY REFERENCE

The ordinary CALL with USING makes a CALL by reference. The CALLed program receives only the address of the shared item in memory:

```
CALL 'PGM1' USING data-name.
```

```
CALL 'PGM1' USING BY REFERENCE data-name.
```

The CALLed program accesses the same memory as the CALLing program and can change values in this shared memory. When the CALLed program ends, the main program can check to see what the CALLed program did to the memory. CALL by reference is how the main program receives communication back from the CALLed program.

C.2 CALL BY CONTENT

You can now pass information to a CALLed program and prevent it from being altered if you code a CALL this way:

```
CALL 'PGM2' USING BY CONTENT data-name.
```

When you make this type of CALL the compiler makes a copy of the data item and passes the address of that copy to the CALLed program. This makes it impossible for the CALLed program to change the value in the original shared data field of the CALLing program. CALL by content involves additional overhead.

C.3 MIXING DATA REFERENCES IN A SINGLE CALL

You can pass some data items by reference and others by content:

```
CALL 'PGM3' USING BY CONTENT TAX-TABLE
                             DEPT-NAME
                   BY REFERENCE PAY-AMOUNT
                   BY CONTENT QTY-DEPENDENTS
                   BY CONTENT LENGTH OF TAX-TABLE.
```

TAX-TABLE and DEPT-NAME will be passed by content and the CALLed program will not be able to change them. PAY-AMOUNT will be passed by reference and the CALLed program will be able to change it. QTY-DEPENDENTS will be passed by content and the CALLed program will not be able to change it.

C.4 LENGTH OF FEATURE

The fifth item coded in the example above—BY CONTENT LENGTH OF TAX-TABLE—is a new feature of VS COBOL II. The VS COBOL II compiler will automatically supply a PIC S9(9) COMP data item carrying the length of an elementary or group name field to the CALLed program if you specify BY CONTENT LENGTH OF data-name. If you want to pass a length value in this way, the CALLed program has to have a PIC S9(9) COMP field in its LINKAGE SECTION to receive it.

You do not have to pass any length information to make a CALL. I included this just as an example of the syntax VS COBOL II makes available to you.

C.5 HOW YOU CODE THE CALLED PROGRAM

Whether you make a CALL by reference or by content, you code the CALLed program the same way. As under VS COBOL, you need to code the USING phrase on the PROCEDURE DIVISION heading specifying the names of 01 or 77 levels in a LINKAGE SECTION:

```
PROCEDURE DIVISION USING TAX-TABLE
                        DEPT-NAME
                        PAY-AMOUNT
                        QTY-DEPENDENTS
                        TT-LENGTH.
```

As under VS COBOL, you don't need to code the descriptions of the shared data items in the same sequence in the CALLed program LINK-AGE SECTION as they exist in the CALL verb data-name list. You don't have to use the same data-names in the CALLing and CALLed programs. But the data-name lists of both the CALL and PROCEDURE DIVISION heading have to match in data-name sequence.

   The fifth item in this list of shared items is present only to match the previous example in which BY CONTENT LENGTH OF TAX-TABLE was coded. TT-LENGTH must be coded PIC S9(9) COMP to receive a compiler-generated length field. You don't have to pass data name lengths in order to do any type of CALL.

C.6   INITIAL AND CANCEL

You can now code INITIAL on the PROGRAM-ID of a statically CALLed ("hard-linked") subprogram to put it into its initial state each time it is CALLed:

```
PROGRAM-ID. PGM2 IS INITIAL PROGRAM.
```

With this coding the VALUE clauses on WORKING-STORAGE fields will apply each time the subprogram is CALLed. Without this clause the values in WORKING-STORAGE continue as left by the previous CALL.

   Values carry over from CALL to CALL in a dynamically CALLed program, too. You can use the CANCEL verb to selectively return a dynamically CALLed program to its initial state:

```
CANCEL 'PGM3'.
```

But you can also use INITIAL on dynamically CALLed programs, which is much more efficient than CANCEL. CANCEL lets MVS relinquish the memory space occupied by the subprogram. This forces MVS to reload the subprogram from its disk library the next time the main program CALLs it. If your intention is to have the subprogram in its initial state for every CALL, code the subprogram with INITIAL.

Appendix D

Nested Programs

D.1 WHAT ARE NESTED PROGRAMS?

You can now code programs in groups and compile them together. The end of a program is marked with the special words END-PROGRAM program-name. If the END-PROGRAM for one program is stated after one or more other programs, the other programs are said to be "nested" or contained within the first.

Fully developed support for nested programs became available with Release 3 of VS COBOL II. Nested programs give COBOL features that are associated with Pascal, C, Ada, and other newer languages.

D.2 AN EXAMPLE OF NESTED PROGRAMS

In the example in Figure D.1 PGM1 contains two other programs—PGM2 and PGM3. PGM3 itself contains another nested program named PGM3SUB. When compiled and linkage edited, all programs will be in the same load module (similar to hard-linked subprograms).

For the second and subsequent programs you don't need an ENVIRONMENT DIVISION or DATA DIVISION unless the particular program has statements housed in these divisions. Only the first program in the group can have a CONFIGURATION SECTION.

D.3 INVOKING NESTED PROGRAMS

You invoke a nested program with a CALL. With the use of EXTERNAL or GLOBAL variables you can make the CALL without having to code the USING clause and without having to set up a LINKAGE SECTION in the CALLed program. This form of CALL executes as efficiently as a PERFORM and is much faster than a dynamic CALL.

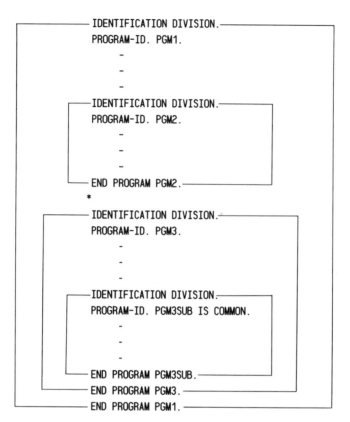

Figure D.1   Nested programs.

Only programs in the group can CALL one another according to rules described in the COMMON section below. Only the first program in the group can be CALLed by programs outside of the group (programs compiled separately from the group).

D.4   EXTERNAL

If you code EXTERNAL on 01 level items in WORKING-STORAGE, you make them accessible to all programs compiled as a group. All programs would define the field in the same way:

```
01 WS-RECORDS-READ-COUNT PIC S9(7) BINARY EXTERNAL.
```

If a field defined with EXTERNAL is a group name, all of the data names under it are available to all programs in the group. You can't code EXTERNAL on items in a LINKAGE SECTION.

You can code EXTERNAL on FDs to allow nested subprograms to access the same file, of any data set organization. This allows one program to open and close the file, but any of the programs in the group can read or write to it:

```
FD INPUT-FILE EXTERNAL.
```

All of the nested programs that access the file need ordinary SELECT/ ASSIGN statements and FDs coded in the same way.

D.5   GLOBAL

Ordinarily the data-names defined in a program are available only to it. They are "local" and are not known to other programs in the group.

You can code GLOBAL in the File Section or WORKING-STORAGE on 01 level items only. It acts similar to EXTERNAL but "opens up" a field only to programs contained by (nested within) the program. For example, a data-name defined as GLOBAL in PGM3 is available only to itself and PGM3SUB. A field defined with GLOBAL in PGM2 is still only available to PGM2 since PGM2 does not contain any nested programs. You can't code GLOBAL on items in a LINKAGE SECTION.

More than one program in the group can use the same data-name in its WORKING-STORAGE. When a program references such a field, the field of that name within the program is accessed if one exists. If no field of that name exists, COBOL searches for the data name in programs in an outward direction from the nested program. The search stops (and the field is referenced) when a field of that name is encountered in this way.

D.6   COMMON

You can code COMMON on the PROGRAM-ID of a contained program to make it CALLable by any program in the group. Unless COMMON is coded on a contained program, it can only be CALLed by a program that directly contains it. COMMON coded on PGM3SUB makes it CALLable by PGM2.

D.7   SHOULD YOU USE NESTED PROGRAMS?

While nesting offers some advantages, it can significantly complicate program maintenance. Consult your management about this feature and initiate discussion about installation standards before implementing nested programs.

Appendix E

Using Microcomputer-Based 1985 COBOL Compilers

E.1 MICROCOMPUTER-BASED COMPILERS VERSUS IBM VS COBOL II

Microcomputer-based 1985 COBOL compilers are marketed by Micro Focus Ltd., Ryan/McFarland Corporation, Computer Associates, and others. In addition, Microsoft markets the Micro Focus product under its own name, Microsoft COBOL.

Microcomputer-based 1985 COBOL compilers support (by definition) the 1985 COBOL standards. You can use all of the new language features discussed in this book with microcomputer-based compilers. Microcomputer-based compilers support the expanded VSAM File Status values but usually not the extended VSAM communication codes.

Differences exist between microcomputer-based compilers and VS COBOL II in several areas. Most of these differences don't affect your source code but they do affect procedures for compiling and testing.

In this appendix I cover first the differences between microcomputers and VS COBOL that affect all microcomputer-based compilers and then cover specifics about Micro Focus, RM/COBOL-85, and CA-Realia compilers.

E.2 BUILDING YOUR SOURCE CODE

You do not use TSO/ISPF to build your source code on a microcomputer. Instead, you can use any word processor that creates an ordinary ASCII text file to house your source code. You can use a simple editor like PC-WRITE or a more complex editor like WordPerfect or DisplayWrite to construct your code. (If you use a word processor like WordPerfect that ordinarily creates files with special formatting codes, make sure you output your source code as a DOS file.) A TSO/ISPF look-alike product named SPF-PC simulates TSO/ISPF on PCs and produces ASCII files suitable for microcomputer-based compilers.

Many installations standardize on certain word processing software by decree. That is appropriate for word processing documents that are highly formatted. But there is no need to standardize on a text editor for source code building since ASCII files do not contain any word processor-specific formatting codes. There is no difference between ASCII files created by one word processor or another.

Microcomputer-based compilers are relevant for program maintenance work as well as for new program development. You can also download programs from TSO/ISPF to a microcomputer to work on them, manipulate them using your word processor, and compile and test them on your PC. You can then upload your source code for final compiling and testing on the mainframe.

Figure E.1 shows you the source code of a renumbering utility I wrote using Micro Focus COBOL. In addition to giving you a handy tool for microcomputer-based source code development you can learn about compiler-specific SELECT/ASSIGN coding and file handling from it.

E.3 MICROCOMPUTER-BASED PROGRAM TESTING

Many microcomputer-based compilers offer sophisticated interactive debuggers that exceed VS COBOL II in responsiveness and speed. These debuggers are particular to the specific compilers themselves. Training on them is usually obtained from the compiler manufacturer.

In order to test a program thoroughly on a PC, you need to establish all of the test files and copy libraries available on the mainframe. Practically speaking, few installations have yet come to grips with the maintenance of the infrastructure necessary to make full-fledged microcomputer-based development and testing a smooth and reliable fit with mainframe VS COBOL II applications.

You should be aware that most microcomputer-based COBOL 1985 compilers are more accurate in numerical computation than VS COBOL II. I cover many of these differences in Chapter 9. The impact of this is that full-fledged program testing on the mainframe is still critical even if you have thoroughly tested a program on a microcomputer.

E.4 COMPILER OPTIONS

Most microcomputer-based 1985 COBOL compilers use different compiler options than VS COBOL II. You need to review product documentation about the specific compiler you use to become familiar with the options you can use.

A handy option provided by some microcomputer-based compilers is EBCDIC support. Microcomputers are ASCII machines, that is, they use the character set of the ASCII coding scheme, not EBCDIC as do mainframes. Your upload/download software translates from ASCII to EBCDIC, so code transfer is not the issue addressed by ECBDIC compatibility. Rather, an ASCII/EBCDIC option deals with the way alphanumeric data is compared in IF/ELSE and EVALUATE statements and the collation order used in sorting.

E.5 COMPILE LISTING

Microcomputer-based compilers optionally produce source code listings as separate ASCII files on your microcomputer hard disk. To print these listings you use the DOS COPY command to copy them to LPT1 (your printer port). You may also be able to view and work with these listings using your word processor. You generally don't need to print the compile listing in order to use it. Most microcomputer-based COBOL compilers display error messages on the screen as the compile proceeds.

E.6 ERROR MESSAGES

Messages produced by microcomputer-based COBOL compilers are not the same as the messages from VS COBOL II. In some cases microcomputer-based compilers produce only brief messages carrying an error number code. You have to look up the error code in documentation supplied with the compiler.

E.7 PRODUCT-SPECIFIC INFORMATION

In the following pages I have listed for you the product-specific information for the Micro Focus, RM/COBOL-85, and CA-Realia compilers that usually present the greatest stumbling block to newcomers. These topics include:

- Format of the SELECT/ASSIGN statement
- DECLARATIVES needed for File Status
- Indexed file creation

```
000100 IDENTIFICATION DIVISION.
000200 PROGRAM-ID.    RENUM.
000300 AUTHOR.        J. JANOSSY.
000400*================================================================
000500*  Renumber a COBOL Source Code File  (Microsoft/Micro Focus 3.0)
000600*
000700*  Copyright 1992 James G. Janossy   All rights reserved
000800*  From VS COBOL II: Highlights and Techniques  (Wiley, 1992)
000900*================================================================
001000 ENVIRONMENT DIVISION.
001100 INPUT-OUTPUT SECTION.
001200 FILE-CONTROL.
001300     SELECT SOURCE-FILE      ASSIGN DYNAMIC WS-FILE-IN
001400            ORGANIZATION IS LINE SEQUENTIAL.
001500     SELECT NEW-FILE         ASSIGN DYNAMIC WS-FILE-OUT
001600            ORGANIZATION IS LINE SEQUENTIAL.
001700 DATA DIVISION.
001800 FILE SECTION.
001900*
002000 FD  SOURCE-FILE
002100     RECORD CONTAINS 80 CHARACTERS.
002200 01  SOURCE-RECORD               PIC X(80).
002300*
002400 FD  NEW-FILE
002500     RECORD CONTAINS 80 CHARACTERS.
002600 01  NEW-RECORD.
002700     05  NR-NUMS                 PIC 9(6).
002800     05  FILLER                  PIC X(74).
002900*
003000 WORKING-STORAGE SECTION.
003100 01  WS-FILE-IN                  PIC X(25)   VALUE SPACES.
003200 01  WS-NAME                     PIC X(25)   VALUE SPACES.
003300 01  WS-SUFFIX                   PIC X(3).
003400 01  WS-FILE-OUT                 PIC X(25)   VALUE SPACES.
003500 01  WS-FILE-FLAG                PIC X(1)    VALUE 'M'.
003600 01  WS-COUNT                    PIC 9(6)    VALUE 0.
003700 01  WS-COUNT-FORMATTED          PIC ZZZ,ZZ9.
003800 01  WS-LOWER  PIC X(26)   VALUE 'abcdefghijklmnopqrstuvwxyz'.
003900 01  WS-UPPER  PIC X(26)   VALUE 'ABCDEFGHIJKLMNOPQRSTUVWXYZ'.
004000 01  MSG-1  PIC X(57)   VALUE
004100     '+---------------------------------------------------+'.
004200 01  MSG-2  PIC X(57)   VALUE
004300     '| VS COBOL II: Highlights and Techniques Renum Utility |'.
004400 01  MSG-3  PIC X(57)   VALUE
004500     '| Renumbers ASCII file source code on a microcomputer. |'.
004600 01  MSG-4  PIC X(57)   VALUE
004700     '| Copyright 1992 James Janossy (John Wiley & Sons, Inc.)|'.
004800 01  MSG-5  PIC X(57)   VALUE
004900     '+---------------------------------------------------+'.
005000 01  WS-CTR                      PIC X(10) VALUE SPACES.
005100 01  WS-MSG  PIC X(28)   VALUE 'Learn VS COBOL II fast!===> '.
005200 01  WS-CONFIRMING-MSG           PIC X(79) VALUE SPACES.
005300 01  WS-END  PIC X(73)   VALUE 'Isn''t COBOL on a microcomputer the
005400-     ' best thing since sliced bread?   -JGJ-'.
005500*
005600 PROCEDURE DIVISION.
005700 0000-MAINLINE.
005800     PERFORM 1000-BOJ.
005900     PERFORM 2000-PROCESS UNTIL WS-FILE-FLAG = 'E'.
006000     PERFORM 3000-EOJ.
006100     STOP RUN.
006200*------------------------------------------------------------
006300*
006400*
006500 1000-BOJ.
006600     DISPLAY WS-CTR, MSG-1.
006700     DISPLAY WS-CTR, MSG-2.
```

Figure E.1 *(see legend on page 326)*

```
006800          DISPLAY WS-CTR, MSG-3.
006900          DISPLAY WS-CTR, MSG-4.
007000          DISPLAY WS-CTR, MSG-5.
007100          DISPLAY WS-MSG,
007200              'Enter full name of source code file to renumber:'.
007300          DISPLAY WS-MSG WITH NO ADVANCING.
007400          ACCEPT  WS-FILE-IN.
007500          INSPECT WS-FILE-IN CONVERTING WS-LOWER TO WS-UPPER.
007600*
007700          UNSTRING WS-FILE-IN DELIMITED BY '.'
007800              INTO WS-NAME
007900                   WS-SUFFIX.
008000*
008100          STRING WS-NAME DELIMITED BY SPACE
008200              '.REN'      DELIMITED BY SIZE
008300              ' '         DELIMITED BY SIZE
008400              INTO WS-FILE-OUT.
008500*
008600          STRING WS-MSG                   DELIMITED BY SIZE
008700              'Renumbering '             DELIMITED BY SIZE
008800              WS-FILE-IN                 DELIMITED BY SPACE
008900              ' creating '               DELIMITED BY SIZE
009000              WS-FILE-OUT                DELIMITED BY SPACE
009100              INTO WS-CONFIRMING-MSG.
009200*
009300          DISPLAY WS-CONFIRMING-MSG.
009400          OPEN INPUT SOURCE-FILE.
009500          OPEN OUTPUT NEW-FILE.
009600          PERFORM 2700-READ.
009700*
009800  2000-PROCESS.
009900          MOVE SOURCE-RECORD TO NEW-RECORD.
010000          ADD 100 TO WS-COUNT.
010100          MOVE WS-COUNT TO NR-NUMS.
010200          WRITE NEW-RECORD.
010300          PERFORM 2700-READ.
010400*
010500  2700-READ.
010600          MOVE SPACES TO SOURCE-RECORD.
010700          READ SOURCE-FILE
010800              AT END
010900                  MOVE 'E' TO WS-FILE-FLAG.
011000*
011100  3000-EOJ.
011200          CLOSE   SOURCE-FILE  NEW-FILE.
011300          COMPUTE WS-COUNT-FORMATTED = WS-COUNT / 100.
011400          DISPLAY WS-MSG,
011500              'Renumbering ended, lines written = ',
011600              WS-COUNT-FORMATTED.
011700          DISPLAY WS-MSG,
011800              'Renumbered program exists as ',
011900              WS-FILE-OUT.
012000          DISPLAY WS-END.
```

Figure E.1   Source Code for a Renumbering Utility for Your Microcomputer.

If you use a text editor or word processor to build your COBOL source code on a microcomputer, you will find a renumbering utility helpful. This program reads your ASCII file source code and applies COBOL line numbers in columns 1 through 6 in increments of 100. When you run it, this program prompts you for the full name of the input source code file. It outputs an ASCII source code file of the same name with suffix .REN. I wrote this utility using Micro Focus COBOL. In addition to representing a handy tool for you this program shows you a lot about Micro Focus-specific file handling coding.

- Procedure for compiling and linkage editing
- Overview of the compiler's debugging environment

The information I provide about each of these products is focused on these areas. Consult your product documentation for additional information about your compiler.

Regardless of the compiler you use, read the information about the Micro Focus compiler first. I have included there much information resulting from my experience with it, and most of this information applies to RM/COBOL-85 and CA-Realia compilers as well.

E.8   MICRO FOCUS COBOL

Micro Focus COBOL is a highly regarded commercial compiler that has received IBM's blessing as a Systems Application Architecture approved product. Microsoft distributes this product under its own name as Microsoft COBOL. The compiler supports Report Writer and internal sorting. Like VS COBOL II, error messages are embedded in your source code listing after each line with an error.

E.8.1   SELECT/ASSIGN Statement and the DOS SET Command

You will need to code your SELECT/ASSIGN statements for sequential files with extra phrases. You should put SELECT/ASSIGN statements for both Micro Focus COBOL and VS COBOL II in your programs and comment out the one that does not apply to the environment you are using.

```
001400 ENVIRONMENT DIVISION.
001500 INPUT-OUTPUT SECTION.
001600 FILE-CONTROL.
001700*---------------------------------------------------------
001800* FOR MICRO FOCUS COBOL:
001900     SELECT TICKET-FILE       ASSIGN EXTERNAL TICKDATA
002000        ORGANIZATION IS LINE SEQUENTIAL.
002100     SELECT TICKET-REPORT     ASSIGN EXTERNAL TICKLIST
002200        ORGANIZATION IS LINE SEQUENTIAL.
002300*---------------------------------------------------------
002400* FOR VS COBOL II:
002500*    SELECT TICKET-FILE       ASSIGN TO TICKDATA.
002600*    SELECT TICKET-REPORT     ASSIGN TO TICKLIST.
002700*---------------------------------------------------------
002800*
002900 DATA DIVISION.
```

```
003000 FILE SECTION.
003100*
003200 FD  TICKET-FILE
003300     BLOCK CONTAINS 0 RECORDS
003400     RECORD CONTAINS 80 CHARACTERS.
003500 01  TICKET-RECORD               PIC X(80).
003600*
003700 FD  TICKET-REPORT
003800     BLOCK CONTAINS 0 RECORDS
003900     RECORD CONTAINS 133 CHARACTERS.
004000 01  TICKET-REPORT-PRINTLINE      PIC X(133).
```

To use Micro Focus COBOL smoothly, you need to use a little MS-DOS. Before running the program use the DOS SET command to associate your SELECT/ASSIGN DDname (such as TICKDATA and TICKLIST here) to an actual file name:

```
C> set tickdata=tickets.dat
C> set ticklist=ticklist.rep
```

This equates TICKDATA (which would become a JCL DDname in the IBM mainframe environment) to TICKETS.DAT, an actual file name on my microcomputer, and TICKLIST to TICKLIST.REP. You can see the current names in the environment by using the SET command without any names:

```
C> set
```

To remove a name from the environment, use the name followed by an equal sign but no assignment name. For example, this removes TICK-DATA from the environment:

```
C> set tickdata=
```

E.8.2 Clearing the Sequential File Buffer

You OPEN your files in the same way in Micro Focus COBOL as you do in VS COBOL II, but you should put a MOVE of SPACES before each execution of the READ verb. This has no effect on operation of the program on the mainframe. But it clears the record buffer on the microcomputer so that a shorter record read after a long one does not carry over any retained characters at the end:

```
PROCEDURE DIVISION.
    -
    OPEN INPUT TICKET-FILE.
    -
2700-READ.
    MOVE SPACES TO TICKET-RECORD.
    READ TICKET-FILE
        AT END
            MOVE 'E' TO WS-EOF-FLAG.
```

Your test files need to be ordinary ASCII files having a line feed/ carriage return at the end of each line. It's a mistake is to put an extra carriage return at the end of a data file. This will be interpreted as an empty record. Depending on what you program is doing, the extra carriage return may or may not cause it to abend.

E.8.3   File Status

Micro Focus COBOL supports the same File Status (but not extended File Status) as VS COBOL II for program-resolvable error situations. You can abandon INVALID KEY coding and develop the program exactly as in VS COBOL II, except for File Status '97' at OPEN (that value is IBM-specific).

E.8.4   Indexed File Creation

There is no such thing as VSAM in the Micro Focus COBOL environment. To create an indexed file you do not use IDCAMS. Instead, you need to write a simple program that reads records from a sequential text file and writes them to an indexed file. The compiler itself generates the instructions to create an indexed file. It uses the information you code in the SELECT/ASSIGN statement of your loading program for the file as well as the key field locations and sizes you specify in the FD for the indexed file. Figure E.2 shows you the source code of a Micro Focus COBOL program that creates and loads an indexed passenger ticket file like the master file discussed in Chapter 12 Figure 12.9.

There are no separate cluster, data, and index components for indexed files on a microcomputer with the Micro Focus COBOL compiler. The index is stored in a separate file named with the suffix .IDX and associated with the data file by the file name before the suffix. Don't use .IDX as a file suffix of your own!

IDCAMS is strictly mainframe software. Your IDCAMS PRINT commands will not work on a microcomputer. To see the contents of an indexed file (after a test, for example) write a simple program to read the records in the index file sequentially and DISPLAY them on the screen.

E.8.5 Procedure for Compiling and Linkage Editing

Build your source code in a file as ASCII code with COBOL line numbers in columns 1 through 6. Name the file housing your code with the program name and the suffix .CBL. Compile the program by entering:

```
C> cobol a1new
```

where a1new is the program name (and the name of the file housing the source code). Pressing *<Enter>* causes several prompts to appear:

```
Object file-name [a1new.OBJ]:
Source listing [NUL.LST]:
Object listing [NUL.GRP]:
```

Press the *<Enter>* key to bypass each prompt. The file name shown in square brackets is the default name for the item. You can enter a name to replace the name shown. Your source code listing will be put into the file named at "Source listing." Replace NUL.GRP with an actual name if you want to see the object file listing (not usually very handy). If you don't want to see the prompts, enter the compile command with four trailing commas:

```
C> cobol a1new,,,,
```

You need to linkage edit your program before you can run it:

```
C>link a1new
```

Pressing *<Enter>* leads to the following prompts. You can override the default file name in each case:

```
Run File [a1new.EXE]:
List File [NUL.MAP]:
Libraries [.LIB]: LCOBOL
Definitions File [NUL.DEF]:
```

```
000100 IDENTIFICATION DIVISION.
000200 PROGRAM-ID.    PASSLOAD.
000300*AUTHOR.        J JANOSSY    INTERNET: JANOSSY@CSCVAX.DEPAUL.EDU
000400*INSTALLATION.  DEPAUL UNIVERSITY, CHICAGO, ILLINOIS, USA
000500*=================================================================
000600*              Program to Create/Load Indexed File
000700*          General Purpose Indexed File Loader  5-05-92
000800*          ** MICRO FOCUS COBOL MICROCOMPUTER COMPILER **
000900*
001000*     Reads records from a sequential file and copies them to
001100*     an indexed file.  Once this program has been run the
001200*     indexed file exists and can be accessed.
001300*=================================================================
001400 ENVIRONMENT DIVISION.
001500 INPUT-OUTPUT SECTION.
001600 FILE-CONTROL.
001700     SELECT SEQ-FILE              ASSIGN TO 'PASSFILE.SEQ'
001800         ORGANIZATION IS  LINE SEQUENTIAL.
001900     SELECT MAST-FILE             ASSIGN TO 'PASSFILE.XXX'
002000         ORGANIZATION   IS  INDEXED
002100         ACCESS MODE    IS  SEQUENTIAL
002200         RECORD KEY     IS  MF-KEY
002300         ALTERNATE RECORD KEY    IS  MF-SALES-AGENT
002400             WITH DUPLICATES
002500         FILE STATUS   IS  WS-STATUS.
002600*------------------------------------------------------------------
002700 DATA DIVISION.
002800 FILE SECTION.
002900*
003000 FD  SEQ-FILE
003100     LABEL RECORDS ARE STANDARD
003200     RECORD CONTAINS 80 CHARACTERS.
003300 01  SEQ-RECORD                   PIC X(80).
003400*
003500 FD  MAST-FILE
003600     LABEL RECORDS ARE STANDARD
003700     RECORD CONTAINS 80 CHARACTERS.
003800 01  MAST-RECORD.
003900     05 MF-KEY                    PIC X(5).
004000     05 MF-LAST-NAME              PIC X(14).
004100     05 MF-FIRST-NAME             PIC X(15).
004200     05 MF-CRUISE-DATE            PIC X(6).
004300     05 MF-TICKET-QTY             PIC 9(3).
004400     05 MF-DECK-CODE              PIC X(2).
004500     05 MF-SALES-AGENT            PIC X(23).
004600     05 MF-DATE-BOUGHT            PIC X(6).
004700     05 FILLER                    PIC X(6).
004800/
004900*------------------------------------------------------------------
005000 WORKING-STORAGE SECTION.
005100 01  WS-STATUS.
005200     12 WS-STATUS-BYTE1           PIC X(1).
005300     12 FILLER                    PIC X(1).
005400*
005500 01  WS-INPUT-COUNT               PIC 9(5)    VALUE 0.
005600 01  WS-REC-LOADED                PIC 9(5)    VALUE 0.
005700 01  WS-REC-NOT-LOADED            PIC 9(5)    VALUE 0.
005800 01  F1-EOF-FLAG                  PIC X(1)    VALUE 'M'.
005900/
006000 PROCEDURE DIVISION.
006100 0000-MAINLINE.
006200     PERFORM 1000-BOJ.
006300     PERFORM 2000-PROCESS
006400         UNTIL F1-EOF-FLAG = 'E'.
006500     PERFORM 3000-EOJ.
006600     STOP RUN.
```

Figure E.2 *(see legend on page 332)*

```
006700*
006800 1000-BOJ.
006900     DISPLAY '*** Start of program PASSLOAD'.
007000     OPEN OUTPUT  MAST-FILE.
007100     IF WS-STATUS-BYTE1 NOT = '0'
007200         DISPLAY '*** Error opening indexed file, program ended'
007300         DISPLAY '    File Status = ', WS-STATUS
007400         STOP RUN.
007500     OPEN  INPUT  SEQ-FILE.
007600     PERFORM 2700-READ.
007700*
007800 2000-PROCESS.
007900     WRITE MAST-RECORD FROM SEQ-RECORD.
008000     IF WS-STATUS-BYTE1 = '0'
008100         DISPLAY MAST-RECORD
008200         ADD 1 TO WS-REC-LOADED
008300     ELSE
008400     IF WS-STATUS = '21'
008500         DISPLAY '*** Err next rec   File Status = ', WS-STATUS
008600         DISPLAY MAST-RECORD
008700         ADD 1 TO WS-REC-NOT-LOADED
008800     ELSE
008900         DISPLAY '*** Loading failed!   File Status = ', WS-STATUS
009000         DISPLAY MAST-RECORD
009100         STOP RUN.
009200     PERFORM 2700-READ.
009300*-------------------------------------------------------------
009400 2700-READ.
009500     READ SEQ-FILE
009600     AT END
009700         MOVE 'E' TO F1-EOF-FLAG
009800     NOT AT END
009900         ADD 1 TO WS-INPUT-COUNT.
010000*
010100 3000-EOJ.
010200     CLOSE  SEQ-FILE  MAST-FILE.
010300     DISPLAY 'File status at indexed file close = ', WS-STATUS.
010400     DISPLAY 'Seq file records read ',
010500         WS-INPUT-COUNT.
010600     DISPLAY 'Records loaded         ',
010700         WS-REC-LOADED.
010800     DISPLAY 'Records not loaded     ',
010900         WS-REC-NOT-LOADED.
011000     DISPLAY '*** Program ended normally'.
```

Output:

```
*** Start of program PASSLOAD
31256NILLY        WILLIE     900216002S1HOBBIT INTERNATIONAL     890718
31257IPPI         MRS.       900216001B2JACK SPRAT TRAVEL        890817
31260MALLOW       MARSHA     900216001B HOLIDAY TOURS, INC.      890805
31307WARE         DELLA      900216004B1WORLD TRAVEL, INC.       890909
31310SHAW         ARKAN      900216007S1HOLIDAY TOURS, INC.      890911
31573WALLBANGER   HARVEY     900216002B HOBBIT INTERNATIONAL     891214
31574AH           GEORGE     900216001S1HOBBIT INTERNATIONAL     900103
31668ZOORI        MOE        900216004S1FOX VALLEY TRAVEL        900103
31778SLEEPING     R. U.      900216001B1UWANNAGO TRAVEL, INC.    900107
31779HEAD         M. T.      900216002C KOOK'S TOURS             900113
35112CABOOSE      LUCE       900331001B2HOBBIT INTERNATIONAL     900121
35189HOE          IDA        900331002S HOBBIT INTERNATIONAL     890603
File status at indexed file close = 00
Seq file records read  00012
Records loaded         00012
Records not loaded     00000
*** Program ended normally
```

Figure E.2 Micro Focus COBOL Source Code to Create an Indexed File.

You create indexed files with Micro Focus COBOL by reading records from a sequential file and writing them to the indexed file. The program itself automatically establishes the index and data using the information provided in the standard SELECT/ASSIGN statement and FD. You can adapt this program to load any indexed file in the Micro Focus environment. The same program will work for RM/COBOL-85 if you add the DECLARATIVES coding discussed in section E.9.3. You can also adapt this program to work in CA-Realia COBOL.

When you linkage edit a program that accesses an indexed file, you have to enter LCOBOL at the Libraries prompt. LCOBOL.LIB contains the Micro Focus service routines your program needs for indexed file work.

If you want to bypass the linkage editor prompts without having to press *<Enter>* at each one, enter the LINK command with five trailing commas:

```
C>link a1new,,,,,
```

The compile and link process produces executable machine code. You execute the program simply by entering its name:

```
C> a1new
```

Don't forget to do your DOS SETs to equate file names with actual files, or you will get runtime error 004! You can find all error codes in *Micro Focus Error Message Manual,* usually bound with the *Optimizing Compiler Operating Guide.*

To use subprograms and the CALL verb, compile each subprogram first, creating its .COB object file in the same subdirectory as your main program and the linker. The Micro Focus environment handles dynamically-linked subprograms so you do not have to hard-link the object files of main (CALLing) and (CALLed) subprograms. Just linkage edit main and subprograms separately but make sure they all reside in the same subdirectory.

E.8.6 Debugging Environment

Micro Focus provides the Animator debugging environment to allow you to step through a program, examine variables during execution, and set breakpoints. This is similar to COBTEST interactive debugging. Consult Micro Focus documentation for information about using Animator.

E.9 RYAN/MCFARLAND COBOL-85

RM/COBOL-85 is a capable microcomputer-based compiler, which is available for less than $25 in an educational version with *Structured COBOL Programming,* 6th ed. (Nancy and Robert Stern, John Wiley & Sons, Inc., 1991). You can use RM/COBOL-85 to process the programs I show you in this book. The information that follows applies to the educational version of this compiler. RM/COBOL-85 does not support Report Writer but does support internal sorting. As with VS COBOL II, error messages are embedded in your source code listing.

E.9.1 SELECT/ASSIGN Statement

The format for the SELECT/ASSIGN statement differs from Micro Focus COBOL:

```
SELECT TELEPHONE-REPORT    ASSIGN TO DISK 'JIM.REP'
   ORGANIZATION IS LINE SEQUENTIAL.
```

Consult RM/COBOL-85 documentation if you would like to use a symbolic DDname at the right side of the statement rather than a hard-coded file name.

E.9.2 Declaratives and File Status

Include a dummy DECLARATIVES section at the beginning of the PROCEDURE DIVISION. DECLARATIVES must be present if you want to abandon reference to INVALID KEY, but it does not have to take any action. Instead, modern practice is to test File Status directly yourself.

RM/COBOL-85 supports ANSI standard File Status values. You can test for the same File Status values indicating program-resolvable error situations as with VS COBOL II. An exception exists for '97' on an OPEN, which is specific to IBM VS COBOL and VS COBOL II.

E.9.3 Indexed File Creation

As with Micro Focus, you create indexed files using a program you write yourself that reads records from a sequential file and writes them to an indexed file. Your SELECT/ASSIGN statements appear like the following and tell the operating system everything it needs to know to create the indexed file:

```
SELECT SEQ-FILE          ASSIGN TO DISK 'TICKETS.DAT'
   ORGANIZATION IS  LINE SEQUENTIAL.
SELECT MAST-FILE          ASSIGN TO DISK 'TICKETS.XXX'
   ORGANIZATION  IS  INDEXED
   ACCESS MODE   IS  SEQUENTIAL
   RECORD KEY    IS  MF-KEY
```

```
ALTERNATE RECORD KEY    IS  MF-SALES-AGENT
    WITH DUPLICATES
FILE STATUS   IS  WS-STATUS.
```

If you use indexed files and want to use File Status checking exclusively (abandoning INVALID KEY coding), you will have to code a dummy DECLARATIVES section at the start of the Procedure Division. In the ANSI standard this is where you might code logic to interrogate the File Status value. VS COBOL II makes these DECLARATIVES optional but RM/COBOL-85 requires the presence of this section or you will abend when you receive program-resolvable File Status values:

```
*-----------------------------------------------------------------
*  In RM/COBOL-85 you need declaratives (even in dummy form) to
*  avoid abends even when non-zero File Status values such as
*  '23' are received for a key-not-found condition. Since
*  DECLARATIVES are a ''section'' MAIN-PROGRAM must be a section.
*-----------------------------------------------------------------
DECLARATIVES.
0000-ERROR SECTION.
     USE AFTER STANDARD ERROR PROCEDURE ON MAST-FILE.
0000-DUMMY. EXIT.
*
END DECLARATIVES.
*-----------------------------------------------------------------
0000-MAIN-PROGRAM   SECTION.
```

This DECLARATIVES logic does not actually do anything. It is just necessary to please the RM/COBOL-85 compiler and a strict implementation of 1985 COBOL standards. Its presence doesn't harm your VS COBOL II program and you can leave it in place after you upload the program to the mainframe.

RM/COBOL-85 does not segregate the index in a separate file. Instead, it places index information at the beginning of the data in an indexed file. This has no effect on program access to the indexed file.

Access records in your indexed file exactly as you would using VS COBOL II. The RM/COBOL-85 compiler supports File Status but not the extended File Status communication fields.

E.9.4 Procedure for Compiling and Linkage Editing

Prepare your program as an ASCII file with COBOL line numbers in the first six columns and name it with suffix .CBL. Use any word processor you like. The educational version of the compiler is supplied with a text editing environment you can optionally use.

The RM/COBOL-85 compiler is named RMCOB85. To compile a program enter:

```
C> rmcob85 b:a1new L
```

The "L" option creates a program listing for you named name.LST. The above command will create A1NEW.LST. You can view this with your text editor to see error messages, which (as with VS COBOL II) are embedded in the source code listing.

RM/COBOL-85 produces object code that is processable by its runtime environment module, a program named RUN.EXE. Your object code is housed in a file named with a suffix of .COB. For example, the compile shown above will produce a file named a1new.COB. To process a program, you compile it then run it. You do not do a linkage edit, simplifying your work. You can run a program immediately after successfully compiling it:

```
C> run a1new
```

The educational version of the RMCOBOL/85 compiler always starts execution in a debugging mode. The prompt changes to an unusual line such as:

```
ST 140 a1new e
```

This indicates that a1new is set to "start" at line 140. To make the program run, type "e" and press *<Return>*. The "e" command means "execute without debugging."

To use subprograms and the CALL verb, compile each subprogram first, creating its .COB object file in the same subdirectory as your main program. When you RUN your main program, the runtime environment will automatically associate the subprogram with your main program as CALLs are executed.

E.9.5 Debugging Environment

The debugger supplied with the RM/COBOL-85 compiler allows you to set breakpoints and examine the contents of data names during operation. Looking at a variable involves entering its hexadecimal displacement. You learn this displacement from a column printed at the left side of the source code listing. To debug code you need to have the listing handy, as well as documentation on the specific debugging commands.

The extensive documentation supplied with the educational version of the compiler provides instructions on using the debugger and the error codes the compiler and runtime module produce.

E.10 CA-REALIA COBOL

Computer Associates provides a microcomputer-based 1985 COBOL compiler that it claims is so compatible with VS COBOL II that the company supplies IBM manuals as part of its product documentation! But a few minor differences do exist. Like VS COBOL (but not VS COBOL II), CA-Realia COBOL produces error messages at the end of your source code listing, not embedded within it. It expects to find the CONFIGURATION SECTION in your program and complains with a warning if you omit it, so it does not allow you to streamline programs quite as much.

An educational version of this compiler is supplied bound with *COBOL: From Micro to Mainframe,* volume 1 (Robert T. Grauer and Carol Vazquez Villar, Prentice Hall, 1991). To use this you must supply your own copy of the Microsoft linkage editor.

E.10.1 SELECT/ASSIGN Statement

The SELECT/ASSIGN statement for CA-Realia COBOL resembles older IBM standards in that prefixes before the "DDname" can be present to inform the compiler about some characteristics of the file. This makes it unnecessary to include extra lines such as ORGANIZATION IS LINE SEQUENTIAL for sequential files. A SELECT/ASSIGN for a sequential file and an indexed file appear like this in CA-Realia COBOL:

```
SELECT SEQ-FILE        ASSIGN TO UT-S-TICKETS.
SELECT MAST-FILE        ASSIGN TO DA-TICKXXX
    ORGANIZATION  IS  INDEXED
    ACCESS MODE   IS  SEQUENTIAL
    RECORD KEY    IS  MF-KEY
    ALTERNATE RECORD KEY IS MF-SALES-AGENT
        WITH DUPLICATES
    FILE STATUS   IS  WS-STATUS.
```

Use the MS-DOS SET command to associate your DDnames, such as TICKETS and TICKXXX, with actual file names before running your program.

E.10.2   Declaratives, File Status, and Index Files

Declaratives are optional in CA-Realia COBOL even when you omit any reference to INVALID KEY and do your own File Status checking. If you code a dummy DECLARATIVES section it causes no harm.

CA-Realia COBOL supports the ANSI standard 1985 File Status values in the same way as does VS COBOL II. The File Status Values above values in the 40s are specific to IBM VS COBOL II and you won't receive them from CA-Realia COBOL. You can test for all of the customary File Status values as usual, with the exception of '97' on an OPEN, which is specific to IBM VS COBOL and VS COBOL II.

As with Micro Focus and RM/COBOL-85, you can create an indexed file with CA-Realia COBOL by reading records from a sequential file and writing them to an indexed file specified in the SELECT/ASSIGN statement. But CA-Realia also provides the REALCOPY utility which can create an indexed file directly. To use REALCOPY you need to read documentation concerning the command parameters it expects you to enter.

E.10.3   Procedure for Compiling and Linkage Editing

Prepare your source code in an ASCII file with the word processor of your choice. Either use actual line numbers in columns 1 through 6 or leave them blank. If you use line numbers, name your file of source code with the suffix .CBL. If you do not use line numbers (meaning the first column at the left is to be regarded as column 7), name your source code file with a suffix .COB. When you enter just the front part of the source code file name (without a suffix) at the compile command, the CA-Realia COBOL compiler first seeks a source code file with that name and the suffix .CBL. Compile your program with the command:

```
C> realcob/r a1new
```

This produces a sequence of prompts with defaults similar to those from Micro Focus COBOL. The compile produces a listing of your source code with the suffix .LST and an object file with a suffix of .OBJ, which must be linkage edited:

```
C> link a1new
```

This linker is the standard Microsoft linkage editor and produces the same prompts as listed above for the Micro Focus environment. You run the resulting machine language load module by entering its name:

`C> a1new`

To use subprograms you compile each separately and linkage edit the subprograms with the CALLing (main) program by coding all of the subprogram names after the main program name:

`C> a1new,sub1,sub2`

E.10.4 Debugging Environment

Computer Associates Realia provides the RealDBUG debugger to allow you to step through a program, examine variables during execution, and set breakpoints. This is similar to COBTEST interactive debugging and makes extensive use of screen formatting and color. Consult CA-Realia documentation about using RealDBUG.

Appendix F

Summary of COBTEST Debugging Commands

GO	Start or resume execution, stop at next breakpoint
STEP	Execute the specified number of program statements
VTRACE	Animate the program highlighting statement executing
RUN	Execute program ignoring all breakpoints
RESTART	Load a new copy of the program and begin execution
QUIT	End the debugging session
DUMP	End the debugging session and provide a dump
FLOW	Turn on control flow trace
FREQ	Turn on verb execution counting
SET	Initialize or change values of program variables
AT	Set breakpoints by line number
LISTBRKS	List current breakpoint locations
NEXT	Set temporary breakpoint at the next verb
OFF	Remove breakpoints that were established with AT
OFFWN	Remove only the breakpoints that use WHEN
WHERE	Show where in code execution has been suspended
SOURCE	Open, close, or change size of the source code area
SEARCH	Search source, log, and auto-monitoring area for string
SUFFIX	Open or close suffix area within the source code area
RESTORE	Restore source code area to last point of execution
WHEN	Set up continuous monitoring for command execution
IF	Cause conditional invocation of debugging commands
ONABEND	Execute specified commands if an abend occurs
AUTO	Display variables in the auto monitoring area
TRACE	Display the flow of program execution
LIST	Display contents of specified data-names
LISTFREQ	Display tally of verb executions since last FREQ
SELECT	Allow viewing frequency count on one line
PEEK	Show line numbers covered up by breakpoint info
EQUATE	Create abbreviations for data-names
LISTEQ	Display abbreviations created with EQUATE
DROP	Delete abbreviations created with EQUATE
LINK	Simulate a non-existing main (CALLing) program
PROC	Trap calls to a non-existent subprogram
PROFILE	Set COBTEST session parameters
COLOR	Set color and intensity attributes of the screen
HELP	Provide information about COBTEST commands

Appendix G

Suggested Shop Standards

VS COBOL II is coming to your shop, whether you are anxious for it or not. It would be wise for your installation to take a few steps immediately to ease its eventual implementation. Then, regardless of where you are in the transition to VS COBOL II, convene a committee to review and revise your shop standards for COBOL coding. I suggest topics for that committee agenda here.

G.1 ACTIONS YOU SHOULD TAKE IMMEDIATELY

1. Make the VS COBOL Release 2.4 MIGR option active by default by having your systems programmers update your VS COBOL compile procs. Notify programmers to look at the MIGR warnings and take simple actions as described in Chapter 2 to minimize them.
2. Start ACCEPTing your current date from DATE instead of using CURRENT-DATE for page headings. Use STRING to assemble the current date in the format you need, as in Chapter 2.
3. Put RETURN-CODE values in the range 1000–1999 off limits. If you happen to be using values in this range for production work, change policies now.
4. Adopt a standard format for the IDENTIFICATION DIVISION making all but the heading and PROGRAM-ID comments. You might want to choose a format as in Figure G.1.
5. Review the material in Chapter 9 on numeric precision and how ROUNDING works. Begin coding any financial computations with

excess precision and using a final COMPUTE with ROUNDING to minimize numeric imprecision.

6. Start coding the table row field (the data name that carries the index) first in all WHEN statements in SEARCHes. This will eliminate syntax errors in using SEARCH ALL in VS COBOL II.

7. If you are developing or maintaining COBOL code on a microcomputer and uploading it to the mainframe for execution, be sure to retest the program completely on the mainframe. You may obtain correct results on the microcomputer but incorrect numeric outputs on the mainframe due to the way the COMPUTE and the arithmetic verbs are implemented in VS COBOL and VS COBOL II.

G.2 ACTIONS FOR A STANDARDS COMMITTEE TO CONSIDER

VS COBOL II provides many new capabilities. I have already seen eager-beavers and hackers revel in nested programs, complex in-line PER-FORMs, and intricate reference modification. This is certain to cause program maintenance problems in their shops in the next few years! Guidelines for locally appropriate feature usage help everyone to be productive in development and maintenance. Adherence to reasonable standards and guidelines also provides a useful gauge in personnel evaluation.

Here are topics that should be decided by your installations standards committee before your shop starts using VS COBOL II (I've shown chapter references for your convenience):

1. Decide on default compiler options that will be activated in your compile procs. Ask your systems programmers to make NOCMPR2, NUMPROC(PFD), XREF, OFFSET, and FASTSRT active by default (Chapter 3).

2. Will you permit elimination of the word FILLER where possible? A minor point but it has pro and con aspects. If you don't make a rule,

```
000100 IDENTIFICATION DIVISION.
000200 PROGRAM-ID.    PRODMODL.
000300**********************************************************************
000400*                                                                    *
000500*              BY JIM JANOSSY    DEPAUL UNIVERSITY  3/15/92           *
000600*                                                                    *
000700*              THIS PROGRAM READS A FILE OF TICKET RECORDS            *
000800*              FOR A PLEASURE CRUISE AND PRINTS A REPORT THAT         *
000900*              LISTS EACH WITH VALIDATION OF QUANTITY FIELD           *
001000*                                                                    *
001100*     CHANGES:    5/05/92   CONVERTED TO VS COBOL II                  *
001200*                                                                    *
001300**********************************************************************
001400 ENVIRONMENT DIVISION.
```

Figure G.1 Suggested Shop Standard for IDENTIFICATION DIVISION Coding.

different people will go different ways and the variation will introduce maintenance problems (Chapter 5).

3. Consider how deeply nested you would like to see in-line PERFORMs. Establish a standard similar to a standard you probably already have in place for IF/ELSE nesting (Chapter 6).

4. Consider a shop standard for explicit scope terminators. Perhaps every IF/ELSE doesn't need them? A related standard should deal with how periods are used since scope terminators now make it possible to eliminate almost all periods. A suggestion: require coding with periods in traditional format and common-sense use of scope terminators to ease program maintenance. Not everyone feels comfortable with arbitrary new styles. (Chapter 7).

5. Will your shop permit the use of or will it abandon SECTIONs? I suggest you abandon SECTIONs, at least for non-CICS programs. With VS COBOL II there is no requirement to use SECTIONs for internal sort input and output procedures. Review Chapter 14 and see why SECTIONs are entirely obsolete and problematic.

6. Will your shop permit the use of nested programs? If so, what steps will you take to educate maintenance programmers about them? To fully consider this issue, squarely address the issue of what problem you are trying to solve by allowing them. Before allowing their use, justify why their additional complexity and learning curve are cost beneficial in your environment (Appendix D).

7. Consider making the use of SET mandatory for condition names, as opposed to perpetuating MOVEs of values to flags or switches for which 88-level names are defined. SET significantly increase the reliability of flag and switch setting and decreases maintenance time (Chapter 7).

8. Consider adopting the standard VSAM File Status checking pattern shown in Chapter 12. You need to regard 0 and 97 as valid OPEN values. Consider abandoning INVALID KEY entirely in favor of standard File Status checking. Make coding of the extended file status fields mandatory and require them to be output when a program-uncorrectable File Status value is received (Chapter 12).

9. Will your shop allow use of the VS COBOL II Release 2 "compatability" option COMPR2? It's a time bomb that requires subsequent management until programs are fully converted from Release 2 to Release 3. Be especially wary of this if you are contracting for the development of software by personnel who will have gone by the time your own personnel have to perform program maintenance (Chapter 3)!

10. Insist on the use of VALUE on table row fields rather than initialization of tables using loops. In cases where VALUE is appropriate, it is much more efficient than use of a loop (Chapter 8).

11. Insist on the use of INITIALIZE to reinitialize variables rather than moves, loops, or clever separate groups of synchronized values moved by group name. INITIALIZE is more efficient and reliable than the alternatives (Chapter 5).

12. Publicize the batch debug JCL illustrated in Chapter 15 so that everyone knows how to get output analogous to that provided by READY TRACE. A majority of personnel will continue to feel most comfortable with batch debugging (Chapter 15).

13. Develop a guideline for the use of interactive debugging; it does use expensive mainframe time. If your shop will favor interactive debugging on a mainframe, plan on giving personnel a brief course on TSO ready mode commands for file access, such as ALLOCATE, ATTRIB, and FREE (Chapter 16).

14. Will your shop permit use of PROCESS statements to set compiler PARMs or not (Chapter 3)?

15. Decide on a new standard format for the FD to streamline it (Chapter 5).

16. Decide on a rule for when hex literals should be used. Prohibit hackers from using hex just to be clever when ordinary characters are sufficient (Chapter 5).

17. Should NOT AT END be a standard for input record counting? It eliminates an IF statement and makes record counts more reliable (Chapter 5).

18. Should PERFORM ... THRU an exit be the shop standard, permitted, frowned upon, or banned? It becomes a bit less reliable since EXIT can now be followed by code that will execute. Whether your shop favors or disfavors this technique is entirely a local issue (Chapter 5).

19. Lowercase letters in source code statements should be prohibited. There is no benefit to them and you have to go out of your way in TSO to use them (Chapter 5).

20. Your shop should insist on use of the new operators $<=$ and $>=$ for IF limit and ranges, instead of perpetuating the old negated complement coding of VS COBOL. This makes code more reliable now and will without doubt save maintenance time in the future (Chapter 7).

21. Will your shop allow compound EVALUATE? If it does, I'd suggest limiting them to two conditions or three at the most (Chapter 7).

22. Publicize the fact that in VS COBOL II the break-even point for efficiency gains with SEARCH ALL is a table size of 70 rows. This is a higher figure than for VS COBOL (Chapter 8).

23. Consider formation of a standard REPLACE and house it in a copylib for use in all converted programs or at least in specific applications (Chapter 11).

24. Consider common-sense limits on the way reference modification can be used locally, in the interest of more productive program maintenance (Chapter 11):
    • Use of literal numbers on the left side of the equal sign is acceptable.
    • Use of data names in reference modifiers on either side of the equal sign and computation of terms should be avoided.

25. Should you establish a limit on how deeply nested COPY directives can be (Chapter 11)?

26. Consider the impact of the NUMPROC option and how it is set by default in your installation. I would suggest using the PFD setting instead of the default usually set as NOPFD. PFD is the most stringent and most efficient. Programs likely to have any problems are those that read data produced by PL/I or FORTRAN programs with sloppy (by COBOL standards) numeric sign treatment (Chapter 9).

G.3   THINGS YOU SHOULD HAVE YOUR SYSTEMS PROGRAMMERS DO NOW

1. Set your compile and link procs to default to AMODE(31) and RMODE(ANY), rather than (24).

2. Examine your IMS and CICS linkage edit procs in view of literature available from IBM concerning efficient use of linkage editor options. Remove linkage editor options for IMS and CICS from application programmer concern. Have systems personnel research your local compatibility of VS COBOL and VS COBOL II modules in concert with their IBM technical contacts (Chapter 13).

3. Form a joint systems and CICS programmer task force and have it study CICS changes in VS COBOL II like LENGTH OF and other simplifications. Move toward adoption of revised standards for use of GOBACK and elimination of BLL cell coding. My suggestion about pointer fields: make written justification of their use a requirement. They are tricky and unnecessary for almost all applications purposes (Chapter 13).

Index

A

A1NEW program, 34–56
A1OLD program, 18–25
ABEND information, 73
ACCEPT, 247, 257
ACCESS MODE IS DYNAMIC, 237, 238
ACCESS MODE IS RANDOM, 231, 233, 238
ACCESS MODE IS SEQUENTIAL, 238
ADDRESS OF, 252
Advance II, 16
ALLOC command, TSO, 293, 298
ALPHABETIC-LOWER and -UPPER, 214
Alternate index, 229–230, 237, 239, 242–246
ALTERNATE RECORD KEY, 237
AMODE, 5, 6
ASCENDING KEY IS, 152
AT, 285
AUTHOR, 84
AUTO window, debugging, 299–301, 304

B

B1NEWRC program, 72–75
B1OLDRC program, 62–67
B2COINS program, 79–83, 113
Batch debugging, 273–286
BDAM, 216
Binary fields (COMP), 88
BINARY, 88
BLDINDEX (IDCAMS), 229–230
BLL cells in CICS coding, 250, 253, 254
BLOCK CONTAINS 0 RECORDS, 85
BPAM, 221
BSAM, 216
BY CONTENT, 316
BY REFERENCE, 316

C

C1HEX program, 90
C2INIT program, 93–95

CA-Optimizer/Migration Option, 16
CA-Realia COBOL, 7, 89, 337–339
Calculations, speeding up, 170
CALL and CICS, 249–250
CALL, 316–318, 319
CANCEL, 318
CICS, 247–256
CLASS, 187
CLIST (VS COBOL option), 58
CLOSE, 221, 247, 256
CMPR2 option, 58, effect on file status, 226
COB2UCL, 275
COB2UCLG and related procs, 26
COB2UCLG, 274
COBDBG, 273, 275, 282, 291
COBOL Conversion Aid, 16
COBTEST, 13, 14, 25, 273, 275, 276–277, 282, 287, 340
COMMON, 321
COMMUNICATION SECTION, 16
COMP, 88
COMP-3, 87, 168
Compound conditions, and EVALUATE, 133–137
Computational accuracy, 173–183
COMPUTE accuracy problems, 173–183
COND CODE, 35, 57, 61
Conditional statement, 121
CONTINUE, 122, 137
Converting lowercase to uppercase, with INSPECT, 197–198
CONVERTING option, INSPECT, 197–200
Copy library, and user-defined data class, 195
COPY statement and new REPLACE feature, 200
COPY, nested, 212, 213
COPYDEMO program, 213
Cross reference of data names, 47
Cross reference of procedures, 49
CRP, current record pointer, 238–241
Current record pointer (CRP), 238–241
CURRENT-DATE, 9, 10, 208

D

D1PERNEW program, 101
D1PEROLD program, 101
D2PERIF program, 105
D2PERNEW program, 103
D2PEROLD program, 103
D2PEROLD program, 103
D3NESTIN program, 109
D3OLD program, 107
D3PERIF program, 105
D4AFTER program, 110
D4BEFORE program, 110
D4NESTIN program, 109
D4NESTOT program, 108
D5NESTED program, 111–113
DATA RECORD IS . . . , 85
Date centering logic, 270, 272
DATE-COMPILED, 84, 85
DATE-WRITTEN, 84
DAY-OF-WEEK, 201
DCBS, double byte character set, 212
De-editing numbers, 171–173
Debugging CICS programs, 256
Debugging commands, summary, 340
DEBUGJCL JCL, 283
DECLARATIVES SECTION, 335
DEFINE AIX (IDCAMS), 229–230
DEFINE CLUSTER (IDCAMS), 229–230
DELETE (IDCAMS), 229–230
DELETE and NOT INVALID KEY, 91
DELETE, 217, 221, 233, 247, 256
DFHCOMMAREA, 250
DISPLAY, 13, 247, 257, 277
DMAP option (VS COBOL), 23, 58
Double byte character set, 212
DUP, 83
DYNAMIC access mode, 237, 238

E

E1EVAL program, 126
E1OLDIF program, 125
E2OLDIF program, 132
E3EVAL program, 135
E4EVAL program, 136
E5SET program, 141
ECAR3035 program, 262–269
Embedded error messages, 72
END-ADD, 119
END-CALL, 119
END-COMPUTE, 119
END-DELETE, 119
END-DIVIDE, 119
END-EVALUATE, 119
END-IF, 118–121

END-MULTIPLY, 119
END-PERFORM, 101, 102, 106, 113, 114
END-PERFORM, 119
END-READ, 119
END-RETURN, 119
END-REWRITE, 119
END-SEARCH, 119
END-START, 119
END-STRING, 119
END-SUBTRACT, 119
END-UNSTRING, 119
END-WRITE, 119
EVALUATE, 115, 124–141
EXAMINE, 9, 12, 196, 197
Execution interface block, CICS, 250
EXHIBIT, 12, 277
EXIT PROGRAM and CICS, 248
EXIT, 89, 98
Expanded file status values, 226
EXT, 83
Extended file status communication, 217, 218
EXTERNAL, 319, 320

F

F1TABLE program, 148–149
F2TABLE program, 158–166
FASTSRT (VS COBOL II option), 58
FD, 85, 245, 328
FDUMP option (replaces SYMDMP), 61, 71, 74, 75, 76, 77, and CICS, 256
Feedback codes, VSAM, 308–310
File status checking logic pattern, 223, 225
File status values (reference), 311–315
File status, 217–236, 329
FILLER omission, 86
FLAG(I,W) option (replaces FLAGW), 33, 57, 58
FLAGE (VS COBOL option), 58
FLAGSAA (VS COBOL II option), 58
FLAGW (VS COBOL option), 58
FLOW option, 13, 14, 67
Forced abort, 221–225
Foreground compile and link, 289–294
FORTRAN-created data, and NUMPROC option, 184, 186
FREE command, TSO, 293, 298
FREQ, 285
Function codes, VSAM, 307

G

G1DEEDIT program, 174–177
G2MATH program, 179–180

G3MATH program, 181
Generated DDname, alternate index, 237
GLOBAL, 319, 321
GO, 285
GOBACK and CICS, 248

H

H1USER program, 190–191
H2USER program, 192–193
H3USER program, 194
Help screen, interactive debugging, 301–302
Hexadecimal literals, in user-defined data classes, 195
Hexadecimal literals, in VALUE clause, 88, 89, 90

I

IDCAMS, creating VSAM KSDS, 229–230
IDENTIFICATION DIVISION, simplification, 84
IF/ELSE operators < = and > =, 115–118
IGYCRCTL, 28
IMP, 45, 83
Imperative statement, 121
IMS/DC, 256–257
Indexed field and reference modification, 207, 209–211
Indexed file creation, Micro Focus COBOL, 329
INITIAL, 318
INITIALIZE, 89, 91–97
INSPECT, 196–200, 257
INSTALLATION, 84
Interactive debugging, 287–305
Intermediate fields, unintended rounding, 182
Internal sorting, 261–269
INVALID KEY, 218–221
Invocation parameters (JCL), 69, 71
ISAM, 12, 216

J

J1CHAR program, 198
J2CHAR program, 199
J3REPL program, 202
J4REPL program, 204–205
J5REFMOD program, 208
J6REFMOD program, 211
J7WHEN program, 214
JCL, VS COBOL II compile, 32

K

K1DEBUG program, 278–280
K2DEBUG program, 303–304
KANJI, 212
Key of reference (KOR), 238–241
KOR, key of reference, 238–241

L

LABEL RECORDS ARE STANDARD/OMITTED, 85
LANGUAGE(UE) (VS COBOL II option), 58
LENGTH OF register, 251, 317
LIBKEEP option, 258
LINK, CICS, 255
LINKAGE SECTION, 250, 253, 320, 321
LIST option (replaces PMAP), 33, 37, 55, 58
LISTCAT (IDCAMS), 230
LISTFREQ, 285
LOAD (VS COBOL option), 58
Locate mode coding, CICS, 250, 253, 254
LOG DSN, 297
Lookup tables, 147
LOW-VALUES, 243
Lowercase letters, ALPHABETIC-LOWER, 214
Lowercase letters, in source code, 98–99

M

Macro level CICS, 247
Map and cross reference, 41, 43, 45, 113
MAP option (replaces DMAP), 33, 37, 39, 41, 51, 58
MERGE, 247
Message suffixes, compiler, 57
Micro Focus COBOL, 7, 89, 161, 173, 176, 180, 206, 327–333
MIG, NUMPROC option, 186
MIGR option, 16, 28
MVS/ESA, 2, 217

N

Negated complement, 116, 117
Nested COPY, 212, 213
Nested in-line PERFORM, 105, 109
Nested programs, 49, 319–321
NEXT SENTENCE, 122, 138
NOCOMPILE option (replaces SYNTAX), 58
NOENDJOB option (VS COBOL), 257
NOPFD, NUMPROC option, 186

NOSEQ (VS COBOL II option), 58
NOSRANGE, 167
NOT AT END, 89, 91
NOT INVALID KEY, 89, 91, 220
NOTE, 9
NULL, in pointer field, 252
NUMBER (VS COBOL II option), 58
NUMPROC option, 184–186

O

OBJECT option (replaces LOAD), 58
Object, selection, 124, 126, 128, 129
Occurs depending on (ODO), 143–144, 149
OFFSET option (replaces CLIST), 33, 37, 53, 55, 58
ON SIZE ERROR, 183–184
ON, 9
OPEN, 221, 247, 256
Optimizer, 75
OPTIONAL data sets, 236
OTHER, 137–138
OTHERWISE, 123

P

Packed decimal number storage, illustration, 169
Packed decimal numbers and NUMPROC option, 184–186
PACKED-DECIMAL, 87, 168
PARM.COB, 28
PARM.COB2, 32
Passing addressability, CICS, 255
PASSLOAD program, 321–322
Penny-dime-dollar game (B2COINS), 79–83
PERFORM, in-line, 100–106
PERFORM, out-of-line, 100–106
PERFORM . . . WITH TEST AFTER, 107, 110
PERFORM . . . WITH TEST BEFORE, 106, 110
PFD, NUMPROC option, 184
PFDSGN option (VS COBOL II Release 2), 184
PIC G(nn), 212
PL/I-created data, and NUMPROC option, 184, 186
PMAP (VS COBOL option), 58
POINTER fields, 252, 253, 255
Preloading, IMS, 257
PRINT (IDCAMS), 229–230
PROCESS statement, 33, 37
Procs, VS COBOL II, 26

Q

QSAM, 51, 85, 221, and file status, 235, 236
QUALIFY, 283–285, 297

R

RANDOM access mode, 231, 233, 238
Range tests, 117
READ and NOT INVALID KEY, 91, 92
READ, 217, 221, 233, 247, 256, 329
READ . . . NEXT, 237, 239
READY TRACE output, 281
READY TRACE, 12, 25, 276, 281
Realia COBOL, 7, 89, 337–339
Receiving field and reference modification, 209
RECORD CONTAINS, 85, 86
Reference modification and subscripted/indexed field, 207
Reference modification, 203, 207–212
Relative indexing, 145–146, 149
Relative subscripting, 145–146, 149
REMARKS, 9, 39, 84
RENT option, 250, 257, 258
RENUM program, 325–326
REPLACE feature, 200–206
REPLACING, and INITIALIZE, 94, 96, 97
Report Writer collator, 15
Report Writer precompiler, 14, 15
REPRO (IDCAMS), 229–230
RERUN, 247
RES option, 250, 257
Return codes, compiler 57
Return codes, VSAM, 307
RETURN-CODE, 61, 63
REUS option (linkage editor), 258
REWRITE and NOT INVALID KEY, 91
REWRITE DATASET, 252, 253
REWRITE, 217, 221, 233, 247, 256
RM/COBOL-85, 7, 89, 161, 173, 177, 180, 271, 272, 333–337
RMODE, 5, 6, 254, 257
ROUNDING, 178, and problems of accuracy, 179–183
Runtime options, 58

S

Scope delimiters/terminators, 102, 104, 119–122
SD, sort description, 265, 269
SEARCH ALL, 150–153
SEARCH, 150–153
Section exit, 261
SECTION, 259–262, 269

SELECT/ASSIGN statement, 218, 223, 225, 237, 244, 265, 269, 327, 334, 337
Selection object, 124, 126, 128, 129
Selection subject, 124, 126, 128, 129
SEQUENTIAL access mode, 238
SERVICE RELOAD, 251
SET, and 88-level names, 139–141
SET, and CICS, 254, 255
SET, and index, 139–40, 150
Signs, unintended change by COBOL, 184–186
Sort input procedure, 261, 267–268
Sort output procedure, 261, 267–268
SORT verb, 247, 261, 267, 269
Source code window, debugging, 299–300
SPECIAL-NAMES, and CLASS, 187
SSRANGE option, 154, 156–167, 209
START and NOT INVALID KEY, 91
START, 217, 221, 233, 240–247, 256
STATE (VS COBOL option), 67
Statement level indicator, 45, 77, 83
STOP RUN and CICS, 248
STOP RUN and IMS, 257
STRING, and date, 11, 215, 271
Subject, selection, 124, 126, 128, 129
Subscripted field and INITIALIZE, 94
Subscripted field and reference modification, 207, 209–211
SXREF option (VS COBOL), 24, 58
SYMDMP (VS COBOL option), 63, 67, 75
SYNTAX (VS COBOL option), 58
SYS1.COB2COMP, 27
SYS1.COB2LIB, 27, 293

T

Table and INITIALIZE, 94
Table dimensions, 153–155
Table size limits, 142–143
TCTUA, CICS, 253, 255
TEST (VS COBOL II option), 58
TESTCOB, 273
Testing, microcomputer source code development, 323
THEN, in IF/ELSE, 123
TIME-OF-DAY, 9, 11
TITLE statement, 39, 41, 45, 47, 49, 53, 60
TRACE NAME output, 282, 284–285
TRANSFORM, 9, 12, 197
TRUE, and EVALUATE, 127–130
TSO foreground operations, 288

U

UND, 83
UNSTRING, 257

User parm, and runtime parm, 167
User return code, 61, 76
User-defined data classes, 187–195
USING, 250, 317, 319

V

VALUE, on table definition, 144, 148, 149
VARYING, with in-line PERFORM, 102
Verb count option, 13, 14
VS COBOL II Releases 1 and 2 and 3, 8
VS COBOL, obsolescence, 1
VS2DATE program, 270, 272
VSAM feedback codes, 308–310
VSAM file status values (reference), 311–315
VSAM function codes, 307
VSAM return codes, 307
VSAM, 216–246
VSAMDEMO program, 231–232
VSAMJCL JCL, 229–230
VSAMLIST JCL, 246
VSAMLIST program, 244–245
VSAMRUN JCL, 234
VTRACE command, debugging, 299–300, 304–305

W

WHEN, 124, 126, 128, 129
WHEN-COMPILED register, 214, 215
WITH TEST AFTER, PERFORM option, 107, 110
WITH TEST BEFORE, PERFORM option, 106, 110
WRITE and NOT INVALID KEY, 91
WRITE, 217, 221, 233, 247, 256

X

XREF (VS COBOL option), 58
XREF option (replaces SXREF), 33, 37, 47, 49, 58

//SYSUT5 and SYMDMP, 75
16 megabyte line, 254
1974 COBOL, 1
1985 COBOL, 2
24-bit addressing, 4, 254
31-bit addressing, 4, 254, 257
88-level condition names, 127, 138–141
<= and IF/ELSE, 115–118
== and REPLACE feature, 200–206
>= and IF/ELSE, 115–118
>= and START, 241, 242